# Publications by the same author

*HISTORICAL*

*Gold in Dean Forest*: Transactions of the Bristol and Gloucestershire Archaeological Society, 1944 (7 pp).

*The Extent and Boundaries of the Forest of Dean and Hundred of St Briavels*: John Bellows, Gloucester, 1947 (70 pp).

*The Verderers and Speech-Court of the Forest of Dean*: John Bellows, Gloucester, 1950 (70 pp).

*The Commoners of Dean Forest*: British Publishing Company, Gloucester, 1951 (179 pp).

*Laws of Dean*: British Publishing Company, Gloucester, 1952 (70 pp).

*The Free Miners of the Royal Forest of Dean and Hundred of St Briavels*: British Publishing Company, Gloucester, 1953 (527 pp).

*Lord Bledisloe, of Lydney*: The Forest of Dean Newspapers Ltd, 1957 (76 pp).

*'101 Not Out': The Story of Lydney Cricket Club*: The Forest of Dean Newspapers Ltd, 1963 (68 pp).

*Watts of Lydney*: The Forest of Dean Newspapers Ltd, 1965 (72 pp).

*Royal Forest: A History of Dean's Woods as Producers of Timber*: Oxford University Press, 1966 (367 pp).

*Archaeology in Dean: A Tribute to Dr C. Scott-Garrett, M.B.E.*: John Bellows, Gloucester, 1967 (68 pp).

*The Industrial History of Dean*: David & Charles, Newton Abbot, 1971 (466 pp).

*The Verderers and Forest Laws of Dean*: David & Charles, Newton Abbot, 1971 (240 pp).

*Coleford: The History of a West Gloucestershire Forest Town*: Alan Sutton Publishing, Stroud, 1983 (573 pp).

*FORESTRY*

*Practical Forestry for the Agent and Surveyor*: The Estates Gazette Ltd, 1967: Third Edition, Alan Sutton Publishing, 1991; reprinted 1995.

*British Trees in Colour*: Michael Joseph Ltd, 1974. Also Paperback Edition published 1986 by Michael Joseph Ltd for Mermaid Books.

*English-French, French-English: A Handbook of Forestry and Woodland Terms* (L'Exploitation Forestière: Guide Pratique des Termes) (with J.W.A. Newhouse, Hazelholt Farm, Bishops Waltham, Hampshire SO3 1GA).

*Forestry in Europe*: A Report for the Committee on Agriculture of the Council of Europe: Strasbourg, March 1979 (45 pp).

*Effect of Taxation on Forest Management and Roundwood Supply*: A Report for United Nations, ECE & FAO: Geneva, September 1980 (119 pp).

*Taxation of Woodlands*: (7 Editions), 1986.

*Private Woodlands: A Guide to British Timber Prices and Forestry Costings*: (7 Editions), 1987.

*Alternative Silvicultural Systems to Clear Cutting in Britain*: Bulletin 115 of the Forestry Commission, HMSO, 1995.

# THE FOREST
# OF DEAN

## NEW HISTORY
## 1550–1818

'The Crad Oak' in upper Sallow Vallet – now fast declining – which has witnessed many of the events described in this book. Now about 300 years old. (Photograph by Richard Davies, 1994)

# THE FOREST OF DEAN

## NEW HISTORY
## 1550–1818

CYRIL HART

ALAN SUTTON PUBLISHING LIMITED

First published in the United Kingdom in 1995
Alan Sutton Publishing Limited
Phoenix Mill · Far Thrupp · Stroud · Gloucestershire

British Library Cataloguing in Publication Data

A catalogue record for this book is available from the British Library.

ISBN 0-7509-0957-9

*Jacket illustrations: front:* see frontispiece; *back:* Ecologically, a dead tree is as important
in a forest ecosystem as a live one; a large rotting stump provides habitats for
invertebrates, plants and fungi. (Photograph by Douglas Green); *back flap:* A *c.* 300-
year-old yew tree grows on top of the stonework and debris of 'Cannop House',
built illegally in 1616–17 by George Moore, ironmaster. (Photograph by Martin
Latham)

Typeset in 10/11 pt Bembo.
Typesetting and origination by
Alan Sutton Publishing Limited.
Printed in Great Britain by
Hartnolls, Bodmin, Cornwall.

# CONTENTS

# PLATES

# MAPS

# PREFACE

The Royal Forests of England, designated following the Norman Conquest, were formerly maintained chiefly as places of hunting by our sovereigns and by those they arranged to benefit; incidentally the hunted supplied their larders. Forests have been at all times subject to peculiar laws and regulations. The Acts concerning them (from the eleventh century to 1535, when Henry VIII seized possession of the monasteries) did not have the increase or preservation of timber for their object; but were intended principally for the protection of deer and other beasts of the forest, while appropriately complementing the regulation of privileges of common and estovers enjoyed by the local populace, and for the use of some trees for charcoaling to sustain primitive industries – notably iron mining and refining. The laws on the one hand could be extremely severe; on the other they could be tolerable and beneficial.

During the sixteenth and seventeenth centuries, as the demand for timber for shipbuilding and other industrial uses increased, the forests became a source of revenue for the crown. Consequently they received somewhat more care and protection; and the laws passed contained little relating to deer and more to the increase and preservation of timber; the intentions were not always achieved.

The Royal Forest of Dean, at least equal in importance as the New Forest, was notable throughout the foregoing periods.

When writing previous books on the Forest*, insufficient time was available to me to undertake additional research in several items of relevant history. The omission of those items is compensated by the present treatise, which relates significantly to the woods and iron industry in Dean from about 1550 to 1667, as well as to the attempts at enclosing and planting during the period 1668–1818; also to the grants within it, and their effect locally. No ordering of the eleven Sections could be wholly satisfactory; they interact and some are closely interlinked.

It has not been possible to provide herein maps adequate to show the names and boundaries of woods, enclosures and plantings (the extents of the two latter were not always the same) at various relevant points in time within the period 1550–1818; the chief reason being the various changes which occurred in the relevant administration and recording of the Forest. A map of 1848 indicated, in various colours, enclosures made in: (a) 1810, 1811 and 1812; (b) 1842, 1843, 1844 and 1847; and (c) enclosures thrown open; but the colours have faded, making them too indistinct for an appropriate map to be based upon them. Nevertheless, the map of *c.* 1710 (Map VIII) and Map IX are helpful in this respect. Other available maps are noted in the Bibliography.

The documents researched – some of them included here *in extenso* – throw light on many economic and social aspects of the times – including yields of iron, value of cordwood and coppices, and the enterprises of neighbouring landowners in

---

* In particular, *Royal Forest: A History of Dean's Woods as Producers of Timber* (1966) and *The Industrial History of Dean* (1971).

conjunction with partners or financiers. The local populace's opposition to enclosure, and their tenacious hold on customs, privileges and what they termed rights, are described. So too are the methods followed to inform government ministers in London of the happenings in remote Dean – and what were the outcomes. The eventual enclosing and planting of about 11,000 acres in Dean during 1810–18 is recorded in great detail.

The book pays little attention to the woods alienated from the original Forest of Dean on the west and north-west, although some information in Sections I to III is relevant. In 1817 many of them, notably Hadnock Wood and Mailscot Wood were reunited with the Forest by the crown's purchase of what became known as the High Meadow Woods.

Photocopies of much of the resource material used will eventually be added to my 'Forest of Dean Collection' deposited in the Gloucestershire Record Office (Reference D3921).

Today, except for the New Forest, Dean remains the largest ancient forest in public ownership in Britain. This treatise helps to explain how broadleaved trees, significantly oak, have dominated much of Dean's history: even now it is Britain's premier oak forest, and the general perception of its character is of oakwoods. Overall, the Forest – currently both broadleaved and coniferous – is regarded as a 'working Forest' managed by Forest Enterprise for multi-purposes – chiefly timber production, the conservation of nature, and the protection and enhancement of the landscape, in particular as an environment for compatible outdoor recreation. Because of the composition of the industrial past – significantly connected with iron, coal, stone, and their transport – there remains a wealth of diverse industrial archaeology which today is generally regarded as an asset to the Forest rather than a detraction.

## ACKNOWLEDGEMENTS

Thanks are recorded to the staff of the British Library (London), the Public Record Office (London and Kew), the Gloucestershire Record Office and the Gloucester Library; also to Vernon Daykin and family who efficiently typed my manuscript, and to Gordon Clissold for some of the maps and Brian Johns and John White for their help noted in Section VI. Warm acknowledgement is also recorded to a late friend, Dr George Hammersley (died Edinburgh 1992). Before, during and after George completed his PhD thesis (unpublished), University of London, 1972, we mutually enjoyed and benefited from co-operating by way of correspondence, publications, notes and maps relating to the Forest of Dean iron industry 1562–1660. I cherish the generous tributes to that co-operation given in his thesis on pages 5, 207, 248 and 556. His published works are noted in my Bibliography.

CYRIL HART

Chenies,
Coleford,
Forest of Dean,
Gloucestershire, GL16 8DT

June 1995

# PRINCIPAL ABBREVIATIONS USED IN FOOTNOTES

| | |
|---|---|
| Add.MS | British Library, Additional Manuscript |
| Bankes MSS | Bodleian, Bankes Manuscripts |
| Br. Liby. | British Library, London |
| *Cal. Cttee for Comp.* | *Calendar of the Committee for Compounding with Delinquents* |
| *Cal.Pat.Roll* | *Calendar of Patent Rolls* |
| *Cal.SPD* | *Calendar of State Papers Domestic* |
| *Cal.Treas.Books* | *Calendar of Treasury Books* |
| *Cal.Treas.Books and Papers* | *Calendar of Treasury Books and Papers* |
| *D.N.B.* | *Dictionary of National Biography* |
| *E.H.R.* | *English Historical Review* |
| *Ec.H.R.* | *Economic History Review* |
| GG. | Gage Manuscripts, Gloucester, D1677 |
| Glos.R.O. | Gloucestershire Record Office |
| Glouc.Liby. | Gloucester Library |
| Harl.MSS | British Library, Harleian Manuscripts |
| *H.M.C.* | *Historical Manuscripts Commission* |
| *I.P.M.* | *Inquisitiones Post Mortem* |
| Lansd.MSS | British Library, Lansdowne Manuscripts |
| N.L.W. | National Library of Wales |
| P. | Conventional for 'Planting Year', e.g. P. 1995 |
| PC | Privy Council (Registers) |
| P.R.O. | Public Record Office, London and Kew |
| Rawl.MSS | Bodleian, Rawlinson Manuscripts |
| SP | State Papers |
| *Trans. B.&G.A.S.* | *Transactions of the Bristol and Gloucestershire Archaeological Society* |
| 3rd Rept. of 1788 | Third Report of the Commissioners appointed to inquire into the State and Condition of the Woods, Forests, and Land Revenues of the Crown (London), 3 June 1788. |

# INTRODUCTION

The Forest of Dean in south-west Gloucestershire – designated in the eleventh century by William the Conqueror as a royal 'forest' (not wholly wooded) – lies in the angle formed by the confluence of the Severn flowing on the east and the Wye on the west. It borders on Monmouthshire across the Wye, and slightly merges in the north into Herefordshire. Physically the central part of the region, largely wooded to this day, occupies a modest hilly plateau with a few shallow rounded tops, deeply scored by a number of small streams, in early days powerful. Eastwards the plateau slopes towards the Severn Vale; westwards it is cut more abruptly by the ancient deep valley of the Wye.

The region was a royal hunting area from Saxon times, and a royal forest after the Norman Conquest; most of the present central remnant has always been part of this. The boundaries of 'forest' have repeatedly contracted and expanded by perambulations made on behalf of the sovereign; the widest bounds followed the Wye in the west, the Severn in the south and east, and a line in the north joining the Wye from Monmouth and Ross to Newent and the outskirts of Gloucester. Forest law extended to the whole of the designated area.

Dean's position, on the Welsh frontiers of civilization, tended to make it an economic backwater; its wooded hills, valleys and plains preserved both its isolation and its trees. Forest law accentuated its segregation. Much of Dean's peculiar character was owed to a specific combination of features – location, topography, deposits of rich haematite iron-ore, many seams of coal, abundant wood, and water-power when harnessed; also to the jealously guarded privileges and customs of the local populace and their abhorrence of so-called 'foreigners', as well as of enclosures.

The royal central woods (broadleaved, mainly oak and beech) were kept virtually void of cattle, horses, sheep and goats (the two latter in any case were 'uncommonable animals'). Lawns[1] and other areas were allowed as common except during the Fence Month and Winter Heyning. The woods likewise were void of dwellings, except a few required to house forest officials; and, following the advent of charcoal blast furnaces, temporary cabins were authorized or tolerated for occupation by miners, woodcutters and charcoal burners, and (under lease) houses and outbuildings for smelters of ore and refiners of iron.

Dean's statutory boundaries as well as its wooded extent – the two have never been the same – were gradually reduced in size;[2] but much of its attractive mineral wealth in iron-ore and coal lay near the central more wooded portion. Mining,

---

[1] In the thirteenth century, commonable lawns [*landeas*] in the Forest of Dean included Moseley, Sainteley, Konhope [Cannop], Wychmead [Whitemead], Oldeford, Habehale, Kenesley, Crumpmead and Walemore. Only the last was not eventually brought into woodland. See Hart, C.E. *The Regard of the Forest of Dene in 1282*, 1987, pp. 19, 20.

[2] Hart, C.E., 'The Metes and Bounds of the Forest of Dean', *Trans. B.&G.A.S.*, LXVI (1945), pp. 166–94; in 1947 published as a booklet (77 pp.) entitled *The Extent and Boundaries of the Forest of Dean and Hundred of St. Briavels*.

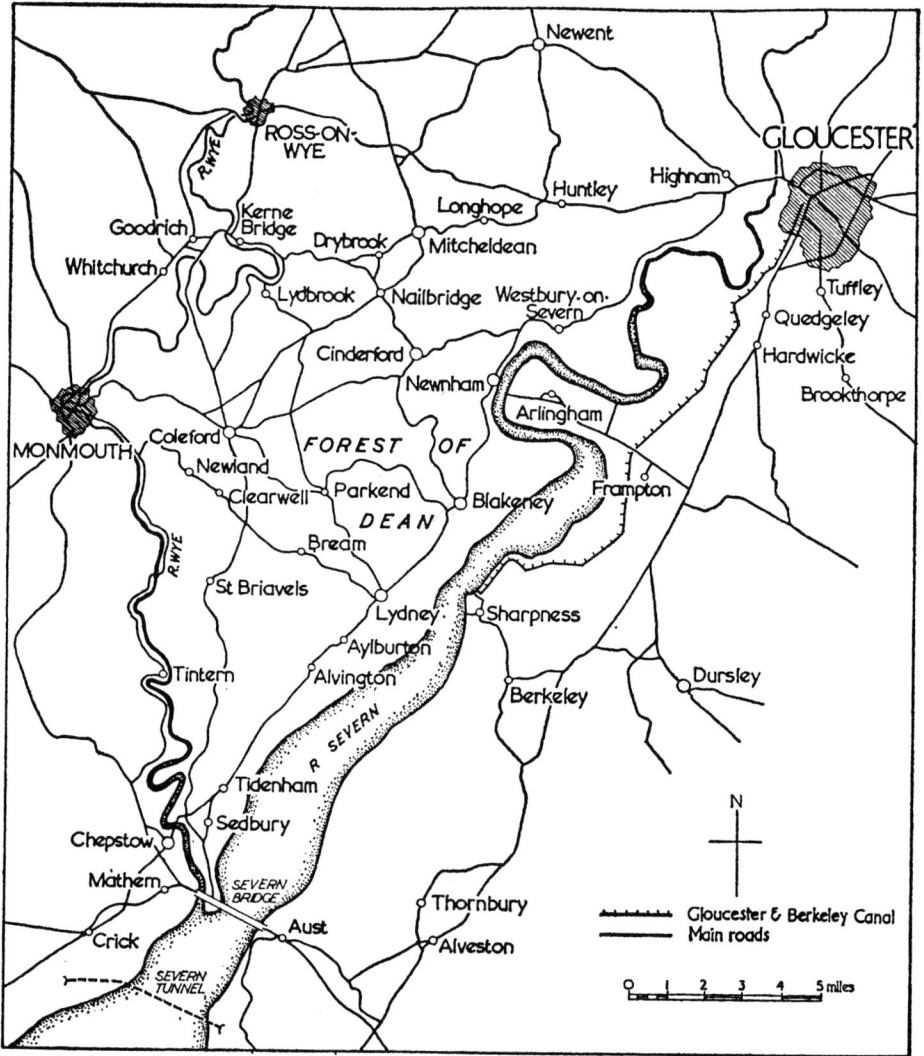

Map I. The Forest of Dean and its neighbourhood.

Ross-on-Wye

Newent

• The Lea

Huntley

Churcham

• Mitcheldean

Gloucester

Ruardean • Drybrook

Upper Lydbrook

Flaxley

Cinderford Westbury

F O R E S T • Littledean

Staunton

Monmouth

O F

Coleford • Speech House

• Rodley

D E A N

• Parkend

Blakeney

• Whitecroft

Bream •

St Briavels •

Lydney

Aylburton

N

• Tidenham

Chepstow

Coal measures

Carboniferous Limestone (yielding Iron ore)

0 1 2 3 4 5 Miles

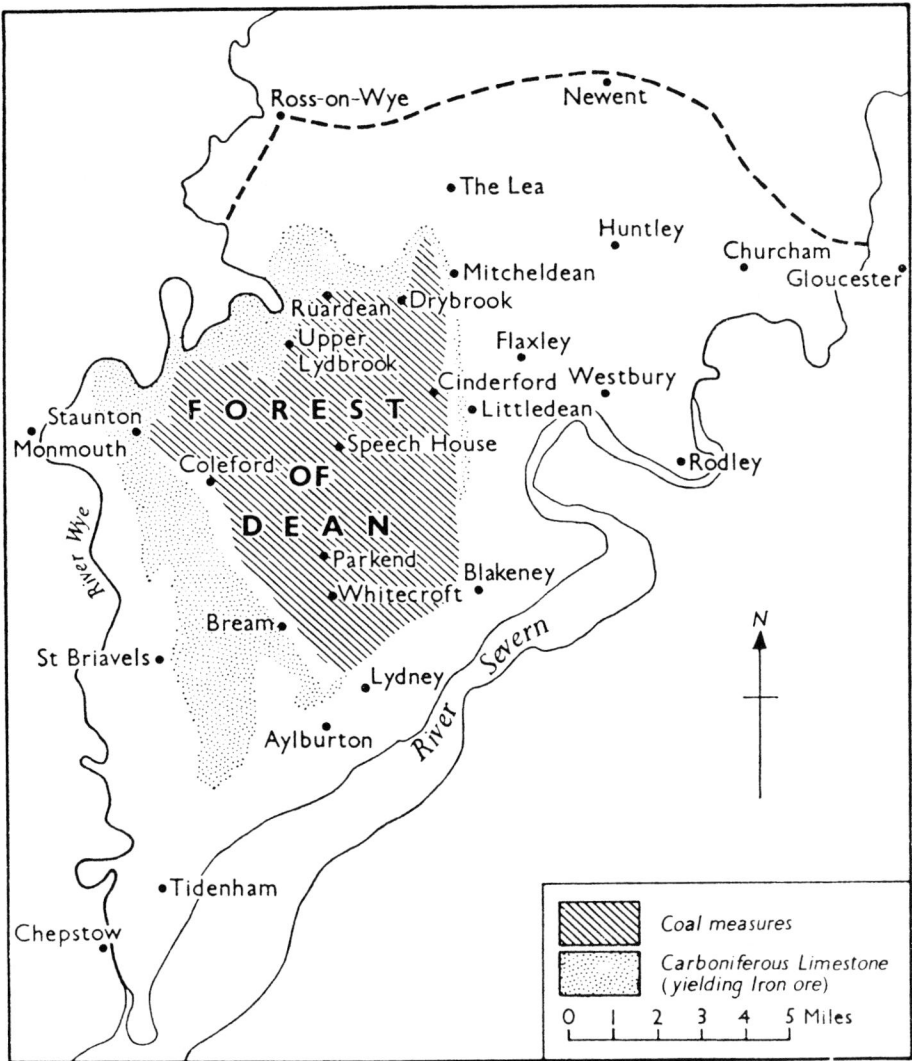

Map II. Schematic map of the Forest of Dean which in early times extended northwards to Ross-on-Wye–Newent–Gloucester, but is now approximately represented by the extent of the coalfield.

smelting and refining, with the inevitable demand for wood for charcoaling, at least from Iron Age and Roman times were conducted on a small scale and intermittently. Bloomeries and primitive forges, not being dependent upon water power, were set up almost anywhere, some were itinerant, and continued during Saxon, Norman and medieval times. Thereby, Dean became one of the principal iron-producing regions in the British Isles. Although the bloomery left about 4 tons of cinders (slag) to each ton of iron produced, the resultant cinderbeds scattered throughout Dean remained evidence of impressive activity; they became of much value following the advent of charcoal blast furnaces in the late sixteenth and early seventeenth centuries. (Approximately half the metal-bearing charge was generally made up of cinders.[3])

Forest law, the conservation of the habitat and sustenance of deer and boars (increasingly used to replenish the larders of the sovereign and his assigns), and the customs and privileges of commoners, miners and the other local populace, restricted early agriculture and ensured a low level of exploitation. Although the central woods of the royal forest were sparsely inhabited, illegal encroachments upon them by way of assarting and purprestures increased in momentum.

During much of the sixteenth and seventeenth centuries the one-time approximately 100,000 acres designated as 'forest' (not wholly wooded) extended only to about 24,000 acres, and comprised: about 18,000 acres of central woods with trees mixed in age- and size-range and quality; 1,000 acres of Lea Baily in the north, containing the best and least disturbed woods; 1,000 acres of the Cannop valley woods, alienated from the crown by lease from 1615 to 1668 (except for about eight years under the Protectorate and the Commonwealth); and 4,000 acres of 'waste' (often then spelled 'wast') recognized near villages ('townships') as common. Outside the above reduced extent were private landed properties, some largely wooded, alienated from the crown by gift, lease, or sale; they included those of the Winters in the south, the Throckmortons and Halls in the west, and the Villiers in the north. At times, by command of the sovereign, the extent under forest law was virtually the central woods; at other times the alienated areas too were 'forest' in the legal sense.

The crown's central broadleaved woods contained a mixture comprising: (i) medium-sized and large oaks and beeches reserved for use as naval timber (some conserved beyond their suitability for that purpose); (ii) young to about thirty-year-old coppices; (iii) lawns and commons, scattered groves and spinneys along with isolated trees (some 'shredded' up to parts of their crown); and (iv) throughout most areas, underwoods of hazel, birch, alder, thorn, willow, holly and the like, of reduced value as wood but important as habitat and sustenance of deer and other wildlife.

Relatively few timber-trees and smaller trees were needed and released for the king's works (castles, bridges and other construction), religious houses, relatives, courtiers and favourites; some, when authorized by the Speech Court, were 'delivered' to miners of iron-ore and coal; and some to the local populace as estovers (housebote, firebote, hedgebote, etc.). Otherwise there was little demand except for firewood; hence the price attainable was low, and woods were of little value commercially. Increasingly the main demand came from the iron industry.

---

[3] Hart, C.E., *The Industrial History of Dean* (1971), pp. xxiv, xxv.

PART ONE

The foregoing conditions and situations in Dean existed well into the seventeenth century. After the crown in 1611–13 permitted charcoal blast furnaces to be built, under contract, for lease, the demand for wood for charcoal soared and its price more than doubled and later increased further; woods, especially renewable coppices, likewise increased in value, so too did cinders.

The indirect process of ironmaking arrived nearby during the 1590s.[4] By about 1611, at least four charcoal blast furnaces and four fining forges were set up on private land adjacent to the royal forest.[5] During 1611–13 the crown followed other great landowners to obtain from its woods an income from sale of cordwood (while reserving timber-trees for shipbuilding), thereby generating fierce competition between a number of enterprising landowners and investors for the crown's iron industry 'concession' in Dean itself.[6] By a series of contracts, leases and sales, the crown became owner in Dean of several specially built blast furnaces and forges (1611–13) sited alongside adequately powerful streams, without any cost to itself other than a few timber-trees and locally available building materials.

The high quality ores, the helpful natural conditions, and the wireworks at nearby Tintern and Whitebrook, focused innovation in Dean. The industry was profitable, even after paying the crown for cordwood and certain fines and charges, but the involvement of crown and court, the interests of the local populace, and an otherwise backward economy created conflicts. The 'concession' in Dean covering the 'King's Ironworks' along with adequate cordwood, and iron-ore and cinders available from the local Free Miners, was not only income-producing to the crown but also a valuable prize to the successful applicants. However, like other favours the 'concession' could be won or lost by intrigue or favouritism at court, for which the complex local relationship of neighbouring families offered much information and exerted pressure. There was too the social effect of the 'divide' of two religions, Protestant and Catholic.

Meanwhile, despite the enormous consumption of wood by the blast furnaces being a potential danger in this respect, there was need always to safeguard the interests of deer (though their numbers were diminishing). Concurrently, continuing crown policy was to grow and conserve oaks and beeches to meet the increasing demand for shiptimber for the Royal Navy and the merchant fleet. There was too recognition of the needs of the local populace. The whole was a rational and sensible use of resources, especially of otherwise virtually unmarketable wood; particularly when, after cutting, attempts were made to perpetuate the woods by enclosing them against grazing by domestic animals and browsing by deer – thereby enabling the stools to recoppice and natural seedlings to survive. Yet enclosure was abhorrent to the commoners and other members of the populace; they were reluctant to concede the crown's right to enclose, regarding it as an attack on the basis of their traditional economy, which the forest laws themselves had safeguarded. Those who were compelled to live under forest

[4] E134/44 Eliz. I/Trin.3; /39 Eliz/I/Hil.23; Chas.I/East.40, suppl. 902/22; Br. Liby., Harl. MS. 4850, f. 47d; Longleat, Devereux MS. 1648, lease of 2 Jan., 12 Jas.I; Devereux Papers, f. 172.
[5] E112/82/310 and MR. 879; Br. Liby., Lansd. MS. 166, ff. 350, 352, 356, 362, 366, 368; Bodleian, Gough, Glouc.I, ff. 61d, 62; Glos. R.O., D421 Winter Papers, E1 and T22.
[6] Br. Liby., Lansd. MS. 166, ff. 350, 372, 374, 388; SP38/10, 16 May 1611; SP14/63/76; C66/1904, 14 June 1611.

law had come to regard it as beneficial; it was the crown which might reasonably resent it as restrictive.[7] To some extent the hereditary forest officials and other holders of ancient forest privileges, remained as buttresses of royal rights and prestige.

Forest law continued to take precedence over common law and partly excluded it in general[8] and significantly in Dean.[9] The laws were well known and observed in principle; only malefactors and corrupt forest officials blatantly abused them. Designed to establish a royal privilege, forest law now safeguarded the inhabitants' interests; it maintained part of the Forest as a waste or wilderness. Overall, there was a royal monopoly in the hunt, often granted or delegated by the sovereign.

In compensation for the forest law restrictions on the local populace, privileges of commoning, pannage and estovers were generously interpreted. Part of the Forest grazed herds of cattle and many horses, and at times fattened numerous pigs; sheep and goats, though legally excluded from 'forest', were generally tolerated in the commons and lawns; the taking of estovers were authorized at the Speech Court, whereby virtually free timber was 'delivered' for buildings, repairs, fences, hedges and tools, and sometimes firewood likewise.

Within a generation twelve charcoal blast furnaces and at least thirteen substantial forges were at work inside the approximate triangle formed by the Severn, Wye and a line from Ross to Gloucester; a further five furnaces and four forges closely adjacent to this area also relied to some extent on Dean's ore, cinders and cordwood. The intensity of exploitation of so small an area, almost unprecedented for the period, caused some justifiable misgivings regarding its effects upon the woods of Dean, especially in relation to shiptimber.[10] In less than forty years following the advent of blast furnaces, Dean became one of the foremost iron-producing regions in the British Isles – a centre of large scale industry and of technical invention. However, it was a time of endless recriminations between crown, industrialists, officials and local populace.

Relevant to the foregoing periods are: the enterprises of the powerful local families of Winter and Hall (Catholic) and Throckmorton (Protestant); the activities of John Broughton (the first deputy surveyor of Dean, 1633) and his contemporary, Charles Powell; also the Justice Seat in Eyre of 1634. Part One (i.e. Sections I to V) should be read as being under the conditions and situations noted above.

---

[7] Hammersley, G., 'The Revival of the Forest Laws under Charles I', *History*, XLV, No. 154, June 1960, pp. 86–7.

[8] Turner, G.J., *Select pleas of the forest*, Selden Society, 1901, pp. ix–cxxxiv; Coke, E., *Institutes*, pt. iv, ch. 73; Manwood, J., *Treatise of the laws of the forest* (1615); Nielson, Nellie, *The English Government at Work, 1327–1336* (1940), The Mediaeval Academy of America, Cambridge, Massachusetts, 'The Forests', Section ix, pp. 394–467; Wright, Elizabeth Cox, *Speculum* (April 1928), The Mediaeval Academy of America, Cambridge, Massachusetts, 1928, 'Common Law in the Thirteenth Century English Royal Forest', pp. 166–91; Petit-Dutaillis, C., *Studies and Notes supplementary to Stubbs' Constitutional History, II*, Manchester University Press 1935, 'The Forest', pp. 147–251.

[9] Hart, C.E., *Royal Forest* (1966) and *The Verderers and Forest Laws of Dean* (1971); Bazeley, Margaret L., 'The Forest of Dean in its Relations with the Crown during the Twelfth and Thirteenth Centuries' (1910), *Trans. B.&G.A. S., XXXIII*, pp. 153–285.

[10] Hart, *Royal Forest* (1966) and *The Industrial History of Dean* (1971).

## PART TWO

The Civil Wars (1642–7) had an adverse effect on the Forest of Dean; they ended the explosive expansion of the local iron industry. Under them and the Commonwealth and the Protectorate, ironworks (and licences to take ore, cinders and cordwood) changed hands frequently, partly as a result of Parliamentary politics, causing production of iron to falter. However, the Protectorate, pressed by necessity for iron and untrammelled by previous traditional fears and procedures, found a way to exploit the resources of the Forest rationally. In 1653 it appointed a trustworthy and competent semi-local Parliamentarian serving-soldier, Major John Wade, as sole administrator of Dean, and instructed him to build a new furnace at Parkend and a new forge at Whitecroft. It placed him under the Admiralty Committee, and permitted him to link the smelting and fining of iron with the production of shiptimber, first for the naval dockyards and then for the local construction of ships. Between the end of 1653 and the beginning of 1660 the accounts of the ironworks and associated enterprises were conscientiously kept by Wade (despite his continued commission in the Army), and carefully audited by the Protectorate. Wade's management proved that a large area of woodland could be used sensibly and productively for timber and cordwood while at the same time improving its yield and condition, and by enclosing along with a modest amount of planting making some provision for future growth. Throughout the period there was always some concern for the protection of disappearing reserves of shiptimber. Following the Restoration of the Monarchy (1660) the whole of the local iron industry 'concession' was soon abandoned by the crown, which suffered in equal measure from unsatisfied creditors and traditional attitudes.

Information relevant to the foregoing period includes accounts of: John Wade's administration; 'Cannop House' and its associated Cannop valley woods; and the Justice Seat in Eyre of 1656. Part Two (i.e. Sections VI to VIII) should be read as being under the conditions and situations noted above.

## PART THREE

By the time of the Restoration (1660), despite attempts at enclosing and planting, chiefly under the Commonwealth, the stocks of timber-trees and coppices in Dean were far from satisfactory. The ironmasters, other lessees, forest officials, and the local populace had taken their toll, but natural increment had made good some of the loss. Relatively few large timber-trees of sound quality remained; some enclosures were ruined, and most were insecure.[11] New measures were needed to replenish and to enhance what remained.

A commission in 1661–2 made constructive proposals for enclosing and planting. However, these as well as helpful 'Proposals' by some of the local populace in 1662 and 1667 were frustrated by the demands and actions of Sir John Winter of Lydney. Eventually, the Dean Forest (Reafforestation) Act 1668 made arrangements ostensibly acceptable to most interests, whereunder the sylvan cover could be enriched and enlarged, with a view to making Dean again a storehouse of timber.

---

[11] Well might John Evelyn bemoan in 1663 (*Sylva*, Edn. 1776, p. 568; Hart, *Royal Forest*, p. 175): 'Nature has thought fit to produce this wasting [iron-]ore more plentiful in woodland than any other ground, and to enrich our forests to their own destruction'.

However, enclosure continued to be abhorrent to the commoners. The demolishing of the 'King's Ironworks' in 1674 helped: the crown having opted out and evaded relevant problems. (Several ironworks outside the Forest continued to draw from it much of the best ore as well as cinders and cordwood.) Continually, the attempts at enclosing and planting were frustrated. Section IX explains why the situation was still unacceptable by 1687, almost twenty years after the Act of 1668.

PART FOUR

Section X, covering the period 1688–1787, describes renewed attempts at enclosing and planting. Previous attempts had been largely unsuccessful, significantly due to the resistance of many of the local populace. Despite increased attention being given by succeeding surveyor-generals of woods and supervisors, as well as several commissions, surveys and reports, the effect continued to be unsatisfactory. Much misappropriation of trees took place as well as excessive taking of perquisites by forest officials of both the old and the newer regime. Continued abuses were the significant factor. In 1788 commissioners were appointed to investigate the state and condition of all crown woods and forests – among them Dean – and to redress abuses in their management, to protect them, and to increase the production of timber for the navy.

PART FIVE

Section XI concerns the period 1788–1818, and relates the forestry surveys of Dean, the inadequate amount of enclosing and planting up to 1787, and the recommendation for further urgent attempts to fully afforest 11,000 acres. The Dean Forest (Timber) Act 1808 provided the necessary powers. Thereunder, Edward Machen, deputy surveyor for the Office of Woods, employing forestry contractors (Messrs Driver) undertook the required operations. The local superintendent, 1810–18, was William Billington. His efforts, problems and accomplishments, along with those of Machen, in enclosing and planting about 11,000 acres, are recorded in great detail. The Section contains a brief comment on the management of the Forest after 1818, along with some criticisms made by later silviculturalists; and also includes some mitigation of those criticisms. Finally included is a mention of the important roles Dean has played and continues to play locally and nationally.

# PART ONE

## I. THE WINTER FAMILY OF LYDNEY

The Winter (Wintour, Wynter) family of Lydney possessed for several generations considerable property and influence in the southern part of the Forest of Dean. The family's history, from the sixteenth century to late in the seventeenth century, is briefly provided by Nicholls,[1] Harris[2] and Whitecross School.[3] This present account relates almost wholly to the Winters' connection with the iron industry and woods of the Forest.

### SIR WILLIAM WINTER

Sir William Winter, the Elizabethan admiral, bought the manor of Lydney and settled there in the early 1560s. On 4 June 1561 he obtained a pardon for the alienation to him of the manor of Lydney.[4] William, Earl of Pembroke, from whom he had bought the manor, had reunited in his hands the two manors known as Lydney Warwick and Lydney Shrewsbury, after their respective former owners.[5] Sir William's official naval duties may not have left him much time to enjoy his new estates; but there is some evidence that he employed his wealth, much of which he may have acquired as Master of the Naval Ordnance and Surveyor of Ships,[6] in order to enlarge his estates judiciously. By 1565 Sir William, although he already owned estates at Dyrham and Kings Weston, had built himself a new mansion in Lydney,[7] presumably the building later known as the 'White Cross House'. He was officially granted the manor of Lydney in 1588 in recognition of his services against the Armada. He died in 1589.[8]

### SIR EDWARD WINTER

Sir William's son and successor, Edward, did not remain quietly at home but such distinction as he attained was confined in a smaller compass. Like his father, he went to sea. In 1589 and again in 1601 he sat as MP for Gloucestershire; in 1595 he was

[1] Nicholls, Rev. H.G., *The Personalities of the Forest of Dean*, 1863, pp. 112–27.

[2] Harris, Frank H., *Wyntours of the White Cross House*, 1923.

[3] *Wyntours of the White Cross: an extended family history*, 1986; a Whitecross School Project directed by B. Rendell and K. Childs.

[4] *Cal. Pat. Roll*, 3 Eliz.; Glos. R.O., D421 Winter Papers, E1, 1604; ibid., App. II, 5 (1603).

[5] Ibid. 1549–51, 16 Jan. 1551 and 6 Edw. VI, 24 Nov. 1552; Hart, *Royal Forest*, p. 76.

[6] Glos.R.O., D421 Winter Papers, A1–3, 1557. Glimpses of the naval career of Sir William Winter are to be found in *Acts of the Privy Council* Vols. VIII (1570) to XVI (1588); some typewritten extracts are in Glouc. Liby. SR24.10. There are mentions of 'William Winter the younger' (1580); also (1577) of taking 12 miners from the Forest of Dean 'to be employed on a voyage'.

[7] Ibid. G54/679; *Cal. Pat. Rolls*, 1549–51, 16 Jan. 1551; ibid. 6 Edw.VI, 24 Nov. 1552; ibid. 3 Eliz.I, 4 June 1561; C54/679.

[8] *D.N.B.*

Map III. A portion of Christopher Saxton's map of Gloucestershire showing the Forest of Dean, 1577.

knighted and in 1598–9 he served as sheriff. In 1595 he married Anne, the third daughter of Edward, fourth Earl of Worcester.[9]

Sir Edward's property included the manors of Lydney, Aylburton, Purton and Allaston with about 3,000 acres lying in the wider bounds of the Forest of Dean alone.[10] This probably described merely part of his lands, as both law suits supplying those descriptions were merely concerned with his claim to rights of common in Dean. At any rate, he was one of the major landowners in Gloucestershire and a power in the county, as befitted one of the Queen's godsons.

In 1594 or 5, Sir Edward obtained the office of deputy constable of the Forest of Dean, under Henry, Earl of Pembroke. He may have bought the office from his predecessor, because it set off a dispute lasting over two years between him and Pembroke. The latter demanded payment of £100 and a bond; the former at least a security for the quiet exercise of his office.[11] Pembroke died in January 1601; on 6 August the Privy Council appointed Sir Edward as one of the deputy lieutenants for Gloucestershire and, on 9 September, he was appointed warden of the Forest of Dean and constable of the Castle of St. Briavels.[12] From 29 September 1604 to 29 September 1609, he along with the verderers supervised the sessions of the Speech Court.[13] In 1604 he was a Subsidy Commissioner for Gloucestershire.

All Sir Edward's offices increased his prestige rather than his income. He must have been wealthy to support their burden but the loss of £6,000–£7,000 due to his Spanish imprisonment and ransom caused him to seek compensation. On 23 October 1604 he was granted a licence to charcoal even his timber-trees for the manufacture of iron, penal statutes to the contrary notwithstanding.[14] Possibly in 1606 but certainly in 1608 and 1610 the existence of a charcoal blast furnace (at Maple Hill north of Lydney) and a forge in Lydney were independently asserted.[15]

The accession of James I (24 March 1603) was followed by an intensified campaign to rationalize the administration and exploitation of land revenues which included the income from royal woods.[16] The landed population was made to compound for land assarted from the forests. In Dean, in 1606, the crown granted a licence permitting the export of iron-ore and cinders for smelting in Ireland.[17] In March 1610 the crown was urged to smelt iron in Dean but to refine it in Ireland.[18] The foregoing occurred when blast furnaces were soon to arrive in Dean.

No direct evidence survives to confirm the size of Sir Edward's ironworks, though scattered indications leave the impression of regular and uninterrupted activity. The furnace may have made as much as 300–400 tons a year; it would be surprising if the forge had a greater output than 150 tons. They would have used

[9] D.N.B., 'Sir John Winter'; H.M.C., Salisbury, V, p. 479, Nov. 1595.

[10] E134/14 Jas. I/Hil.8; E112/82/310; Gage MS. GG 568 (1600).

[11] H.M.C., Salisbury, V, pp. 460 and 479; VI, 48; Acts of the Privy Council, 1597–8, p. 73.

[12] Acts of the Privy Council, 1601–4, p. 161; C66/1562.

[13] Hart, Royal Forest, p. 86.

[14] Glos. R.O., D421 Winter Papers, E1 23 Oct. 1604; all Sir Edward Winter's lands lay less than the statutory 14 miles from the navigable Severn and Wye. The Statute 1 Eliz. I, c. 15 prohibited the charcoaling of trees more than one foot square at the stub, within 14 miles of navigable water.

[15] Schubert, H.R., History of the British Iron and Steel Industry c. 450 B.C.–A.D. 1775 (1957), pp. 380–1, refers to the existence of a forge and furnace on Winter's lands in 1608.

[16] Hammersley, G., 'The Crown woods and their exploitation in the sixteenth and seventeenth centuries', Bull. of the Inst. of Historical Research, XXX, 1957, pp. 136–61.

[17] C66/1705, 20 April 1606.

[18] Cal. SP Ireland, 1608–10, pp. 419, 530.

some 4,500 cords of wood in a year or from 150–300 acres of coppice. With a coppice rotation of sixteen years, such a rate of production could then have been maintained on about 3,000 acres of woodland or less. Winter owned almost as much as that: in the Manor of Lydney alone he held 1,200 acres of woodland.[19] In addition, around 1610, he held subject to the King's Court of St. Briavels, among 'new sett [? suite] lands' – 'in his park from the woodside to the launde [? lawn], together with two highways which have been inclosed over the Forest this 20 years – rent £30 per annum'.[20] By 1610[21] he began to negotiate for the purchase of six coppices in Dean standing about 1 mile north-west of Lydney, 530 acres (later reduced to 444 acres).[22] A survey of the six coppices made for the crown in March 1610 reads:[23]

> Right Honorable [Sir Julius Caesar, Chancellor of the Exchequer],
>
> According unto your Lordship's warrant, we repaired unto and have viewed and duly considered the several woods known by the names of Great Bradley, Little Bradley, Stonegrove, Pigslade, Buckholle Moore, and The Copps. All lying together and containing by the measure of 16½ foot to the pole, 530 acres. In which grounds we think (the woods being much differing in quality, by an equal proportion) there may be raised for every acre 30 cords of wood (reserving sufficient staddells according to the state) which according to the measure of the same grounds, amounts unto the number of 15,600 cords of wood. Upon conference with divers in the country, we find that such a quantity of wood is not suddenly to be vented in any other sort than to the iron works which causeth either the cheapness or dearness of the same; the country not valuing the said woods upon the stem above 14d the cord, although to the iron works it may be valued at 2s.6d. the cord.
>
> So that according to the rate of the country, the said proportion of wood is worth £505.
>
> And according to the computation for the iron works, the same may be valued at £1,960.
>
> We imagine that the charge of fencing [inclosing after felling] the said woods circuiting 4 miles, will cost to be done and kept according to the state, about CC marks [£13.6s.8d.]. The rent is £20 per annum.
>
> [Signed]        Robert Treswell [surveyor-general of woods]
>                      J. Norden [a surveyor of crown woods and forests]
>                      Tho. Morgan [a verderer, previously surveyor-general of woods]

The suggestion of such a deal generated rivalries and jealousies which delayed the completion of the 'bargain'. In consequence Winter was forced to cut some of his own coppices two years before their trees had reached the dimension usual for charcoaling. Early in 1610 he issued the following statement:[24]

---

[19] Glos. R.O., D421 Winter Papers, T23, 1618.
[20] Br. Liby., Lansd. MSS 166, f. 358. Some of the folios have been renumbered in recent years.
[21] Ibid. ff. 347, 348, 350.
[22] Ibid. f. 356.
[23] Ibid. f. 348.
[24] Ibid. f. 352.

A true Answer to the objections made against my late bargain for some of his Majesty's coppices or colletts adjoining to the Forest of Dean:

1.   That contrary to the intention of this bargain I have already cut down a great number of timber-trees, whereas to this hour not any one is felled of that kind or any other.

2.   That a following of my Lord of Worcester's should survey these woods is a wilful mistaking, since by the particulars it appears that one Mr. Hervye made this survey by warrant from the late Lord Treasurer.

3.   That I should gain £1,000 per annum by this bargain is so vain and impossible a thing as deserves no answer.

Yet that your Lordship may see how much the informer hath exceeded therein, himself or any man else shall purchase my interest for a tenth part of his valuation. Which I write not in any sort to capitulate with your Lordship; for without any consideration at all, I am ready to yield up this bargain, rather than by retaining thereof to harbour in your noblest thoughts the least ill conceipt of me or my proceedings. But now, Sir, how profitable a bargain you have made for the King, these considerations following will easily demonstrate. For whereas in former time a greater profit was never raised out of these woods than 25s. per annum until my Lord your Father and Sir Walter Myldemaye did let them by lease, and so made £7 rent, without any fine, your Lordship hath now made £500 fine, and £20 rent, which is no small improvement, considering that these 25 years last past not one penny rent or profit otherwise hath been made out of them, but left as a thing forgotten. That the coppice wood or underwood through the abuse of the last Farmer, who never inclosed these woods, and the continual spoil and havock of the country thereabouts, is utterly destroyed. That there is nothing now left in 4 of those 6 coppices for which I have bargained but old beeches, heretofore topt and lopt, whereof many of them now are scarce worth the cutting out to any man but myself, in respect of my iron works being so near to them. That the other two coppices which are well stored have nothing in them but young beeches, and some other wood of 20 or 30 years growth. That in divers of these coppices there are many acres which have no manner of wood standing upon them at all. Lastly, that the enclosing of these coppices with a sufficient mound will cost me 200 marks the least, besides the great quantity of wood that must necessarily be spent therein, for which no manner of allowance is made me at all.

Now, Sir, if I should not have power by my lease to cut down such trees as are there remaining (timber-trees excepted) considering the underwood is quite destroyed, I should neither have wherewith to recompence my £500 fine, nor my £20 dead rent within 21 years amounteth to £1,000 the least.

To conclude, since according to your Lordship's order I have already paid into the Exchequer £200 and the other £300 by the same order, I will pay the last of this November.

That I may know your Lordship's further pleasure and resolution herein, and can but refer the consideration of all to your good liking and judgment.

Eventually, on 14 March 1610, a lease to Winter was agreed:[25]

A Remembrance of that which passed between the right honorable Sir Julius Caesar, Kt., Sir Walter Cope, Kt, and Sir Edward Wintour, Kt. concerning the bargaine of wood

[25] f. 356. Br. Liby., Lansd. MSS 166, f. 356. Some of the folios have been renumbered in recent years.

heretofore compounded for by Sir Edward Wintour, the day and year above written [14 March 1610].

After much arguing and debate, concerning that business, it was concluded: That whereas Sir Edward Wintour had formerly compounded for those woods, for a lease for 21 years at £500 fine and £20 yearly rent, and he to have the profit of the next cutting [of the six coppices or collets] upon the expiration of the lease. Because Sir Edward Wintour is willing to offer those conditions which to such honorable personages should (upon due consideration) seem reasonable.

He hath voluntarily and willingly yielded to relinquish the first contract and to pay besides the £500 which he hath disbursed already, £300 more, which is £800 in the whole.

So as he may have a bargaine and sale of the woods now growing upon those coppices, and liberty of ingress, egresse, and regresse, to cut, cole and carry away those woods, so converted into cole, for the space of five years, viz. the term to begin at or Lady day next 1611, and to expire at or Lady day which shall be in the year of our Lord 1616.

And in consideration that the said Sir Edward Wintour shall be freed of the £20 yearly rent, and likewise of the charge of fencing and mounding of those coppices, he is likewise willing to relinquish the benefit which may accrue unto him by the next cutting; to the end his Majesty may reap so great a benefit thereof himself as is pretended.

The £300 to be paid as followeth, viz. £100 at Midsummer next, £100 in Hillary term following, and £100 at Midsummer following.

I do agree to this bargaine, 14 March 1610. [Signed] Edward Wyntour.

The arguments, accusations, and answers to them[26] suggested to rivals and the crown the possibility of using Dean for iron production on a larger scale.[27] Much opposition was generated in and around Dean. Other people, notably (a) Winter's nephew Herbert, Earl of Pembroke and his co-governors of the Mineral and Battery Society with wireworks at Tintern and Whitebrook just across the Wye, and (b) local magnates, the earls of Shrewsbury and Clanricarde, anxious to obtain substantial grants of cordwood, iron-ore and cinders in Dean. Blast furnaces had arrived in the neighbourhood by 1600.

In about April 1611 Sir Giles Brydges (a local landowner of the Chandos family, later advancing to a minor member of the Villiers entourage), acting on Sir Edward Winter's behalf, offered to buy 14,000 cords annually for ten years from Dean, in partnership with William Hall and Thomas Culpepper. (Brydges and Culpepper were possibly contact men at court, and probably nominees.) Their tender was accepted and the grant sealed, but local opposition and the Earl of Pembroke combined to obstruct and withdraw it;[28] compensation was given by the crown. However, Winter had at least obtained the grant of the six coppices for five years from 1611, probably to his trustees, including his nephew, Henry Lord Herbert and two local landowners, Sir Henry Poole and Sir George Huntley, none of them likely

---

[26] Br. Liby., Lansd. MSS 166, ff. 353, 356, 360, 366, 367, 368. Some of the folios have been renumbered in recent years.
[27] Ibid. ff. 350, 370.
[28] C66/1904, 11 May 1611; Br. Liby., Lansd. MSS 166, ff. 374–6, 388, 29 April 1611; LR 6/38 and 12/35/1.

to be interested in Dean coppices for themselves.[29] (For the loss of his profits from the greater grant Sir Edward received £450 in November 1616 as compensation.[30])

Later in 1611 there emerged a grant to William Herbert, Earl of Pembroke – the most powerful man in the region, being the constable-warden and a governor of the Mineral and Battery Society. The 'concession' was made out to him personally and he was regarded as the responsible tenant until its termination.[31] The grant included 12,000 cords of wood a year at 4s. a cord, plus £33.6s.8d. a year towards enclosing after cutting. Timber for buildings and repairs was to be free, on assignment by forest officials. The tenure was twenty-one years from Michaelmas 1612. Marked oak timber-trees were to be exempt from cutting. The cordwood could be cut anywhere in the Forest but in compact areas to facilitate subsequent enclosure. Ore, cinders, coal, earth, sand, stone and marl could be taken freely and used at discretion. Any kind of works, apart from wireworks, could be built in the Forest in any number on any site and altered. Houses could be built for all employees with free timber, firebote and hedgebote, and be given an enclosure of twelve acres for each ironwork. All houses, cabins and enclosures were to be demolished either when no longer in use or after twenty-two years. Nobody else was to be permitted to have ironworks in the Forest or to have wood, timber, ore or cinders from it without the earl's permission. All cordwood arising from timber-trees intended for shipbuilding was to be offered to the earl at 4s. a cord.

The furnaces and forges under Pembroke's grant were built and managed by Edmund Thomas and Thomas Hackett.[32] Thomas had been a clerk in the Tintern wireworks; Hackett had been a managing clerk. The earl first of all appointed Hackett and his steward Thomas Morgan as his officials for the ironworks;[33] but within seven months he replaced Morgan by his servant Edmund Thomas. However, in February 1612 Pembroke sublet to Sir Richard Catchmay the fee-farm of Dean, excepting mining rights.[34] The Dean 'concession' and the tenancy of the two wireworks were now under the same management. By about 1612[35] building of what came to be known as the 'King's Ironworks' had been completed – charcoal blast furnaces at Lydbrook, Cannop, Parkend and Soudley; and forges near each of them except Cannop.

The farmers of the 'concession' found that their success offended some local landowners, particularly the Winters, Halls, and the neighbouring estate owners Devereux and Clanricarde. The Earl of Northampton on 14 August 1612[36] made criticisms and averred that cutting of the woods had caused 'some fifteen desperate knaves' on 9 August to set cordwood on fire 'and then dancing about the fire cried God save the King; they still walk the wood with weapons and oft I hear weak shot; they call their neighbours cowards for not assisting them; they give out that they look for more help; the Justice has given order for their apprehension but the country [i.e. the local populace] favour them.' Northampton added: 'A man may see that upon bad foundations worse buildings arise for had the matter been put into

[29] SP38/10, 16 May 1611.
[30] LR 12/35/1271.
[31] C54/2103, 17 Feb. 1612.
[32] E178/3837.
[33] C99/34, m.11, 2 March 1612.
[34] C99/22.
[35] E178/3837.
[36] SP14/70/49. The Earl of Northampton was lord lieutenant of Gloucestershire.

the hand of the gentlemen who could have tempered the wild humours of those Robin Hoodes things had been carried in a better fashion but the earl [of Pembroke] is extremely odious and with attributes that concern himself will give other matters in distemper.'

However offensive Pembroke's success and his behaviour to his competitors, much of the antagonism came from commoners who regarded timber, wood, grazing and pannage in the Forest as partly theirs, hence to be protected. Their suit against Pembroke in the Exchequer Court, probably begun towards the end of 1612 (not the first attempt to bar all outsiders from use of the Forest), really tried to deny the crown any right to the rational exploitation of its forest land.[37] They claimed that cutting down of wood and timber would destroy their herbage, pannage and estovers; implicit in their attack was the resentment of all enclosure, which would have been necessary to restore the woods. While the woods were exploited extensively, the commoners gained; but intensive exploitation was more profitable but excluded the commoners.

Privileged ironmasters also tended to collide with the older privileges of the Free Miners, most of them also commoners and many of them small freeholders. The miners were rebuffed by the Exchequer Court.[38] The 'concessionaires' were to be offered the right of first purchase of ore, but not the control of mining.[39]

Attacks on the 'concessionaires' persisted. Late in 1613 woodcutting was suspended.[40] The grant was officially surrendered by Pembroke on 29 May 1615[41] by which time the crown had received much money, and gained the 'King's Ironworks' without cost except for some building materials. Two days later two separate partnerships each acquired half of the 'concession' at a higher price – (a) Sir Basil Brooke and Robert Chaldecott, and (b) George Moore and Richard Tomlins. (For the second partnership, see Section VI.)

Sir Edward Winter's ironworks may have given him some satisfaction outweighing the loss of his high office as constable-warden of Dean in January 1608.[42] That he should lose a valuable concession to the man who had displaced him from his office, the Earl of Pembroke, cannot have increased Winter's love for the family. Winter himself did not remain immune from legal prosecution: twice at least he was attacked for alleged offences in the Forest including misappropriation of wood and timber.[43] In June 1618 he, along with William Bell of Newland, obtained a grant or disafforestment of many lands in Dean,[44] some of which they sold 22 September of that year to George Wyrrall gent.[45]

[37] E112/82/300.
[38] Ibid./83/411, Pembroke v. the Free Miners, 1613.
[39] E124/14; E126/1, f. 270.
[40] *Acts of the Privy Council*, 1613–14, pp. 279–80; E178/3837, Jan. 1614.
[41] LR 1/15, f. 182.
[42] C66/1741.
[43] E112/82/310, 6 Jas. I; E134/14 Jas. I/Hil.8.
[44] F20/1(8), 9 pages in Latin. See Hart, *Coleford*, 1983, pp. 102–4. Cf. GG 655, 22 Sept. 1618.
[45] Glos. R.O., D33 Wyrhall Deeds, bdle. E. 138/1889, 22 Sept. 1618. Bargain and sale of Jayfords Mill and land, the Sterts, Blackthornes, Yarworthshill, Edingwalle, Patwaie, Gaishome and Thornesland (reserving Stowlays field and the Hoggins) being 457 acres of assarted land in the Forest of Dean in English Bicknor, Staunton, Bers, Newland and Churching granted by letters patent to William Winter and William Bell gent., 30 June 1618, and compounded for by George Wyrrall as worth £56 a year, consideration £225.13s.4d. paid to Otho Nicholson Esq (receiver for assarts appointed for the king), rents of 6s.8d., 7s.3d., 12d., 17s.10d. paid for the different lands to the king. See also Deeds in Hereford Cathedral (copy in Glos R.O., D3921, Hart Collection).

Sir Edward died some time before May 1619.[46] He left to his son, John, a considerable legacy, in wealth, reputation and prospects.

## SIR JOHN WINTER

John Winter, son and heir to Sir Edward Winter, was born about 1602; he was at most 17 at his father's death (that was his age as known to the Court of Wards).[47] He was knighted on 7 August 1624. He stirred little locally until about 1625. Around 1624–5 the king was recommended to permit Sir John to have 2,500 cords of wood at 6s. the cord.[48] Then he began to negotiate for additional wood from the Forest,[49] perhaps because his own woods in and near Lydney again required further growth. He may, however, simply have intended to expand his production. His furnace at Guns Mill south of Mitcheldean may have been built about 1625.[50] Certainly he was alleged to own two furnaces and two forges by August 1628 and neither of them was then described as new.[51] In March 1627 he obtained a grant of 4,000 cords of wood from the Forest for £1,266.13s.4d., paid in advance, with permission to buy enough cinders and iron-ore to use up the wood.[52] By the end of the year, he came to a provisional agreement with the surveyor-general of woods for another 4,000 cords from Coverham etc., this time in partnership with Benedict Hall of Highmeadow, his brother-in-law and co-religionist – see Section III.[53] In 1629 Winter succeeded in obtaining a share of the principal Dean iron industry 'concession', tacked on to the end of the grant to Sir Basil Brooke and George Mynn (via the Earl of Pembroke). He was to have 2,500 cords of wood yearly for twenty-one years as from Michaelmas 1628, with permission to build new ironworks using crown timber and to acquire ore – but no cinders – and in general to have equal privileges with Brooke, Mynn and Thomas Hackett (of Chapel Hill, Mon.) in proportion to the amount of wood granted, for 6s.8d. the cord payable to the crown and 1s. the cord payable to Pembroke. The crown had been paid an advance of £1,500 by Sir John.[54]

By 1629 Winter had increased his works and now owned, along with the furnace at Guns Mill, one at Maple Hill north of Lydney, also an ordinary forge, a double-forge and a slitting mill, all in or near Lydney.[55] The year 1628 was that in which Winter began to expand seriously: in April 1629 he paid £28 to a Mr. Boyle for hammers and anvils, which he had probably at least received by then.[56]

Litigation pursued Sir John as it appears to have done all prominent local landowners and certainly all who signed contracts with the crown in Dean. In 1626 he, with Benedict Hall and others, was charged with misappropriation of wood:[57]

[46] Glos. R.O., D421 Winter Papers, T23.

[47] Ibid.

[48] Br. Liby., Add. MS 69909, Coke Papers (Series II), XLII, 57/7/11.

[49] H.M.C., 12th Rept., Coke, p. 294.

[50] Bodleian, Gough MSS, Glouc. I, f. 61d.

[51] E178/5304.

[52] C99/23, 17 March 1627; SP16/57/96; Hart, Royal Forest, p. 102.

[53] Glos. R.O., D421 Winter Papers, E2; H.M.C., 12th Rept., Cowper/Coke MSS, I, p. 294; C99/23.

[54] C99/22, 17 July 1629 and C99/36, 18 July 1629.

[55] E178/5304, 4 Chas. I; Bodleian, Gough MSS, Glouc., I, f. 61d; Br. Liby., Harl. 4850, f. 48; SP16/282/127, p. 3.

[56] Lismore Papers of the first Earl of Cork, ed. A.B. Grosart, 1st Ser., II, 308.

[57] E112/179/17.

perhaps this was the crown's retaliation for the attempt of the freeholders, headed by Winter, to stop the crown from selling parts of Dean for enclosure.[58] In 1630 Sir John was charged, along with the other ironmasters, with taking timber and wood beyond the authorization of their grant;[59] this prosecution appears to have petered out, perhaps because it had been based on the information of Robert Treswell junior, a surveyor who had himself committed peculation on a considerable scale in Dean.[60] Around 1630–1 it was reported:[61]

> The ground called the Sneade that Sir John Winter did inclose in the Forest contains in compass round about 540 luggs, every lugg containing 5½ yards or 16½ foot. The length contains 1,290 yards. The breadth thereof is 700 yards. Measured by Richard Burte, William Morse, Giles Powell, Griffith Morgan, James Trested, Thomas Wapper, Richard Partridge, Edward Worgan.

Early in 1631 Winter was found to be experimenting with the mechanized production of iron wire, employing methods which the Mineral and Battery Society regarded as infringing their monopoly. Winter explained that he was merely experimenting and that the wire was used for a bird cage, but probably the slitting mill had been built with iron wire in mind.[62] By March 1632 he had acquired from Mrs. Eleanor James the lease of her furnace at Rodmore on the south-western boundary of the crown woods along with her grant of the roots and stumps of trees felled in the Forest and in her woods at £280 a year.[63] On 11 January 1632 John Broughton of Ruardean (see Section IV), writing to Sir John Coke, Secretary of State, when suggesting new rents for the crown ironworks, commented:[64]

> The rates [rents] (£3,100) that are set down (suggested) upon Sir John Winter's works at Lydney will hold if he be put to it and he will not refuse it . . . Sir John Winter has a furnace at Guns Mill near Micheldeane, built by the King's timber, and chiefly maintained by his Majesty's wood. Because Sir John has wood of his own to obtain this furnace he may refuse to give the rate of £1,300 set down by me in the notes. But then he should have none of the King's woods to that furnace. The sooner that Order is sent for stay of cutting wood in the Forest of Deane for the ironworks, the sooner this rent will begin.

By 1632 Winter controlled three large furnaces and three forges, one being a double-forge, probably at Lydney Pill. (With this equipment he later admitted to having made more than 11,000 tons of iron between 1628 and 1634.[65]) It is possible that John Typper, the tenant of the two Flaxley forges, was also Winter's employee;[66] Winter had a lease of the nearby Abbotswood from the Kingstons of Flaxley.[67] By 17 September 1632 Winter was purchasing timber in the Cannop valley woods from John Gibbons (see Section VI). Some (allegedly illegally) had been cut

[58] E112/179/28, possibly before August 1624.
[59] E112/179/37.
[60] E178/5304, 6 Chas. I.
[61] Br. Liby., Add. MS 69909, Coke Papers (Series II), XLII, 57/7/14, c. 1630–31; Cp. H.M.C., I, 429.
[62] Mineral & Battery Society Min. Bk., II, ff. 53 and 59, 11 Feb. and 28 June 1631.
[63] SP16/257/94; H.M.C., 12th Rept., Cowper/Coke MSS, I, 474.
[64] Br. Liby., Add. MS 69909, 57/7/13, 11 Jan. 1632.
[65] SP16/289/105.
[66] Ibid. /282/127; Bodleian MSS, Gough, Glouc. I, f. 61d.
[67] Bodleian, Bankes MSS, 40/2.

down by Winter's appointment and by the agreement of 'Mr. Surveyor [Treswell]'
who 'heretofore hath been Steward to Sir Edward Winter, and Sir John, and hath
kept their courts, and without question he will not fail to do Sir John Winter what
favour he can'.[68] Around 1633, Charles Powell of Ruardean (see Section IV),
reported to Coke:[69]

> Now touching Sir John Winter, he hath at Lidney one furnace and two double forges. In
> his furnace he casteth yearly at least 800 tons of raw iron, which doth cost him 2,000
> cords for [char]coale at least. Which cole with the best husbandry possible cannot be made
> with less than 4,000 cords of wood. This raw iron he bendeth into bar iron, whereby he
> maketh 600 tons of bar iron, which must spend 1,800 loads of coales, which coales are
> made with 3,600 cords of wood. Sir John Winter hath by Micheldeane another furnace
> [Guns Mill] in which if the year be not very dry (as this is) he makes about 800 tons of
> raw iron, but this dry year he hath made but 600 tons. You may guess by the former
> accompt what coales he may spend in making this quantity of iron at this second furnace.
> He hath no woods for those works at Lidney, but what he hath out of the Forest; it is true
> he hath large woods and coppice of his own but they are all too young to cut. But he
> cutteth for his second furnace at Micheldeane [Guns Mill] some quantities of wood in his
> wood at Newent, and he doth buy some small quantities up and down the country, but
> the main cometh from the Forest of Dean to serve that furnace also.

There is little doubt that Winter aimed, from now on, at the complete industrial
domination of Dean. In 1633 he offered Mynn £12,000 for his half of the major
Dean ironworks 'concession';[70] probably in April 1634, while the grant to Brooke
and Mynn (assigns of the Earl of Pembroke) was still in force, he offered the crown
to replace their contract by one which would secure to the crown all the timber-
trees and all the young woods in Dean, while allowing him all the cordwood, at a
perpetual rent of £4,000 a year, of which £8,000 was to be paid in advance, and
£4,000 had already been paid.[71] In about 1633 Sir John Coke noted:[72]

> Sir John Winter is allowed by contract 2,500 cords per annum for 15 years unexpired. He
> keeps in work:
>
> | | |
> |---|---|
> | 2 Furnaces which spend | 8,000 cords |
> | 2 Double forges which spend | 4,000 cords |
> | | 12,000 cords = £4,000. |
>
> Of this quantity he cuts out of his own woods at Newent about 2,000 cords. Besides these
> 12,000 cords Sir John imployeth upon his colepits and his cutting and slitting mill 1,000
> cords.

On 5 June 1634 Winter entered into partnership with Brooke; between them they
bought out Mynn for £8,000 plus agreements on the delivery of Osmund iron at
reduced rates to Mynn.[73] Winter's offer to the crown was accepted, 'yet with this

[68] Br. Liby., Add. MS 69909, Coke Papers (Series II), XLII, 57/7/9, by John Broughton.
[69] Ibid. 57/7/16.
[70] E112/182/163.
[71] SP16/266/69.
[72] Br. Liby., Add. MS 69909, 57/7/17, c. 1633.
[73] E112/181/155; /182/63; E133/157/55 and 56; SP16/266/69; C99/36.

proviso that if upon a survey or other information at a Justice Seat we find that greater yearly revenue will be raised . . . for the woods aforesaid . . .' the better offer was to be preferred and Winter to be repaid an advance of £4,000 with interest.[74] If no other offer had been received by 13 September 1634, the grant to Winter was to stand.

Sir John Winter's hoped for success was disrupted by the Justice Seat in Eyre of July 1634, where his offences in the Forest were made evident; he was alleged to owe for 60,700 cords (see Section V). He spent a day or two listening to the proceedings; on 15 July, in the words of the prosecuting council, 'perceiving his case to be like that of Sir Basil Brooke's and Mr. Minne's in open Court *relicta verificara* he confessed the Indictment. So the Court gave Judgment against him and fined him according to his confession £20,230.' Undoubtedly Sir John's change of plea saved him some hours of useless argument laced with unrequited insults without increasing his sentence.[75]

As an immediate result, the further cutting of all wood in Dean under the 'concession' ceased. Brooke and Winter could use up the charcoal and wood already handed over, because the Justice Seat had no powers over the ironworks and the terms of a royal patent, apart from those dealing with Forest wood and timber. But then came deadlock; Winter claimed the full rights to which his patent entitled him and refused to surrender it without legal process: like all his fellow sufferers, he petitioned for a reduction of his fine.[76] In the course of his arguments he pointed out that his total production of iron for the last six years had amounted to 11,080 tons of iron, by which he possibly meant pig-iron: in any event, he was not likely to exaggerate his production in this context.[77] A yearly output of 1,800 tons of pig-iron would have made Winter one of the greatest ironmasters in England: the combination of his works with the crown works in Dean would have given him and Brooke an output more than half as great as that of the whole Weald.

Whereas Winter managed to have his fine reduced to £4,000, which he paid,[78] he was persuaded to surrender his share of the grant. Moreover, a new 'concession' to Baynham Throckmorton and partners (see Section II) incorporated an explicit grant of monopoly within the boundaries of the Forest, so that Sir John was compelled to enter into negotiations with them in order to be able to use his furnaces at Maple Hill and Guns Mill as well as one of the Lydney forges. He was forced to agree to employ Rodmore furnace for only another year and to draw his cordwood from his own woods and from the Abbotswood exclusively: on those conditions he was to have all the ore and cinders he needed.[79]

[74] SP16/266/69, Sir John Winter's warrant, April 1634. The draft for a contract (which proved abortive) is in GG 1545(1) *c.* 1633. It is notable because of two arrangements therein whereby Sir John Winter (i) be allowed 'to shroud [shred] the timber trees, cutting the boughs one foot at the least from the body of the trees if by so doing the timber be not impaired'; (ii) 'should suffer officers to encoppice [enclose for regrowth] such part of the said Forest as we shall appoint after the felling of the trees and he shall not cut or fell any of the said woods so coppiced until they shall be fifteen years growth.'
[75] Br. Liby., Add. MS 25302, ff. 65, 65d, of which SP16/271/67 is an incomplete copy; Hart, *Royal Forest*, p. 113; pardon and release – Glos. R.O., D421 Winter Papers, E.4, 1637.
[76] SP16/285/7, /289/105, /293/40 and 68, /294/99, 307/11.
[77] SP16/289/115.
[78] C66/2766.
[79] Bodleian, Bankes MSS, 40/2, 18 Dec. 1635. Benedict Hall financially aided Winter in 1635 (GG 800).

Winter found himself faced by the bonds with which he and Brooke had secured to Mynn the completion of their agreement; they sued Mynn to recover their bonds: while the case dragged on from Court to Court and from one technicality to another, they were at least spared the payment.[80] In 1637 John Broughton, now local deputy surveyor (see Section IV), commented:[81]

> Sir John Winter with his 2,500 cords which he hath yearly granted unto him by patent cannot possibly make above 500 tons of raw and bar iron. If the propounder of this offer be Sir John Winter, and if he by this bargain do hedge in wood for his own ironworks, he may very well give the [suggested] great rent for the wood that doth at this present serve his Majesty's works and Sir John Winter's works, is proved plainly in my proposition to be worth £12,000 per annum.

In the same year, 1637, Winter wrote to Secretary of State Sir Francis Windebank:[82]

> His Majesty having declared by you that he holds me not unfit to serve him, I have been elected verderer by the freeholders on Wednesday last. And because there has been great opposition made for the place by Sir Robert Cook [of Highnam], assisted by many of this county that deny payment of ship-money, I beseech you to be the first that made it known to the king for prevention of sinister information.

Winter's wealth, standing and influence were not easily exhausted. If his coalmining on his own estates, albeit within the limits of the Forest, interfered with the coal patent given to Edward Tyringham by the crown, he was quite prepared to fight back.[83] The crown, having extended the bounds of the Forest, proceeded to ask for bids to compound for the disafforestation of affected estates. Sir John bought the disafforestation of his lands for £1,000.[84] His reputation had been so little tarnished that Queen Henrietta Maria appointed him as her secretary and master of requests in May 1638.[85] This probably helped Winter in his own ambitions. On 20 January 1639 he was added to the commission set up to compound for the disafforestation of the Forests of Essex, and Dean.[86]

Early in 1639 the crown decided to cancel a large grant of wood and ironworks made to Throckmorton and partners (see Section II), and to sell most of the crown relevant rights and lands to Sir John Winter. Perhaps he had expunged his alleged misappropriation of wood by eight months' royal service, or the crown had never taken it very seriously. Negotiations lasted for more than a year. The eventual sale to Winter, dated 20 February 1640 (but not operative until 31 March) is noted below.[87]

Winter, by letters patent, gained most of the iron industry 'concession' and a lease in fee-farm of most of the soil of the Forest of Dean. The extent of the royal

[80] E112/182/163; E133/137/55 and 56.
[81] Br. Liby., Add. MS 69909, 57/7/12, 13 c. 9 June 1637; Cp. Cal. SPD, 1637–8, p. 205.
[82] SP16/367, 412, No. 52; Hart, The Verderers and Forest Laws of Dean, 1971, p. 103.
[83] E112/181/155, 12 Chas. I, 1636–7.
[84] E401/1924 & 1925, 29 July and 5 Dec. 1637, 22 Feb. and 12 June 1638.
[85] D.N.B.; Glos. R.O., D421 Winter Papers, 1/5, 25 Apl. 1638.
[86] Bodleian, Bankes MSS, 43/12, 18 Dec. 1635; T. Rymer Foedera, 1744, XIX, pp. 20–2.
[87] Glos. R.O., D421 Winter Papers, E5, May 1639, and T24; also App. II, 20, 21, 22 (1640); C66/2843, 20 Feb. 1640; C66/2876; LR 1/1, ff. 279–84, 31 March 1640; 3rd Rept. of 1788, App. 6, pp. 60–3; E178/5321; Hart, Royal Forest, p. 125.

property virtually sold was 18,000 acres within the old perambulation, excepting eight items stated in detail and including six items formerly let to other individuals. The most important exception was 4,000 acres of land, allocated to the local populace in perpetuity; the second was the Lea Baily woods in the north of Dean. The total woodland contained an estimated 153,209 cords of wood and 61,928 tons of timber of which 14,350 loads were fit for the navy (later revised to 15,319 loads). Excepting 15,000 tons of naval (standing) timber, the remainder was sold. Included in the sale were all the ironworks, and all mineral rights, neither excepting privately owned lands nor the lands now granted in common, but excepting mines royal (silver, gold, etc.). All the land in the grant was to be disafforested at royal expense by letters patent, as also the land of all commoners agreeing to the partition and enclosure; the land of dissenters from the scheme was to remain subject to forest law at Winter's full discretion. Numerous other privileges were included; lands and privileges were to be held in free and common socage of the manor of St. Briavels. (Throckmorton and his partners, as compensation for loss of their grant, were to have a lease of Parkend and Soudley furnaces, along with Soudley, Bradley, Parkend and Whitecroft forges and 13,500 cords of mixed wood a year with iron-ore and cinders at 10s. a cord of wood for six years from Lady Day 1640.) Payments (excluding some minor deductions) were to be: £10,000 before the letters patent were passed; £16,000 a year for six years, half each at Michaelmas and Lady Day beginning at Michaelmas 1640; and a perpetual fee-farm of £1,950.12s.8d. payable in the same fashion. A loan of £8,000 at 8 per cent per annum to the crown from Winter was to be repaid by defalcations of £750 plus interest from each half-yearly payment, the last two instalments being of £250 each plus interest, ending at Lady Day 1646.

This 'bargain' can be regarded as Sir John's attempt to clarify, analyse, determine, lay down and settle the use and exploitation of the soil, woods, minerals and privileges claimed by any interested party in Dean. Two detailed surveys of the Dean woods showed the crown precisely what there was to sell and Sir John what he was buying. In fact the crown had, under the severe pressure of financial needs, found the reasonable solution of placing the whole Forest under single undivided management.

The deal seems eminently fair. The price corresponds to an income of approximately £7,250 yearly reckoned at 5 per cent: rather more than the crown had been getting from Dean and a regular income and very much more than the cash which reached it after the cost of administration, commissions, litigation and riots had been taken into account. Moreover the scheme was the first reasonable design for the future of the Forest, with clear delimitation of responsibilities, privileges and boundaries. (It bears little sign of that ruthless endeavour to destroy Dean for the sake of iron smelting, which was later alleged against Winter. His administration of his own woods suggests that, had he been permitted to keep his purchase, he would have preserved the woods as carefully as any other sensible landowner-cum-ironmaster.)

For the next two years, Winter became the greatest ironmaster in the country bar Richard Foley of Stoke Edith in Herefordshire: six furnaces and eight forges. Winter's lands lay mainly to the south of the Forest, whilst Benedict Hall's (see Section III) lay to the west and north-west. Together they were strategically placed to participate in the Dean industry; both had much wood of their own; Winter's land had some iron-ore deposits and some coal seams,[88] Hall's had iron-ore and

---

[88] E112/181/155.

cinders – the latter being the most valuable raw material of the Dean smelter.[89] Winter and Hall may have co-operated more regularly than appears from their occasional joint or mutual transactions: their neighbours regarded them as tolerably friendly with each other; they never clashed directly and openly.[90] About 1641 between them they controlled almost three-quarters of all the wood connected with Dean: nine furnaces out of fifteen, fifteen forges out of twenty. Hammersley[91] suggests that Winter 'was a not unfamiliar type: the wealthy, able, vigorous landowner whose catholicism forbade him an outlet in ordinary public service and who turned his energies to making more money and to experimenting with technical innovation'.

Local opposition and Parliamentary antagonism to a Roman Catholic official of the Queen's household outweighed Winter's personal popularity and the rational advantages of his scheme. He was compelled to relinquish his purchase: it was terminated 21 March 1642 by resolution of the House of Commons.[92] His use of the Forest was investigated.[93] Meanwhile Parliament had ordered the local sale of some timber from Dean and, when this proved fruitless, the wood and some of the works were offered to John Browne of Brenchley, gunfounder, in part payment of money due to him. When Winter demurred that he would want his accounts settled first, considerable pressure was put on him to comply.[94] His calculations suggest that he was owed about £15,000 on the deal. In any event, the disposal of the Forest, the repayment of debts and even the formal surrender of the patent were all swallowed up in the Civil Wars (1642–7).

Winter's main accuser was a Protestant, the local Sir Baynham Throckmorton[95] (see Section II). What evidence about his alleged misdeeds had been collected was characterized as contradictory and insufficient by the Exchequer auditors sent to investigate Winter's claims for compensation;[96] his accounts were taken on oath and, while no compensation was in fact paid now, the sworn and countersigned statement was to be useful to him after the Restoration (1660).[97] The compensatory sub-lease to Throckmorton and his partners was, at least for the moment, permitted to stand. At first Parliament only renewed their grant until Michaelmas 1642; perhaps as a consequence of the outbreak of the Civil Wars, it then intended to allow the full term of their lease to stand.[98] The furnaces at Cannop and Lydbrook as well as Lydbrook forge, were let to the gunfounder John Browne by order of Parliament for two years and three months from 6 July 1942[99] in spite of Winter's strenuous opposition; not unreasonably but perhaps undiplomatically, he wanted to

[89] GG 515, 673.

[90] Hammersley, G., *pers. comm.*

[91] Ibid.

[92] *Commons Journal*, II, 489, 21 March 1642.

[93] *The Journal of Sir Simon D'Ewes*, Ed. W. Notestein, Yale, 1923, pp. 119, 488–9; SP16/489/35, 14 Feb. 1642 and E178/6080, pt. i, m.s. 20–21d; SP16/491/62, 68, 70, 14 July 1642 and E178/5304, 17 & 18 Chas. I, with his account in 18 Chas. I.

[94] SP16/487/77, misplaced in the *Calendar* under 1641; SP16/491/50, 21 March 1642; ibid., /86.

[95] Notestein, W. (ed.), *op. cit.*, p. 119 – the petition of Throckmorton and other local men against Winter's lease; *Commons Journal*, II, 131.

[96] SP16/491/62, 11 July 1642: report by W. Kingscote, deputy surveyor-general of woods, and two auditors.

[97] E178/5304, 9 Aug., 18 Chas.I.

[98] SP16/489/35; LR12/1014; E407/50, 8 Sept. 1642.

[99] E178/6080, pt. i, m.20d; L.R.R.O. 5/7A; SP16/491/50.

have his claims for compensation settled first. An explicit threat from the clerk of Parliament was necessary to make Winter co-operate.[100] Thus ended the largest consecutive era in the administration of the Dean iron industry 'concession'.

During the Civil Wars, Winter became one of the king's most active partisans in Dean.[101] He garrisoned his fortified 'White Cross House' at Lydney for the king. He was the lieutenant colonel of the Welsh Force raised by his cousin, the Marquis of Worcester, in 1643; and the coastal strip between Parliamentary Gloucester and Royalist Chepstow became a flashpoint at the height of the Civil Wars. The house featured several times in local engagements between the Roundheads and Cavaliers, and although it was captured once by Colonel Massey, the Parliamentarian Governor of Gloucester, Sir John succeeded in reoccupying it; when he was turned out again in 1645, he burnt it down. The following letter written by him on 21 April 1645 to someone in authority at Oxford, describes some of his actions:[102]

> May it please your Lordship.
> The occasion of my present address unto your Lordship is to satisfy you with some late passages in these parts; the last week Col. Massey with the Glostershire forces came before my house and (being very numerous and potent) made an assault upon one of our works, which was received and returned by my men with as much valour as could be expected, but being over-powered they gained a Home Worke and took two pieces of Ordnance in it, upon this the Rebells having gained so great an advantage upon me, I was put to it, to do what I could for the safeguard of the garrison, and thereupon to prevent their further doing mischiefe, I appointed some of my souldiers to fire the barns and outhouses, but the Rebells came so fast upon them, that although it took fire, yet it did not prove effectuall, being frequently extinguished by them, and so they got the houses: after this I sent out a partie of 200 horse and foot to beat them out of the houses, but a partie of Rebells got between my men and the house [?horse], fell upon them on both sides and put many of them to the sword, and not one of them escaped to me, by which means this garrison is much weakened. Sir I beseach you not to neglect to use your best indeavours for the sending of speedy supplies for my relief, and suffer him not to perish (my Lord) who is your Lordships humble Servant, J. Winter.

The Royalist army left Gloucestershire in May 1645, and Winter seeing that he was incapable of further resistance 'resolved that his house should never harbour his enemies', and having removed from it the lead and furniture, burned it to the ground, and joined the queen in France. (Little is known about the house: it lay just south of the main road, at the west end of Lydney, and the site was abandoned from the mid-seventeenth century onwards.) Winter's estates and the Dean ironworks passed, for a time, to his conquerors,[103] and his landed property was under Treasury management in spite of appeals by the trustees for his creditors: probably the trust set up for his children in December 1640 fared no better.[104] At least one of his manors was sold although the man who bought it was probably his nominee,[105] his

---

[100] SP16/487/77, probably between 1 and 22 July 1642.

[101] Glos. R.O., D421 Winter Papers, App. IV, 1/6, 1/7, 1/8.

[102] The 'Perfect Diurnal' for 26 April 1645, quoted by F.A. Hyett (pamphlet 'The Civil War in the Forest of Dean, 1643–1645', p. 14.)

[103] Hart, Royal Forest, p. 131; SP23/136/219.

[104] Cal. of Cttee. for Comp.,. 2143 & SP23/103, pp. 503 & 519; SP25/92, p. 49; Glos. R.O., D421 Winter Papers, T23, 23 Dec. 1640.

[105] Glos. R.O., D421 Winter Papers, E22.

ironworks were either let out or simply permitted to fall down and his coppices were sold. When Major John Wade, administrator of the Forest for the Commonwealth (see Section VIII), came in 1653 to start ironmaking again, at least one of the Winter furnaces would have needed extensive repairs, if not rebuilding.[106] There is some indirect evidence that parts of the estate remained or were restored to Lady Winter and Winter's children, as was normal (without a forge of some sort, his son Charles and his agent, John Coster, would not have bought some 400 tons of pig-iron from the state works in Dean between 1656 and 1600.)[107] In 1649[108] it was reported that the following woods of Winter had been devastated: Kernes, Shraves, Dodmore, Ten Acres, Timleys, Horrage, Breames, Norchard, Mill Ruff, Bab Redding, Oakles, Hassell, and Wood Grove. A scathing attack on the Commonwealth ironmasters, as well as on Sir John appeared in 1650.[109] At the Justice Seat in 1656 (see Section VII), Winter was accused thus:[110]

> Sir John Wintour Kt has since the last Justice Seat [1634] inclosed with a stone wall a parcel of land called the Sneed and Kidnells containing by estimate 200 acres, being his Highness [the Lord Protector] wast soyle of the Forest of Dean . . . [also] . . . raised and made a dam-head and thereby impounded the water called Bull Bollock Pond to the over-flowing and drownding of an acre of his Highness wast soyle of the said Forest.

> [Also] . . .encroached with his ditch 20 yards long and 4 foot broad upon his Highness wast soyle at Coverham within the Woodwardship of Staunton.

> [Also] . . . there has been stript by Sir John Winter's order in Kenslyes Edge since the last Justice Seat [1634] 500 oaks.

> [Also] . . . Capt Gifford for cutting without licence one Coppice Grove, 8 acres, within Sir John Winter's Park, being then in the fee of Sir John Winter . . . [also] . . . for cutting without licence one Coppice Grove, call The Shraves, 10 acres, being then in the fee of Sir John Winter.

> [Also] . . . John White, gent. and partners, the late purchasers of Sir John Winter's estate, one Coppice Grove, 7 acres.

There is no evidence of any fine being imposed on Winter.

Altogether the Civil Wars, directly and indirectly cost Sir John a great deal. Following the Restoration (1660), commissioners were at first appointed to succeed Wade, both to clear the accounts and as a holding operation. The uncertainties of the position are shown in the reduction of output of iron.[111] Meanwhile all the different claimants to Dean or parts of Dean began to press their claims to restitution or for consideration. The commoners, and the former holders of concessions in Dean along with the former state ironworks, all found their advocates.[112]

---

[106] SP25/70, pp. 288–90, SP18/40/61 and 73; E178/6080, pt.i, m.s. 18d–19d.
[107] SP18/157B; E178/6080 pt. i, m.s. 25–38d.
[108] LRRO 5/7A; Hart, *Royal Forest*, pp. 136–7.
[109] Glos. R.O., D3921, Hart Collection, II/12 (1650): I. Bromwich, a commissioner. Original in Br. Liby., 577, b.40.
[110] Glos. R.O., D2026 Bond Papers, X.14.
[111] SP18/220/106 and E178/6080, pts. i and iii.
[112] Shaftesbury Papers, P.R.O. 30/24/32 contain copies or the originals of some of the claims.

Henry Lord Herbert, who had been appointed lord lieutenant of Gloucestershire and constable of the Forest, headed a commission appointed 12 September 1660, charged to survey the Forest and to recommend its further disposal. Reasonably they confirmed the soundness of the general policies pursued by the Protectorate: they recommended the resumption by the crown of all grants of and in Dean, a temporary suspension of the ironworks to permit the woods to recover, and the continuation of direct management by the crown; they opposed any suggestion of leasing the ironworks.[113] However, Sir John Winter put in a claim for more than £15,000 in compensation for his former losses; and Sir Baynham Throckmorton claimed the crown's obligation to him.[114] Winter was significantly successful: in March 1661 he obtained the Dean ironworks with stocks worth £4,360 and the right to some wood and underwoods in partial settlement of his claims; he was to grant Throckmorton a sublease.[115] This temporary arrangement was followed in March 1662 by a commission to settle the Forest affairs, on the assumption that Winter was to retain a concession of the ironworks together with wood but without rights to any timber-trees. The commissioners' report discussed the various uses of the Forest, again recommended the direct management of the ironworks by the crown and attempted to apportion the Forest between commons for the inhabitants and enclosures for regeneration.[116] Their estimate of the available timber and wood formed the basis of Winter's new contract,[117] and of instructions for another commission, which was to set out the enclosures and commons and to repeat some of the earlier enquiries.[118]

Winter's estates had survived sequestration and sales of royalist lands better than might have been expected: part was successfully claimed by the trustees for his creditors and his family;[119] some at least of the purchasers of another part of his land may have been his agents;[120] a number of his ironworks had been kept in his family with the remainder of the estate.[121] But the resulting expense was formidable: lawsuits to permit the trust to stand, the temporary administration of some or all of his land by the sequesters and his own prolonged imprisonment in the Tower, all helped to pull him down financially.[122]

Winter's new grant, dated 30 July 1662, term eleven years, was of 60,787 cords of wood, contained in 25,929 oaks and 4,204 beeches, standing on 18,000 acres of Dean formerly granted to him, plus Whitemead Park, plus 4,000 acres of common, plus all the wood from trees blown down in the Lea Baily, except timber contained in the last. Exempt also were 11,334 tons of naval timber; Winter was to pay 15s. for every ton of timber missing from this, the crown likewise for every excess ton of timber. Included were the 'King's Ironworks' and their equipment, also permission

---

[113] E178/6080, pt. iii, 12 Sept., 12 Chas. II.

[114] Shaftesbury Papers, P.R.O. 30/24/32; Cal. Treas. Bks., 1660–7, p. 114, 5 Jan. 1661.

[115] Glos. R.O., D421 Winter Papers, E6e; Shaftesbury Papers loc. cit., 30/24/32; Cal. Treas. Bks., 1681–5, VII, pt. iii, 1531–2.

[116] E178/6080, pt. i, ms.4d–11, 5 March, 14 Chas.II; Br. Liby., Harl. MS 6839, ff.332–8.

[117] C66/3007; Glos. R.O., D421 Winter Papers, E7.

[118] E178/6080, pt. i, ms.3–5, 28 Nov., 14 Chas.II.

[119] H.M.C., 7th Rept., pt. i, Lords MSS, p. 9; Glos. R.O., D421 Winter Papers, T23, 23 Dec. 1640; Cal. of Cttee. for Comp., pt. iii, 2143; SP23/103, pp. 503, 519.

[120] Glos. R.O., D421 Winter Papers, T22, sale of the manor of Pyrton to Francis Finch and others by the Commonwealth Committee, 1655.

[121] Ibid. T16, 20 July 1663; E6b., T22, 12 July 1654.

[122] Ibid. T18, 20 July 1663, E6b, T22, 12 July 1654 and 7 Aug. 1662.

to build one or more new ironworks. The significant part of the new grant was Winter's new associates, Francis Finch and Robert Clayton. Finch was probably Winter's nominee but Clayton was obviously his creditor and the grant was Winter's method of repayment.[123] Neither was Clayton the sole creditor, though clearly he was the most considerable: he had been compelled to mortgage one of his forges for £1,200 and to secure another loan on his share of the Dean 'concession'.[124] The manager was joint agent for Winter, and the moneylender, Clayton, used the works independently from Winter's immediate supervision.[125] Local and Parliamentary opposition to the grant was varied, debated and challenged; the grant was suspended, restored and almost incessantly attacked.[126] However, at that time, Samuel Pepys thought highly of Winter and recorded 20 June 1662:[127]

> Up by 4 or 5 o'clock, and to the office, and there drew up an agreement between the King and Sir John Wintour about the Forest of Dean; and having done it, he came himself, whom I observed to be a man of fine parts; and we read it, and both liked it well. That done, I turned to the Forest of Dean, in Speede's Maps, and there he showed me how it lies; and the Leabayley with the great charge of carrying it to Lydney, and many other things worth knowing.

Winter and partners were repeatedly accused of misappropriating the timber-trees which he had been obliged to reserve to the crown; his tenure was attacked and suspended, the works were seized for damages by the crown but released because the seizing turned out to be illegal (*infra*).[128] In spite of strong opposition, Winter and partners were at last permitted to work out his agreed period, perhaps because the unreliability of even the most sound surveys of timber-trees was at last becoming notorious.[129]

Hostile comment repeatedly accused Winter of destroying the woods in Dean. These accusations were based on no better evidence than those made earlier against other ironmasters and patentees; his essays in their refutation impress as honest and reasonable statements.[130] Even his religious opponents in the Long Parliament were prepared to concede his integrity and honesty.[131]

Hammersley[132] avers that 'it seems out of character for such a man to purloin timber he had agreed to preserve; a successful and experienced businessman like him would also be careful to avoid the penalties set in his contract. Certainly his regime was in no way more harmful to the woods than that of his predecessors or successors. But if the commoners and miners had resented attempts to use even parts

---

[123] Glos. R.O., D421 Winter Papers, T18, 6 Dec. 1664.

[124] Ibid. T18 & T22; also App. II, 28 (1662).

[125] Ibid. E6, a & b.

[126] *Cal. Treas. Bks.*, 1660–7, pp. 673, 699; ibid. 1667–8, pp. 8, 23, 26, 50, 54, 121, 131, 149, 174, 275, 276, 349, 535, 543; cf. *A True Narrative concerning the Woods and Ironworks of the Forrest of Deane . . .*, c. 1667, and *Sir John Wintour's Vindication . . .*, 17 Aug. 1660 (copy in Glos. R.O., D3921, Hart Collection, I/43).

[127] Wheatley, W.B. (ed.), *The Diary of Samuel Pepys* (London, 1904).

[128] *Commons Journal*, VIII, 312; *Cal. Treas. Bks.*, 1660–7, I, 699; 1667–8, II, 23, 26, 29, 39, 50, 54, 87–90, 121, 123, 131, 149, 275, 276, 288–9, 349, 535, 543.

[129] *Cal. Treas. Bks.*, 1669–72, III, pt. ii, 1331, 22 Oct. 1672; 1672–5, IV, 175, 17 June 1673.

[130] *Sir John Wintour's Vindication . . .*, (1660), *op. cit.*, and *A True Narrative . . .*, (c. 1667), *op. cit.*

[131] Notestein, W. (ed.), *op. cit.*, pp. 392, 393, 488–9.

[132] Hammersley, G., *pers. comm.*

of Dean rationally, they would surely fight to the last the permanent limitation of their privileges of common and the considerable privileges over former crown land granted to one man.'

The grant made to Winter in 1662[133] virtually ended in 1664.[134] In 1667 he received a third grant[135] but this soon ended. In that year, on 15 March, Pepys recorded that he felt Winter 'to be a worthy good man and I will do him the right to tell the Duke [of York] of it, who did speak well of him the other day'.[136] However, in that same year, 1667, 'The Freeholders and inhabitants who claim right of common within his Majesty's Forest of Deane' petitioned 'the Honorable Knights, Citizens and Burgesses in this present Parliament assembled':[137]

Sheweth that Sir John Wintour Knight in the year 1639 did obtain of his late Majesty [Charles I] a Grant of 18,000 acres of the wast soil of his Majesty's Forest of Deane consisting of 23,000 acres to him and his heirs for ever under the yearly Fee Farm rent of £1,950 and for the Wood and Timber growing thereon the sum of £16,000 per annum for six years, his Majesty reserving for himself 15,000 tons of Ship Timber for the use of the Navy and the Wood and Soyle of the Woodwardship of the Lea Bayley containing about 1,000 acres, Sir John Wintour laying out but 4,000 acres only of the worst of the Forest for Common of many hundred of families and that in the beginning of the Parliament holden in November 1640 the House of Commons after a full examination of the said patent did Order that the said Sir John Winter was not fit to hold the said bargaine it being disadvantagious to the Common Wealth, and that the said Sir John Wintour's offer to surrender his said patent into the hands of the Crown for the Treasury it was thought fit to be accepted and his patent to be surrendered accordingly.

That in the Convention of his Majesty's happy restoration [1660] the Settlement of the said Forest for the use of his Majesty was again taken into consideration by the House of Commons and the said Sir John Winter thereupon making demands of money due to him was required to state an account which accordingly he so did and pretended a debt of £14,000 only and no more to be due to him from his Majesty upon the said Grant which was thought fit to be allowed him and a Bill to be brought into the House to resettle the said Forest in the Crown but that Convention was disolved before the said Bill could pass. In pursuance whereof in the March following being in 1666 Sir John Winter did agree with the Lord Treasurer to surrender his said Grant to his Majesty upon just satisfaction to be given him for what he had disbursed upon the said patent; that in the said month Sir John Wintour's account was by warrant from the Lord Treasurer referred to Auditors of the Exchequer to be stated and thereupon in the same month had immediately by Warrant from the Lord Treasurer delivered over to him for part of the satisfaction for what should appear to be due to him in iron and debts owing to his Majesty to the value of £4,300 that the Act of Juda..aity being confirmed and by reason of the Agreement no provision made to debarr him of this pretence to the said patent he became in law entitled to the full benefit thereof both as to the soil and wood whereby the arrears of the said Fee Farm rent of £1,950 for the soyle for about 20 years together with the £16,000 payable for about 4 years for the Wood was wholly committed and forgiven. Whereupon he presently demands and obtains an allowance of above £30,000 instead of his former demand of £14,000 besides the £4,300 delivered unto him as aforesaid for payment whereof his Majesty did grant unto him 27,000 cords of wood blown by the Great Wind in the said

[133] Hart, *Royal Forest*, pp. 157–8; Glos. R.O., D421 Winter Papers, T22 and E7 (1662).
[134] Hart, *Royal Forest*, p. 160.
[135] Ibid. p. 161.
[136] Wheatley, *op. cit.*, IV, p. 224.
[137] Glouc. Liby., MS L.F.1.1, p. 9.

Forest worth to be sold £6,000. And also all of the old trees then standing upon the said Forest valued upon an exact survey made by his Majesty's Officers at (?) 120,000 cords of wood and worth at the usual rates in the country £36,000 together with all his Majesty's Iron Works there for 11 years with divers other privileges and advantages which might reasonably under the said Wood converted into iron above £70,000, his Majesty reserving by the last Patent the quantity of 11,335 tons of ship timber for the use of the Navy estimated by the said Survey to be in the trees to be fallen by the said Grant; that upon obtaining the said Grant of the Wood the said Sir John Winter did promise to your petitioners who have right of Common of Estovers in the said Forest that provided they would let him peacefully enjoy his said Grant of the soil and Wood he will never disturb them in their right of Common in the whole wast of the said Forest which they complied with accordingly.

That the said Sir John Wintour upon this his last bargaine for the Wood surrendered his pretended interest in the soyle by virtue of his first patent unto the King. That this Honorable House taking the said last grant of the Wood into consideration Anno 1663 and finding how unfit it was that the said Trees as well as soyle should be disposed of unto private hands did Order the said Sir John Winter to state his account and referred the consideration thereof to a Committee and upon a Report by them made did Order a Bill to be brought in for measuring and settling the said Wood and Soyle in the Crown giving reasonable satisfaction for the same to Sir John Winter which Bill was accordingly committed but before any effective proceedings therein, the Parliament was prorogued but at their rising passed a Vote recommending it to the Lord Treasurer and Chancellor of the Exchequer to take some care for the preservation of the timber of the said Forest and also to consider the interest of Sir John Winter and the persons concerned. Notwithstanding which he hath not only cut down all the trees growing upon the said Forest whereby the aforesaid quantity of timber hath been much imbezelled and fall short and other his Covenants for the manner of the delivery of the said trees by his Majesty's officers not observed by him and also great spoils committed upon the underwood by his agents and workmen in felling and converting of the said trees unto [char]coale and also by setting as many as 100 of acres of underwood on fire but the said Sir John Winter hath after all these great advantages to himself and prejudice to the public and his said promise to the petitioners again set on foot his former designs upon the soyle of the said Forest under pretence of making a Nursery for the future growth of Ship Timber having by judicant practices as on his first patent obtained Articles under the Great Seal for the enclosing 10,000 acres only for his Majesty's use whereas the whole 23,000 acres is apt to wood for which he is to have 8,000 acres to his own use for ever and would compell the petitioners to accept of 4,000 acres of the worst part of the Forest in full recompense of the rights of the Common in the whole whereon he hath used judicial and oppressive practices to force the petitioners to a compliance. Notwithstanding that the petitioners have always been willing to comply with any thing that may really tend to his Majesty's service and public good for the preservation of a future growth but upon all their addresses to his Majesty and his officers hath been by the said Sir John Winter misrepresented and scandalized in order to his own private designs whereby the young woods have been for this three years past and still are exposed to very great spoils and so are a long time like to continue during his tedious and vexatious suites with your petitioners.

Your petitioners therefore humbly pray this Honorable House to permit your petitioners to set forth the great disadvantage of the bargaine to the public the deceitful and judicial practices of the said Sir John Wintour in obtaining thereof and the injuries and oppressions your petitioners have sustained by the said Sir John Winter And that you would be pleased to reasume your former care and consideration of the speedy preservation and settlement of the said Forest which will be suddenly destroyed and counted into private hands and your petitioners ruined. In the settlement whereof your petitioners humbly refer themselves to the justice and wisdom of this Honorable House as to their rights and properties in the said Forest. And your petitioners shall ever pray &c.

| Kedgwyn Hoskin | John White | Duncomb Colchester | John Hawkins |
|---|---|---|---|
| Thomas Morgan | Richard Machen | Thomas Carpender | Henry Hall |
| Abraham Clarke | Willm. Aylberton | James Gouth | |
| Edward Ricketts | Wm Carpender | Wm Bromwich | |
| J. Hyett | Wm Browne | Thomas Pyrke | |
| Thomas H (?) | Richard Hill | Richard Elly | |

On 17 December 1667 'the whole business of the Forest of Dean was before Parliament'. Winter went to great lengths to vindicate himself from accusations.[138] In 'A True Narrative &c to a pretended paper, lately published, wherein divers things most falsely charged on his grants in the Forest of Dean reflecting very much on the integrity of divers of His Majesty's officers, and several other persons of great worth and reputation'[139] it was asserted on Winter's behalf:

This bargain was not sought or obtained by Sir John Wintour upon the score of any former debt or demand from his Majesty, but merely for the accomplishment of that service, and by express command from His Majesty when no other but himself, upon the like terms, would undertake the same, which is well known to his Majesty and the Lords, and acknowledged in the said Articles. And next to his Majesty's said command, the ensuring considerations gave him most encouragement so to do, and to believe his endeavours therein would be very acceptable to the Parliament:

(1)   That it was profitable to his Majesty who neither at present nor future was to be at any expense about the same.

(2)   That it was a most certain and undoubted way for future production of ship-timber there, by reason of the perpetuity of inclosure.

(3)   That it was advantageous to the generality of the freeholders of the Forest, in freeing their lands from subjection to the forest laws, and annoyance by the deer, as also their persons from the chargeable attendance at forest courts, etc.

(4)   That it was most beneficial to the poorer sort that have no freehold land, whereof 200 of them or more in the several parishes within the perambulation of the Forest were to have 5 or 6 acres bestowed upon them gratis for their three lives, the reversion thereof to be hereafter at the dispose of the respective parishes for their poor for ever, besides the relief they might have by the multiplicity of all sorts of work for men, women and children, by means of the improvements.

(5)   That it was not unpracticable, for that the pretended rights of those commoners that only opposed it, depends upon a very clear point of law, which after great endeavours to delay, is now at issue, ready for hearing, in his Majesty's Court of Exchequer, where the major part of the lords of manors and freeholders that claim common as aforesaid, have already consented, and are bound by Decrees of that Court, and particularly by the last clause of that of 3 Charles which therefore was omitted by his adversaries, in recital of the said Decree 3 Charles.

If nevertheless, any other way for his Majesty's greater benefit and increase of ship-timber as aforesaid shall be approved of, Sir John Wintour in all obedience will quit his said bargain, and surrender his said Articles, though passed under the Great Seal, upon reasonable compensation for his charge and expense in prosecution thereof, which was done by his Majesty's direction and command as abovesaid.

On 6 March the following year, 1668,[140] another attempt was made to settle Winter's deficiency of timber. He and one of his nominees, Clayton, were called before the Treasury; Clayton 'refused to join in the security and would rather stay

---

[138] Br. Liby., MSS 726, c.1.(2), 8, c. 1667.
[139] Ibid.; Hart, *Royal Forest*, p. 167; Glos. R.O., D3921, Hart Collection, I/43.
[140] *Cal. Treas. Bks.*, II, p. 269.

till the King's debts be satisfied', while Winter prayed 'for any overplus that may remain after satisfaction of this debt'. On 11 March[141] a warrant was issued to seize Winter's stock of iron and charcoal.[142] He and Clayton appealed, and on reference to the attorney-general it was found that seizure would be illegal.[143] Lawrence Bathurst, May, and Furzer were told to discontinue the seizure,[144] 'but not to suffer any more wood to be converted into charcoal, and to continue the seizure of the forges'.[145] Winter's debt for timber was £6,691.6s.1d.;[146] he was not even to have '200 dotard trees which are yet unfelled'.[147]

On 30 June 1668[148] Winter was given a release of £6,692.6s. due to the king for 8,921 tons, 35 feet of shiptimber; also of his covenant concerning 'the improvement of the waste soil in the Forest of Dean and of his recognizance of £2,000 entered into in pursuance of the same'. Probably Sir John and his nominees were permitted to work out their term. Winter's own ironworks continued in production, if on a smaller scale than before the Civil Wars.[149] (Guns Mill was described as not rebuilt in 1680;[150] the Lydney works on the other hand stood in 1673 and in 1723.[151])

The administration of the Forest was reformed and settled by the Dean Forest (Reafforestation) Act 1668 (see Section IX), which specifically exempted Winter's grant from all its restrictions. The Act did not include directives or suggestions for the ironworks: the crown eventually in March 1674 sold its four remaining ironworks in Dean to Paul Foley of Stoke Edith in Herefordshire for demolition[152] – thus resigning from the iron industry. Yet the crown continued to sell huge quantities of cordwood from Dean to the neighbouring ironmasters for the remainder of the seventeenth century at least.[153]

Winter in about 1670 may have started to build a new family house (the Old Park House) on a site further west, but it is traditionally said to have been completed by his son, Sir Charles Winter, in about 1677 (infra). The date of his conversion to Rome is unknown. He may have become a recusant under the influence of his cousin Edward, from 1640 the second Marquis of Worcester.[154] But Winter does not appear a weak character, easily influenced by others; his sister married Benedict Hall of Highmeadow (see Section III), another Roman Catholic. It seems improbable but not impossible that their father might have returned converted from his Spanish captivity.

Winter was the chief cause of discontent in Dean over several decades, during which the stock of timber-trees and coppices was much reduced. However, he clearly remained a highly respected man: a man who was alleged to have stolen royal property and destroyed shiptimber without warrant would hardly have remained a trustee of the estates of Henrietta Maria the Queen Mother. He died between

[141] Cal. Treas. Bks., II, p. 275.
[142] Ibid. p. 276.
[143] Ibid. pp. 288, 543, 581.
[144] Ibid. pp. 535, 543, 581.
[145] Ibid. p. 288.
[146] Ibid. p. 535.
[147] Ibid. p. 321.
[148] Cal. SP Dom. 1667–68, p. 466.
[149] Ibid. pp. 166–8; A True Narrative . . ., c. 1667, op. cit.; Br. Liby., MSS 726, c.1(2), 8, c. 1667.
[150] Hart, The Free Miners, p. 103.
[151] Glos. R.O., D421 Winter Papers, T22, 27 May 1673; ibid. T18.
[152] Cal. Treas. Bks., IV, 227–8, 489, 27 Feb. and 11 March 1674.
[153] LR1/19/40, 41, 78, 153, 173.
[154] D.N.B., 'Sir John Winter'; Collins's Peerage of England, London, 1812, I, 233.

17 January 1685 (when he was one of the surviving trustees of the Queen Mother's estates) and 27 January 1687 (when the Earl of St. Albans was the sole surviving trustee).[155] His long and active life – born in the reign of Elizabeth and surviving Charles II – spanned the most intensive development of the iron industry in Dean.

Thus ended Sir John Winter's long and often unfortunate connection with the Forest. In 1669, after he had relinquished his post as Secretary to the Queen Mother, he attempted to work a colliery near Coventry.[156] He was unsuccessful, and by 1676 he was of 'mean and low estate'.[157] The family were still running 'Lydney ironwork' in 1699–1700.[158] His descendants were holding several hundred acres in the Forest in 1719.[159] In 1714 William James of Soilwell informed the Treasury that the Winter family had without right continued in possession of the Snead and Kidnalls woods. He requested preferential treatment in regard to the woods, 'the present Lady Wintour being a papist and married to James Nevill a papist'; they had lately cut at least 1,500 cords of wood, 'part of the Forest'.[160]

Sir John's son, Sir Charles, completed the building of the Old Park House in about 1677.[161] He died in 1698, leaving his widow Frances in possession, there being no heir. She later married Thomas Neville, and died in 1720. But already in 1718 the estate had been sold to mortgagees, who in their turn conveyed it to Benjamin Bathurst of Mixbury (the younger brother of the 1st Earl Bathurst of Cirencester Park) in 1723.[162]

Plate I. Lydney Park House of the Winter family. This view, in Samuel Rudder's *A New History of Gloucestershire*, 1779, shows that the late seventeenth-century house had been added to.

---

[155] *Cal. Treas. Bks.*, 1681–5, VII, 1500 and ibid. 1685–9, VIII, pt. iii, 1164: these dates, approximate though they remain, approach the truth more clearly than does the *D.N.B.*

[156] S.P.1671–2, pp. 159, 181.

[157] *Cal. Treas. Bks.*, IV, p. 169.

[158] Glos. R.O., D421 Winter Papers, E9, is 'The Furnace account that began the blast 11 Sept. 1699 and ended 6 May 1700'. The statement summarizes a genuine working account.

[159] *Cal. Treas. Papers*, V, pp. 457, 461, 473.

[160] Ibid.

[161] Kingsley, N., *The Country Houses of Gloucestershire*, Vol. II (1992) pp. 174–5.

[162] Glos. R.O., D421 Winter Papers, Introduction.

# II. THE THROCKMORTON FAMILY OF CLEARWELL

The Throckmorton (Throgmorton) family of Clearwell (originally of Tortworth, Gloucestershire) had great influence for several generations in the western part of the Forest of Dean. The family's history, from the sixteenth to late in the seventeenth century, is briefly provided by Nicholls.[1] This present account relates almost wholly to the Throckmortons' connection with the iron industry and woods of the Forest.[2]

## SIR WILLIAM THROCKMORTON BT.

Sir William Throckmorton junior was the son and heir of Sir William Throckmorton of Tortworth, who was made a baronet in June 1611, and of Cicely Bainham, the daughter of Thomas Bainham of Clearwell and the granddaughter of Sir William Winter of Lydney.[3] This, and probably his two subsequent marriages to Alice Worgan and to Sarah Hall,[4] gave Sir William much property, office and influence in the Forest of Dean. He acquired the offices of master forester-in-fee and woodward of the Bearse Woodwardship, probably as his wife's inheritance (they were entailed upon his son Baynham). In addition he became a deputy constable to William, Earl of Pembroke. He had certainly come from outside the Forest and may not have settled there until 1614 or 1615; perhaps he therefore became all the more rigid in his defence of forest privileges against the crown and its farmers and all the more alert in asserting his own.[5] He agitated against Sir Basil Brooke and George Moore and their partners while they shared the iron industry 'concession' in the Forest.[6]

On 21 February 1618 Sir William complained to the king of transgressions in the Forest of Dean by Castle and Callow, crown overseers for cordwood.[7] On 23 February he likewise complained about the activities of George Moore and Richard Tomlins (ironmasters) in building 'Cannop House' without licence and misappropriating timber in the Cannop valley woods[8] (see Section VI). However, on the same day[9] counter complaints were made against Throckmorton himself:

---

[1] Nicholls, Rev. H.G., *The Personalities of the Forest of Dean*, 1863, pp. 103–8.

[2] For a brief introduction, see Hart, *Royal Forest*, pp. 105, 111, 116–18.

[3] G.E.C., *Complete Baronetage*, Exeter, 1900, I, 65.

[4] Glos. R.O., P227, IN, 1/1, 1669, contains notes by Sir Baynham Throckmorton, Bt. regarding his birth and two marriages, all of which took place 11 December, each on a Saturday.

[5] E112/82/343; Br. Liby., Lansd. MS 166, f. 384; Add. MS 36767, f. 379.

[6] Br. Liby., Lansd. MS 166, f. 380.

[7] Ibid. ff. 378, 380.

[8] Ibid. f. 380.

[9] Ibid. f. 384.

Exceptions against the proceedings and demeanour of Sir William Throgmorton as well as in his complaint as in the business in the Forest of Deane:

That Sir William Throgmorton hath ever from the beginning been a maintainer of the unjust title of himself and of the Country against the king:

1. At his being at Coleford 1612, he publicly declared himself speaking then for the Country's Right, where now upon experience by law it is found they have not any at all.

2. Being a [Forest] officer till very lately, he never seemed to restrain any man.

3. To justify the title of the Country, he for his own use, 1611 or thereabouts, did cause to be fetched out of the Forest 40 loads of wood being ready cut at his Majesty's charge, for which as yet he never answered anything, but justified the same as his right, and so continueth fetching wood, cutting out timber-trees for firewood to this day.

4. Since he came to be Deputy Constable, he hath been so free as everyone demanding warrants at the Speeche Courte, and presuming upon authority which he hath not, hath given out his warrants to those that have no manner of right, whereby his Majesty hath been damnified above £1,000 within these two years, as shall be proved.

5. That under colour of being Deputy Constable, he hath and doth unjustly claim all windfall trees and otherwise casually fallen, by the Country digging cinders, and notwithstanding he was forewarned by the Commissioners to meddle therein, hath lately sold divers of them both timber and firewood to the Country, to the value and loss to his Majesty £1,000 at least, being a matter whereof himself hath formerly complained.

To maintain the said unjust title, he hath caused some of the timber felled for the Navy to be converted by his warrant for building up of his neighbours houses which have no manner of interest in the Forest.

That he hath no interest in the said Forest either in himself as an inhabitant or otherwise as an officer, neither thereby any power to dispose of his Majesty's woods:

All the land he hath in the Forest is Ancient Assart land.

His Woodwardship is the Baylewick of Berse within which is confined for his relief to gather dead and dry wood, as all other woodwards are, as appeareth by their Claims; without which by vertue of his woodwardship he hath nothing to do in the Forest; and which woodwardship is, by negligence of his ancesters, now so wasted, that there is not left any wood at all therein, except what he hath in several, so that nothing being left, the King hath lost his right which his father Mr. Bayneham was fined for in the Exchequer.

To his Forestership belongeth no manner of Estovers.

The Constable hath no power to fetch wood out of the Forest not for repairing the King's Castle of St. Brevylles for so it appeareth by Record, that ever the King's Privy Seal did pass if but for 4 trees to repair the Castle of St. Brevylles as appeareth, much less to dispose of the King's woods at his pleasure as he doth to himself and others that have no right.

On the same day, 23 February 1618, it was noted:[10] 'That since the Restraint and Sir William Throgmorton's undertaking, that no timber or green wood should be

[10] Br. Liby., Lansd. MS 166, f. 378.

felled, many of these trees have been felled by his allowance, and some good timber-trees cut out for firewood, to serve his own house, as will be proved.' Eventually Sir William was asked to draw up the interrogatories for a Commission over which he himself presided at Coleford on 1 September 1618, which was decisive in ending the then iron industry leases.[11] His success neither stopped him from helping himself to more wood from the Forest[12] nor did he himself refuse payment in wood or collaboration with the ironmasters when it suited him.[13] When his son and heir, Baynham, ran away from home at the age of nineteen and sought protection in the home of his father's enemy, Sir Richard Catchmay (of Bigsweir and Coed Ithell on Wye side), the fault may have been due to both or either of them.[14] By 1620 Sir William held The Copes or Coppice Woods, 100 acres in the bailiwick of Bicknor (later to be held by the Hall family).[15] He died in 1628.[16]

## SIR BAYNHAM THROCKMORTON BT. SENIOR

Sir Baynham Throckmorton Bt. succeeded his father William as the second baronet upon the latter's death in 1628.[17] Like some of his neighbours, he owned extensive woods on his estates; in 1628 he settled on his wife 6 mills, 2,000 acres of land, 1,400 acres of pasture and 500 acres of woodland held in Forest manors; also 'the office of Master or Principal Forester of the whole Forest of Dean'.[18] He inherited his mother's family office and prestige in the Forest and from his father hostility to outside intervention therein.

During his father's lifetime, Sir Baynham around 1624 had been associated with his championship of forest rights and privileges of the commoners and miners of Dean against the crown and outsiders[19] but after his father's death he seems to have kept quiet for some time, neither attacking the farmers of the 'King's Ironworks' nor using his woods to enter the iron industry himself – although he may well have sold some wood for charcoaling.

In 1633 Sir Baynham became impressed with the mounting opposition to the then farmers, Sir Basil Brooke and George Mynn, and proceeded to attack them. He interviewed their patron, Philip, Earl of Pembroke, who had recently inherited this patronage from his deceased brother, together with the title. The Earl disclaimed any special interest in the ironworks 'concession', and Sir Baynham thereupon informed Endymion Porter (a contact man at court) that their project could continue unchecked and that he would send him someone with more detailed information about the farmers' misdeeds in Dean.[20] When Sir John Finch in 1634 appeared in Gloucestershire a few days before the Justice Seat for the Forest

[11] Br. Liby., Lansd. MS 166, f. 378. and SP39/9/40; Glouc. Liby., MS, L.F 6.3.

[12] H.M.C., 4th Rept., de la Warr, p. 312.

[13] SP14/147/66, 7 June 1623.

[14] H.M.C., 5th Rept., Cholmondley, p. 345.

[15] GG 673, 677.

[16] G.E.C., Complete Baronetage, Exeter, 1900, I. 65.

[17] Ibid.

[18] GG 735, 6 Oct. 1628.

[19] E134/22, Jas. I, Easter 8, Sir William Throckmorton and Thomas Bainham v. Attorney General, on behalf of the Free Miners, 1624.

[20] SP16/375/34, dated (?)1634 in Cal. SPD, Chas. I, 1637–8, pp. 53–4 but dated 18 May in the original.

was due to begin (see Section V), in order to prepare his case more thoroughly as King's Counsel, he 'had great light from Sir Baynham Throckmorton' regarding the misdeeds of the farmers.[21]

At the same Eyre of 1634 Sir Baynham claimed: to be chief forester of the Forest of Dean and to have under him a forester called a bowbearer to make attachment of vert and chase; to be entitled to ten bucks in summer and ten does in winter each year; and 16d. profit on each charcoal pit within the Forest. He further claimed that he was seized in fee of his bailiwick, also a virgate of land in St. Briavels called Hathwayes alias Hathwayes Manor alias Hathwayes Place; and that he and his ancestors had held the same of the king as of his Castle of St. Briavels, rendering 28s.4d. yearly. He likewise claimed, along with many other claimants, privileges of common, and windfallen trees.[22]

Brooke, Mynn and Sir John Winter were heavily fined at the Eyre and their wood deliveries suspended. Consequently the crown temporarily lost its revenue from cordwood to fuel the ironworks, which was firmly tied to specific deliveries of complement wood. Even before Winter and Brooke had agreed to surrender their patent, new tenders for the 'concession' appeared and were considered by the Treasury Commission and the Privy Council. If the welfare of the Forest had been Sir Baynham's sole motive in appointing himself 'chief private prosecutor' of the farmers, he would presumably have joined Sir Richard Catchmay, a local landowner and ironmaster, in proposing that the crown should administer its woods and ironworks on its own account. But in 1635 he was one of the first to tender for 7,000 cords of wood yearly at about 8s.7d. the cord;[23] in March 1635 he offered the king £7 of each ton of iron made in Dean; in May he made another offer and in September he had entered into partnership with Sir Sackville Crow, ironmaster, of Langharne, Carmarthen, to make iron in Dean, with a promise of the grant as soon as the old patent should have been surrendered.[24] Thus Crow and Throckmorton had succeeded, in spite of their reputation for poverty; perhaps they had overcome this by their alliance with John Taylor and John Gonning, merchants of Bristol: in one document, which probably refers to Crow and Throckmorton as the opposite numbers to Brooke and Winter, Secretary Windebank had called the former 'bankrupts', not without some cause.[25]

The patent for the new grant of the Dean iron industry 'concession' to the four partners was sealed on 8 July 1636.[26] The grant to Throckmorton, Crow, Taylor and Gonning[27] was for twenty-one years from Midsummer 1636. It included 12,000 cords a year, 8,000 of them from trees cut for the purpose, and 4,000 from windfalls, trimmings, etc., at the unprecedented high price of 11s. a cord for thirteen and a half years and 10s. a cord for the remainder of the lease, plus all wood of less than 4 inches circumference at £250 a year. Timber could be taken for repairs and new building either by official assignment or after fourteen days' notice if left on the

[21] Glouc. Liby., MS L.F. 1.1, f. 33. This unsigned and undated MS contains Sir John Finch's own notes about the Justice Seat in 1634 (see Section V).

[22] Hart, *The Commoners . . .*, p. 169; Claim No. 120 (Glos. R.O., D3921, Hart Collection, I/42); copy in Northamptonshire Record Office, IL 1374.

[23] SP18/282/127, Jan. 1635.

[24] SP16/285/7, /288/55, /297/45.

[25] Ibid. /307/12.

[26] C66/2740.

[27] Ibid.

ground for seven days after cutting and a note of the full amount given to an official and later presented at the next forest court. Payment was to be made in arrears at Christmas and Midsummer, including £25 a year for mining rights; the £25 to be paid to the surveyor-general of woods for enclosing, at Midsummer from 1637 onwards. The first other payment to be at Christmas 1636, an advance of £3,125 being paid. Fellets for cordwood were to be set out by 1 November each year for the contractual amount, and cords to be 'delivered' (released) within at most three months, but on request within six weeks or every six weeks; demarcation, marking of timber and delivery to be effected by four men, including two of the constable or deputy constable, the surveyor-general of woods or his deputy, and one verderer; the others may be these or other forest law officials. The crown was to pay a fine of £100 for any failure to set out fellets by 20 November or to 'deliver' cordwood at most fourteen days after the due date. The trees cut could be inspected for timber quality but the cost of felling the timber to be repaid for any taken over. The trees to be cut one foot above the spreading of the roots; roots could be taken, at 4s.6d. a cord, in addition. All cordwood to be removed from each fellet before 25 March following demarcation of it (to give the stools a better chance to re-coppice). Further works could be built; but not more than two furnaces and four forges or three furnaces and two forges were to be used simultaneously without official permission. All unauthorized ironworks within the old perambulation of the Forest were to be demolished. Former tenants were to be recompensed for two new forges they had built. Ore and cinders should only be taken for their works in the Forest and for one other furnace (perhaps Sir John Winter's); and no one was to sell or obtain any ore and cinders from the Forest without their consent. Common was to be made available for 100 horses. The patentees were to be heard before any interference with or interruption of their operations on any pretext.[28]

Throckmorton's position as chief forester-in-fee of Dean and ostensibly the defender of the inhabitants' rights and privileges (as well as his own) may have brought the partnership a little more peace: they were not pursued quite as persistently as previous ironmasters and patentees. But when the accusations inevitably came, they were like all that had gone before and relied on the same type of evidence. Additional complaints were that the partnership was unduly monopolizing the iron industry in and around Dean and that it used its favoured position to depress workers' wages and to make them pay truck.[29]

Of the four partners, Crow was probably the only one with expert knowledge of iron-smelting, but his role appears to have remained almost entirely passive, once the grant had been obtained. Sir Baynham continued to act as the partnership's front, representing them before the Privy Council when the usual investigations and local accusations came to be examined there.[30] On 7 January 1637[31] (see Section IV) John Broughton complained to Sir John Coke:

> They [the Farmers] have likewise wronged his Majesty in the oversize of their cords, and in divers other particulars. And it is generally observed that when Sir Baynham Throgmorton is present, at any delivery of wood, or about any other Forest business, the officers of the Forest are so awed with his Authority and stern carriage, they dare not

---

[28] The lease was surrendered before 1 April 1640 (SP38/18).
[29] E112/181/159; SP16/361/48, 9 June 1637; PC/48, p. 493.
[30] PC 27/48, pp. 493–4, 17 Dec. 1637.
[31] Br. Liby., Add. MS 69909, XLII, 147/8.

speak, nor offer to contradict any of the Farmers' actions, be they ever so prejudicial to his Majesty.

Sir Baynham probably conducted the negotiations for compensation when the crown in 1639 demanded the surrender of the grant, prior to the comprehensive agreement with Sir John Winter (see Section I). At any rate Sir Baynham's claims for additional compensation implied that he had been subjected to a special commission in 1637[32] and to legal proceedings in 1638[33]. The case against them was not dropped until June 1639;[34] they were granted a pardon dated as from the beginning of Winter's new grant on 1 April 1640.[35] Again, when Winter's grant had been annulled by Parliament, Sir Baynham attended the commission investigating the future of the Forest and offered a new farm;[36] he himself may well have agitated for the repeal of Winter's grant. Throckmorton was the main accuser of Sir John Winter.[37]

The partners managed to put up a successful defence against some accusations.[38] The defence improved their treatment but did not prolong their tenure. Early in 1639 the crown decided to sell most of the crown rights and lands in the Forest to Sir John Winter (see Section I). Throckmorton and partners were compensated by a sublease of two furnaces and four forges with 13,500 cords of wood yearly for six years, for which they were to pay Winter at 10s. a cord.

Under Winter's purchase of most of the Forest of Dean on 20 February 1640,[39] Throckmorton and partners, as compensation for loss of their earlier grant, were to have a lease of Parkend and Soudley furnaces with Soudley, Bradley, Parkend and Whitecroft forges, and 13,500 cords of mixed wood a year, also with iron-ore and cinders, at 10s. a cord of wood for six years from Lady Day 1640. When Winter's purchase was nullified, the sublease still held.[40] However, in 1642 the partners' grant was assigned to Thomas Dunning and Richard Skinner (possibly agents for Winter and Throckmorton together with Gonning);[41] this apparently ended in 1644.

Sir Baynham may also have supervised the activities of officials in the Forest, for which his offices and residence would have qualified him admirably. He was high sheriff of Gloucestershire in 1643. But there is no evidence that he took more than a passing interest in the ironworks themselves; no doubt the partners had agreed to the appointment of the clerks but only one of the chief clerks, named Richard Skinner, reappears later in connection with John Gonning (an ironmaster).[42]

While Sir Baynham remained a partner in the subsequent grants, both when the partners became Winter's under-tenants[43] and when Winter had lost his grant,[44] he did not engage in the industry outside the partnership. He sold some wood to

[32] E178/5304/13 Chas. I.
[33] E112/181/159.
[34] H.M.C., 12th Rept., Coke, II, p. 225.
[35] SP38/18.
[36] E178/5304, 17 and 18 Chas. I.
[37] Notestein, W. (ed.), op cit., pp. 119, 392, 393, 488–9; Commons Journal, II, 131, 489, 21 March 1642.
[38] SP16/323, pp. 210–11 and /403, pp. 78–9; SP38/18, 1 April 1640.
[39] C66/2843.
[40] E178/6080, pt. i, ms. 20–21d; SP16/489/35.
[41] L.R.R.O., 5/7A.
[42] E112/181/159; Gonning MS, acc. 331.
[43] C66/2876.
[44] SP16/489/35, 14 Feb. 1642; E407/50, 8 Sept. 1642.

Gonning in autumn 1649[45] and, after the Restoration, he successfully pressed his claims for some compensation by a farm of some woods and works in Dean.[46] Sir Baynham's principal interest in the works was clearly financial. Perhaps the description of him as bankrupt (*supra*) had not been quite inept: for compounding purposes his estate was passed as £624 per annum but in May 1637 a total indebtedness of £3,000 had compelled him to set up a trust for his creditors.[47] Statements made in this context need not be taken at their face value but Sir Baynham sold land in 1633 and 1640, worth perhaps £500 (giving bond in £1,000 for the completion of the sale)[48] and he appears to have anticipated his share of the ironworks profits with much regularity, at least in 1639–41.[49] It seems probable that Sir Baynham invested his title and his local status in the industry, driven by the urgent need for cash; even if pure concern for the fate of the Forest was his first motive, it soon turned to pure source of income, defended tenaciously but administered by others.

During 1639–43 Throckmorton helped Dean's commoners against the attorney-general.[50] He found favour with the Free Miners[51] but occasionally opposed some of them.[52] At the eyre of 1656[53] (see Section VII) he was accused thus:

[With others] since the last Justice Seat [1634] cut down and charcoaled great numbers of trees in the Forest to maintain ironworks.

For cutting without licence a Coppice Wood, 10 acres, and one Coppice Grove, 1½ acres, all in the parish of Newland and in his own fee.

With his partners, farmers of the Ironworks, misappropriating timber and wood and cinders for furnaces and forges.

[Incidentally] Richard Skinner, gent. for taking and converting to his own use the [?] utenses of iron from the works of Sir Baynham Throckmorton and his partners.

There is no evidence of any fine being levied. At the Restoration of the Monarchy (1660), Throckmorton on 5 January 1661 claimed 'wood and some of the ironworks contested between him and Winter'.[54] He died in May 1664.

## SIR BAYNHAM THROCKMORTON BT. JUNIOR

Following the death of Sir Baynham senior in May 1664[55] his son Sir Baynham junior held the family's property. He was soon defending himself in a law suit actioned by the attorney-general, Sir Jeffery Palmer Bt., his defence being:[56]

45 Gonning MS, acc. 331 and 331/7/50.
46 *Cal. Treas. Bks.*, 1660–7, p. 114; P.R.O. 30/24/32; Glos. R.O., D421 Winter Papers, E66.
47 SP23/195/549.
48 GG 735.
49 Gonning MS, acc. 331/5, /7/7, /7,8, and two documents dated Feb. and June 1641 in same box.
50 Hart, *The Commoners . . .*, pp. 47, 51, 52.
51 Hart, *The Free Miners*.
52 Glos. R.O., D3921, Hart Collection, I/56.
53 Glos. R.O., D2026 Bond Papers, X.14.
54 Hart, *Royal Forest*, pp. 153–4.
55 Glouc. Liby., MS L.F.1.1, p. 5.
56 Ibid.

The several Answers of Sir Baynham Throckmorton Knight and Baronet one of the Defendants to the Information of Sir Jeffery Palmer, Knight and Baronet his Majesty's Attorney General Complainant.

The said Defendant saving and reserving unto himself now and at all times hereafter all benefit of exceptions to the sucuffiency [sic] of the said Information for Answer thereunto or to so much thereof as materially concerns him, this Defendant to make Answer unto says that he believeth it to be that his late Majesty King Charles I was in his lifetime in right of the law of England seized in fee of and in the Forest of Deane in the said Information mentioned and extending and with such libertyes as in the said Information is alleged. And the Defendant hath heard and believeth and there did send forth such a Commission under the Great Seal of England for the Deafforestation of such Forest about the time in the said Information for that purpose mentioned and that there were such proceedings and returns made thereupon as in the said Information is at large set forth. And whereunto for more certainty of the same may be produced the Defendant confirms more at large appeareth. And this Defendant hath heard and believeth that the enclosing of some parts of the wast for his said late Majesty's use was began and some progress made therein which this Defendant conceiveth could not be without expense of money. And that there might be such opposition therein from the Commoners as by the Information is alleged. And this Defendant believed that there was by the said late Majesty's then Attorney General an English Bill or Information exhibited unto the Honorable Court against the said several persons in the said now Information named and amongst the rest against Sir Baynham Throckmorton Bt. this Defendant's late Father about the time and to the effect in the now Information set forth but how many of the said persons nocated [sic] for Defendants to the Information exhibited in his Late Majesty's reign did appear and put in their Answers thereunto and[?] declare to consent to the Improvement or Inclosure of the said Forest or how many of such persons descended therefrom this Defendant doth not know. But this Defendant sayeth that it hath appeared unto this Defendant by the copy of an Answer of the Defendant said that which was by him put into the same Information by this Defendant's said Father did (as much as in him lay for more this Defendant conceiveth he could not do) assent or submit to the said Deafforestation, Improvement and Inclosing but what proceeding, Information or other Orders or proceedings were had in that suite this Defendant sayeth he is a stranger thereunto but believeth the same will appear by the Records of this Honorable Court.

This Defendant sayeth that his said Father Sir Baynham Throckmorton died in or about the month of May in the 15th Year of his now Majesty's reign [May 1664] upon whose death . . . this Defendant came to have some interest in the profits of the said Forest as appertaining to the Manor and lands lying within the liberties of the said Forest which came to this Defendant by the means aforesaid which he this Defendant holdeth and standeth seized of as follows (Viz.): That he and his Ancestors and all those whose estate he hath in the Manor of Hathwayes, St. Briavels situate lying and being in the parish of St. Briavell within the liberties of the said Forest have and time out of mind of man have had as this Defendant expects to make appear unto the Honorable Court and used to have the office of the Master Forestership of the said Forest as belonging to the said Manor which was heretofore holden of his late Majesty in Capite and is now holden of his Majesty by Fee and Comon Soccage by virtue of the late Act of Parliament which hath destroyed all Capite tenures and converted the same into Fee and Comon Soccage.

This Defendant taketh it but by the [?]Act of [?16]28 or thereabouts And the Defendant and his Ancestors and those whose Estate this Defendant hath in the said Manor by all the time aforesaid have had and used to have and keep as this Defendant doubteth not to prove unto this Honorable Court one manservant which hath been called the Bowbearer who hath used to walk the said Forest and to see to and preserve his Majesty's Game and Deer there from destruction and the woods there growing from wasts or spoils and to make Attachments and presentments of all such abuses as he should find in the said Forest either in Vert or Venison. And all the foresters of inheritance within the said Forest have been and ought as this Defendant conceives to be at the appointment and direction of the said Master Forester for the preservation of his Majesty's Game of Deer and Woods there, and that there is belonging to the office of Master Forester 18d in money for every pitt of [char]cole that is or shall be now made within the said Forest by the Founder or maker of such new pitt of cole and so for every six weeks after that the same shall be continued. And the right shoulder of every deer killed within the said Forest and ten Fee Bucks and ten Fee Does to be taken at the season of every year yearly with free liberty to hunt kill and carry the same away at all seasonable times of the year at the will and pleasure of this Defendant and of his said Ancestors Lords and Owners of the said Manor of Hathwayes for the time being which this Defendant for this time hath and his said Ancestors for their times before him as this Defendant verily believed enjoyed and taken accordingly. And this Defendant sayeth that he is likewise seized of the Capitall Messuage Manor and Lands called Clowerwall lying within the liberties of the said Forest and holden of the said Castle of St. Briavells.

Following the Dean Forest (Reafforestation) Act, 1668, Sir Baynham junior was appointed as one of the Inclosure Commissioners.[57] On 18 April 1674[58] he was

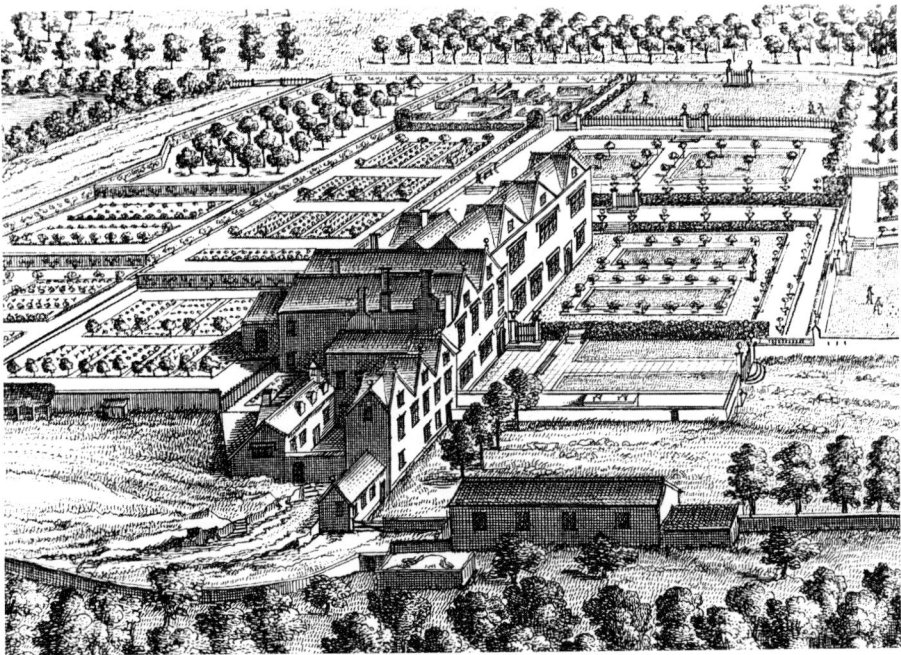

Plate II. Clearwell House was a late sixteenth-century manor house of Thomas Baynham (until 1609). His daughter and heiress, Cecily, married Sir Baynham Throckmorton of Tortworth Court, Gloucestershire, and the house became at first a secondary house. The next occupant was Sir Baynham Throckmorton junior, a leading figure among the county gentry and one of the foremost forest officials of the Forest of Dean. In the late seventeenth century the house came into the hands of Francis Wyndham. His heir, Thomas, inherited it in the 1720s and replaced the house with a new one, its appearance being known only from this engraving by Kip in Atkyns' *The Ancient and Present State of Gloucestershire*, 1712. A later rebuilding is known as 'Clearwell Castle', currently used as a hotel.

[57] Hart, *Royal Forest*, p. 169.
[58] *Cal. Treas. Books*, IV, p. 508. On 14 March 1676 it was confirmed that Throckmorton 'is entitled to fee deer – 10 bucks in summer and 10 does in winter' (SP29, 1676–7, pp. 27–8).

appointed by the Treasury as conservator and supervisor of Dean; its officials were put in his charge. He held office until 1681.

In 1680 Sir Baynham settled Hathaways Manor on his three daughters – Elizabeth and Mary (both d. 1684) and Carolina.[59] In 1710 Carolina and her husband James Skrymster sold the manor to Francis Wyndham of Uffords Manor in Norfolk.[60] When his heir, Thomas, inherited in the 1720s, the old Clearwell Court House (see engraving by Kip)[61] was pulled down and replaced by a new house ('Clearwell Castle').[62]

Many of the Throckmorton family rest in the chapel on the south side of the chancel in Newland Church. The Elizabethan mansion (to which Sir Walter Raleigh is reputed to have come to claim his bride, Elizabeth Throckmorton) was replaced in 1727 as one of the first of the Gothic Revival houses by the Wyndham family, and called 'Clearwell Castle'. It came into the hands of Caroline who married the future second Earl of Dunraven in 1810. In 1911 the whole estate and 'Castle' were purchased by Colonel Charles Vereker who saw the 'Castle' gutted by fire in 1929. He restored it, but on his death it was sold and once more fell into disuse until it was purchased in 1953 by the son of a one-time gardener there and refurbished as a hotel. Subsequent owners continued to use it as such.

[59] Nicholls, op. cit., pp. 108–110.
[60] N.L.W., Dunraven MSS 271; Bigland, Glos., ii, pp. 261–2.
[61] Atkyns, Gloucestershire, plate facing p. 574; Kingsley, N., The Country Houses of Gloucestershire, Vol. I (1989), pp. 78–9.
[62] Rowan, A., 'Clearwell Castle' in Colvin & Harris (eds.), The Country Seat, 1970, pp. 145–9.

# III. THE HALL FAMILY OF HIGHMEADOW

The Hall family of Highmeadow between Newland and Coleford possessed for several generations considerable property and influence in the west of the Forest of Dean. They purchased lands and ironworks in Gloucestershire, Monmouthshire and Herefordshire. The family's history, from the fifteenth century to the mid-eighteenth century, is briefly provided by Nicholls.[1] This present account relates almost wholly to the Halls' connection with the iron industry and woods of the Forest.[2]

The family was Roman Catholic in the seventeenth century and had probably never changed its faith.[3] It rose and prospered, without the help of public office, on the profits of estate management and ironmaking. By the second half of the sixteenth century the Halls were categorized as gentlemen;[4] if they did not yet make iron themselves they still held some forges and bought more amongst their numerous purchases of land.[5] Highmeadow itself lay close to the oldest centres of iron mining in Dean and their lands contained ore and cinders as well as much wood.[6]

Probably in 1604 William Hall, gent., built his first (the 'Newland') blast furnace, alongside the road from Highmeadow to Upper Redbrook, where the Halls had recently been buying mills, ponds, woods and forges,[7] a little east of the junction with the road from Staunton.[8] In 1634 a Hall furnace was said to be either twenty or thirty years old[9] but in 1614 William Hall's furnace was mentioned as if it had stood for some time.[10] By 1611 William was so far engaged in the industry that he applied for and almost obtained from the crown a share in a Dean iron industry 'concession' in partnership with nominees of Sir Edward Winter.[11] (Some time later the crown felt compelled to offer William compensation for its withdrawal and, after his death in 1615, his eldest son Benedict benefited by £100 worth of bar iron.[12])

Benedict Hall's wife Anne was Sir John Winter's sister[13] and amongst local gentry

---

[1] Nicholls, Rev. H.G., *The Personalities of the Forest of Dean*, 1863, pp. 69–72.

[2] For a brief introduction, see Hart, *Royal Forest*, pp. 100, 128, 134.

[3] The first Benedict Hall was a Catholic; his name suggests that his parents may have been of the same faith.

[4] GG 515.

[5] GG 413, 419, 515, 541, 593.

[6] GG 419, 515, 541, 603, 673.

[7] GG 535, 579, 603.

[8] P.R.O. MR 879, Glos. 1608. This map, along with another of 1608 (P.R.O. MPC 108, Mon.) give indications of the Hall family's properties at that time.

[9] Bodleian, Gough MSS, Glouc. I, f.62; Br. Liby., Harl. MS 4850, f. 48.

[10] E178/3838, 11 Jas.I.

[11] C66/1904; Hart, *Royal Forest*, p. 89.

[12] LR 12/35/1271; LR 6/38, 14 Jas.I.

[13] Bodleian, Selden MSS 113, f. 26.

his rise was only less great than that of Winter himself. He may have inherited some land in Monmouthshire and Herefordshire; his Gloucestershire inheritance lay in the western portion of the Forest and perhaps most of it consisted of the 800 acres in Newland and Staunton for which the Baynham family had compounded as assart lands and with which they enfeoffed Benedict in 1619.[14] On this land stood two ironworks; in 1623 he added to them by a lease of Pontrilas forge for twelve years plus an option for nine more;[15] by 1628 he had built a forge near Monmouth;[16] possibly in 1629 he built a second furnace;[17] in 1633 he bought Bishopswood furnace and Lydbrook upper forge from the Earl of Essex[18] and Lydbrook lower forge for £45 from John Gardiner.[19] Between 1640 and 1645 he bought Lydbrook middle forge for about £300;[20] in 1645 the forge was reckoned part of Benedict's sequestered estate.

At times, Benedict Hall associated with the enterprises of Sir John Winter, his brother-in-law and co-religionist (see Section I). By the end of 1627 they jointly purchased 4,000 cords of wood from the crown.[21]

In 1620 Benedict bought a part of Staunton and Coleford as well as Mailscot and Hadnock Woods;[22] in 1633 alone he bought more than £1,000 worth of land in Herefordshire[23] as well as the manor and lordship of English Bicknor (with the ironworks) from Robert the second Earl of Essex for £2,400.[24] By about 1640 Benedict held a solid block of land bordering on the north-western side of the Forest from Redbrook and Highmeadow to Lydbrook and Ruardean and reaching as far as the Wye at least at Hadnock's Wood. When he settled his Gloucestershire lands in 1657 to establish a jointure of £800 for his eldest son Henry Benedict and his wife Francis, the yearly value of all the manors settled came to £2,500, excluding two Lydbrook forges and all the woods on the estate.[25] This sort of wealth explains how Benedict could take over £4,500 of Sir John Winter's debts in 1635, repayable in 300 tons of pig-iron a year at £6 per ton.[26]

At the Justice Seat in Eyre of 1634 (see Section V), Benedict Hall claimed rights and privileges in his manors of Staunton and English Bicknor.[27] He was fined £150 for building his 'upper furnace' without licence. In all, he paid £800 of other fines totalling £1,300. By 1640 he had two to three furnaces – there is nothing to show

---

[14] GG 656, 657. For the Baynham family of Clearwell, see Maclean, Sir John, 'The History of the Manors of Dene Magna and Abenhall', *Trans. B. & G.A.S.*, VI, 1881–2, pp. 123–209.

[15] GG 684.

[16] E178/5304, 4 Chas.I.

[17] Bodleian, Gough MSS, Glouc. I, f. 61d; Br. Liby., MS 4850, f.48; SP16/282/127, p. 3.

[18] GG 784.

[19] GG 780.

[20] GG 821, 867; E407/50; E112/300/30.

[21] *H.M.C.*, 12th Rept., Cowper/Coke MSS, I, p. 294; C99/23; Glos. R.O., D421 Winter Papers, E2.

[22] Maclean, Sir John, 'History of the Manor and Advowson of Staunton in the Forest of Dean', *Trans. B.&G.A.S.*, VII, 1882–3, pp. 227–66. See also GG 666, 17 June 1620, GG 673, 10 Feb. 1620, and GG 1340,1341.

[23] C54/2958; D23 Probyn Papers, E29 (Mailscot in 1625).

[24] C54/2978; GG 784–6, 820; Maclean, Sir John, 'Remarks on the Manor, Advowson, and Demesne Lands of English Bicknor, Co. Gloucester', *Trans. B.&G.A.S.*, I, 1876, pp. 69–95; Hill, Mary C., 'Wyrall Lands and Deeds', ibid. LXIII, 1942, pp. 190–206.

[25] Gage MSS, D1677, GG, various.

[26] GG 800.

[27] Hart, *The Commoners . . .*, p. 167; Claims Nos. 8 and 9 (Glos. R.O., D3921, Hart Collection, I/42). GG 1259 is a copy of Hall's claims.

how long the second Newland furnace existed beyond 1634 – and four to five forges. His purchases were mainly for investment, with the tenants remaining undisturbed at least for the moment.

By the early seventeenth century Benedict Hall had interests in woods other than those traditionally held by the family in or around Newland and Coleford; for example, in the area now known as High Meadow Woods, parts of, or groves in, Hadnock Wood and Lady Park Wood, Cawvall, Braceland, Bunjups and the Copes (or the Coppice Wood, 100 acres).[28] However, it is often uncertain whether the interests were freehold or simply leasehold. Most were probably connected with ensuring supplies of cordwood for the family's iron industry.

During and after the Civil Wars, Benedict's luck or sense allowed him to escape relatively lightly. In 1641 he had established a settlement for his children.[29] In 1645 he was sequestered as a catholic recusant; he attempted to compound locally and obtained letters of protection from Major General Edward Massey.[30] But the county committees disregarded this; his ironworks were taken over by Capt. Thomas Pury, Capt. Griffantius Phillips, Capt. John Braine and Lt. Col. Robert Kyrle who used force and influence to obtain wood from Benedict's Gloucestershire estates and who bought 12,000 cords from his Monmouthshire wood.[31] Meanwhile the validity of his trust was discussed before the compounding committee which eventually accepted Hall's contention that the trust antedated his conviction for recusancy; for the time being Benedict was ordered to pay two-thirds of his reserved rent from the estate as a fine.[32] In 1650 two of the Hall forges in Lydbrook, probably the upper and the middle ones, were destroyed by the state 'Preservators' along with his Bishopswood furnace;[33] the middle forge was rebuilt and the lower forge may have remained undisturbed so that both of them were in the Halls' possession in the late 1650s.[34] In 1650 Pury and his associates were expelled from Hall's property. At the Eyre of 1656, Benedict Hall was accused of:

Having cut several Coppice Groves within the perambulation of the Forest though in his own fee:

In the parish of Bicknour:
   Stowfield Grove, 20 acres
   The Copes, 60 acres
   A Grove, 16 acres
   Brookes Head Grove, 5 acres
In the parish of Newland:
   Dingle Grove and Astredge Grove, 5 acres
In the parish of Stanton
   Bungeps Grove, 40 acres
   Ellens Reding Grove, 5 acres
   Winnell Grove and Blake Grove, 10 acres

[28] Gage MSS, D1677, GG, various; Map of 1608 (P.R.O. MPC 108, Mon.); Map of 1608 (P.R.O. MR 879, Glos. F.17/1).
[29] GG 871. Benedict Hall had 5 sons and 7 daughters living.
[30] E178/6080, pt. i, ms. 21d. 22.
[31] LRRO 5/7A; E178/6080, pt.i.ms. 21d–23; Glos. R.O., D421 Winter Papers, E9; LR 7/55, 1646; E112/300/30; H.M.C., 7th Rept., Lords MSS, p. 117.
[32] Cal. Cttee. for Comp., pp. 2200–4; SP23/110, pp. 918–19, 929–32.
[33] E112/300/30; SP25/63/634 and 635; /64, pp. 21–2.
[34] Gage MSS, GG, various.

Having within 6 years last past enclosed with a stone wall the Rudge and Nockolls, 200 acres, in The Protector's wast soyle of the Forest of Deane.

Having encroached with his ditch 20 yards long and 2 foot broad at Coverham in the Woodwardship of Stanton.

Having within 28 years last past built a furnace at Redbrooke in the parish of Newland.

Having within 7 years last past built a forge at Lidbrook.

There is no evidence of any fine being levied on Hall. At least by 1657 he had recovered control of his estates and could resettle them.[35] In that year his Gloucestershire properties alone brought him almost £3,000 a year.[36] There was nothing to stop him from operating his ironworks, and Redbrook furnace and forge

Plate III. Highmeadow House (east of Newland), built around 1672, the seat of Benedict Hall. Drawn by Kip, *c.* 1712. The house faces east, and Newland church is depicted top left of centre. It was demolished in 1805 when owned by the Gage family. The site is now a grass field overlooking Newland to the west.

[35] The 1640 settlement had been made for 15 years (GG 871). For the Hall family charity, see Glos. R.O. D34.

[36] Gage MSS, GG, various.

were apparently working at the beginning of 1660.[37] He had built an early Highmeadow House. He died 16 April 1668, aged 78, and was buried at Newland.

By 1672 a new Highmeadow House had been built by his son and heir, Henry Benedict. Between 1668 and 1671 he was evidently in some financial difficulty and repeatedly borrowed money.[38] But by 1668 the upper forge is no longer mentioned. In 1671 Hall let the furnace at Redbrook and the Lydbrook forges to Paul Foley of Stoke Edith in Herefordshire;[39] by that time at least only Lydbrook middle and lower forges were mentioned in the Hall manuscripts;[40] and in 1702 these two forges appear to have been called upper and lower in an agreement between Benedict Hall and the partnership of Richard Avenant and John Wheeler.[41] In 1681 Benedict Hall was challenged by the Treasury as to the title to about 500 acres at Mailscot to the north of the Forest.[42] William Hall, Henry's brother, had apparently taken over the Herefordshire part of the family estates.[43] In 1702 when the last Benedict Hall let his ironworks to Avenant and Wheeler only Redbrook furnace and two Lydbrook forges, now called upper and lower, were included in the contract.[44] The same contract also indicates that the Hall estates could reckon to produce at least 2,000 short cords of wood a year and that they contained a fair amount of ore and cinders. These works could still have been repaired without too much difficulty in 1764.[45]

Henry Benedict Hall died 1687 and was buried at Newland. His only daughter and heiress, Benedicta Maria Theresa, married Thomas Gage, MP for Tewkesbury for thirty-three years, later to be given the title of Sir Thomas Viscount Gage. Their Highmeadow House was demolished around 1804, and most of the family's estate sold to the crown in 1817, to become High Meadow Woods.[46]

Most of the properties built-up by the Hall family and acquired late in the seventeenth century by the Gage family are indicated on a map of 1792.[47] Numerous relevant deeds are extant.[48]

---

[37] Gage MSS, GG, various.

[38] GG 950, 952–4, 981, 983, 986, 1338, 1346.

[39] Hereford R.O., F/VI/DBc/2.

[40] GG 950, 952–4.

[41] GG 1557.

[42] Cal. Treas. Bks., VII, p. 279.

[43] Hereford R.O., F/VI/DBc/3.

[44] GG 1557, Articles of Agreement with the Foleys, 10 Aug. 1702. Cf. ibid. the account for 1709 and 1710 between Hall and William Rea. See also GG 1545 (14).

[45] Gage MS (unlisted) survey of ironworks, 1764.

[46] GG 1146, 1150, 1152; Hart, *Coleford* (1983); *The Dean Forest Guardian* 30 Dec. 1893, and 30 May 1991; Kingsley, N., *The Country Houses of Gloucestershire*, vol. II (1992), pp. 161–3.

[47] P.R.O. F17/88 (map), /117 (terrier). By George Richardson.

[48] D1677 Gage MSS, in particular: as regards (a) properties: GG 1358–60; (b) mortgages and debts: GG 1405–31, 1438–85; (c) settlement proceedings: GG 1378–1404, 1432–38; (d) Lord Gage's claims to part of Hangerbury Wood, and to windfallen trees and bark in his bailiwicks: GG 1173–1332; D23 Probyn Papers, E29, 35, 38, 42.

# IV. JOHN BROUGHTON: THE FIRST DEPUTY SURVEYOR IN DEAN: 1633

John Broughton of Ruardean, during the 1630s in the reign of Charles I, was one of several local minor gentry with brief prominence in the Forest of Dean. He achieved some notoriety in the affairs of Dean's iron industry. He had contacts with the Vaughan family of Courtfield, near Lydbrook,[1] with Charles Powell of Ruardean (of the Powell family of Preston, Herefordshire)[2] and, through John Powell, with Sir John Coke (Secretary of State)[3] who had married John Powell's daughter,[4] also with Sir John Bridgman, Lord Chief Justice of Chester.[5]

Broughton's first known interest in Dean was with the iron industry. In May 1630, along with Henry Rudge, he took a lease of George Vaughan's Lydbrook middle forge (under the Earl of Essex), said to fine 160 to 200 tons of iron a year. Allegedly they repaired the forge with Dean's timber, and used illicit wood from Dean for charcoal.[6] Broughton also had licence to use the underwood in Bishops Wood between Lydbrook and Ross-on-Wye. In 1632 he sold the lease to Charles Powell, gent.; but repurchased it for £130 in 1635.[7] During 1631–3, Broughton occasionally briefed Sir John Coke on conditions in Dean.[8] (Likewise did Charles Powell of Ruardean – see Appendix.) On 11 January 1632[9] Broughton wrote to Sir John:

> The rates [rents] (£3,100) that are set down [suggested] upon Sir John Winter's [iron] works at Lidney will hold if he be put to it and he will not refuse them. The rates (£1,600) for Bishopswood furnace and for the two forges at Lidbrook Mr Charles Powell offers to give and to pay his half year's rent beforehand. The farmers [of the 'King's Ironworks'] deserve favour because they have built two forges upon the king's land and repaired newly all the other forges that are his Majesty's in that Forest; they are well dealt withall if they may have the works they now hold at £5,600 per annum for 7 years. But then the Earl of Pembroke's patent must be called in, or evicted, or compounded. Sir John Winter has a furnace at Gunns Mill near Micheldeane built by the king's timber, and chiefly maintained by his Majesty's wood. Because Sir John has wood of his own to maintain this furnace he may refuse to give the rate of £1,300 set down by me in these notes; but then he should have none of the king's wood to that furnace. The sooner that Order is sent for stay of cutting wood in the Forest of Deane for the ironworks, the sooner this rent will begin. I shall be ready at any time to make answer to any other question or difficulty that may occur. Only I beseech your Honor to be mindful of the [my] present trouble of your Honor's servant.

[1] SP16/307/6.
[2] E112/182/188.
[3] Ibid. /102/188; *H.M.C.*, 12th Rept., I, p. 474; Cowper MSS., Coke, II, pp. 5, 51, 157, 231.
[4] *H.M.C.*, 12th Rept., Cowper MSS., Coke, I, p. 474; II, pp. 5, 51, 157, 231.
[5] SP16/349/24; /236/82.
[6] SP16/307/6; E178/5304, 6 Chas. I.
[7] E112/182/188.
[8] *H.M.C.* 12th Rept., Cowper MSS., Coke, I, p. 474.
[9] Br. Liby., Add. MS 69909, Coke Papers (Series II), XLII, 57/7/3.

It appears that Broughton was in some kind of difficulty, perhaps not financial, in London. His letter was written in a neat and clear hand. The next day, 12 January 1632,[10] he wrote again to Coke:

> If this increase of his Majesty's revenue be fixed to be effective with speed, the only way is first cause a sudden stoppage of cutting within the Forest any more wood to be converted into [char]cole until further Order. Then to send down a Commission to able honest gentlemen to examine all wrongs done to his Majesty as well in his woods as in his lands. I can name divers men fit for that imployment. But if it be thought a more legal way that before the Commission a Bill be preferred in his Majesty's attorney-general name, I can give in very material points for such a Bill. And your Honor at half an hour's warning may command.

In April 1632[11] Broughton reported to Coke:

> In my duty to his Majesty, my obligation to your Honor, and my care of this poor commonwealth in the Forest, I have since my coming from London endeavoured to make good by effects what I gave in writing to your Honor. And now I can assure your Honor that Sir Basill Brooke and Mr. Mynn, how averse soever they have showed themselves in London towards the new course of taking his Majesty's woods and works at a yearly rent, yet now they are at this instant so satisfied as whensoever it pleaseth my Lord Treasurer and your Honor whom this cause may concern to send for them they will give satisfaction in every particular. So as these conditions may be to them performed: First that none of his Majesty's woods shall be given or sold to any other iron works whatsoever. Second that his Majesty's myne [ore] and cynders shall be likewise preserved for his own works, and not suffered to be exported to any other iron works. Third that the Deputy Constable of the Forest shall be always a man that hath no means within the Forest whereby his Majesty's Farmers may be hindered in their Myne and Cynders.
>
> These Conditions are so reasonable, and necessary, as being carefully observed, his Majesty's works within the Forest will continue for ever, and the present rent will very much increase. Being neglected, these his works within very few years will come to nothing and his Farmers at these great rates cannot but be infinitely prejudiced, if not utterly undone.
>
> The people of the Forest, especially the better sort and those that have no iron works adjoining to the Forest, are so pleased with this course as, besides subscribing unto it with all their hearts, they desire to know wherein they may declare or express their forwardness in assisting or furthering it.
>
> His Majesty's two officers, Mr. Rolls and Mr. Cous [commissioners among others for sale of crown log-wood and timber], came unto me 23 March to know of the new thought on course, and I freely and friendly acquainted them with some particulars, with which they showed themselves not only to be well pleased but to my face in presence of others they did extoll the business. And Mr. Cous (who seemeth a very able man) did confess it to be a thing so possible as what might concern his office therein he undertook to perform in every point; yet being departed from me they both, fearing a decay in their own interests, changed their minds and presently made known to their friends their great dislike of it. And because the Farmers' chief clarke did applaud it, Mr. Cous did not fail to complain of him to Mr. Mynn; and upon the 27th of March following he by a trayne apprehended Skimmington [a riot-leader] and brought him to Gloucester gaol, a thing which he, or any other by the like means might have done at any time many months before. I will not say that he did this of purpose to imbroyle the Forest in new tumults, for

---

[10] Br. Liby., Add. MS 69909, Coke Papers (Series II), XLII, 57/7/1.
[11] Ibid. 57/7/6.

many men thrive best by fishing in troubled waters, but the people of the Forest being beforehand informed of this new course resolved upon for his Majesty's profit and the Country's good and trusting in his Majesty's gracious lenity and mercy, for their late transgressions, showed no great alteration at the matter but do promise to continue in all obedience and quietness.

I beseech your Honor to further what in London I gave in writing for the Country's ease, and your Honor shall by God's grace see very speedily a constant revenue settled to his Majesty within this Forest like to which no county in England yieldeth. Your Honor shall see likewise by your means this poor Country settled in such peace and happiness as all succeeding people within this Forest shall be bound to pray for your Honor and your posterity, and in particular the first Moover of this service.

Broughton ended his letter thus: 'I have sent unto your Honor a small present – a few Shropshire cheese; if I may understand that they prove well, I shall be bold to send more unto your Honor.' His aim was to ensure that the king received the best rent for his ironworks along with an adequate rate per cord of necessary wood, and to ensure the inhabitants were contented and co-operative. On 18 June 1632[12] Broughton again wrote to Coke:

Being commanded by your Honor to show the way by which his Majesty might appease the troubles of the Forest of Deane, might avoid the wrongs and spoils done there, and might make the best profit of his woods and ironworks in that Forest.

I did set down in writing to your Honor an assured means of procuring the quiet of that Forest viz. if the King by composition with the parties would be pleased to take into his own hands all his late inclosures let and granted unto others.

I showed a Course whereby his Majesty without injuring any man might presently increase his revenue there which is now not above £4,200 per annum to £8,200 per annum, and how he might also save £4,000 per annum of wood which is now spent in other iron works and uses for which his Majesty doth not receive one farthing.

I made it evident that within five years his Majesty might raise this rent of £8,200 per annum to £9,000, £10,000, £11,000 and £12,000 per annum. And that with a small charge this greater rent might be continued for ever.

Because I would injury no man, I desired your Honor the present Farmers might have the refusal of the works and woods upon this course, and that they might be considered for their buildings. And in case they refused to take the works at these rates, I assured your Honor of other sufficient chapmen. Men well known to your Honor. So that whensoever it pleaseth my Lord Treasurer, and those to whom the King's revenue doth concern, they may at any time of leisure call the Farmers before them, and settle this great business in half an hours space.

Broughton added: 'I have done my duty; and for this service your Honor promised to free me of my present trouble and to procure me to be secured from further trouble in this kind. I do rely upon your honorable word, which I do humbly intreat may be performed to your Honor's most humble servant.' He continued his plea in a postscript:

That your Honour should not mistake my cause, and the way of taking of my trouble, in a Case which is without example, and as I think never yet practiced in England. I dwelling 100 miles from London by the malicious and injurious testimony of William Waynewright and John Gray am indicted at Newegate for a Priest. I am told that by the course of the

---

[12] Br. Liby., Add. MS 69909, Coke Papers (Series II), XLII, 57/7/8.

law I shall be convicted within 4 or 5 days unless your Honor do give present Order to stop proceedings against me. I am violently prosecuted and the more earnestly (as I conceive) for this present service I have set on foot for his Majesty's profit, for which I hope by your Honor's favour and grace with his Majesty I shall the rather be protected and defended.

On 17 September 1632[13] Broughton reported to Coke troubles which had arisen in the Cannop valley woods leased to John Gibbons (see Section VI):

The woodward of Ruardean gave in the writing to Mr. Surveyor [Treswell] in the presence of Mr Cous [Cowse] and Mr. Rolls, before whom it was read, and afterwards he did prove the contents thereof concerning the [Cannop etc.] quantity of acres, the spoils of the coppice, the value of the wood both cut already, and yet standing, not only by his own oath but also by the oaths of divers other substantial men, amongst whom Mr. Rolls was one. In conclusion he desired the Surveyor that he would be pleased to give some Order for a present stay of cutting any more trees in Mr. Gibbons' fellett [Cannop etc.] until further Order were given by the Lords of the Council whom he did intreat the Surveyor to acquaint with the business, for (sayeth he) at this instant many cutters are set at work in that fellett, and they do at this hour, cut down for cordwood as goodly trees as are in the Forest. The Surveyor did ask him, who did cause these trees to be cut down; he answered that they were cut down by Sir John Winter's appointment who (as he thought) had bought them of Mr. Gibbons. Henry Rudge tells me that when Mr. Surveyor heard Sir John Winter named he said no one word to it. So he fears all will come to nothing. I do understand that heretofore Mr. Surveyor hath been Steward to Sir Edward Winter, and Sir John, and hath kept their courts, and without question he will not fail to do Sir John Winter what favour he can. This is all I can say to this present great business which for any thing I can perceive is like to come to nothing. May be you may know more which I do desire to hear with your first convenience.

In April 1633 Sir Charles Harbord, surveyor-general of woods, appointed Broughton as his deputy surveyor of the Forest of Dean – the first in such office[14] (but without the powers or influence of later deputy surveyors). Broughton related 15 April of that year[15] (he may have been in London) that he 'came to Gloucester Friday, which was the wettest day he ever travelled . . . The spoils in Dean are so great that he will undergo excessive toll to reform abuses.' One of his first tasks was a survey of the number and value of the trees in Dean, completed on 23 August 1633.[16] At least one-third were fit for naval use, and 'an old experienced ship-timber man', George Dunning, had assured him that in the Forest was 'sufficient ship-timber to furnish this Kingdom with shipping'. Broughton reported that after he had numbered the trees (166,848) he did, as directed, spend divers days on reviewing the whole Forest 'viewing the trees very precisely and valuing them as near the truth as possibly we could, yet rather under than at their just value (£177,681.6s.8d.)'. He averred that the majority of trees would most profitably be used as cordwood for the ironworks, adding:

I leave to those that shall read this Paper to judge of the Forest wood. And God Almighty direct them whom it doth concern, in the best way for his Majesty's profit and honour

[13] Br. Liby., Add. MS 69909, Coke Papers (Series II), XLII, 57/7/9.

[14] SP16/236/82; C99/25; Hart, *Royal Forest*, p. 109.

[15] SP16/236/20; Hart, *Royal Forest*, p. 109.

[16] SP16/245/191 [22 pp]; Hart, *Royal Forest*, pp. 274–77; photocopy in Glos. R.O., D3921, Hart Collection, No. 36.

and for the public good. But if I may give a scarthing of my thoughts in this great business, I think that if this Forest did belong to any private man, and if this private man had therein ironworks of his own that had cost him £10,000 the building, as these ironworks in the Forest have cost the Crown and the present farmers, and if these works would constantly yield unto him £6,600 per annum for the space of 15 years, and afterwards £12,000 per annum as long as there was wood to supply these works, which by good husbandry might be continued a long time and perhaps for ever, if care was used in coppicing the grounds, I think that this private man would never entertain a thought of selling the Forest wood from his own ironworks, nor of giving or selling any part of the Forest to any man whatsoever, but would preserve the timber for his own uses, and best and fit, the offal wood for his own ironworks, and would enclose and encoppice the ground of the Forest to breed wood and timber, the grounds being for wood worth 10s. an acre, and for any other use scarce worth ten groats an acre. But I submit all I have written to graver and better judgment. And craving pardon for my boldness take my leave, being ever your Honor's humble and devoted servant.

Broughton's comments indicate that he was not lacking in knowledge, and was not necessarily thinking of his own interests. He grumbled frequently about the severity of his duties – which would suggest that they were congenial – and he was kept busy chasing after offenders in the Forest although the effect of his efforts was perhaps not great.[17]

On 19 November 1633[18] Broughton reported that 'Thomas Dean and William Jones had built a ship of 70 tons of the King's timber without leave or order'. John Purnell was building a ship in like manner; 'for her keel he took a beech 80 feet long which was sealed with his Majesty's mark'. The Lords of the Admiralty ordered Broughton 'to seize and stay all barks or building in the Forest of his Majesty's timber, by Dean, Jones, Purnell, or anyone else'.

At this time, with so many offences and abuses in the Forest by commoners, other inhabitants and ironmasters – the situation being in turmoil – a Justice Seat in Eyre was decided upon (see Section V). On 1 April 1634 Broughton wrote to Sir John Coke, following riots in Dean:[19]

I persuaded Mr. James Kyrle of Walford, the present deputy constable of the Forest, to obtain a commission from Sir John Bridgeman out of the Court of the Marches by virtue of which we call in all offenders of what quality or degree soever, binding some to the Council Board, some to the Council of the Marches, and others the Constable sendeth to the Castle of St. Brevills. Already this service worketh wonderful effects with all people of the Forest and especially with the officers who I fear by this means will come upon the stage.

From April to June of that year, part of Broughton's time was employed in assisting forest officers (especially those of the ancient forest law regime) to prepare information for the Justice Seat in Eyre (see Section V), opened on 10 July at Mitcheldean and adjourned to Gloucester castle.[20] In preparation for the eyre, the

[17] SP16/250/80, 19 Nov. 1633; *H.M.C.*, 12th Rept., Coke MSS, II, 51, 11 April 1634.
[18] SP16/250/292; /307/23.
[19] Ibid. /275/50; *H.M.C.*, Cowper MSS, II, p. 5; Hart, *The Commoners . . .*, p. 29.
[20] References in Hart, *The Commoners . . .*, pp. 29–32 and *The Verderers and Forest Laws of Dean, 1971*, pp. 98–101; Hammersley, G., 'The Revival of the Forest Laws under Charles I', *History XLV*, No. 154, June 1960, pp. 92–102.

swanimote (the Dean forest court of presentment) had drawn up its roll with amazing speed.[21]

Following the eyre, as official agitation over Dean receded, Broughton concentrated on other matters. By October 1634 he had surveyed the Forest twice more on the orders of the Earl of Holland (Chief Justice of forests south of Trent); he had 'numbered the trees twice, including cords cut and corded, and timber and logs uncut on the ground'.[22] On 23 September 1634 Sir Charles Harbord, surveyor-general of woods, himself had been on an inspection of Dean 'which has been as unlucky to itself as to its merchants'; his work was hindered because his deputy, Broughton, who held a forge at Lydbrook, was accused of misappropriating timber.[23]

To add to Broughton's troubles, 'on 11 October 1634 at about 7 am, a vehement wind within two hours blew down at least 1,000 trees'.[24] He and other officials were trying 'to preserve them from being cut out by the rude country people who claim these windfall trees as their dues'. On 16 October[25] he asked the Secretary of State what was to be done with the windthrows; if cut into cordwood he could sell for 6s.8d. a cord. On 9 January 1637[26] Broughton again wrote to Coke (ostensibly making an offer for the ironworks 'concession' on behalf of himself and associates. By this time his office was shared by Michael Meredith, probably because he was mixing commerce with duty.):

The farmers of the Forest of Dean do cut yearly 13,500 cords of wood by vertue of a Privy Seal (as it is conceived) and not by their Patent granted unto them under the Great Seal, for which wood they pay 10s. per cord which is £6,750 per annum. We, for the same wood and the same number of cords, undertake to pay his Majesty £9,450 per annum which is £2,700 yearly more than they pay. The farmers with their 160 cabins and cottages cannot but spend in firewood, hedging and timber great quantities of his Majesty's wood. We (because we will avoid that expense and the cries of the country by entertaining of strangers) will be tied and confined to 20 cabins at most. And we will quit and disclaim all other crying privileges that they pretend to be granted unto them in their late Patent. By which privileges they restrain whom they please from making iron in their own ironworks from cutting and coaling their own woods. And although it is most certain that there is in myne [ore] within the Forest abundantly sufficient to consume all the woods of his Majesty's Dominions, yet these farmers in a pretended fear of wanting myne restrain the mynors and coliers from getting their living by their accustomed labour, whereby these poor people are impoverished and will be disabled to pay unto his Majesty the dues of ship money and other services.

By 2 March 1637[27] Broughton was adjudged by Sir John Bridgman to be 'an honest and discreet man'. Broughton on 14 April 1637 wrote to Coke:[28]

[21] Copy of the Swanimote roll for 10 June 1934 in Bodleian, Gough MSS, Glouc.I, ff. 17–68d; and Br. Liby., Harl. MS 4850, ff. 10–53d. See also Hammersley, op. cit., 1960, pp. 92–102.

[22] SP16/275/50/257; Hart, Royal Forest, p. 119.

[23] SP16/288/393; /307/23.

[24] Ibid. /275/237.

[25] Ibid. /347/32.

[26] Br. Liby., Add. MS 69909, Coke Papers (Series II), XLVI, 147/8; Cp. Cal. SPDom. 1637–8, p. 205.

[27] SP16/349/482; /361/205; Hart, The Industrial History of Dean, p. 15 and Royal Forest, p. 119.

[28] H.M.C., 12th Rept., Cowper MSS, II, p. 157; Hart, Royal Forest, p. 119.

The [present] farmers [of the ironworks] in Dean Forest by their new grant have 13,500 cords granted yearly to them at 10s. a cord, annual rent £6,750. My undertakers will pay £9,450 and will be tied to have at most 20 cabins in the whole Forest whereas the present farmers have lately had 159 cabins there, whereby besides contentment to the commonwealth by strangers being excluded there will be saved about £2,000 of wood and timber which is usually spent by them. If your honour can procure this petition to be granted, the present farmers will in a snuff make a show to yield up their patent, and then his Majesty may take them at their words and thereby obtain his right.

Broughton then listed 'wrongs done to his Majesty by the present farmers':

1.  These farmers have cut into cordwood for [char]cole most of the special timber-trees what stood in their felletts and were marked by the king's officers to stand and remain for timber-trees, to his Majesty's great wrong and prejudice.
2.  They have lately cut out into cordwood for cole divers tons of timber that were specially reserved for the king's use and delivered to the Woodwards by indenture to be preserved for that end.
3.  They have cut out into cordwood for cole divers timber-trees that were marked and appointed to stand by his Majesty's ship carpenters and by the Surveyor-general.
4.  Though much of the wood they cut prooveth excellent good timber and fit for many uses in the commonwealth yet they convert all to coles contrary to the laws of this kingdom and contrary to their own handwriting exhibited by petition to my Lord of Holland at the last Justice Seat [1634].
5.  They have likewise wronged his Majesty in the oversize of their cords and in divers other particulars. And it is generally observed that when Sir Bayneham Throgmorton is present at any delivery of wood or about any other Forest business the officers of the Forest are so awed with his authority and stern carriage as they dare not speak nor offer to contradict any of the farmers' actions, be they ever so prejudicial to his Majesty.

These and many other abuses done to his Majesty by these farmers will be proved by divers witnesses of good quality if it please his Majesty to have them examined legally. But it is humbly desired that the Lord Treasurer and the Lord Cottington will be pleased to command these farmers for the present immediately to cease the further cutting down of trees in the Forest. Until as well our abovesaid offers for the increase of his Majesty's revenue may be considered. As also these farmers' devastation and cutting down for cole of the best timber-trees of the Forest in which execution they are now very busy, may be speedily prevented and the trees saved for better uses. And their misdemeanors committed against his Majesty particularly examined.

On 9 June 1637[29] Broughton supplied to Coke notes relating to the output and commercial value of ironworks:

Upon my knowledge the present farmers of his Majesty's ironworks did never in any one year (however well soever the year did prove) cast within his Majesty's four furnaces 2,800 tons of raw iron. They did never yet make in one year in his Majesty's five forges 700 tons of bar iron. The Earl of Essex's forge and Mr. George Vaughan's forge did never yet make in any one year 300 tons of bar iron. Sir John Winter with his 2,500 cords which he hath yearly granted unto him by Patent cannot possibly make above 500 tons of raw and bar iron.

[29] Br. Liby., Add. MS 69909, Coke Papers (Series II), XLVI, 57/7/12, 13; Cp. Cal. SPDom. 1637–8, p. 205.

These 4,300 tons, at 35s. per ton according to this new proposition amounts to the yearly rent of £7,525; my proposition for the same wood and works offers yearly £8,033.6s.8d.

I leave that man's judgement to be considered of that offereth £9,000 per annum with addition of another great service for wood to serve the above named works only and no other works and does offer to be bound that those very works shall cast and make yearly so much iron as that at 35s. per ton the rent of £9,000 per annum shall accrue to his Majesty when it is not possible that those works only should make that quantity of iron which he propoundeth which is about 900 tons per annum more than ever was yet made in those works or by those 2,500 cords of wood granted yearly to Sir John Winter.

If the party be an able sufficient man in estate to secure this rent, a better bargain cannot be made for his Majesty's profit, for it exceeds my proposition at least £1,500 per annum if the party be confined to the king's works.

If the propounder of this offer be Sir John Winter and if he by this bargain does hedge in wood for his own ironworks, he may very well give this great rent for the wood that doth at this present serve his Majesty's works and Sir John Winter's works is proved plainly in my proposition to be worth £12,000 per annum.

But whosoever makes this proposition of paying to the king 5s. for every ton of iron that shall be made in the king's works must of necessity make yearly 5,200 tons of iron to make his yearly rent of £9,000 a thing (I have said already) impossible to be performed in the king's works only and if he could make so much iron he must allow very near five cords and a half of wood to every ton of iron he makes, which in the whole sum cannot come to less than 28,000 cords of wood and this wood at 6s.8d. per cord is worth £9,333.6s.8d.

So his Majesty by this proposition, besides an even greater proportion of wood yearly spent which will utterly cross the hoped perpetuity of those works in the Forest will by that way lose yearly in the price of his wood at the least £333.6s.8d. And also his Majesty will be put to an endless trouble of keeping Clarkes for every work to watch and to take account of the tons of iron that shall be there made which is a business of trust and subject to much fraud and abuse.

About this time, *c.* 1637,[30] Broughton gave 'an estimate of damage to the king *super totam materiam,* done by the farmers which comes upon the 2nd and 3rd charge, viz: for cutting marked trees, and for cutting trees into cordwood before view':

In the first year it appears by the Ledger Books the Farmers had 14,300 cords:

Tho. Gunr. B.fol.i, Int.9: the half of the cords were good timber fit for shipping and building; and the king lost 5s. in every cord at least, which comes to £3,575.
John Artex.B.fol.29, Int.9:                   }   fit for shipping
Alex Morgan.B.fol.52, Int.9:                }   and
Humfrey Mason.B.fol.76, Int.9.             }   building [and loss likewise].

Note that all timber that is fit for building is fit for shipping, either for the outward or inward parts of the ship, but there are pieces of timber that are fit for shipping and not for building.

[30] Br. Liby., Add. MS 69909, Coke Papers (Series II), XLVI, 202/25.

In the second year before the Bill filed it appears by the Books their number of cords was 10,903 cords in the which the same loss proved by the same witnesses which comes to £2,725.15s.

The oversizing of the cords: the number of the first year's cords appears in above:

> Alexander Morgan.B.fol.52, Int.16: From the time of the defendants entry, for one year and a half, the Farmers far exceeded the assice, and the king was damnified 2 cords in every score in his judgement, he having duly weighed and considered the measure.
> Humfrey Mason.B.fol.76, Int.16: 2 cords in every score.
> John Artex.B.fol.19, Int.16: well nigh 2 cords in every score.
>
> £7,727.15s. [It is not clear how this total was calculated.]

Additional notes written by Broughton between March 1635 and December 1637[31] are:

> The farmers stand upon the strength of their Patent, and say that by law and justice they cannot be deprived of their bargain. But they say that if his Majesty will assuredly and constantly preserve all his woods within the Forest for his own ironworks, from all other ironworks whatsoever, upon this condition they will willingly give unto his Majesty £1,000 per annum more rent than now they pay.

> This offer, or like to this, they intend to make unto your Honor whensoever they shall be called about this Forest business. And if it appears unto your Honor that there will be some difficulty to bring them favourably to accept of this new course, your Honor may then join with them in this sort:

> That you accept of the £1,000 per annum and that you give it back again unto them on these conditions: that hereafter, they shall make no loggwood but all cordwood, that they shall cut all their wood fairly before them and leave not one tree or logg behind them uncut, except the trees that are marked to be preserved for timber. And that they pay hereafter for every cord of wood 6s.8d. per cord.

> This being done and security being given by them for performance of this point, your Honors may shortly after give express Order to your officers within the Forest that by all means they do cause the farmers to cord up their wood in whole cords and not in half cords, that is cords four foot thick, and not two foot thick. This one observation will be worth unto his Majesty at the least £2,000 per annum. And the changing of loggwood into cordwood will be worth £1,500 per annum. And a good overseer over his Majesty's officers there will keep them all in awe and in their duty and see this course performed.

Early in 1636 Broughton had given a demonstration, arranged under official supervision and before the verderers, asserting that careful operation of the direct process on a small scale could save about one-third of the charcoal (and hence trees) at present consumed.[32] For his forge at Lydbrook he had an 'improved bloomery wherein was made in 2½ hours a bar of iron of 55 lbs. weight from one sack of charcoal and a quantity of cinders and small ore'. On 7 March 1636[33] he wrote to Coke:

[31] Br. Liby., Add. MS 69909, Coke Papers (Series II), XLVI, 57/7/2.
[32] SP16/347/32.
[33] Br. Liby., Add. MS 69909, Coke Papers (Series II), XLII, 90/11.

What I did undertake to your Honor for my new way of making iron in the Forest of Dean, is now made good even by the judgement and approbation of Sir John Bridgeman [Lord Chief Justice of Chester] and by the certificate of those officers of the Forest to whom it pleased him to refer the examination of all particulars, which I do send here enclosed to your Honor. Now my humble request is that your Honor having received this satisfaction will vouchsafe to take this my small ironwork into your protection, whereby I may not be interrupted nor molessed in the practice of this invention, which every day is bettered and is brought to further perfection. This your Honor may easily procure by speaking one word in my behalf to his Majesty whose intimation to my Lord of Holland [the Chief Justice] or rather to the present farmers of the Forest of Dean and that it is his pleasure I shall proceed therein will be sufficient. If I may not obtain this favour, I must be forced to remove the work out of the Forest to a place two miles off, which will be very chargeable unto me. But I trust by your Honor's assistance that I shall not be put to that exigent. And this I humbly crave.

Nothing came of Broughton's petition.[34]

On 2 June 1639 Broughton wrote to Coke:[35] 'The country prayeth for my Lord Berkeley and that he may have the Forest, if Sir John Winter cannot perform his bargain'. He continued to criticize the 'concessionaires' but failed to substantiate his case before the privy council; they referred him to the exchequer court but here too the prosecution failed and was finally settled with a pardon in 1640.[36]

In 1641[37] Broughton, still residing in Ruardean, deposed to the attorney-general, Sir John Bankes, that he had known 'great store of timber and fallow deer' in Dean. Many of the 'greatest and chiefest freeholders had offered his Majesty half a year's value of their land so that it might be freed from the forest laws, provided that they were allotted a reasonable proportion of waste for their commoning'. He further deposed that 'he had seen a map taken about 20 years since, when the Forest consisted of 16,000 acres and 8,000 to 12,000 plains'.[38] Thereafter from being the first deputy surveyor of Dean, he had aspired to become a more substantial ironmaster than he had been before the appointment, and his mixing of commerce with duty may have been one of the reasons why from 1636 to 1639 his office had been shared by Michael Meredith.[39] After this, although Broughton is occasionally heard of, nothing significant appears to have been done by him in the Forest. He embodied in himself the then normal mixture of local connections, public service, and private advantage. Without any pretensions to great importance, his activities illustrate the close configuration of local affairs, in which the neighbours knew more of other men's business than of their own and where all men almost were related to one another or a friend.[40]

One day it may be discovered in which year John Broughton died, and where he was laid to rest.

[34] *H.M.C.*, 12 Rept., Coke MSS, II, p. 157; SP16/307/5; /361/49; /361/49; /364/118; /375/33.

[35] *H.M.C.*, 12th Rept., Coke MSS, II, p. 231; Hart, *Royal Forest*, p. 124.

[36] *H.M.C.*, Coke MSS, II, pp. 225, 233; SP38/18, 1 April 1640.; PC 2/48, pp. 493–4.

[37] E134, 16 Chas. I, Mich., Glouc. 36.

[38] Hart, *Royal Forest*, pp. 126–7.

[39] E101/141/5.

[40] Hammersley, G., *pers. comm.*

# APPENDIX

## CHARLES POWELL, GENT.

During the 1630s in the reign of Charles I, Charles Powell of London and later of Ruardean had an intensive although brief interest in the Forest of Dean. He had a degree of intimacy with Sir John Coke (Principal Secretary of State and Master of Requests to Charles I) who married Mary Powell of Much Marcle and corresponded with his father-in-law, John Powell of Preston in Herefordshire; this may suggest that Charles Powell was either brother of Eleanor James of Soilwell in Dean or at least closely related to the Powells of Preston. By 1632 he had become a minor ironmaster near the Forest. For a few years, while residing at Ruardean, he found time to inform Sir John Coke of much that was happening in Dean particularly as it related to the iron industry and to offences connected with wood suitable for charcoaling. For a few years he was virtually the local 'eyes and ears' of Sir John, yet seeking some advantages for himself.[41]

In January 1632 Powell entered into partnership with George Kemble of Pembridge Castle in Herefordshire to build a furnace at Whitchurch near Goodrich, paying £1,200 as his share of the required capital. The partners soon quarrelled and agreed to dissolve the partnership in April 1633, Powell being bought out for £1,064.[42] The furnace was built in August 1632. In 1632 Powell acquired from John Broughton and others the lease of Bishopswood ironworks (held under the Earl of Essex). He resold the lease to John Broughton in September 1935.

During 1632 and 1633 Powell, writing usually from Ruardean,[43] supplied to Coke information on Dean, notably as to ironworks and wood for them, as well as to local disturbances. In 1631 he supplied measurements of woods illegally felled at Mailscot by the Villiers family, and of inclosures made at Cannop Vellet by John Gibbons, and at The Sneade by Sir John Winter.[44] On 11 January 1632 Powell offered to pay £1,600 rent for Bishopswood furnace along with two forges at Lidbrooke, and to render his half year's rent in advance.[45]

On 2 April 1632[46] Powell informed Sir John of the apprehending of the notorious anti-inclosure rioter Skimmington (by two local officials, Cowse and Rolls).[47] He enclosed a letter dated 2 March from Steven Varner ('one of the Gibbins' men') to a Mr. Goodman Browne[48] seeking his protection from threats

[41] *H.M.C.*, 12th Rept., Cowper MSS, Coke I, p. 474; II, p. 5; Br. Liby, Add. MS 69909, Coke Papers (Series II), XLII.
[42] E112/182/188.
[43] Br. Liby., Add. MS 69909, XLII, *op. cit.*
[44] Ibid. 57/7/14.
[45] Ibid. 57/7/13.
[46] Ibid. 57/7/5.
[47] Hart, *The Commoners . . .*, p. 27, and *Royal Forest*, pp. 107, 114, 124.
[48] Br. Liby., Add. MS 69909, Coke Papers (Series II), XLII, 57/7/5.

made by Skymmington and his accomplices (at Cannop). Powell further proffered information and recommendations as to the management of the king's ironworks, and the wood required for them. On 24 April[49] he supplied additional information relating to the riots, especially as to the role of Rolls and Cowse, particularly at Newland; and added further advice on the use of the ironworks for the benefit of the king and the contentment of the inhabitants. He was again in touch with Sir John Coke on 20 December, writing from London.[50] Soon afterwards[51] Powell set down the conditions under which he would like to obtain a lease of named ironworks in Dean, at an annual rent of £4,300, following up with further relevant references,[52] and especially on information he had gleaned as to the making of gun ordnance, for which he said the Forest 'metal' was unsurpassed.

[49] Br. Liby., Add. MS 69909, Coke Papers (Series II), XLII, 57/7/7.
[50] Ibid. 57/7/10.
[51] Ibid. 57/7/15.
[52] Ibid. 57/7/16.

# V. THE JUSTICE SEAT IN EYRE OF JULY 1634

In 1633 the government of Charles I, through Lord Treasurer Portland, made known its intention to hold a Justice Seat in Eyre for the Forest of Dean. It was to be a revival of exploitation of the medieval forest laws by the crown. The sudden resurrection of an institution after a lapse of over 300 years was a revolutionary step (although elsewhere – at Windsor, Bagshot and Waltham – eyres had been held in 1632). In Dean, the protection of disappearing reserves of naval timber was perhaps one objective, but the protection of crown woods emerged as pretext rather than purpose. Reasons why Dean was chosen for an eyre, instead of others under consideration by the crown (e.g. Windsor, New Forest, Waltham, Chute, Alice Holt and Northampton) may have been some or all of the following:[1]

1.  Dean was one of the royal forests which had long been somewhat abandoned to their inhabitants. Hunting and other real interests to the crown were rarely used. Over 300 years had elapsed since the previous eyre.

2.  Only local use saved its trees from rotting where they had grown. Its large oaks and beeches were reserved for shipbuilding though many of them were past maturity for that purpose.

3.  Dean contained a large proportion of open crown land (wastes, lawns, commons) also huge deposits of iron-ore, masses of bloomery cinders and seams of coal, all increasing in value.

4.  Privileges of commoning, pannage and estovers were administered by forest officials with the authority of an attachment court, locally known as the Speech Court; there was a rarely used swanimote court. Together with the miners' ostensible rights to pitwood, all generated complications. Often there were jarring interests, and opposition to enclosure for regeneration.

5.  Since 1612, Dean had acquired new prominence: alone of all the forests it was beginning to produce a considerable and increasing revenue for the crown. The sale of cordwood to be charcoaled and used in the king's four furnaces and five forges specially built in the demesne forest, made the most substantial and regular contribution to this. The crown had repeatedly broken its long-term contracts with the farmers of the iron industry 'concession' for cordwood, iron-ore and cinders in order to re-let the 'concession' at a higher rent with perhaps a higher charge for the necessary 'complement' cordwood. They thought they were entitled to do so because of the patentees' abuses of terms of contract, and

[1] Relevant records are included in Hart, *Royal Forest*, pp. 111–14.

the overlapping of responsibilities of forest law officers and crown overseers (along with the declining influence of the ancient regime of hereditary foresters-in-fee, and the like), which led from accusation and bickering to open hostilities. Throughout all, timber-trees were to be reserved for the navy (though many were past maturity for shipbuilding). There were many abuses and spoils, yet the eyre was to prove the majority minor compared with those of four major malefactors.

6.   Some local gentry (as well as intruding ironmasters) were at odds with one another (significantly Throckmorton, Crow and the Kyrles against Winter, Brooke, Mynn and Gibbons). Between 5,000 and 6,000 acres, particularly coppices, were precariously enclosed to ensure the future supply of wood to the ironworks. Thus almost a third of the Forest had been fenced by walls, pales, banks and hedges. The commoners, in self-defence, as they conceived it, blackened all intruders, thus further exacerbating the ordinary distortion and magnification of each minor event or symptom. The anti-enclosure rebellion of 1628, led by John Williams alias Skimmington, quickly took hold amongst them; and was not completely put down until 1632. By itself, that was enough to attract the government's attention.

7.   There were bitter struggles for leases of the woods and ironworks: like other favours, the 'concession' could be won or lost by intrigue at Court, for which the complex local relationships offered much ammunition; significant were Sir Baynham Throckmorton of Clearwell and Sir John Winter of Lydney.

In April 1634[2] Charles I informed Sir John Bridgman (Chief Justice of Chester and vice-president of the Council of Wales) that he had ordered the Earl of Holland (Chief Justice in Eyre south of Trent) to hold a 'court of justice in eyre' within Dean 'for redressing the great abuses which through the discontinuance of the forest laws are there grown so high'. Bridgman was to assist sheriffs in choosing regarders and to instruct them in their duties. Hammersley[3] has discussed how far part of the policy pursued was an intrigue by the attorney-general, Sir William Noy, against Lord Treasurer Portland. At least part of Noy's intended policy against offenders was to base proceedings on a series of Exchequer enquiries into conditions in Dean which had already served in some inconclusive prosecutions of concessionaires, officials, and inhabitants, past and present.[4] But a fatal illness removed Noy from the preparations, and his place was taken in April 1634 by Sir John Finch as King's Counsel (he had been attorney-general to the Queen, and Speaker of the Commons in 1628). On 6 June 1634 the king commanded 'our trustie and welbeloved Sir William Jones Knt. one of the Judges of our Court of King's Bench':[5]

Trustie and welbeloved we greet you well. Whereas we have appointed a Justice Seate to be held for our Forest of Deane by our right trustie and right welbeloved Cosen and

---

[2] *Cal.* SP16/266, p. 576; Hart, *Royal Forest*, p. 111.
[3] Hammersley, *op. cit.*, 1960, p. 93; Dietz, F.C., *English Public Finance 1558–1641* (1931), p. 273.
[4] E178/3837 and 5304.
[5] C99/31, 1634.

Councellor Henry Earl of Holland, Chief Justice and Justice in Eyre of all our forests, chases, parks, and warrens on this side Trent, to commence the tenth day of July next at Michell Deane in our County of Gloucester and so to be continued there or at any other place where our said Chief Justice shall think fittest for our service till our affairs for that Forest shall be setled according to our forest lawes. We require you therefore according to the trust and confidence we repose in your wisdome, learninge and fidelity, to be there present and assistant unto our said Chief Justice and Justice in Eyre, the better to advice him in such points of lawe as may fall out before him. That so many the abuses happening and increasing dayly in this as in other forests for want of the due observance of our forest lawes may be reformed. Given under our signett sett at our Palace of Westminster the sixteenth day of June in the tenth year of our reign [1634].

Similar writs were sent to Sir Thomas Trevor, one of the barons of the Court of the Exchequer and to Sir John Bridgeman, Chief Justice of the County Palatine of Chester. On 4 July 1634 the king commanded 'our right trustie and welbeloved Cosen and Counsellour Richard Earl of Portland our High Treasurer of England and our trusty and welbeloved the Chamberlaines of our Exchequer and their deputies':[6]

Whereas by our especial direction and appointment an Iter and Justice seate is to be houlden the tenth day of this instant July in our Forest of Deane in our countie of Gloucester by and before our right trustie and right welbeloved Cosen and Counsellour Henry Earl of Holland our Chief Justice and Justice in Eyre of all our Forests &c. this side Trent – where (for the furtherance and advancement of our service) there will be special occasion to make use of the Regard Rolls and other the rolls of former ancient iters of that Forest and of the claims formerly made in former iters there and of inquisitions taken of offences done in the said Forest remaining in our Treasury among our records in your custody. Now for the better furtherance of our said service our will and pleasure is and we do hereby require and command you to deliver the said rolls, inquisitions, and claims to our trustie and welbeloved John Kelinge Esq. principall clarke of the same Iter, whose receipt of them under his hand shall be your discharge, for which this shall be a sufficient warrant. Given under our signe manuall at Wansted this fourth day of July 1634 in the tenth year of our reigne.

Regarders were ordered to make a perambulation of the Forest (see Appendix V). Sir John Finch (King's Counsel) later made notes (see Appendix I) of his actions in the Justice Seat of Eyre of 1634.[7] He used them to set down for Charles I a comprehensive report of the proceedings at the eyre. Following a swanimote court held at Mitcheldean, the Justice Seat in Eyre opened on 10 July 1634 at the same village and was adjourned to Gloucester Castle. There it reopened, with due ceremony, before Henry Earl of Holland (the Lord Chief Justice in Eyre). The assistant judges were Baron Thomas Trevor (solicitor to Charles I as prince), Sir John Bridgman (Chief Justice of Chester), and Mr. Justice William Jones (a judge of the King's Bench). Finch acted as Crown Counsel – a man of great ability and greater ambition, who coveted the king's attorneyship.[8] The Court continued until 18 July 'and then adjourned *de die in diem*'.

On Saturday 12 July 1634 in Gloucester the parade of the forest officials with their regalia was followed by the formal presentation 'by all the officers of the Forest

---

[6] *Palgrave's Antient Kalendar's and Inventories of the Treasury*, vol. 3, Appendix, pp. 437–8.
[7] Glouc. Liby., MS L.F.1.1, pp. 33 *et seq.* See Appendix I to this Section V.
[8] Hammersley, *op. cit.*, 1960, pp. 86–102.

and freeholders of the Hundred of St. Briavels and other persons bordering on the Forest' of written claims to 'estovers, commoning, fees, liberties, franchises and privileges within the Forest'.[9] The 120 presentments (see Appendix IV) ranged from rights of common, pannage, and estovers to offices within the Forest. They did not include rights of mining 'except that the Keeper of the bailiwick of Blakeney claimed seacole, and the Earl of Pembroke, as Constable of the castle of St. Briavels and Warden of the Forest, claimed to be chief judge of the King's Court within the Forest called the Mine Law Court, from the time whereof the memory of man was not to the contrary, held and used for the government of the mines of ore and coal and the workmen within the Forest'.[10] No 'claim of the miners appears, the same having been rejected as illegal they not being a Corporation'.[11]

Brief extracts of each of the 120 claims have been published (see Appendix IV).[12] Most of the claims were for 'housebote and heybote for repair and rebuilding of messuages and buildings by view and delivery of the foresters and verderers at the Speech Court, and firebote of dead and dry wood',[13] also for 'common in all open wastes and places of the Forest', making a small payment for the same, and for pannage for which were paid a few pence called 'swine-silver'. Holders of woodwardships further claimed by ancient custom the lop and top of trees given by the king and all wind-thrown trees. (The court did not pronounce judgment on the claims but 'they remained on Record in the Tower of London').

On the same first day, Saturday 12 July, in the presence of the Grand Jury (being fifteen), the twelve regarders, with the officers of the Forest and the 'fayremen' (four men) and reeve of each of the Forest townships, the matter concerning the perambulation of the Forest was solemnly debated. Finch, the King's Counsel, took steps to dispute and then to widen Dean's current perambulation which had stood since the reign of Edward III (see Appendix I and II). He had collected documents purporting to invalidate the then reduced bounds, and copies of those perambulations of Edward I within whose bounds were seventeen 'vills with their woods and plains' long treated as deforested. The bounds of Dean were based on perambulations of 1298 and 1300, which had been confirmed by letters patent in 1301; the statute I Edward III, c.1, had settled all forests in their reduced bounds.[14] Finch now challenged them with an undated document of unknown provenance which declared the reduced perambulation false and void. He argued that the reduced perambulation had been *ultra vires* in disafforesting what had been forest before the time of King John and ancient demesne. He also adduced in his favour the fact that some of the supposedly disafforested villages had continued to claim common in the Forest. 'The legal validity of Finch's argument from fundamental as against royal and statute law cannot easily be decided; it remained arguable to some of his learned opponents'.[15]

The jury of local men, unexpectedly confronted with Finch's case, deliberated from Saturday afternoon till Monday morning. Reluctantly and under some

[9] F20/1/(17), p.7; Hart, *Royal Forest*, pp. 111 *et seq.*
[10] F20/1/(17), p. 7; 3rd Rept. of 1788, p. 12.
[11] F20/1/(17), p. 7; 3rd Rept. of 1788, p. 12.
[12] Hart, *The Commoners . . .*, pp. 29, 167.
[13] C99, X, 133 membranes. See Appendix III and IV to this Section V.
[14] Hart, *The Metes and Bounds of the Forest of Dean, Trans. B.&G.A.S.*, LXVI (1945), 166; Br. Liby., Harl. MSS 738, ff. 306–311 (photocopy in Glos. R.O., D3921, Hart Collection, I/42).
[15] Hammersley, *op. cit.*, 1960, p. 95.

pressure from the judges it found for the crown, adding a rider that, in consideration of one patent, one statute and the custom of 300 years, the present bounds should be allowed to stand. Finch thereupon appealed to the judges for a statement of the law and, with its aid, persuaded the jury to drop its reservation. 'By this the King hath much enlarged the Forest', Finch wrote, 'but the King's Counsel in regard to their being but new brought in . . . thought it not fit to proceed with any of them at that Justice Seat'.[16] 'Small wonder that others found a decision unpalatable which left crown counsel uneasy.'[17] The Grand Jury, the twelve regarders, the officers of the Forest, the fayremen (four men) and reeve of each township subscribed their names accordingly.[18]

In the afternoon of Monday 14 July, fortified by dinner, the eyre turned to consider offences in the Forest. The Dean court of presentment, the swanimote, had drawn up its roll with amazing speed. It had met a mere month before the eyre, on 10 June 1634, and found 420 cases of cutting, taking or selling wood, 260 of illegal enclosure or other encroachments, 80 of poaching, 10 of unauthorized building of ironworks, and some 30 miscellaneous ones; many of these concerned more than one person and some of them referred to events forty years old.[19]

The eyre must have passed sentence after only the briefest consideration; some £130,000 worth of fines were endorsed against the 800 presentments. Finch himself thought these procedures open to criticism; he also wished to make an example of three notable ironmasters Sir Basil Brooke, George Mynn and Sir John Winter as well as of John Gibbons (Lord Treasurer Portland's secretary). The four were most prominent amongst all those affected; on the presentments they were liable to be fined almost £80,000 between them. Their fines would be high enough for them to complain about the summary procedure and trial without representation; their influence sufficient to make such complaints effective. Considerations of this type decided Finch to deal with them 'by way of a Special Indictment and not upon the Swanimote roll'.

John Gibbons (see Section VI), who was called first, had allegedly taken and enclosed more land than he had been granted in Dean (in the Cannop valley); he had then wangled a perpetual lease of the total and a licence to cut all the trees on it. The full relevant record is:[20]

On Monday [14 July] after Dinner a presentment and conviction of the Swanimote Court was read against Mr. Gibbons by which he was convicted for cutting down 4,000 oaks and 2,000 beeches worth 20s. apiece, between the last of March 5 King Charles [1630] and the

---

[16] For Finch's account of the proceedings, see Br. Liby., Harl. MSS 738, ff. 306–311 (photocopy in Glos. R.O., D3921, Hart Collection, I/42); Glouc. Liby., MS L.F.1.1, pp. 33–37; Bills and Answers, Exchequer K.R. E112/181/131; Hart, *The Commoners . . .*, p. 29; and Appendix I and II of this Section V.

[17] Hammersley, *op. cit.*, 1960, p. 95.

[18] Hart, *The Metes and Bounds . . ., op. cit.*, 1947, p. 33, where 17 townships are named; but the relevant townships are likely to be either those mentioned (1676) in Appendix V to Section IX, or those mentioned (1713) in the Appendix to Section X.

[19] Two copies of the Swanimote roll, June 1634: Bodleian, MS Gough, Glouc., 1, ff. 17–68d and Br. Liby., Harl. MS 4850, ff. 10–53d. The latter appears to be the working copy of one of the clerks to the Eyre. A brief note of the same is in Br. Liby., Lansd. MS, 151, f. 87.

[20] Br. Liby., Harl. MSS 738 ff. 306–311 (copy in Glos. R.O., D3921, Hart Collection, I/42); Bills and Answers, Exchequer K.R., E112/181/131; Northamptonshire R.O. IL 3006; Br. Liby., Add. MS 25302, ff. 56–66. See Appendix I and II to this Section V.

last of April 10 King Charles [1634] and for spoiling certain coppices to the damage of the King £1,200, and for inclosing 940 acres valued at £113.13s.4d. per annum with a wall, against the assize of the forest.

At the same time an Indictment found by the Grand Jury was read against Mr. Gibbons for cutting down divers goodly timber trees marked by the King's officers for shipping and other uses for his Majesty.

To his Indictment one Mr Haupe [? Thorpe] with a Letter of Attorney from Mr. Gibbons appeared and desired a copy of the Indictment, and time to plead, which was granted him.

On Tuesday morning Mr Haupe on the behalf of Mr Gibbons pleaded to that Indictment not guilty whereupon a trial was had and upon evidence, witnesses being heard in open Court, Mr Gibbons was caused to answer concerning the presentment and the Indictment, set out to be thus:

King James [I] at his great charge inclosed with a pale [fence] two several parcels of land for coppice, of which Mr Gibbons afterwards got a lease for 41 years by the measure of 574 acres more or less under the yearly rent of £28.14s., which came to so much as 12d. an acre, which was the contract rate the King was to reserve, and for a fine of £280, the timber trees and wood being thereby specially reserved to the King.

Whilst the Lease was obtained and before it was passed, Mr Gibbons set some on work to join in one inclosure those two parcels of inclosures, and by that means drew into the inclosure so much more not intended him; and made the 574 acres to be between 1,000 and 1,100 acres; and therein the King was deceived of 500 acres or thereabouts; which at 12d. an acre comes to £25 per annum, or thereabouts; and the true value of what he had is now £200 per annum at the least and would be worth twice as much within few years.

After his Lease was thus obtained Sir Allen Apsley[21] having a patent for divers lands in fee farme from the King, Mr. Gibbons excused his to be included in that patent by particular names of land containing by estimation 574 acres more or less in the possession of John Gibbons; And in that patent there being a general clause whereby no timber trees and woods growing upon any of the manors or lands passed to Sir Allen Apsley was granted, Mr Gibbons under Sir Allen Apsley's title claimed the fee farm of the land, but no conveyance was produced to that proof, though the King's Councell much tried to have sight of it.

What Mr Gibbons really paid for this, did not plainly appear; it was alleged he paid very near £1,000.

Since Mr Gibbons purchased and not long before the Justice Seat it was affirmed he had sold the lands to Sir Robert Bannester for which it is said Sir Robert paid £3,000; But Sir Robert (although he was at Gloucester) did not appear in it, neither was there any proof of it.

The timber growing upon these lands were as goodly timber trees as any in the Forest, and a good number of them marked for the King; all which were cut down by Mr Gibbons.

For all this, the Court finding the King deceived in the quantity of acres, to the number of 500 acres or thereabouts, yet Mr Gibbons under Sir Allen Apsley's title had no power to cut down any timber, or wood; Because being in a forest the grant of wood gives no

[21] Sir Allen Apsley (1569–1630) of Pulborough, Sussex, 'Lieutenant of the Tower', etc.

power to cut them unless there be special words to that purpose; And finding (as well by the reservation in the Lease, and by the marking of the trees for the King) that the King never intended that Mr Gibbons should fell the timber trees; it was thought fit to repair the King's losses procured by the ways aforesaid, fining Mr Gibbons £6,000, according to the value of the trees found upon oath.

And for his offence in that, and in cutting down marked trees, destruction of the coppices, and inclosing with a wall contrary to the Forest Lawes, with the former £6,000, came to about £9,000, the Court conceiving the King hath lost so much by Mr Gibbons means.

Gibbons paid £8,000 of his fine of £8,600, a much higher proportion of his sentence than anyone else.[22] Sir Robert Bannister was allowed to retain his lease. It appears that the Earl of Portland did not support Gibbons: he 'drove his Secretary from his house and forbade his making any defence. As a result Portland could not be involved in the disaster of his minions.'[23] Another source[24] asserts that Portland wished to remove suspicion and 'has driven Gibbons from his house' and forbid him to make any defence.

Sir Basil Brooke and George Mynn were charged with the alleged theft of 178,200 cords of wood, worth 6s.8d. each, during the past six years. This charge was buttressed by the ordinary complaints of most woodsellers against ironmasters: cords made too large, timber-trees charcoaled and/or paid for as inferior, officials corrupted, and woods destroyed. Finch offered two calculations in proof, one based on the amount of cordwood which all their ironworks, working to full capacity, must have used over the years, the other one an attempt to estimate the number of acres they had cut, the number of trees per acre and the cubic content of an average tree. The statement was comprehensive rather than accurate.[25] The defence claimed that they had used less wood and that they had paid not only for their 10,000 cords a year but for considerable amounts in addition. But they merely quoted the original accounts and refused to produce them in court. They were rebutted, according to Finch, because the procedure laid down in the patent had been disregarded; but according to Justice Jones,[26] because the Chief Justice of Forests had not been asked to countersign their grants. The full relevant record is:

Sir Basil Brooke and Mr Mynne (as assignees of the Earl of Pembroke [Constable and Warden of the Forest]) have a grant from the King for divers years yet to come of 10,000 cords of complement wood yearly, and of the windfalls, offalls, and loggwood for the maintenance of the ironworks in Deane Forest, paying the King 6s.8d. a cord for the complement wood, and 3s.4d. a cord for the logwood, windfalls and offals; these to be delivered by the officers of the King appointed for that purpose or, in case of the officers neglect upon request, to make proclamation in the parish church there of Great Deane, and so to take them.

The Swanimote Court presented and convicted them for felling divers great quantities of wood; But because the Swanimote Court had not presented all; And to the end all particular abuses and deceits might justly appear upon oath when they might have liberty to make their defence, which at the Swanimote Court they did not, being then absent; it

[22] Receipt Book (Pells), E401/1924, 3 Jan. 1637/8.
[23] Dietz, F.C., *English Public Finance 1558–1641* (1931), p. 273.
[24] *Cal. SP. Venice* MSS. vol. 23, 1632–6, No. 372, p. 293, 3 Nov. 1634.
[25] Hammersley, *op. cit.*, 1960, p. 97.
[26] Jones, *Reports* (London, 1675), 16, pp. 347–8.

was thought fit by the King's Councell that an Indictment should be preferred against them, to which they might plead, and be admitted to examine what witnesses they would for clearing themselves.

Accordingly an Indictment was preferred charging them to have taken of the King's wood within six years last past, they conniving in by assignment from the Earl of Pembroke in June 1628: to the number of 178,200 cords of wood to the value of £59,400.

The Indictment being found upon evidence to the Grand Jury in open Court, they had time given them by the Court to plead to it, and after that Wednesday morning the 16th of July assigned for trial; At which time the Jury of the best rank and quality, there being sworn, the matter was at large charged by Councell, as well on their behalf, as for the King, and seven hours spent in hearing the cause:

The Charge: The King's Councell charged them with two things, viz. 1. With the number of cords, 2. the abuses in taking them.

For the number of cords of wood there were produced divers witnesses, who deposed that the Farmers having four furnaces for making raw iron; and five forges, whereof three were double forges, and two single forges for making bar iron; those furnaces and forges could not (being all set on work) spend less than that quantity of wood wherewith they were charged as they demonstrated by their several quantities of raw iron made in their furnaces, and of bar iron made in their forges by the quantity of [char]coales that served for the making of that iron, and by the quantity of cord wood, that must needeth be spent in making those coales.

This being but a probable argument, the King's Councell rested not there, but by several witnesses, made it clear to the Court what number of acres had been fallen by them, how many trees were on every acre, how much cordwood those trees would make, and so particularly charged them with the quantities of the Indictment. For the abuses in taking the cordwood, the King's Councell urged many particulars, and fully proved them all; And namely:

1.   That they caused great quantities of cordwood to be wheeled into their [charcoal] pittes, without delivery of the King's officers, and so of all them the King was deceived.

2.   That where cordwood was delivered by tally, they had 23 for the most instead of 20.

3.   That by the bargaine with the King, the cordwood being agreed to be a certain size, they have exceeded the size, and therein also much abused the King.

4.   That they have invented a way of making half cordwood instead of whole, and by that hath so increased the size that in every two whole cords they gained a fourth part; it being proved that every three half cords went as far as two whole cords.

5.   That they had taken great quantities of great timber, fit for the complement wood, for which they were to pay 6s.8d. a cord, and reckoned it for logwood, and for windfalls, and offall, for which they paid but 3s.4d. the cord, and so deceived the King half in half.

6.   That they have by cutting glades, and destroying the shelter of the great timber trees left them open for the wind upon the side of hills, and in wet ground, so that as winter came those winds, having power upon them, blew down a great number of goodly timber trees, a thousand in a night, many of them marked for the King, and those they took as windfalls.

7.   That they have felled some young spring [natural regeneration], good for nothing, to the great destruction of the Forest in the future.

8.   That having by bargain from some other patentee divers roots and stools [of felled trees] they have caused excellent timber trees to be felled and mingled amongst them; of all which the King was deceived, and no accompt made.

9.   That contrary to the express agreement they have made, they have felled divers marked trees reserved for the King's store, and with which they ought not to have meddled.

10.  That they had destroyed woods in which were arieries of hawkes, contrary to express directions.

11.  That notwithstanding a restraint by the now Lord Treasurer, of which they had notice, they since that restraint, and in contempt of it, felled timber and wood to a great or a greater proportion, than before the restraint.

12.  That they have sufferred and brought in others to cut down wood, and to make [char]coale of it, and serve them with coales at a price.

13.  That they had brought in multitudes of cottagers and cabbeners who all made their cottages and cabbins of the King's wood, and live upon spoil of the wood.

14.  That they had threatened officers to have them turned out of their places if they did prie too narrowly into their accounts; whence it came that the officers for the most part were connivers and confederates with them to deceive and abuse the King.

Their Councell by way of defence brought some of their own agents to depose what quantity of iron was made by them in the several furnaces and forges, and so for the quantities of coales that served for the making that iron, and of the wood that served for the making those coales, whereof estimation the Court did not much weigh in regard that they would not produce their original Books of Accompt which they were commanded by the Court to do; But deposed and made to serve their turn.

And for the justification of the quantity; in part they read the Grant to the Earl of Pembroke under which they claimed 10,000 cords a year to which they had accompted in the Exchequer, and paid the King.

But the King's Councell repressing them to prove delivery by the King's officers according to the words of the patent, they answered they could not, and thereupon took occasion to desert their defence, and proceeded no further, but left themselves *in Misericordia Regis*; Upon which the King's Councell took occasion to let the Court, and Auditorie know how just it was not to allow them more wood deliveries by the officers of the King; Because had the King's officers delivered all the cordwood as it was agreed, and directed by the patent, the Farmers could not have put the deceit and abuses above mentioned upon the King; And therefore it was no reason they should take advantage of their own wrong. They then giving over the cause; the Judges directed the Court they had failed of their justification.

After Dinner, viz. about five of the clock, the Court coming on purpose to receive the verdict, the Jury found them guilty, to the value of £57,939.16s.8d.; Whereupon the Court gave judgement against them; And the Lord Chief Justice set the fine only proportionable to the value found by the Jury, and not according to the Forest Laws, being twelve times the value.

Sir John Winter (see Section I), charged with taking 60,700 cords, was fined £20,230.[27] The full relevant record is:

> Sir John Winter had by grant (as assignee of the Earl of Pembroke) 2,500 cords of wood a year at 6s.8d. a cord. Sir John Winter was presented and convicted for cutting down and taking within 6 years last past, three score thousand and seven hundred [60,700] cords of wood to the value of £20,230. Sir John Winter was also indicted for the same quantity and on Tuesday the [blank] day of July pleaded *non culpabilis*.
>
> Then the King's Councell was produced for the Trial; Sir John Winter conceding his case to be like Sir Bassil Brooke and Mr Minne, in open Court *relicta vareficara*, he confessed the Indictment; so the Court gave judgement against him, and fined him according to his confession £20,230.

The four principal sufferers appealed, on a technical point, to the King's Bench; they all failed.[28] Following the eyre, Brooke and Winter (who had bought Mynn's share) retained the letters patent of their grant; these had been issued under the great seal and could neither be confiscated nor abrogated by the eyre. The Chief Justice of Forests however could and did suspend supplies of woods to the ironworks.[29]

The crown extracted from the three farmers verbal assent to the strict legality of the proceedings at the eyre.[30] Mercifully, the crown at length admitted in mitigation most of the arguments which had been rejected at the eyre.[31] First it expressed the intention of collecting the great fines in full,[32] then it reduced all but a few of them. (Before June 1636 a general settlement had been agreed: the old grant was surrendered and the fines had been reduced to about a fifth, leaving Brooke and Mynn to pay £12,000, Winter £4,000,[33] while the new iron industry 'concession' went to the highest bid, submitted by Sir Sackville Crow, Sir Baynham Throckmorton and partners, at a rent increased by £2,500 a year.[34])

Other fines amounted approximately to £55,000.[35] Local ironmasters and past farmers of the ironworks concession had become liable for £17,000 between them, not all for offences connected with the ironworks. The rest ranged from 2s. for taking a few branches, or from £2 to £10 for the illicit building of cottage or house, to £100 or more for taking some tons of timber or acres of coppice. The fines had often been reduced on appeal. Only forty-two payments were registered on one of the copies of the swanimote roll to survive. A fine of £2,400, on a minor official, was reduced to £50. Benedict Hall (see Section III), a local recusant, considerable landowner and ironmaster, paid £800 of his £1,300. Another £420 worth of assorted fines brought in £160; altogether sixteen fines of under £10 and

[27] *Cal.* SP16/289, p. 100; Br. Liby., Harl. MSS 738 ff. 306–8 (copy in Glos. R.O., D3921, Hart Collection, I/42); Br. Liby., Add. MS 25302; Hart, *Royal Forest*, p. 113; Bills and Answers, Exchequer K.R., E112/181/131; Northamptonshire R.O. IL 3006; Jones, *Reports* (London, 1675), 16, pp. 347–8.

[28] K.B., Controlment Roll, Hil. 10 Chas.I, KB 29/283, m.s. 146, 147, 148, 161; Coram Rege Roll, Hil. 10 Chas. I, pt. iii, KB 27/1014, Rex. Roll, 41, 42.

[29] See Section I.

[30] SP16/293/69.

[31] Ibid. and /285/7, p. 5; /285/71; 288/55; /307/10 and 11.

[32] *Cal. SP. Dom.*, 1634–5, p. 350.

[33] E401/1923, 9 and 19 Aug., 2 Dec. 1636; E401/1924, 27 May 1637; C66/2766; Glos. R.O., D421 Winter Papers, E4, 1637: 'Pardon and release to Sir John Winter of fines incurred in the Swanimote Court [1634]'.

[34] C66/2740.

[35] Br. Liby., Harl. MS 4850.

six of £10 and over were paid in full. There is no evidence to show how much of the remaining £40,000 worth of fines was collected. Hammersley[36] suggests that all the fines might have produced rather more than £26,000 and rather less than £30,000, about one-fifth of the original figure.

The Dean eyre, planned without concealment since the middle of 1633, proved to become chiefly an inquisition. (It was to prove a model for eyres in other forests – among them Waltham, New Forest, Chute, Alice Holt and Northampton.) As one of Charles I's fiscal expedients, the restoration of forest law was only moderately successful. The strict legality of the proceedings became almost irrelevant. The Long Parliament (1640–60) regarded the exploitation of the medieval forest laws by the crown, between 1632 and 1640, as a major grievance. It cited Sir John Finch's part in the forest eyres as one of the principal charges against him.[37] (Nonetheless, in 1656 a resurrection of forest law by the State was attempted – see Section VII – only to be mitigated by the State with an Act in the following year.)

In the year following the eyre, 1635, the justices sent instructions to be carefully observed by the 'lieutenants' and deputy constables.[38] They were to ensure that the perquisites of trees and deer were to be taken only by those who could prove their right; only dead and dry wood was to be taken for firewood; taking of housebote was to be regulated; alehouses, being the cause of much disorder in the Forest, were to be suppressed; cabins, except those required for the ironworks, were to be demolished; and stealing, shredding, lopping and browsing were to be prohibited. Furthermore, sheep and goats were not to be permitted; they were despoilers of young trees, and were not commonable animals in a forest.

The old regime of forest officials eventually resumed prominence. A Swanimote Court for the Forest was held at Littledean 9 June 1637[39] before Charles Bridgman Esq. (of Poultons Court, in the parish of Awre) and John Berrowe Esq., verderers of the Forest. At this time, besides the Earl of Pembroke, constable-warden, and Sir Baynham Throckmorton, the chief forester, there were 10 foresters-of-fee, 15 regarders, 7 woodwards, and 6 keepers or foresters. Attending the court were 15 sworn jurors, as well as 4 men and the reeve of each of the Forest's 17 townships. The list of officials is given in Appendix VI to this Section.

---

[36] Hammersley, *op. cit.*, 1960, p. 100.
[37] J. Rushworth, *Historical Collections* (1654–1701), III.1.136–9; *D.N.B., sub.* Sir John Finch.
[38] C99/31, m. 2; Hart, *Royal Forest*, pp. 114, 115.
[39] Glos. R.O., D4431, Phillipps Documents, Box 17.

# APPENDIX I

Notes made by Sir John Finch (King's Counsel) of his
Actions in the Justice Seat in Eyre of 1634[40]

About Easter [1634] I received the King's [Charles I] pleasure to attend the Justice
Seat and to wait upon his Attorney [Sir William Noy] for some directions. The
directions from him were: that for the bounds 28 Edw.I [1300] a perambulation
would direct me, and the Confirmation 29 Edw.I [1301]. For the offences they were
chiefly in suite, of which I must inform myself by the proceedings of the Swainmote
Court and by such information as might otherwise be given me. His indisposition
of health hindered further conference with him about particulars.

And although divers came to me to give information and abuses, and divers
Commissions had formerly issued, yet the present information was in general and
such Commissions as I could so had produced little whereupon to ground any
judgment that I was fayne to resolve with myself to rest upon the fruite of the
Swainmote Court and upon such further sight as might be given me when I came
to Gloucester, for which purpose I went down hither some days before the Justice
Seat.

Touching the bounds, when I searched in the Tower and the Tally Office for the
perambulation 28 Edw.I [1300] and the Confirmation in 29 Edw.I [1301] and to see
what was done in former Iters held there, I found the ancient bounds of the Forest
had been far larger for the perambulation of 28 Edw.I which might well be and yet
the bounds be well and truly settled by that perambulation.

So by the Charter of the Forest 9 Hen.III [1225] whatsoever was the inheritance
of the Subject and afforested by King Hen.II. King Richard or King John was by
that Act to be disafforested but if either it were the demesne land of any of those
three Kings or if were the inhabitants of the Subject that had been afforested before
Hen.II time it was by *Carta Foresta* to remain forest still. While I had the
confirmation of this in my thoughts I heard a rumour that there was some fear
apprehended in the country of enlarging the bounds and I found divers very busy in
the Tower and in the Tally Office to get copies of the perambulations of 28 Edw.III
and exemplification of that and of the Confirmation in 29 Edw.I. This quickened
my care and gave me reason to believe there was some cause of their fear.

Thereupon I was careful to search among the Records and to arm myself fully for
that point and at last sight upon some Records that gave me assurance there was
reason to question the perambulation of 28 Edw.I. But because I found it was a new
Case and met with some difficulties in point of law I kept my resolution of
questioning the bounds formel to myself till the night before the Justice Seat; at that
time I desired my Lord of Holland [Chief Justice] I might in private confer with

---

[40] Glouc. Liby., MS L.F.1.1., pp. 33 *et seq.*

him and the Judges his assistants. They being altogether I explained to them the true state of the Cause together with the difficulties that I foresaw might arise in point of law and not trusting my own judgment in a matter of so great weight not daring to question such a thing wherein, if I failed, your Majesty might remain of point of law in questioning bounds so long quoted, I desired their Lordships' opinion whether upon that I acquainted of which I had no reason to question the bounds. Then all agreed I had and thereupon the next day I visited some towns to be called which were held out of the forest and the perambulation that the Regard now made (which I found was the same with it and moved the Court it might not be received). This and the calling the towns reputed not forest made some that were of Counsell for the Towns to allege that those Towns were clearly out of the forest. I thereupon desired them to let me have a Note what Towns they were of Counsell with, and I would the next morning let them know which of them I would question, and which I would not. Thereupon they sent me a Note of some few and in the morning I gave them public notice in court that on Saturday morning the bounds should be examined and bade them appear themselves against that day for I meant to question those towns and many more.

And because it is a new Cause as may concern your Majesty in divers other Forests I will if your Majesty please upon the true state of the Cause as shortly as I can as it was handled in Court.

On your Majesty's part it was alleged: That before 9 Hen.III the Forest went on the east side Severn to Bristol. By Hen.III was enacted *at supra*. 12 Edw.I: this perambulation was allowed at a Justice Seat then holden [1282] and offences done in those bounds presented and punished. So the large bounds continued without contradiction for 6 [?70] years from 12 Hen.III to 26 Edw.I. And the time of the perambulation and disaforestation [sic] being within 3 years after 9 Hen.III when things were fresh in memory, and the Subject not willing to lose any privilege was against that authority I desired to have what could be said against it.

On the Towns' part were alleged three objections: (1) Matters of Record was two perambulations, 26 Edw.I and 28 Edw.I; (2) Act of Parliament 1 Edw.III, cap.i whereby is enacted that the perambulation made in the time of Edw.I shall be observed; (3) Long usage – usage ever since 28 Edw.I. And concluded it against law to question those bounds. And against all probability of reason to do it after so long time of usage to the Country.

My reply on your Majesty's Part:

(1) Record: That 26 Edw.I and 28 Edw.I were false and erroneous perambulations having disaforested [sic] divers towns as afforested by King John whereas in truth they were afforested before Hen.II time and so ought by 9 Hen.III to remain forest though they had been Subjects' inheritance. And if divers of them had been afforested by King John, as 28 Edw.I sayeth, yet they were the demesne lands of the Crown and so ought to remain forest though newly reforested by King John. And all this I made appear by a Record I had in the Tower whereby it appeared that for those reasons 28 Edw.I was revoked. Then had no date but was after 28 Edw.I. And for 29 Edw.I the Charter of Confirmation that could not bind your Majesty according to many Cases of Law because the King was deceived. And his deceiving of the King.

(2) For the Act of Parliament: 1 Edw.III it was doubly answered:
(i) That gave no strength to 28 Edw.I because the words are general and so refers as

well to 10 Edw.I as to 28 Edw.I, and so in a Case of uncertainty that must be taken which is best for the King especially truth being so.

(ii) It was never the meaning of that Law to undo *Carta Foresta* but to confirm it. And to exclude aforestation whether of the King's demesne lands or of Subjects' lands aforested before Hen.II time was to undo *Carta Foresta*.

(3) For the wrong, it was thus answered prior usage cannot prejudice your Majesty's right for *nullum tempus occuril Regi*. The usage could not be well known because no Justice Seat hath been since 10 Edward III [1336]. But the truth is usage hath been otherwise for the owners of land in those towns near the King's wast have used common of pasture, pannage and estovers in the King's soil of the forest which by *Ordinance Foresta* 33 Edw.I they are barred if they be out of the forest. And the truth is that accordingly in 9 Edw.III being about 37 years after 28 Edw.I the owners of land in most of those towns were presented for cutting wood without licence and for assarts and other offences against the assize of the forest which is a manifest proof that the perambulations were observed according to 12 Hen.III and of 10 Edw.I and not according to 28 Edw.I. This I then had not and divers other matters will be found to corroborate it.

Upon all this I left it to the Jury of 15, all the officers of the Forest and fayre men [four men] and reeve [from each township] of the towns in the Forest. The Judges all three for matter of law declared that 28 Edw.I, 29 Edw.I and Act of Parliament, and usage were not binding if 28 Edw.I were a false and erroneous perambulation and for matter of fact touching the truth of the perambulation and upon consideration of all the Records they left it to the Jury. The Jury could not that day agree but asked further time, which was granted. After some days of consideration they brought in a Special edict that the true metes and bounds were according to 12 Hen.III [1228] and 10 Ed.I [1282] but in regard to the Confirmation of 29 Edw.I and of the Act of Parliament I Edw.III and long usage they left it to the Court's consideration whether 28 Edw.I ought not to stand for a good perambulation.

All three Judges thereupon delivered their opinions fully as before. And upon the Jury allowed their verdict by unanimous consent and made it thus: We present that the metes and bounds of the Forest of Deane are and ought to be according to the perambulation made in the 12 Hen.III and 10 Edw.I. And all of them have subscribed it in a parchment roll made upon Record. By this 30 towns are brought in and divers are the best and most populous places of the Forest.

What advantage it will bring to your Majesty and how it is a Consideration fit for your Majesty wherein whensoever your Majesty shall command it I shall employ my humblest and faithful Service.

Offences: For the offences in the Forest in the matter of the woods (for other things were not so considerable), when I was at London the noise was great against your Majesty's farmers [of ironworks] there – Sir Basil Brooke and Mr Mynn and against Sir John Wynter and Mr. Gibbons. And when I came to Gloucester I heard the Bell ring out against them and with all had information given me that all art and diligence was used to obscure things and to prevent things coming clearly to the notice of the Regard and by them to the Swainmote Court and so to the Justice Seat. Thereupon I endeavoured to satisfy myself in the truth of every thing as near as I could and upon inquiry found the abuses in the Forest to be very great and to rest principally upon those four before-named. And in this I had great light from Sir

Baynham Throckmorton [of Clearwell] but for further satisfaction I sent to the woodwards and other officers of the Forest that I might have particular accompt of the destruction of the wood, and when I had sufficiently as I thought informed myself, I attended my Lord of Holland [Chief Justice] and the Judges to know what course might be taken to having the offenders present. Sir Basil Brooke and Sir John Wynter were there but Mr Mynn and Mr Gibbons were away. My Lord of Holland was Resolved to address himself by Letter to your Majesty for Mr. Mynn coming down and to send Mr Gibbons. But while this was in consultation Sir Basill Brooke appeared for Mr Mynn who was his partner [in the ironworks 'concession'] and Mr Gibbons sent down an attorney with power to answer for him. And upon that I resolved to prove against them without expecting their presence. The proceedings against them I resolved should be by way of a Special Indictment and not upon the Swainmote Roll and my reasons were these:

(1)  I found the abuses complained of and offered to be verified upon oath were much greater than appeared upon the Swainmote Roll.

(2)  Upon the Swainmote Roll I found the bare offences presented but the particulars of the abuses and deceit did not appear without such an examination as was not so proof upon the Swainmote Roll.

(3)  I considered with myself that they were absent and had been absent at the Swainmote Court, and if now they were fined they had excuses ready that they were absent that they could not now be allowed to the Swainmote Roll (being a full Commission in Law admitting no ........[?]) which if they had liberty to do they would have justified themselves. And so by this means I foresaw that your Majesty would be as for all most from an undoubted knowledge of the truth as you were before the Justice Seat.

Whereas upon Indictment they have all advantage of Counsell pleading what they could and of producing witnesses or what they could to outthrow the evidence that might be given on your Majesty's part and so the Cause might come fairly and entirely to a full discussion and examination. And for all these reasons I took the Cause by way of Indictment holding it the fittest for your Majesty's honourable profit and for Justice (All which, God willing, I shall ever most truly endeavour to my power in what place shall be to your service.)

The particulars I shall now open to your Majesty:

*Sir Basil Brooke and Mr Mynn Case*: Indictment: within 6 years last past cutting the timber-trees of the King of which they made 178,200 cords: King's damage £59,400. The Indictment proferred to the Grand Jury in open court evidence given publicly upon proportion of iron, wood and [char]coale. Enough to find *Billa vera*. Sir Basil Brooke appearing for himself and Mynn plead not guilty. A day fixed for trial. A sufficient Jury taken of gent. and others in Court. Exception to Sir Baynham Throckmorton. Evidence on the King's part:

1.  For quantity proved by proportion of the wood spent in the four furnaces and five forges whereof two double.

2.   By particular quantity of trees.

For the manner. In which divers abuses proved:

1.   Wherein proved without delivery or knowledge of officers and without cording.

2.   Taking 28 for 20 [cords] where it was delivered by officers.

3.   Exceeding the size:      In the long cords to a 5 or 6 part
     In half cords a 4 part
     And workmen durst not cut it in whole.

4.   Turning the complement wood into logwood. There the King lost half.

5.   Mingling complement wood with [char]coale wood, in which the King lost
     5s.2d. in every 6s.8d.

6.   Bringing in men and suffering them to cut the woods and [char]coale it, and
     they bought the coale. And had 9 bushells in a [?] stack for 7, for the coles had
     no [?] care.

7.   Bringing in multitudes of cottagers.

8.   [...?...] 1,000 in a night.

9.   When one tree fell, cut down three above it.

     In all which the King lost 3s.4d. Yet they saved the charge of felling for they
     were felled to their hands.

10.  Marked trees.

11.  Destroying aeries of hawkes which they were restrained from. Making
     [char]coale Pitts under them for to drive away the hawks with the smoke. So
     felling them next year for they were the best timber.
     Nine acres now none.

12.  Three [...?...] officers. Under workmen discharged.

13.  Never any cord taken legally.

14.  The Stowles [stools]. My Lord of Holland saw them.

15.  Cutting contrary to a warrant 28 February. They were growing lawless.

Their defence opened: They justified:        10,000 cords under the Lease
                                             6,000 cords
                                             2,900 cords of Logwood and windfalls
                                             in 5 years
                                             3,839 of [...?...] year

Read the patent. Gave out the evidence. The Jury found them guilty of 172,800 cords valued £57,937.16s.8d. less the Judgment they were found but less the value and £100 apiece for a fine. Note the Forest Law 12 times. (1) Surprised in his defence. Time given. (2) No evidence but by guess. (3) Partial Jury. (4) Objections against me for caryage [?]. Acknowledgement in open court and to me in person of Mr Whitfold. (5) My not allowing what was paid unto the Exchequer.

*Sir John Winter's Case*: Indictment: first Indictment:

| 60,700 cords | } | 84,000 cords |
|---|---|---|
| value £20,230 | | value £28,000 |

This found by the Grand Jury and made less, he confirmed. Fined but £10.

Objections: (1) The proof but guess. That the Grand Jury; (2) much of it was his own woods; (3) promised he should suffer no inconveniences.

*Mr Gibbons' Case*:

1. Mr Gibbons and Stephen Winder [? Varner] convicted at Swainmote for cutting 4,000 oaks and 2,000 beeches, value £6,000.
2. For inclosing lands with a wall.
3. For spoiling coppices at Morestocke.
4. For building a house and taking 20 tons of the King's timber.

He was indicted for cutting 3,000 marked trees value £4,500, he by his attorney having pleaded not guilty upon evidence by Counsell on both sides.

King James [I] inclosed two parcels for coppice. Mr Gibbons gets a particular of those and other lands, 574 acres more or less. Then promised all to be inclosed, and inclosed with it other lands where the aery of hawkes was. While this was in doing 14 March 8 Chas. [I] [1633] for £280 obtained a lease from the King by content of 574 acres more or less for twelve years, rent £28.14d., except all timber-trees and saplings. By this means got possession of almost 1,100 acres.

Sir Allen Apsley &c passed in the patent by that content at the rent for which the King had 30 years perhaps of £861. Mr Gibbons pretended a conveyance from Sir Allen Apsley that was not produced. Takes upon him before or after to sell him all the timber upon the 1,100 acres. And among the rest the marked wood and the trees where the hawks treed [nested]. And destroyed the coppices. By colour of general words whereas the words gave no interest because no words [?] *luct sit infra metas*. After he did inclose all the 1,100 acres with a wall and built a house with timber of the King taken out of other lands. The Jury upon full evidence on both sides found him guilty of 3,000 marked trees value £4,500.

The Court fully satisfied (1) unduly obtained were passed; (2) that before he had the inheritance he felled so his was upon destruction; (3) The wood well worth £6,000; (4) Informed he had £8,000 of Sir Robert Banister. Fine for all these offences:

£3,000 upon [?] wast
4,500 upon indictment
  500 for destroying coppices
  500 for the wall
   30 for the house
   80 for the timber
£8,610

# APPENDIX II[41]

## THE BOUNDS OF THE FOREST OF DEAN, 1634

On Saturday the 12th of July 1634 in the presence of the Grand Jury (being 15), the 12 Regarders, with the Officers of the Forest and the Fayremen [four men] and reeve of the several townships within the Forest, the matter concerning the perambulation of the Forest was solemnly debated.

The King's Counsell [Sir John Finch] produced two ancient perambulations: the one in 12 Hen.III [1228] and the other in 10 Edw.I [1282] both agreeing that the bounds of the Forest began at Gloucester Bridge, and so went to Monmouth Bridge, and Chepstow Bridge, and came round again by the Severn to Gloucester, taking in all those seventeen towns.[42]

The Counsell for the towns produced two perambulations, one in 26 Edw.I [1298] and another in 28 Edw.I [1300] both agreeing that the seventeen towns were not anciently Forest, but were afforested by King John, and so by the Statute of *Carta de Foresta* ought to be disafforested; and produced also Letters Patent in 29 Edw.I [1301] whereby that perambulation of 28 Edw.I [1300] was confirmed; and, lastly, insisted upon an Act of Parliament in 10 Edw.III [1337] whereby the perambulation made in the time of Edw.I were confirmed; and they urged also the long and constant usage ever since, agreeing with the perambulation of 28 Edw.I [1300], concluding that by the law the metes and bounds ought not to be questioned contrary to that perambulation, confirmed by Letters Patent and an Act of Parliament.

The King's Counsell replied that the perambulation of 28 Edw.I [1300], and so consequently of 26 Edw.I [1298], were false and erroneous perambulations, prejudicial to the King, and contrary to the Charter of the Forest; and whereas by that Charter of the Forest no disafforestation should be of any lands that were afforested before Henry II's time, nor any of the King's demesne lands, though afforested after the beginning of the reign of Henry II. Yet this perambulation did disafforest those seventeen towns afforested by King John; whereas the truth is, that they were forest long before, and divers of them were of the King's own demesne lands, and for that cause the perambulation of 28 Edw.I was afterwards revoked as a void and erroneous perambulation; and to prove it, produced an old Record[43] in the Tower which had no date, but by the body of the Record it appeared to be after 28 Edw.I, reciting it as a void and revoken thing.

---

[41] Copies in: Br. Liby., Harl. MSS 738; Northamptonshire R.O., IL 3006; Glouc. Liby., MS L.F.6.2. and L.F.1.1., pp. 33–37; Glos. R.O., D3921, Hart Collection No. I/42; Hart, *The Metes and Bounds . . .*, 1947, pp. 47–9; 3rd Rept. of 1788, pp. 59, 60.

[42] As to the probable 17 townships see footnote 18 *supra*.

[43] Doubtless P.R.O. Chanc. Misc. bdl 12, No. 45, see Hart, *The Metes and Bounds . . .*, 1947, p. 51.

For the long usage it was answered that no *Iter in Eyre* had been there since 10 Edward I [1282] and so no man could say what was the usage. But divers of those towns had since claimed common in the Forest, which showed they took themselves to be forest and not purlieu, because by *Ordinationes Forestae*, 33 Edw.I, no Purlieu Man can have common within the forest.

For the confirmation in 29 Edw.I it was answered that the perambulation being void and erroneous, the Letters Patent confirming it was also void, the King doing it upon false information; and for the Act of Parliament in 10 Edw. III, that did not confirm the perambulation of 28 Edw.I by name, but the perambulations throughout England of all forests made in the time of Edw.I generally.

And therefore that of 28 Edw.I being a void perambulation, the Act of Parliament wrought not upon that, but had its operation upon the perambulation of 10 Edw.I which was written with the words of that Act as well as the 28 Edw.I, and was within the meaning, being a true perambulation, and the King's Counsell demanded judgment of the Court whether this question of the bounds were not, for all the reasons aforesaid, agreeable to law.

To which the said Judges' Assistant answered that it was legal and not contrary to the Act of Parliament in 10 Edw.I, and left it to the country to consider of the Record of the Tower produced by the King's Counsell as an evidence to overthrow the perambulations of 26 and 28 Edw.I; and if those perambulations were void it must follow that the perambulations of 12 Hen.III and 10 Edw.I were true ones. On Monday the Grand Jury and the rest brought in their verdict touching the perambulation, which was to this effect:

> We agree that the metes and bounds of the Forest of Dean ought to be according to the [wider] perambulation made in 12 Hen.III and 10 Edw.I; but because we find the perambulation of 28 Edw.I to be granted by Patent of 29 Edw.I and because of the Act of Parliament of 10 Edw.III and a possession of 300 and odd years concurring therewithal, we therefore refer it to the judgement of this Honorable Court whether the perambulation of 28 Edw.I ought to stand in force.

Whereupon the King's Counsell moved the Judges to deliver their opinion for the matter in law, which they all agreed on as before; and then the King's Counsell moved the Jury, since when their verdict in law was satisfied by the Judges, that they would agree to leave out the latter part of their verdict, and let the first part only stand for their verdict, *viz*:

> We agree that the metes and bounds of the Forest of Dean ought to be according to the perambulation made in 12 Hen.III and 10 Edw.I.

To which the Grand Jury, the 12 Regarders, the Officers of the Forest, and the 'Fayremen' [four men] and reeve [of each township], subscribed their names accordingly.

By this the King hath much enlarged the Forest of Dean, and all within the seventeen towns aforesaid were fearful that they should have been questioned for many things done contrary to the forest law; but the King's Counsell, in regard of their being but new brought in, and long usage, thought it not fit to proceed with any of them at that Justice Seat.

# APPENDIX III

## A TYPICAL CLAIM, 1634

Translation (from the Latin) of a typical claim, being that on behalf of William Skynne, the owner of Plattwell in the south-west of the Forest of Dean, made at the Eyre of 1634.[44]

Forest of Dean \
in County of } And now to this Court comes William Skynne by Edward Offley his attorney and says that he is seised of an
Gloucester / old messuage in Plattwell in the parish of Newland and
of 20 acres of land, meadow and pasture and of various barns and stables (so called in English) and other necessary buildings on the aforesaid land built of old in the parish of Newland within the Forest of Dean aforesaid in his demesne as of fee; and for himself and his heirs he claims these liberties, privileges and franchises following as appertaining and belonging to the messuage, land, meadow and pasture and other buildings aforesaid. Namely:

For the necessary rebuilding and repair of his said messuage and his other old buildings being upon his lands and tenements aforesaid, that he by the view and allowance of the foresters[-of-fee] and verderers of the aforesaid Forest may take and receive from time to time of the wood and timber of the King growing upon the wastes and commons of the aforesaid Forest. And that the foresters and verderers of the aforesaid Forest at the request of William Skynne made to the same at the Court of the King held within the aforesaid Forest called The Speech Court ought to go and see and appoint the wood and timber growing on the wastes and commons of the aforesaid Forest as aforesaid for the aforesaid necessary rebuildings and repairs to the said messuage with the other buildings above said and there to make allowance to the same William Skynne.

And he claims for his necessary estovers to be burnt and used in his said old messuage at his own will to take of the dead and dry trees of the said King being on the wastes and common places of the aforesaid Forest.

And he claims common of pasture in all open and common places and commons of the aforesaid Forest for all his common beasts of burden levant and couchant at all seasons of the year on his lands and tenements aforesaid (the forbidden month [the Fence Month] alone excepting).

And he claims to have pannage for all his pigs levant and couchant upon his aforesaid lands and tenements in all the wastes of the aforesaid Forest at the time of pannage rendering to the King annually the sum of one penny for the aforesaid pannage by the name of swine-silver, and no more.

And for title to these liberties, privileges and franchises aforesaid as above claimed by him the same William Skynne lastly says that he and all his ancestors and all whose estate he now holds in the above said messuage, land and tenements from time wherein the memory of man runneth not to the contrary were used and accustomed from time to time to make suit at the court of the King and his predecessors the Kings and Queens of England at his castle of St. Briavels from three weeks to three weeks and also annually to pay to the King's fee-farmer of the aforesaid Forest for the time being or to his bailiff a

[44] Hart, *The Commoners* . . ., (1951), pp. 30–32.

rent of 8s.8d. for the use of the King. And also annually to pay to the said fee-farmer or his bailiff the sum of 1d. as swine-silver for the use of the King. And that he the aforesaid William Skynne and all his ancestors and all whose estate he now holds in the messuage, lands and tenements aforesaid by suit at the King's court and rent of 8s.8d. aforesaid and the sum of 1d. as swine-silver as aforesaid by him from time to time made and paid to the King were from the whole aforesaid time of which the memory of man runneth not to the contrary used and accustomed to use all and each of the liberties, privileges and franchises in the manner and form as are claimed above by William Skynne as to the aforesaid messuage, land and tenements belonging and appertaining, and each and all of them were used according to the strength form and effect of his claim aforesaid. And the same William Skynne has used them hitherto as is quite lawful to him. And he is prepared to verify this when the court has considered whence William Skynne seeks the aforesaid liberties, privileges and franchises as aforesaid claimed above by him for himself and his heirs to be allowed according to his aforesaid claim.

[Examined by] Tobias Rose.

# APPENDIX IV

## CLAIMS MADE IN 1634

Extracts from the Claims made at the Eyre of the Forest of Dean, held at Gloucester Castle, Tuesday, 10 July, 1634, before Henry, Earl of Holland, K.G., Chief Justice and the Justices in Eyre of all the forests, chaces, parks and warrens of the King, this side of Trent.[45]

| No. | Claimant | Situation of Property, or Subject of Claim |
|---|---|---|
| 1. | Phillip, Earl of Pembroke and Montgomery | Constableship of St. Briavels Castle, etc. |
| 2. | Edmund Berrow | Manor of Blakeney |
| 3. | Joan Vaughan | "     " Littledean |
| 4. | "           " | "     " Abenhall |
| 5. | "           " | "     " Ruardean |
| 6. | Nicholas Roberts. | "     " Lea |
| 7. | "           " | "     " Mitcheldean |
| 8. | Benedict Hall. | "     " Staunton |
| 9. | "           " | "     " English Bicknor |
| 10. | George Fouch. | Office of Ranger |
| 11. | Thomas, Earl of Arundel and Surrey, guardian of Henry, Lord Stafford, the King's ward. | Courts, etc., within the borough of Newnham |
| 12. | Men and tenants of Rodleigh | Rodley |
| 13. | Warren Gough. | Verdererership perquisites |
| 14. | John Berrow. | "                              " |
| 15. | George Wyrall. | Newland |
| 16. | Bridget Wyrall and George Wyrall. | English Bicknor |
| 17. | William Perkins. | Newland |
| 18. | William Skynne. | Plattwell [see Appendix III] |
| 19. | Anthony Calow. | Mitcheldean and Abenhall |
| 20. | Thomas Matthews. | Bream |
| 21. | Thomas Yerworth. | Coleford and Staunton |
| 22. | Edmund Berrow. | 'North Hall', Awre |
| 23. | Lawrence Stedd. | 'Inwoods Farm', Newland |
| 24. | John Court. | Awre |
| 25. | Richard Katchmay. | 'Suitelands', St. Briavels |
| 26. | Anthanasius Ely. | Newland |
| 27. | John Bufford. | Ruardean |

[45] E146, For. Proc. bdl. X, 10 Chas. I (133 membranes). Copies in Glos. R.O., D3921, Hart Collection.

| No. | Claimant | Situation of Property, or Subject of Claim |
|---|---|---|
| 28. | Richard Smyth. | Staunton |
| 29. | Henry Dowle. | " |
| 30. | John Hoskyns. | " |
| 31. | Edward Smyth. | " |
| 32. | Thomas Wysam. | English Bicknor |
| 33. | William Marshall. | "          " |
| 34. | William Godwyn. | "          " |
| 35. | William Gardner. | "          " |
| 36. | John Batchellor. | "          " |
| 37. | James Keare. | Staunton |
| 38. | John Fisher. | English Bicknor |
| 39. | Henry Worgan. | Clearwell |
| 40. | Roger Lewis. | English Bicknor |
| 41. | Frances Carpenter, etc. | St. Briavels |
| 42. | Andrew Horne. | Awre |
| 43. | George Birkin. | " |
| 44. | Charles Bridgman. | Manor of Poltons Court |
| 45. | Robert Yonge. | Awre |
| 46. | Thomas Salence. | " |
| 47. | Edward Morsse. | Mitcheldean |
| 48. | Richard Hopkins. | Awre |
| 49. | John Wintle. | " |
| 50. | John Brown. | " |
| 51. | John Nelme. | Ruardean |
| 52. | Morgan Griffith. | Coleford |
| 53. | Charles Trippett. | Awre |
| 54. | William Hodges | " |
| 55. | Thomas Adeane | " |
| 56. | Gough Chinne | "    and Newnham |
| 57. | Alexander Thorne | Clearwell |
| 58. | John Harris | Blakeney |
| 59. | John Preece | 'Woodfield', Awre |
| 60. | Henry Hulyn | Clearwell |
| 61. | Thomas Whooper | " |
| 62. | Alice and Thomas Partridge | " |
| 63. | Thomas Whooper | " |
| 64. | Thomas Keare | " |
| 65. | John Bucke | Blakeney |
| 66. | Richard Hooper | Gatcombe |
| 67. | Master and Warden of Gonville and Caius College, Cambridge | Awre |
| 68. | William Stevington | Mitcheldean |
| 69. | Ketford Brayne | Littledean |
| 70. | (a) Charles Bridgman | " |
|     | (b) John Birkin | Awre |
| 71. | Warren Gough | St. Briavels |
| 72. | John Gunninge | "    "    and 'Chishall' |
| 73. | William Cachmay | Newland |
| 74. | Hugo Dowle | Clearwell |
| 75. | John Knight | Ruardean |
| 76. | Edward Brown | English Bicknor |

| No. | Claimant | Situation of Property, or Subject of Claim |
|---|---|---|
| 77. | Matthew Dowle | English Bicknor |
| 78. | Richard Morse, Jnr. | " " |
| 79. | Christopher Worgan | Clearwell |
| 80. | Avis Baylie, etc. | Blakeney |
| 81. | William Phillips | 'Le Harp', Lea |
| 82. | Henry Phillips | 'Le Beechgrove', Newland |
| 83. | William Lovell | Newland |
| 84. | Robert Phillips | Lea Lyne |
| 85. | John Berrowe | Blakeney |
| 86. | Thomas James | Newnham |
| 87. | " " | Ruardean |
| 88. | George Bond | Clearwell, Whitson's House in Newland and Redbrook |
| 89. | Blanch Bond, etc. | Newland |
| 90. | Kedgwin Hoskin | Clearwell |
| 91. | Christopher Dubberley | Coleford |
| 92. | John Yerworth | " |
| 93. | Anne Dowle | Clearwell |
| 94. | Sturley Kedgwin | " |
| 95. | Richard Strowde | Coleford |
| 96. | John Kedgwin | " |
| 97. | Richard Moreton | "         and 'Whitecleeve' [Whitecliff] |
| 98. | William Carpender | Coleford and Stowfield, English Bicknor |
| 99. | Robert Jordan | Coleford, Newland and Staunton |
| 100. | Henry Marsh | 'Whitecleeve' [Whitecliff] |
| 101. | Henry Morton | Coleford |
| 102. | Edw. Worgan | 'Millend' in Newland and Clearwell |
| 103. | John Symonds | Clearwell |
| 104. | William Dowle | Coleford |
| 105. | William Ymme | " |
| 106. | Jane Birt | Clearwell |
| 107. | Richard Hill | re Office of Bailiff, etc. |
| 108. | Arthur Ricketts | Newland |
| 109. | John Bullocke, etc. | Awre |
| 110. | Thomas of Awre | " |
| 111. | Charles Bridgman | Verdererership perquisites |
| 112. | Sir John Wintour, Kt. | Office of Forester [-in-fee] |
| 113. | John Jeane of Brockweare | St. Briavels |
| 114. | "     "     "     " | "     " |
| 115. | "     "     "     " | "     " |
| 116. | Richard Worgan | Clearwell and Coleford |
| 117. | William, Bishop of Llandaff | Tithes of iron-ore |
| 118. | "     "     "     " | "     " assarts |
| 119. | William Monmouth | [illegible] |
| 120. | Sir Baynham Throckmorton, Bt. | Office of Chief Forester [-in-fee], etc. |

Among the claims are those for certain lands (totalling about 5,000 acres) at Awre, Blakeney, Gatcombe, Rodley, Bream, Newnham, English Bicknor, Stowfield, Ruardean, St. Briavels, Brockweir, Staunton, Newland, Whitecliff, Coleford,

Redbrook, Clearwell, Lea, Mitcheldean, Littledean, and Abenhall. There is no mention of claims in connection with lands at Lydney, Aylburton, Woolaston, Blaisdon, Westbury and Longhope. There is no contemporary record to show that any of the claims were allowed or confirmed. Furthermore, it seems that no claims were made in respect of lands in what was the wooded central portion of the Forest, for no mention is made of places such as Lydbrook, Cinderford, Yorkley, Pillowell and Parkend.

It can be gleaned from the claims that the closed, or 'non-open', portions of the Forest were not commonable; one claim mentions 'beyond the covert of the forest'. Thus only the open and waste portions of the Forest were commonable. The claims make no mention of payments for common, but pannage was paid for by 'swynesilver'; the last usually amounted to 1d. per annum per messuage: the village of Awre paid a total of 8s.2d. No specific claim was made for commoning with sheep or goats. The claims acknowledged that pigs were required to be ringed.

# APPENDIX V

## PART OF A PERAMBULATION OF THE FOREST OF DEAN, MAY 1634[46]

A Perambulation of the Forest of Deane in co. Gloucester made beginning 12th day of May in 10 Charles [I] 1634 by Warren Gough Esq., Geo. Wyrrall Esq., George Bond, Anthony Arnold, Joshua Deane, Richard [?] Byekyr [?Birom], Nicholas Morse and other gents., Regarders of the said Forest of Deane by vertue of His Majesty's writ to them directed and returned into the Justice Seat for the said Forest in July 1634.

It beginneth at a certain well in Purlow Greene called Hopeswell being a well of small depth and breadth but [?] inclosed with 4 or 5 stones about a foot or 18 inches high above the ground, And so descending from [blank] unto a Greene called Barlings Green, Descending on the left hand down a little valley unto a certain old decayed well called Ashwell by the hedge of Ashwell Mead to Bishops Brook [south of Walford] and thence down that valley or Strait Bottom unto the River of Wye where is a little Green increased by reason of the [?] stones carried into Wye by the violence of the water, Descending from a Furnace in the valley a little above it, And from the said little Green in Wye until it cometh unto a certain place called Juttlyne, and thence from Wye ascending up a certain path or way called Slowpath unto a Yew tree [? V...] below Symons Yatt at which Yew tree is a certain little Meer Stone ditched in the ground being the bounds between the counties of Glouc. and Hereford, And thence descending down overthwarte that craggy rock or hill unto Wye, and so descending down Wye [blank] unto a certain old weare now utterly ruinated which was built to drive a Furnace of the Lord Gray of Ruthen, and from that weare descending down Wye by the confines of Mailscott until it cometh unto a certain little stream [...B...], and so up that little stream until it cometh unto the corner of Lady Park Grove, and so ascending up that Grove unto a certain old oak called Bellmans Oak, and thence up a certain meadow or pasture called Ryddings, etc.

[46] Glos. R.O., D1677, GG1337. The above part of the perambulation can be compared with that of 1667 in Section IX, Appendix I. Lord Gray mentioned in the 1634 perambulation was Earl of Kent, and of the Talbots, Earls of Shrewsbury family.

# APPENDIX VI

## THE SWANIMOTE COURT FOR THE FOREST OF DEAN, 1637[47]

The King's Forest of Dean in Gloucestershire [remainder faded]

Swanimote Court of our lord Charles, by the grace of God, King of England, Scotland, France and Ireland, Defender of the Faith, for the Forest of Dean, held at Littledean in the aforesaid Forest in Gloucestershire on 9 June in the thirteenth year of the King's reign (1637) before Charles Bridgman esquire and John Berrowe gentleman, verderers of the said Forest.

The names of those wardens, foresters, woodwards and other officials of the said Forest

Philip, Count of Pembroke and Montgomery, the King's constable of the castle of St Briavels and warden of the aforesaid Forest
James Kirke, esquire is the deputy of the said warden

Baynham Throkmorton, baronet, chief forester
George Hamblyn, gentleman is his deputy

Foresters in Fee

John Wintour, knight
John Hannys
Thomas Wilse
Hugh Dowle
   Geoffrey Lippiatt his deputy
William [G]ray
   Charles Calowe his deputy
William [G]ower esquire and Richard Durlinge in right of their wives, co-heirs of Anthony Wye, esquire, deceased
   John Baker their deputy
George Roberts
[John] Worgan
   John [Jefferies] his deputy

Regarders: formerly elected

Warren Goughe of Hewelsfield, esquire
George Wirrall of English Bicknor, [gentleman]

[47] Glos. R.O., D4431, Phillipps Documents, Box 17.

Anthony Arnold of le Grange near Walmore, [gentleman]
John A Deane of Etloe, gentleman
[Anthony Bower] of Mitcheldean, gentleman
George Bond of Redbrook, gentleman
[John] Jane of Brockweir, gentleman
Nicholas Morse of Mitcheldean, gentleman
William Wargeant of St Briavels, gentleman
Thomas Arram of Newnham, gentleman
Edward Browne of English Bicknor, gentleman
Richard [Birom] of Hagloe, gentleman

Regarders: recently elected

William Jones of Naas in Lydney, esquire
William [Civildale] of Tayton, gentleman
Edward Sergiant of Mitcheldean, gentleman

Woodwards

Baynham Throkmorton baronet, for the bailiwick of [le Bearse]
    John Dobbs, his deputy
Benedict Hall esquire, for the bailiwick of Staunton
    Richard Smyth, his deputy
the same Benedict, for the bailiwick of English Bicknor
    Thomas Harsfeild, gentleman, his deputy
Edmund Berrowe, esquire, for the bailiwick of Blakeney
    William Treganoe, gentleman, his deputy
Joan Vaughan, widow for the bailiwick of Ruardean
    Henry Rudge, her deputy
the same Joan for the bailiwick of Abenhall
    Walter Baker, her deputy
the same Joan for the bailiwick of [Badcocks Bailey] alias Littledean
    Thomas Sparks, her deputy
[Nicholas] Roberts, esquire, for the bailiwick of Mitcheldean
    [illegible] Gwillam, his deputy
[the same] for the bailiwick of Lea alias Lea Bailey
    [Robert Beeke], his deputy
Richard Hill, gentleman for the bailiwick of Blyths Bailey
    William Browne, his deputy

Keepers or Foresters

Thomas Ch[illegible]ey, gentleman          William Brethers, gent
[David Foxe], gentleman                    John Adams
Thomas Jelfe                               Simon Magretts

[illegible], gent, bow bearer to the Warden of the said Forest
[illegible], gent, bow bearer to the Chief Forester in Fee
[illegible], beadle for the Hundred of St Briavels
[Thomas Smyth], beadle for the Castle of St Briavels

Jurors sworn at the Court

[illegible] Pauncefoot, gentleman
W [illegible] Tyler                    William Skynn
John [illegible]                       Thomas Trigg
William [illegible]                    John Arram
.[Tanner] Morse                        Morgan Griffiths
John Cadle                             Thomas Young
John Smart                             Daniel Morse
John Nash                              Joseph Okey

Four men and the Reeve from the vill of Staunton

Edward Smyth
Anthony Peyne
James Wysam
John Hoskins
Henry [Dowle], constable.

[No other vills are included.]

# PART TWO

## VI. 'CANNOP HOUSE' AND CANNOP VALLEY WOODS: 1616–60

The early seventeenth-century 'Cannop House' – its location, history, and connection with the Forest of Dean – for long has been intriguing. The few remnants of the house in the woods of Cannop Vallet (syn. Fellet) have been known for several decades. Its site and remnants, with a yew tree standing above them, as well as the mounds of an enclosure (now partly obliterated on the west by the spoil tip of the spent Cannop Colliery) stand about 200 yards south-west of the Cannop Villas, part way between 'Cannop Bridge' in the south and Mirey Stock in the north (see Map IV, overleaf).

On 21 January 1947 George Taylor of Coleford, a knowledgeable state forester, recollected often passing the remnants of a house with a yew tree standing thereon, when walking from Wimberry Colliery to Speech House Hill Colliery during the time he was employed at both before joining the Office of Woods in 1897 (he later joined the Forestry Commission).

Plate IV. 'Cannop House' was built illegally by George Moore, ironmaster, in 1616–17 to house himself and his clerks (who supervised his timber fallers, charcoalburners and carriers). In 1618 James I ordered the house to be demolished. A c. 300-year-old yew tree grows on top of the stonework and debris. (Photograph by John White, 1994)

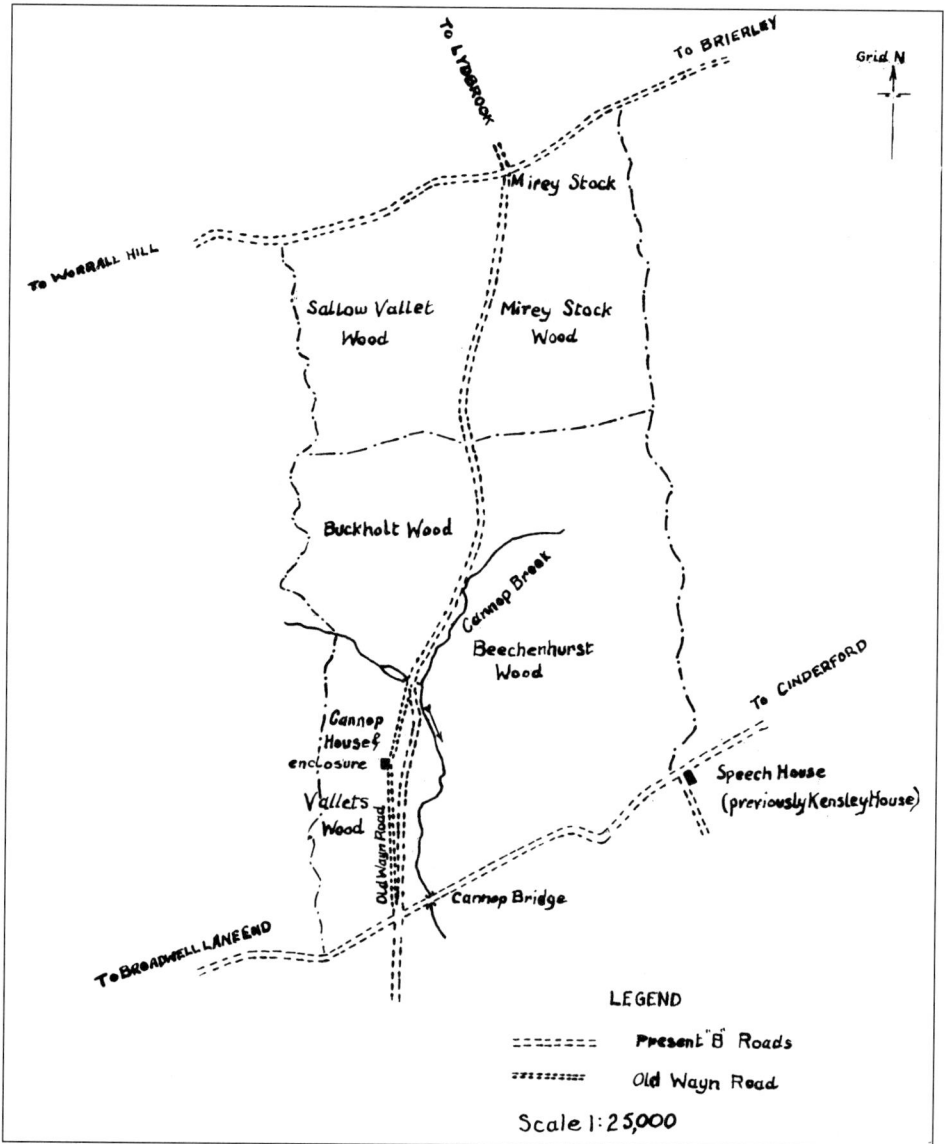

Map IV. Schematic map of the Cannop valley woods, c. 1620–30. In 1628, 574 acres of crown woodland in the south of the Cannop valley were alienated from the Forest of Dean by grant of Charles I to John Gibbons (Secretary to Lord Treasurer Portland) who, later, illegally enlarged to about 1,000 acres, to include the east, west and north. Repurchased in 1668 by Charles II for £1,500. The site of 'Cannop House' is indicated, bottom left. (Drawn by G.L. Clissold, 1994)

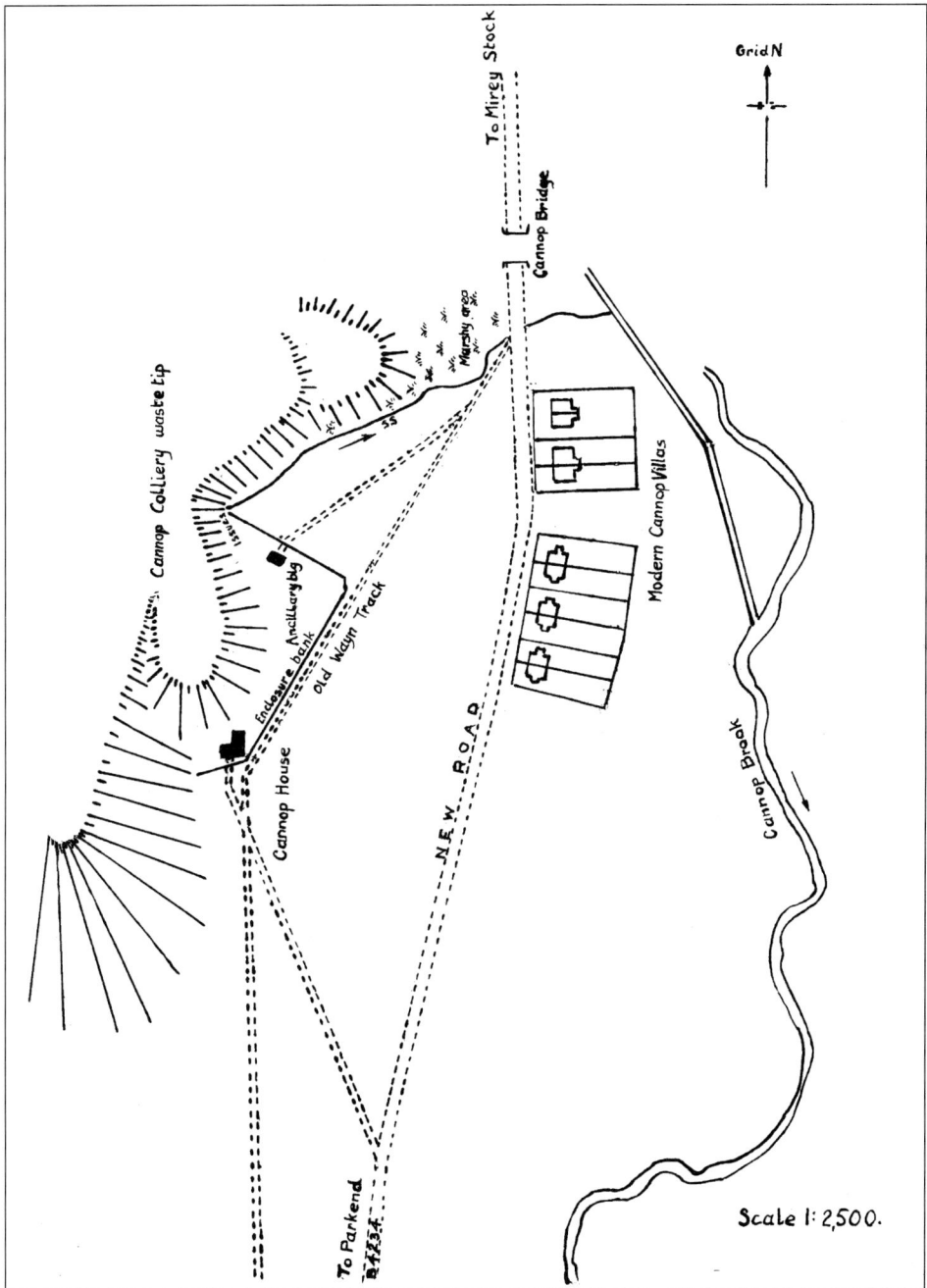

Map V. Schematic map of the terrain around 'Cannop House' and its enclosure. (Based on a dowsing survey by Brian Johns; drawn by G.L. Clissold, 1994).

In 1951, in *The Commoners of Dean Forest*, the present author recorded (p. 24, note 1) that the search for the site of the house had recently ended successfully. In 1966 the site was briefly referred to by the present author in *Royal Forest* (p. 104). Recent additional research in the Public Record Office at London and Kew, and in the British Library, London, has enabled the preparation of a reasonably comprehensive history of the house, its then surrounding woods, and their connection with the Forest of Dean.

(During 1604–6, in the reign of James I, fifteen sessions of the Speech Court of the Verderers, one session every six weeks, were held 'at Cannop', a mile to the west of the usual venue, Kensley House,[1] but this was a decade or so before 'Cannop House' was built.)

## GEORGE MOORE AND 'CANNOP HOUSE'

George Moore of Goodrich was a Roman Catholic whose father had tried to help Mary Stuart.[2] In 1609 he was the steward of Goodrich Castle but had probably not held the office for more than a few years.[3] At that time he was engaged in planning for the construction of a blast furnace at Longhope,[4] part of the Earl of Shrewsbury's estate in this district, and he had evidently examined the potential value of the Forest of Dean for an expanding iron industry with his employer's interests in mind.[5] In 1609, in a letter dated 26 April to his master, Gilbert, Earl of Shrewsbury, Moore projected plans for the erection of ironworks in Dean.[6] He asserted that in Dean were 'divers good rivers and mine of iron-stone in all parts of the same, and the woods were so stately and such planted, as will continue six furnaces and as many forges for at least 20 or 30 years.' (More correctly, the water-courses were streams, the iron-ore deposits lay in certain parts only, and the woods were natural, not planted.[7]) It may have been in consequence of his investigations and reports that Shrewsbury applied for part of an extensive iron industry 'concession' in Dean in 1610–11;[8] he was unsuccessful, and this may have persuaded him not to build at Longhope after all.

'Concessions' for the mining of ore, the digging of cinders and the taking of trees for fuel in Dean were obtained in February 1612 by assigns of William Herbert, second Earl of Pembroke, who had vast possessions in South Wales and Monmouthshire, and was constable of St. Briavels castle. Pembroke's assigns erected in Dean four blast furnaces and three forges, which came to be known as the 'King's Ironworks'.[9]

The Dean iron industry was buoyant during 1612–13, but the actions of the ironmasters brought grave disputes between themselves, the miners, and some other inhabitants; these disputes, and the illegal taking of trees for charcoaling, led James I

---

[1] E137/13/4, m.2.; Hart, *The Verderers and Forest Laws of Dean*, pp. 92, 93.

[2] Br. Liby., Lansd. MS 166, ff. 380–1.

[3] Lambeth Palace, Shrewsbury/Talbot MSS, 707, f. 66 suggests that Moore was not the steward in 1608, but held the office in March and April 1609; ibid. 702, ff. 167, 169.

[4] Ibid. f. 169, 31 March 1609.

[5] E178/3837, 11 Jas. I., 12th Rept., Coke MSS, I, 67.

[6] Schubert, H.R., 'The King's Ironworks in the Forest of Dean, 1612–1674', *Jnl. Iron and Steel Inst.*, CLXXIII, Feb. 1953, p. 153.

[7] Hart, *The Industrial History of Dean*, p. 9.

[8] Br. Liby., Lansd. MS 166, ff. 374, 388.

[9] Hart, *The Industrial History of Dean*, pp. 10 *et seq.* and *Royal Forest*, pp. 89, 90.

in 1613 to suspend the ironworks. Not till 31 May 1615 were they re-let. On that day,[10] the 'office' of 'clerks and overseers of the king's ironworks' was given jointly to (a) George Moore and Richard Tomlins, and (b) Sir Basil Brooke of Madeley Court, Shropshire and Robert Caldecott, gent., of London. The 'office' in effect was a valuable 'concession' in the Forest's iron industry; and may, in the case of (a), have represented success by Shrewsbury at the second attempt and conceivably this was run in conjunction with the Goodrich works and on the earl's behalf. Also on that day Moore and Tomlins obtained a lease for fifteen years of the king's furnace at Cannop, as well as of a furnace and three forges at Lydbrook.[11] The furnace at Cannop, built in 1612, stood just north-west of 'Cannop Bridge' where the Howlers Slade stream flowing from the west joins the Cannop (Newerne) stream flowing from the north, the conjoined stream thereafter flowing through Parkend, Whitecroft and Lydney to the Severn.

Moore and Tomlins under their lease dated 31 May 1615[12] were to have 6,000 cords of wood a year for fifteen years from 4 June 1615, paid for by 160 tons of bar iron a year at £13.10s. per ton (equivalent to 6s.8d. a cord). The rate of payment was to be 20 tons of iron a month during the months of September to April inclusive, no more than 40 tons to be in arrears; shortfalls due to frost, drought, flood, etc. to be made up by June. The cordwood was to be taken from the half of the Forest, decided after survey, nearest to their ironworks (Cannop and Lydbrook); to be cut in compact areas to facilitate enclosure. Cords were to be 8 feet 4 inches long, 4 feet 3 inches high, with sticks (billets) 4 feet 3 inches long and at least 2½ inches in circumference. Three forest officials, one of whom was to be the surveyor-general of woods, were to 'deliver' (release) the cords within fourteen days of a request to do so, otherwise the cords could be taken.

No oak timber was to be felled except 'for their necessary business'; no marked trees to be felled; marking to be done in the beginning of June, September, December and March annually; with 10s. forfeit for felling a marked tree. Timber to be taken for repairs only, free, on assignment by forest officials, or to be taken six days after notice of need given. The ironworks and housing for workmen to be handed over to them and by them kept in good repair; no new ones to be built. Ore and cinders to be taken only as needed to use up the cordwood; none to be for other employment; and both to be bought from the miners. The grantees to be called 'Clarks and overseers of the King's Ironworks'. They were to have three forges and two furnaces in or near Lydbrook (they separately acquired a lease of the furnace at Cannop). Permission was given to stamp bar iron with 'a rose and crown'. Shipment of iron was to be free of cocketts and custom dues. The lessees obtained a reduction of £110 8s.6d. for repairs and the building of stores to service their half of the 'concession' and were at first ordered to pay cash until Sir Richard Robartes offered to take the iron in payment of a crown debt to him.[13]

In order to house themselves and their clerks, and probably some of their workmen from time to time, in 1616–17 without licence Moore built a house in the Cannop valley woods part way between their Cannop furnace and their

[10] C66/2060, 31 May 1615.
[11] Ibid. /2076; Br. Liby. Lansd. MS 166, ff. 380, 388. Two of the Lydbrook forges were later proved to belong to the Earl of Clanricarde and Alexander Bainham (LR 12/25/1271).
[12] C66/2060, 31 May 1615.
[13] LR 12/35/1271; /27/923; /743.

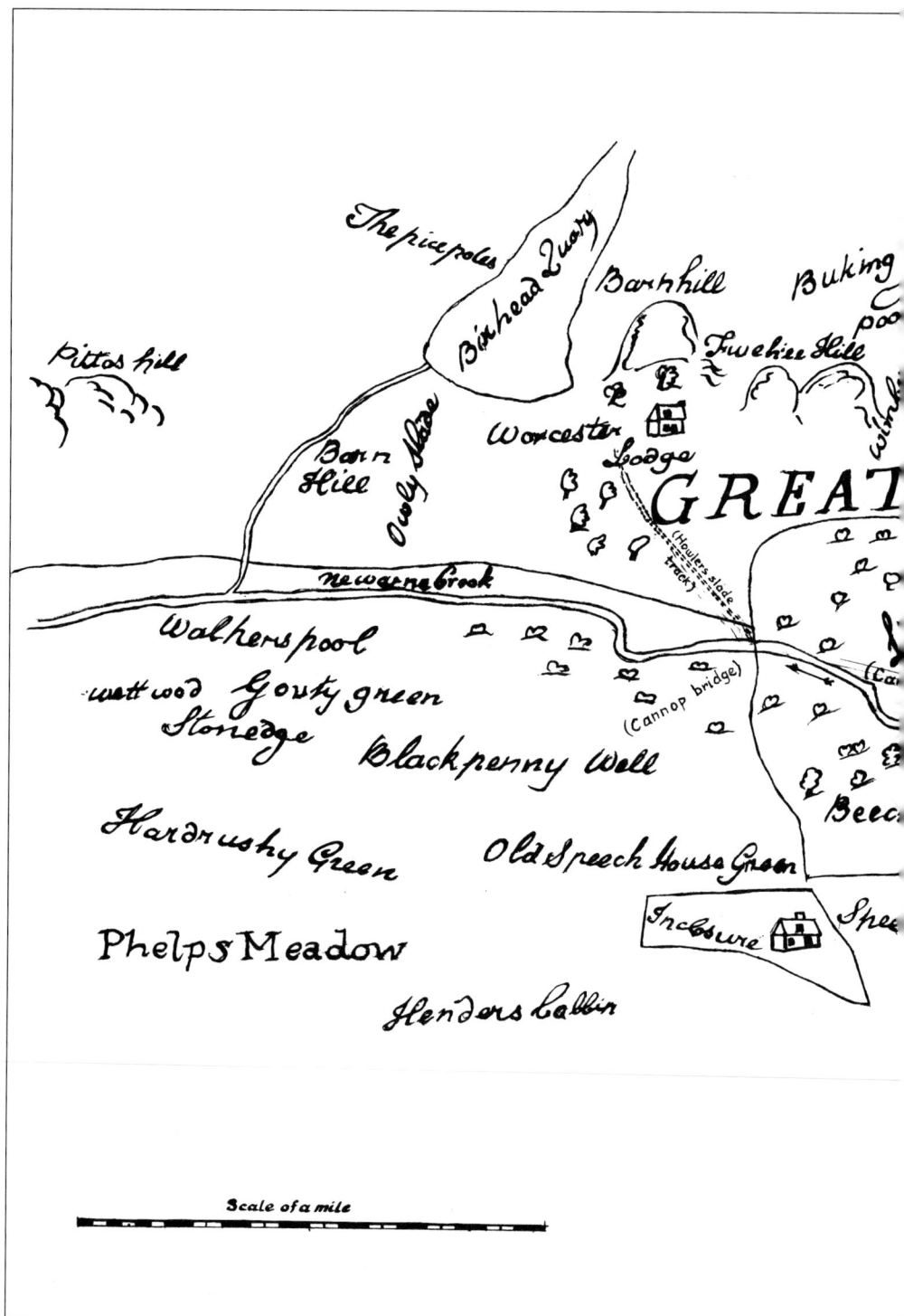

The picepoles

Birhead Quary

Barnhill

Buking
poo

Twehier Hill

Pittos hill

Barn Hill

Owly slade

Worcester Lodge

GREAT

(Howlers slade track)

Newerne brook

Walherspool

wett wood

Gouty green

Stonedge

Blackpenny Well

(Cannop bridge)

Beec

Hardrushy Green

Old Speech House Green

Phelps Meadow

Inclosure

Spee

Henders Cabbin

Scale of a mile

Map VI. Part of a map of the Cannop valley woods, c. 1710 (P.R.O., F17/7). To aid identification a few modern names have been added within brackets. (Drawn by G.L. Clissold, 1994)

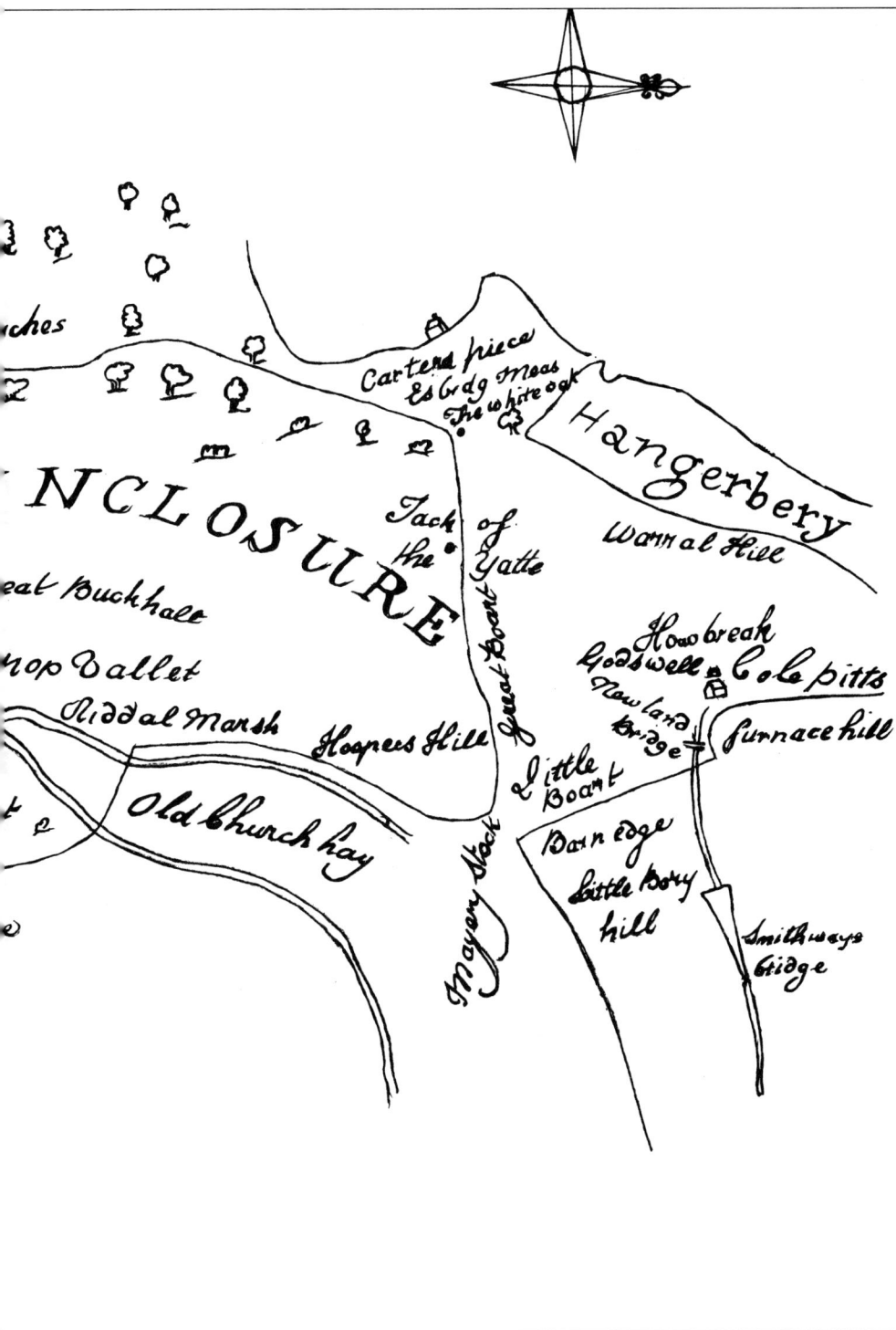

ches

NCLOSURE

Carters piece
Esbrdg Meas
The white oak

Hangerbery

Jack of the Yatte

Warral Hill

eat Buckhall

nop Ballet

Riddal Marsh    Hoopees Hill

Great Boart

Howbreak
Godswell    Cole pitts
Newland bridge    Furnace hill

Old Church hay

Majory Stock

Little Boart

Barnedge
Little Bory hill

Smithways bridge

ironworks in Lydbrook; the house came to be known as 'Cannop House'. Surrounding the house was an enclosure, probably for a cow or two, and even more likely for the great number of horses always needed for hauling ore, cinders, timber, wood and charcoal.

Within a year or two, Moore and Tomlins had taken and used much cordwood. They were reported upon by Sir William Throckmorton, Bt. of Clearwell (himself apparently trying to obtain the 'concession'). As a Protestant, and with a high standing in Dean, he generated 'local pressure' against the Recusant 'spoilers of wood'. Throckmorton carried on a campaign against the lessees, drawing on anti-catholic feeling.[14] He accused the ironmasters of misappropriation of cordwood, as well as of building houses of the king's timber. In answer, on 23 February 1618[15] the following appeal was made on behalf of Moore to the crown:

> *On reverse*:    Concerning the building of the house by Mr. More one of the present farmers to the king in Dean Forest. 23 Feb. 1618.

> *On front*:      For the house built by Tomlyns and More

In the patent is granted that the works are, or shall before the 4th of June [1615], in sufficient repairations together with all necessary houses for workmen, and all other buildings belonging or needful to be used for the same.

The Farmers maintain five Clerks in the oversight of their workmen, pay the king rent amounting to £2,000 p.ann., and pay more in wages to workmen £3,000 p.ann.

They have no house either to lodge themselves, or their Clerks neither can it be intended they should lye under a tree in attendance of so great a charge of danger, and it is submitted to your honorable judgement whither a house be not needful to be used with the work, according to his Majesty's Covenant and whither the king fayling in the performance of his Covenant, it be an office worthie of Sir William Throgmorton's complaint that the Farmers at their own charge supply that defect.

This house is but 40 foot square, the farmers have but a little above 11 years in their lease. The king hath no house in the Forest to lodge his officer, this house likely to last much longer than the Farmers' terme. All the bourdes with much other timber was provided of the farmers' own and not of the king's, building upon any others land is accompted in the buylder rather than prejudice of his land lost. The charge in building the said house is above £200, the king's timber therein spent not worth above £20, and the farmers if they may, will in the end of their terme pay the king for the timber, and carry away the house.

The father of More having indured 3 yeares ymprisonment in the Towre, and the rack, having lost both his houses and land for the service of his Majesty's most gratious mother, which the said More now indureth the want of and whereof it pleased his Majesty to voutch[s]auf to take notice, when Sir William Throgmorton urged before his Majesty this complaint, the whole is submitted to your Lordships' consideration.

On 29 March 1618 all felling of trees was suspended by order of the crown. On 17 July 1618[16] it was recorded on behalf of James I that the four Farmers of the Dean

---

[14] Br. Liby., Lansd. MS 166, ff. 359, 378.
[15] Ibid. f. 380.
[16] SP39, No. 40.

ironworks 'concession' (Brooke with Challenor, and Moore with Tomlins) had misappropriated much wood and timber. Furthermore, that 'great store of timber had been there consumed by the building of a great house within the Forest by George Moore, one of the patentees, for his habitation there, and of various other unnecessary houses; all which have been built there by the said George Moore and the other patentees by their or some of their appointment without any licence, warrant or grant unto them.' The crown further asserted that the building was not within the parameter of any parish or parishes, 'and the persons inhabiting in those houses are recusant papists, and not conformable to the Laws and Statutes of this our Realm as we have been informed.' The 'great house' was 'Cannop House', around which was an enclosure, within which there may have been a few temporary 'cabins' or 'shacks', timber-built, to house woodcutters and charcoal burners (some probably from other counties) and possibly their wives and families; Moore is likely to have employed, where possible, persons of the same faith as his own. Alternatively, some of the 'other unnecessary houses' may have been those which Moore and Tomlins were entitled to around the Cannop furnace (which stood near Cannop Bridge, about half a mile south of the 'great house').[17] 'Cannop House' was obviously very useful to Moore for his own habitation, as he appears to have had no other dwelling, his father having lost both his houses and his land (*supra*).

Because of the offences, as well as 'divers other abuses, spoils and wastes likewise committed, perpetrated and done within the Forest' – allegedly 'through the negligence of our Commissioners or Overseers there', a Commission was appointed to investigate the whole situation. The commissioners – Sir Thomas Brudenhall and six others – were to have the assistance of interrogatories prepared by 'our trusted and well beloved Sir William Throckmorton Kt and Bt.' The Commission was to meet at Coleford on 1 September 1618. No Return of the Commission has been found. The patent to Moore and Tomlins was apparently revoked, or simply stayed through stoppage of supplies of cordwood, towards the end of 1618.[18]

Until some time in 1619 Moore and his partner continued their regular payments, from the end of 1617 apparently entirely in bar iron, but in 1619 they were just under 1,800 cords below their entitlement and this was shown in their payments, which were not resumed.[19] In May 1619 Sir Richard Boyle sent one of his employees to enquire from Moore as to when his 'concession' was likely to be suspended, in the hope that his own market might improve in consequence.[20] Moore's last appearance in the records is in the Star Chamber bill which attempted to bring home the crimes to the holders of the 'concession' but this seems to have petered out.[21] They were never sentenced, and the debts were cancelled by a royal pardon in June 1628.

Whether or not Moore was forced to demolish 'Cannop House' (along with any dwellings around it) is uncertain. In 1628 there is reference (*infra*) to 'a piece of ground [the enclosure] adjoining to Cannop House'[22] but no indication is given as

---

[17] Cannop furnace in about 1631, based on a survey of 1635, had a furnace house, bridge house, furnace keeper's cabin, filler's house, clerk's house, founder's house, and a cabin for the ore cracker: Hart, *The Industrial History of Dean*, p. 32.

[18] Hart, *The Industrial History of Dean*, p. 12; Glouc. Liby., MS L.F. 6.3; LR 1/12, f. 286; 12/743.

[19] LR 6/38, 13–17 Jas. I (5 accounts).

[20] Grosart, *Lismore Papers*, 2nd series, II, 164.

[21] Star Chamber, Jas. I, 8/25/14, 1620; SP39/24/28, 14 June 1628.

[22] E125/4, ff. 269 *et seq.*, 11 Feb. 1628; copy on K.R. Mem. Roll, E159/466, Roll 44; Hart, *The Commoners . . .*, pp. 23, 24.

to whether the house was occupied or even standing. For the same year, 1628, it was noted that under a grant to John Gibbons (*infra*) in that year he 'was seized of fee Cannop house with divers lands thereunto belonging'.[23] Whether or not the house was in ruins is unknown. There is no helpful record of it thereafter. (In 1918 a fire at Easton Lodge in Essex destroyed most of the archives of the Maynard family (see Appendix) who held the land after Moore and John Gibbons (*infra*), which may have thrown further light on 'Cannop House' and Cannop valley woods.)

One day it may be discovered in what year George Moore died, and where he was laid to rest.

[Cannop furnace remained unworked until 1621, when it was leased for seven years to Richard Challenor and Philip Harris.[24] Between June 1621 and the end of 1625 only two campaigns took place. By 1625 the furnace was not working, but was repaired in 1631. A survey in 1635 indicated Cannop furnace to again need repair. In 1642 it was leased to William and Thomas Dunning through John Browne the gunfounder. During the Civil Wars it was put out of action in 1644, and later was seized by Captain John Braine of Littledean.]

## JOHN GIBBONS AND CANNOP VALLEY WOODS

Repeated unrest in the inhabitants of Dean, and abuses by them and the ironmasters, as well as opposition shown by crown officials to commoning,[25] resulted in a Decree being made by the Exchequer Court on 11 February 1628.[26] This regularized the inhabitants' commoning and pannage as well as the taking of estovers (housebote, firebote, ploughbote, cartbote, etc.) except in certain lands granted or leased by the king. Among the exemptions were 'the lands commonly called Cannopp, Moyrey Stock, Beeching Hurst, and Buckholt, and a piece of ground adjoining to Cannop House,' i.e. the lands virtually comprising most of what is now upper and middle Cannop valley. (Other leased lands excepted were Mailscott, Chestnutts, Sneade and Kidnalls.)

Why the lands of Cannop valley were excepted as early as 11 February 1628 is unknown: the first recorded lease of at least part of them was by Charles I on 14 March of that year, when John Gibbons (sometimes spelled Gibbon or Gibbins)[27] procured a lease of 'Cannup, Moirestock, etc., by estimation 574 acres, for 41 years, at the rent of £28.14s. per annum'.[28] Later, the extent was around 1,000 acres. Gibbons was Lord Treasurer Portland's secretary. In 1630–1 it was recorded:[29]

The Compasse of Cannops Vellet, inclosed by Mr. Robert Treswell [surveyor-general of woods] and Mr. John Gibbins contains in measure 9340 yards [*sic*]; in length it contains 2640 yards; in breadth it contains 1980 yards; every yard containing 3 foot. Measured by Henry Rudge the elder, William Yeme, Henry Rudge the younger, John Rudge, Henry Morgan, Thomas Smart, Thomas Rudge, Richard Morgan, Sturley Kedgin, John Fox, Henry Morton, William Morton, William Reynolls, James Fox, Richard Hibbes.

[23] SP29/35.
[24] Hart, *The Industrial History of Dean*, p. 12.
[25] Hart, *The Commoners . . .*, pp. 21–23.
[26] E125/4, ff. 269 *et seq.*, 11 Feb., 1628; Copy on K.R. Mem. Roll, E159/466, Roll 44; Hart, *The Commoners . . .*, pp. 23, 24.
[27] SP 29/35, f. 66.
[28] Ibid.
[29] Br. Liby., Add. MS 69909, Coke Papers (Series II), XLII, 57/7/14.

The degree of precision shown by 'the measurers' is less persuasive when it is calculated that in effect they were recording that the lands were 1.5 miles in length and 1.125 miles in breadth. (1.5 × 1.125 = 1.6875 sq. miles × 640 = 1,080 acres.) The measurements were sent by Charles Powell (ironmaster) of Ruardean to Sir John Coke, Secretary of State. (They were slightly related through the Powell family of Preston – see Appendix to Section IV.)

On 2 April 1632 Charles Powell wrote to Sir John enclosing a letter from 'one of Mr. Gibbins' men [Steven Varner] as one of the Forest who continually is making all the haste he can in the ridding [felling] of the ground of wood within his grounds [at Cannop]'.[30] Varner's letter,[31] dated 2 March 1632 and addressed to Goodman Browne (connected with some relevant parish), included: 'I have heard from workmen and others, some of them dwelling within your parish and all within the Forest; the rumour is that John Williams (alias Skymington) [a notorious anti-inclosure rioter][32] and his accomplices will burn the wood I intend (and have order) to [char]cole'. Varner appealed for help from Browne.

On 17 September 1632[33] John Broughton of Ruardean (see Section IV) wrote to Sir John urging need for an Order 'for a present stay of cutting any more trees in Mr. Gibbons' fellett . . . at this instant many cutters are set at work in that fellett, and they do at this hour cut down for cordwood as goodly trees as are in the Forest. The surveyor-general asked who did cause these trees to be cut down, the answer being that it was by the appointment of Sir John Winter who had bought them from Mr. Gibbons.'

In the same year, 1632,[34] the inhabitants of the Forest became involved in trouble emanating from the actions of John Gibbons in the Cannop valley woods. Under the heading 'The substance and truth of the lamentable case now likely to fall upon the poor innocent inhabitants of the adjacent villages of the Forest of Deane', they asserted:

It being the King Majesty's pleasure to have the decayed woods and ........[?] trees in the said Forest cut down and sold, commanded that all the timber-trees in every Vallett [Fellet] should be marked and left standing for his Majesty's use and service for timber for shipping and for his ancient tenants and inhabitants there for the reparation of their messuages; and that all Valletts and Inclosures there to be made for the raising of young springs [natural regeneration] and coppices after the expiration of nine years should be laid open again to the Commoners and Inhabitants of the said Forest.

That amongst many of the Vallets that were inclosed there, happened 2 or 3 [in the Cannop Valley] to join together, and by means thereof were all brought and inclosed into one and then called by the several names of Cannopp, Morestocke, Beechenhurst and the Buckholte Vallets containing by estimation near 2,000 acres being paled in [fenced] by and at the King's great charge which cost near £1,000, besides timber to pale it, and left well stored with wood and timber worth at least £6,000, being most of it principal timber-trees chosen and marked out by the King's officers to stand, and which had been always

[30] Br. Liby., Add. MS 69909, Coke Papers (Series II), XLII, 57/7/5.

[31] Ibid. 57/7/4.

[32] Hart, *The Commoners* . . ., pp. 27, 28 and *Royal Forest*, pp. 107, 114, 124; Allan, D.G.C., 'The rising in the West', *Econ. Hist. Review*, 2nd series, V (1952), pp. 80–3. Skimmington was captured in 1632. He was released from Newgate prison after five years and bound over in £2,000 to keep the peace (Bankes MS 56/6, before 6 May 1637, his petition, and 45/22, 10 Aug. 1637, his bond.)

[33] Br. Liby., Add. MS 69909, Coke Papers (Series II), XLII, 57/7/9.

[34] Glouc. Liby., MS L.F.1.1, pp. 12 *et. seq.*

excepted from his Majesty's farmers of his iron works, because one of his Majesty's eyries of Gossehawkes should not be disquieted who used yearly to timber [nest] there.

That many years after the same had been inclosed and paled at the King's charge as aforesaid, the same being well come on in new growth again for the preservation and growth of those Inclosures and Coppices, one Mr John Gibbon procured some places in that Inclosure a particular from the Surveyor[-General] containing 500 and odd acres as by the particular appeareth. And then without having any Writ or Commission directed to his Majesty's officers of the said Forest *ad quod dampnum* &c or assertation of Forest Laws as it ought to have been, the said Mr Gibbons obtained at first a demise or grant from the King's Majesty for a term of 41 years pleading the same to be wast ground in the said Forest for and under some small rent.

And by colour of the same demise and grant the said Mr Gibbons entered and claimed the whole Inclosures being near 2,000 acres aforesaid, and excluding the setting open the same again and all the King's ancient tenants from having or taking any timber from there or other benefits, and manured and enjoyed the same wholly for many years and did not only then take and receive the issues and profits thereof but under colour of the same demise or some other did cut down and make spoil of great store of the good timber-trees preserved and marked as aforesaid, and also destroyed the hopeful young springs and coppices esteemed to be worth more than £3,000. And now is cutting down and hath sold the remainder of all the wood and timber-trees being near 3,000 trees yet standing within the Inclosure, each worth one with another 20s. apiece, a parcel whereof being the parcel reserved for Gossehawkes as aforesaid. So that it is conceived that Mr Gibbons of the wood and timber reserved for his Majesty's use as aforesaid having no grant thereof hath and will make above £6,000 besides the destruction of the young coppice wood ground since the inclosure thereof.

That 5th April 7 Chas. [1631] divers riotous persons in a tumultuous manner did throw down the pales about the said Inclosure being formerly made at the King's charge and some hedges and ditches that Mr. Gibbons had therein made, which said riotous persons were then presently suppressed by the power of the Right Honourable the Lord Compton Earl of Northampton Lord Lieutenant of the said County [of Gloucester], the Deputy Lieutenants and Justices of the Peace together with the inhabitants of the adjacent villages who did their best endeavour to suppress them. And at the Quarter Sessions then next held at Gloucester for the County of Gloucester the 11th April aforesaid [1631] being within seven days after, above 50 of the said rioters and malefactors were by the inquest for the body of the said County by particular names and addresses indicated for the same part and divers of the jurors that indicted them were the inhabitants of the ancient villages now questioned, and evidence was given against the malefactors by divers constables also there inhabiting.

And in June afterwards above 60 other persons and malefactors were then also indicted for the same fact by their particular names and addresses before Sir John Bridgeman Kt, by virtue of a Commission of Oyer & Terminer to him directed of purpose for punishing of the malefactors.

That by virtue of the same Commission the most of the malefactors have been fined and tried for the same offence and great sums of money, and recognizancies taken for divers of the malefactors' appearances have been forfeited. And in Easter Term last the fines imposed upon several of the malefactors, and recognizancies forfeited, were then transcripted into the Exchequer amounting to the sum of £386.

And others of the malefactors have been since also tried, convicted and fined by virtue of the said Commission and many remain in prison for the same fact and many that were indicted for the same are fled and divers fines imposed upon most of the malefactors since Easter Term are to be transcripted into the Exchequer this Michaelmas Term and one of the malefactors [a Knight] fined 100 marks and came and enstalled the payment thereof and thereupon set at liberty.

Yet nonetheless on 13th March Anno 7 [1632] produced a Writ issued out of the Court of Chancery to the Sheriff of the County of Gloucester (to enquire of the fact and malefactors) who privately on receipt thereof impannelled a Jury remote from the said

Forest and executed the same without giving any Notice thereof to any of the inhabitants of the said adjacent villages of the said Forest whereby for want of the information the Jury then impannelled the 2nd day of April last did find none of the said rioters or malefactors but that the same was done by unknown persons notwithstanding above 100 persons of the rioters were at the same time fairly indicted for the same fact and then convicted, fined and imprisoned.

That upon the return of the same Writ out of the Chancery returnably any Crown office a Writ of Distraining was awarded from the King's Bench in Easter Term last to distrain the inhabitants of the adjacent villages to repair and make up the hedges and ditches of Mr Gibbons and to make him amends by yielding damages. And as soon as the inhabitants were summoned and had Notice they appeared and desired to plead in excuse of themselves in regard the malefactors were presented and discovered according to the words of the said Statute upon which the first Writ is grounded, but the inhabitants were not admitted to plead as yet.

So that in Trinity Term last, £177 issues were returned by the Sheriff against the inhabitants of the several adjacent parishes upon the Distraining into his Majesty's court of King's Bench and there Ordered the same Term to be estreated into the Exchequer but judgment for £200 damages to Mr Gibbons for amends then after returned was respited to be considered until the same as by the Order appeareth.

And notwithstanding, the issues were ordered by the Court of King's Bench to be transcripted into the Exchequer. Yet before judgment was confirmed made forth of the Crown office and sent down lately to the Sheriff of Gloucester levy the said issues upon the guiltless and innocent inhabitants of the said ancient villages which tendeth to the utter undoing and overthrow of them, their wives and children.

Now, in regard to all the inclosures round about the Valletts containing above 2,000 acres as aforesaid were made and paled at the King's great charge and the malefactors did overthrow the same with the hedges and ditches thereon made by Mr. Gibbons, were indicted for the same according to the Statute and for that divers of them are men of good abilities that have already been punished for the same fact and may uphold damages to Mr Gibbons if he please duly to question them by action. And in regard most of the malefactors sued already as aforesaid in great sums of money amounting upwards £386 and the same fine transcripted in the Exchequer aforesaid.

And for that Mr Gibbons passed the same Inclosure for wast ground supposed to be concealed; and caused all the posts and pales and fences of the said whole inclosure of the Vallets to be [char]coled and sold the same to the iron works for his own benefit, besides the benefit he hath and will make of the trees and woods marked and reserved for timber as aforesaid amounting to above £6,000, besides the destruction of the young coppices.

And for that it is conceived that there will be many hundred of acres of land well stored with timber-trees inclosed that Mr Gibbons cannot challenge by any demise having cut 500 and odd acres at all mentioned in his lease so that if the inhabitants be compelled to inclose the whole Vallett containing near 2,000 acres for Mr Gibbons they may much wrong the King's Majesty and his posterity: And thereby induce future trouble to themselves being altogether innocent of the fact and not knowing what quantity of acres are granted to Mr Gibbons.

Therefore the poor and innocent inhabitants (not any way intending to free or meddle with any of the said malefactors) [blank].

There followed jottings relating to the Statute upon which their 'case' was largely placed, along with other notes relating to relevant forest law. Having set out their case, and 'that the guilty being punished for the fact', they 'pray that the innocent may plead in excuse of themselves having been always ready to obey the Order of the Court, many of them being above 6 miles from the place the fact was committed, and parishes between them and the place'.

A survey of trees in Dean made in 1633 by John Broughton (on his appointment as the first deputy surveyor of Dean) states that 'the trees standing in Mr. John Gibbon's grounds are not numbered or surveyed'.[35] Later evidence discloses that the land comprised both coppices and timber-trees, mainly oaks and beeches. The coppices may have been the source of charcoal for the king's iron furnace at Cannop. The two forges at Bishopswood in about 1633 were being fuelled by cordwood from 'Mr Gibbins woods'; and Sir John Coke noted that an examination was necessary as to 'what is cut by Mr. Gibbins who has wood there standing worth £3,000'.[36]

About the same year, Charles Powell (see Appendix to Section IV) was seeking a farm of ironworks and wood in Dean. He offered £1,200 yearly for 'Cannopp furnace with the house and appurtenances belonging to it';[37] the house was not 'Cannop House'. The lands were enclosed against sheep and cattle of the commoners.

At the Justice Seat for Dean held at Gloucester in July 1634 (see Section V), Gibbons was one of the many people accused of forest offences.[38] 'London rumours had loudly accused him' regarding his lands in Dean.[39] Gibbons, the first offender to be called before the Justices and Judges, 'had allegedly taken and enclosed more land than he had been leased in Dean, and had then wangled a perpetual lease of the total, and a licence to cut all the trees on it'. On 10 June that year he was fined £8,600 of which he paid £8,000,[40] especially related to felling trees there.

The prior Swanimote Court presentment against Gibbons was 'for cutting 4,000 oaks and 2,000 beeches worth 20s. each between 31 March 1630 and 30 April 1634, for spoiling certain coppices to the damage of the king £1,200, and for enclosing with a wall 940 acres valued at £113.13s.4d. annually'.[41] The indictment by the jury was 'of cutting divers goodly timber trees marked by the king's officers for shipping and other uses of His Majesty'. King James 'at his great charge had enclosed with a pale two parcels of land for coppices of which Gibbons obtained a lease for 21 years of 574 acres at a rent of £28.14s. yearly and a fine of £280'. Gibbons 'joined the two enclosures and thereby increased the whole to 1,000 or 1,100 acres'. Gibbons had sub-leased the lands to Sir Robert Bannister, and this transaction was allowed to stand.[42] This was confirmed in 1638 by the lands being omitted from a survey of Dean.[43] It seems that Gibbons was not convicted for sharp practice but either because the extended grant did not use the words 'in the forest' or because he had cut the timber trees before his grant had been sealed.[44]

The Earl of Portland did not support Gibbons: he 'drove his Secretary from his house and forbade his making any defence; as a result Portland could not be involved in the disaster of his minions'.[45] Another source[46] asserts that Portland

[35] Hart, *Royal Forest*, p. 275; *Cal.* SP16/236, p. 191.

[36] Br. Liby., Add. MS 69909, Coke Papers (Series II), XLII, 57/7/17 c. 1633.

[37] Ibid. 57/7/15.

[38] E.401/1924, 3 Jan. 1637–38; *Cal.* SP16/402, p. 123.

[39] C. 99/22 and 36; Hammersley, *op. cit.*, 1960, p. 94.

[40] E.401/1924, 3 Jan. 1637–38; *Cal.* SP16/402, p. 123; Hart, *Royal Forest*, p. 112; Hammersley, *op. cit.*, 1960, p. 96.

[41] *Cal.* SP16/271, p. 143; Br. Liby., Harl. MSS 738, f. 300.

[42] P.R.O., E.112/181/131; Hammersley, *op. cit.*, 1960, p. 96, footnote 38.

[43] Hart, *Royal Forest*, p. 280.

[44] Hammersley, *op. cit.*, 1960, p. 96.

[45] Dietz, F.C., *English Public Finance 1558–1641* (1931), p. 273.

[46] *Cal. SP. Venice* MSS, vol. 23, 1632–36, No. 372, p. 293, 3 Nov. 1634.

wished to remove suspicion and 'has driven Gibbons from his house' and forbid him to make any defence.

## THE BANNISTER/MAYNARD (MAINARD) FAMILIES AND CANNOP VALLEY WOODS

On 8 January 1641 'the same lands, by estimation 1,070 acres, were leased by [Sir Robert] Bannister to his trustees John Mansell and Ambrose Bavin gent. 'their heirs and assignees for ever, under the aforesaid rent of £28.14s yearly with a clause for deafforestation'; and in 1642 'a general deafforestation was settled by Parliament, whereby the lands remain deafforested'.[47] In 1649 the lands were still in the hands of Sir Robert Bannister and his trustees, and on 7 May they conveyed them to Bannister Maynard, grandchild, son of Lord Maynard (so titled by 1661).[48]

In 1656, at a Swanimote Court preceding a Justice Seat in Eyre held in Mitcheldean[49] (see Section VII), two presentments by regarders and other forest officials indicate that they were uncertain of the then respective interests of the Bannisters and Maynards. Thomas [sic.] Bannister was presented that 'he had within the space of ten years last past, made divers loads of charcoal within his Highness [The Lord Protector] wood within the Forest of Dean, and sold the same to Captain John Gifford [an ironmaster]'.[50] Also 'the Lord Maynard by his servants or agents had caused to be cut and corded in Cannopps Fellet, in the year 1649, 118 cords of 3 foot wood, which Captain Griffantius Phillips[51] [ironmaster] took away and converted to his own use.' No fines appear to have been levied.

On 19 March 1657[52] the Council of State noted 'that in 3 Charles [I: 1628] a lease was granted for 31 years of 1,000 acres in the Forest of Dean to John Guibon [for Gibbon] who sold it to Sir Robert Bannister, which sale was confirmed by the king with the fee and disafforestation of the lands; that Sir Robert left it to his grandchild, Lord Maynard, then under age; that as the land lies in the heart of the Forest, convenient for his Highness [The Lord Protector], Lord Maynard consented to sell it for £1,500 from the ironworks in the Forest, and this before the Act [of 1657] voiding the patent, and settling the lands on his Highness'. It was recommended 'that his Highness issue a warrant for payment to Lord Maynard of £1,500, out of the ironworks in the Forest of Dean'. Annexed to the Council's statement was a report from General John Desborow alluding to the matter and adding to the above statement 'that Sir Robert Bannister disafforested the lands, and that he paid £3,400 for them, but was willing to accept £1,500'.

On 20 August 1657[53] the Council of State ordered the attorney-general 'to consider the draft produced of a deed from Lord William Maynard for lands in the Forest of Dean, for his Highness and the State's use, and so to prepare it as to secure the title', and to instruct Major John Wade [the administrator of the Forest] to pay the £1,500 out of the proceeds of the ironworks. On 10 November of the same

[47] SP29/35, f. 66.
[48] Ibid.
[49] Glos. R.O., D2026 Bond Papers, X.14.
[50] Gifford, under General Massey, may have had an interest in Cannop furnace (as he did in several other ironworks in Dean).
[51] Some of Phillips' ironworks were at Lydbrook and Bishopwood.
[52] SP18/156, pp. 316, 317.
[53] Ibid. (16), p. 73.

year,[54] the Council referred to the surveyor-general 'the draft of a deed from Lord Maynard, for sale of lands in Co. Northampton, worth £1,500, for his Highness and General John Desborow, for the use of Banaster and William Maynard, his infant sons, in lieu of woods in the Forest of Dean which they claimed by patent etc., lately made void by the Act [1657] for mitigation of the rigour of the Forest Laws in the said Forest and for the preservation of timber; Lord Maynard to receive £1,500 on passing the deed, and the Attorney-General to prepare the deed and that it may secure the title of the infants'. This was agreed on 22 December[55] and 31 December,[56] and a warrant was issued to Major John Wade 'to pay £1,500 to Lord Maynard in pursuance of the contract'. Wade duly paid the £1,500 from the proceeds of the ironworks.[57]

Cromwell by the above noted Act of 1657[58] 'declared all Letters Patent and Grants of the demesne, wastes and woods of the Forest of Dean to be null and void. Thereafter Lord Maynard received £1,500 in recompense of Cannop etc., 'though nothing near the value of the same, and his lordship was caused to make an indenture in consideration of the said £1,500 to settle certain lands in Northamptonshire called Pouselry pastures etc. upon his son and heirs in lieu of the said Forest lands, and to covenant that the said pastures are worth £100 per annum'. During the Civil Wars and the Commonwealth, the woods in the Cannop valley were managed for the State.[59]

Following the Restoration of the Monarchy (1660), William, Lord Maynard on 15 May petitioned Charles II as follows:[60]

> That Sir Robert Banastre knight deceased, in his lifetime [1628] was seized of fee Cannopp house with divers lands thereunto belonging, formerly part of the Forest of Dean lately inclosed with a stone wall. And being so seized did settle the same upon Banastre Maynard your petitioner's eldest son by Dame Dorothy the daughter of the said Sir Robert Banastre and the heirs of his body, and for want of such issue the remainder to William Maynard your petitioner's younger son and said heirs of his body in remainder to right heirs. And afterwards the said Sir Robert Banastre departed this life. After whose decease your petitioner in right of his son Banastre and as his guardian was in possession of the premises to manage the same for the best advantage of his son being an infant. But so it happens that Oliver Cromwell desirous to have the said lands did procure an Act [1657] as he called it of one of his Conventions. That he [the petitioner] did likewise in that he received such recompense [£1,500] for the same as Cromwell thought fit to afford him, though nothing near the value of the same. [The petitioner] prayeth to enter upon the premises.

The petition is endorsed: 'At the Court at Whitehall 15 May 1661; his Majesty is graciously pleased to refer this Petition to the Right Honorable Lord High Treasurer of England to inform himself of the several particulars therein alleged, and to certify to his Majesty what his lordship conceives to be done therein.' His report thereon dated 28 June 1661 confirmed the statements in the Petition, but added that the

[54] SP18/157 (1), p. 157.
[55] Ibid. /158 (68), p. 225.
[56] Ibid. (14), p. 239.
[57] E.178/6080/Pt. 1, m.1–43; copy in Glos. R.O., D3921, Hart Collection.
[58] Copy in Hart, *Royal Forest*, pp. 284, 285.
[59] Ibid., Chapter 7. See Sections VII and VIII.
[60] SP29/35.

king had a good claim to the £1,500 received by Lord Maynard for the land, or to the land. He annexed a certificate dated 20 January 1661 by Sir Charles Harbord, surveyor-general, of the several leases of the lands, being 1,070 acres. The Petition later succeeded (*infra*). The Cannop valley lands totalled 1,070 acres.[61]

A Report made in 1662[62] advises: 'Canup which we find of an absolute necessity to be reduced into his Majesty's hands as being 1,100 acres of the best land within the Forest, a great part whereof hath been lately fallen by Sir Baynham Throckmorton junior' (of Clearwell, deputy warden, ironmaster, and ostensibly a help to the king and to the Forest's inhabitants).

Under the Dean Forest (Reafforestation) Act 1668[63] the lands were reunited with the Forest, being 'the grounds called by the several names of Cannop Fellett, Buckholt, Beechenhurst and Moyrystock, containing about 1,000 acres, heretofore granted to John Gibbon, John Mansil and Ambrose Bavin, some or one of them, and now belonging unto or claimed by Banistree Mainard, esquire.' Decayed trees not of timber quality were to be sold in Dean to raise £1,500 to recompense Bainistree Mainard. The sum was duly raised and paid. (It appears that two sums of £1,500 may have been paid.)[64] A Report made in 1680[65] confirms 'the Buckholt, Moyry Stocke and part of Cannoppe in Coverham' as being within the crown Forest.

'Cannop House' (NGR SO607122) is not indicated on maps of 1608 or *c.* 1710. In 1741 a wayn-way (track for walking and haulage) ran 'from Moyery Stock and thence along the bottom of a place called Sally Vellet, and so along the same way . . . unto Cannops Brook, and down the said brook to Cannops Bridge'.[66] The house is not shown on Taylor's map of 1777 nor on the Drivers' map of 1787.[67] In much later years, some of the house stonework may have been used as roughage in the building of the Wimberry Railway Bridge near the later Cannop Colliery, or of the Cannop Villas (built 1907 and 1911). The remains of the house, the enclosure boundary around it, and the yew tree are still to be seen. Early in 1994 Brian Johns, an appreciated local archaeologist, undertook a preliminary dowsing survey of the site of 'Cannop House' which signalled:

> A structure formed on a square with sides measuring a maximum of 52 feet. The approach is made from the south where an entrance 15 feet narrows to approximately 6 feet and passes into the structure, possibly as a passage. There is an indication of a narrow passage,

---

[61] *Cal.* SP29/17, p. 295; /29/35 f. 66, 15 May 1661; *Cal. Treas. Bks.*, VII, pt. I, p. 58; Hart, *Royal Forest*, p. 152.

[62] Hart, *Royal Forest*, p. 287.

[63] Act 19 & 20 Chas. II, c.8; copy in Hart, *Royal Forest*, pp. 291–5.

[64] Hart, *Royal Forest*, p. 179. In 1675 Banastre Maynard of Chelsea loaned £1,696 on mortgage to Henry Benedict Hall of High Meadow (GG 981, 1005, 1006, 1007, 1053).

[65] Ibid. p. 298.

[66] Hart, *The Free Miners*, p. 129.

[67] The site of the house does not appear on plans drawn for the 'New road' from Mirey Stock to Cannop, i.e.:
(a) P.R.O. (Kew) F17, No. 97 (1903): Centre road: plans, elevations and sections of the road from Miry Stock to Parkend Culvert and of the bridge under Wimberry Railway. R. Phillips (County Surveyor). 8 sheets, MS. coloured. Various scales and sizes. (Referred to *in re*, Cruyws and Hobrough and the King.)
(b) P.R.O. (Kew) F17, No. 148 (1908): Speech House Walk: Ordnance survey of vicinity of Vallets Wood and Wimberry Bottom showing Parkend to Mirey Stock new road and the road on lease to the Cannop Coal Co. Ltd. Printed, coloured. About 1'2" × 2'5". Scale: 208.33 ft to an inch.

some 6 feet wide, which runs along the south face of the structure: it is not clear whether this is within, or without the actual building line; it could be a courtyard outside, which would reduce the depth of the house to a maximum of 46 feet. The whole area is littered with debris and rocks which have strayed onto the site from the nearby Cannop colliery spoil tip.

A wayn-way extends southwards from the south edge of the structure outline; this bends towards the east where it meets and joins a track line running north to south along the Cannop valley.

The site for the house may have been chosen to take advantage of a low rise, the ground sloping gently to the north, south and west, effectively forming a dry area. An enclosure in the form of a low bank contains the site: the bank is visible for most of its length except on the north side; on the east it lies alongside what was the route of the ancient wayn-way already noted.

The age of the yew tree growing on top of part of the stonework of the house (see Plate IV) has been calculated by John White, dendrologist of the Forestry Authority, to be around 330 years: in which case it arose from a seed (within a pink aril) falling on the debris of the house in about 1665.

# APPENDIX

## I. BIOGRAPHICAL NOTES ON THE BANNISTER/ MAYNARD (MAINARD) FAMILIES

The connection of the seventeenth-century Bannister/Maynard families with the Cannop valley woods is not fully known, but the following notes are pertinent:

1.  In 1620 a grant of barony of Maynard was made to Sir William Maynard. Sir Henry Maynard, MP for St. Albans and Essex, was the first of the family to reside at Easton Lodge in Essex. Unfortunately, in 1918 a fire there destroyed most of the Maynard archives, some probably relating to the Forest of Dean. (F.G. Emmison's *Guide to the Essex Record Office*, 1969, pp. 132, 133.)

2.  William Maynard died 18 December 1639. His son William Maynard, 2nd baron, married first Dorothy, daughter and sole heir of Sir Robert Banaster (sic), Knt., of Passenham, Northants, by whom he had two sons. (Sir Bernard Burke, *Dormant and Extinct Peerages*, 1978, pp. 612, 613.)

3.  The Hon. Banastre (sic) Maynard of Little Easton, Essex (*c.* 1642–1718) was first son of William, and Baron Maynard of Estaines, by first wife, Dorothy, daughter of Sir Robert Banastre of Passenham, Northants. Married 9 November 1655, Lady Elizabeth Grey. Maynard was descended from a lawyer of Devonshire origin who sat for St. Albans in the Marian Parliaments of 1553 and 1554. (B.D. Henning, *The House of Commons 1660–1690*, 1983, p. 38.)

## II. THE LOCATION OF THE NAMED WOODS IN THE CANNOP VALLEY

It is impossible to delineate, through time, the exact boundaries of the individual four components of the woods forming the Cannop valley, i.e. 'Salley Vallets, The Buckholt, Beechenhurst and Mirey Stock'. It appears that 'Cannop Vellets' (a 'vellet' being a felled area, usually enclosed thereafter for recoppicing or natural regeneration) lay in the south of the valley, and 'Sallow Vallets' in the north-west. However, the extent and boundaries changed during the late seventeenth, eighteenth and nineteenth centuries, sometimes merging into one another for purposes of administration, scheduling, reporting and mapping. In 1787 The Buckholt lay in the west of the valley and included the site of the later Cannop Colliery (behind which still stand Weymouth pines planted *c.* 1781 – the first conifers planted in Dean – 3rd Rept. of 1788, p. 113. See Plate IX herein). Beechenhurst always lay in the east of the valley, reaching up to The Speech House. Mirey Stock lay in the north-east of the valley. By 1853 (Report by Edward Machen, Deputy Surveyor; 31st Rept. of the Commissioners of Her Majesty's Woods, Forests and Land Revenues, 1853) the relevant extents were:

Plate V. St. Briavels Castle, the one-time administrative centre of the Forest of Dean. (From a drawing by Isaac Taylor, 1777)

|                | *Year Planted* | *Acres* |
|----------------|----------------|---------|
| The Buckholt   | 1787           | 368     |
| Beechenhurst   | 1810           | 308     |
| 'Sally Vallets'| 1812           | 397     |
|                |                | 1,073   |

The old woods called 'Cannop Vellet' and 'Mirey Stock' had merged with the other woods named above. The total acreage, as hitherto, remained around 1,100 acres.

From the early eighteenth century, maps of the Cannop valley have indicated an extensive area to be 'Crown Freehold'. It lies immediately to the north-west of Cannop Bridge, stretching northwards almost to Wimberry Slade, on the south Howlers Slade, and on the east the Cannop Brook. A map of 1848 and one of 1897 indicate that it may have been about 70 acres in extent. The origin of it becoming Crown Freehold is uncertain, but probably relates to the reacquisition by the crown in 1668. Some notes on the Freehold and the other woods are available in P.R.O., F3/1340.

# VII. THE JUSTICE SEAT IN EYRE OF 1656

*Royal Forest* (1966, p. 148) contains the comment: 'in 1656 the government considered holding a new Dean Eyre to assist in the reformed administration'. By 'government' was meant 'the Council of State and the Office of Lord Protector, Oliver Cromwell'. Little more was found regarding the projected eyre, but some years later the Gloucestershire Record Office made available the Bond MSS. D2026, X.14, which included some relevant (though incomplete) records, enabling research to be continued.

Information found leading up to the Swanimote Court (held at Mitcheldean on 9 June 1656) are the many presentments made by regarders (un-named), preservators, and other officials (named). Those officials had been assisted by Major John Wade (see Section VIII), administrator of the Forest. Their long lists of offences and offenders had been drawn up with much speed, probably in or around Spring 1656.

In readiness for the eyre itself, a request was made on 1 July 1656, by the Council of State, for an Order to the Remembrancer of the Exchequer that – as a Commission was issued in 1645 to Nathaniel Stephens and others,[1] and another in 1640 to Lord Whitelock and others,[2] to enquire concerning spoils in the Forest of Dean – the Master of that Office be ordered to send down the (Returns of) Commissions to the Swanimote by some attorney of the Exchequer Court, the Return of the Commission being too bulky to copy.[3]

A fortnight later, on 15 July, the Master of the Capital Office in the Court of Upper Bench was ordered to appear at the Justice Seat to be held for the Forest on 26 August, with the records of the last Justice Seat for Dean held in 1634. John Keeling of Southill, co. Bedford, in whose hands were some of the records, was to deliver them to the Master of the Office, to be brought to the Justice Seat.[4] A week later, on 22 July, William Ryley, Keeper of the Tower Records, commented:[5]

> I am bound by oath not to permit any record to go into other hands, but if required I will carry them down to the Justice Seat to be held for the Forest of Dean, and will assist in that affair with the knowledge obtained by 25 years experience of the method of Justice Seats, where I have constantly attended with the records, or I would serve as assistant to the Clerk of the Iter, under the Chief Justice of England. I want an order from him, or from the Protector and Council, to carry down and have the sole management of the records; also an imprest to buy 3 horses for myself, my man, and the records, or an order to Mr. Frost to pay me £50 on account of my salary, which I shall spend on this service if I may be reimbursed.

[1] Hart, *Royal Forest*, p. 132.
[2] SP18/129/ (3), p. 2.
[3] Ibid.
[4] Ibid. (11), p. 20.
[5] Ibid. pp. 60–3. Cf. Admiralty 2/1729, ff. 95, 103 of 19 July and 2 Aug. 1656 for other preparatory moves.

On 4 August Major John Wade (*infra* and Section VIII) of Littledean wrote to the Admiralty Commissioners requiring a Council Order to be made to the Exchequer Office to send down the (Return of a) Commission sued out in 1641 concerning the Forest[6] and the proceedings therein, as they were wanted at the Court due to sit at Mitcheldean on 12 August. 'Mr Nutley should be employed, as he knows all about the business'.[7] On 21 August his Highness the Protector gave the necessary warrant to the Keeper of the Records.[8]

The only records found of the Swanimote Court are given below *in extenso*:[9]

## THE SWANIMOTE COURT HELD ON 9 JUNE 1656 AT MITCHELDEAN

'*THE PRESENTMENT OF THE REGARD* presented at the *SWANIMOTE COURT* held at Michel Deane the 9th day of June 1656, and delivered into the *JUSTICE SEAT* holden at the same place upon the 26th day of August following, before John Disbrow[10] Deputy Justice in Eyre to Major General John Lambartt. Judge Attkins and Judge Nicklas being assistants, and Euan [or Evan] Syce [or Siese] Esq.,[11] Attorney to the Lord Protector for the Service.

'*ASSARTS* made within the Perambulation but without his Highness the Lord Protector's wast soyle of the Forest of Dean':

First they say and present that Benedict Hall, Esq. [of Highmeadow], has within the space of 6 years last past assarted our Lord's Coppice Grove (1 acre) in the parish of Staunton, worth 6s.

Then follow three similar presentments (the length of time varies):

Richard Long . . . part of his Coppice Grove, 8 acres, called Rickis Grove within the parish of Flaxley, now sown with corn, worth 13s 4d.

Giles Tower . . . his two Coppice Groves called Hoopers Groves, 4½ acres, within the parish of Newland, now sown with corn.

John Baddam . . . his Grove, 3 acres, within the parish of Newland, now sown with corn, worth 8s per acre.

*NEW ERECTIONS: PURPRESTURES* within the Perambulation but without his Highness demesne woods of the Forest of Dean:

First they say and present that William Wyrrall, gent, hath within two years last past erected one barn upon his own fee land within the parish of Bicknour without his Highness's demesne woods.

---

[6] SP18/129 (3), p. 2.

[7] Ibid. /143 (28), p. 399.

[8] Ibid. /129, pp. 60–3.

[9] Glos. R.O., D2026 Bond Papers, X.14.

[10] For Major General John Lord Desborough [Desborow, Disbrowe], see Hart, *Royal Forest*, p. 149; and Glouc. Liby., MS L.F.1.1., pp. 16, 17. Richard Cromwell had appointed him Constable of the Forest 24 April 1654 [Bodleian Rawl. MS A328, pp. 31–2].

[11] For Sergeant Syce (Siese), see Hart, *Royal Forest*, p. 149.

Then follow similar presentments (the length of time varies):

William Phillipps . . . a dwelling house near the Lea Line, within the parish of Lea.

Charles Crosse . . . a dwelling house near the Lea Bayly on the lands of John Ridge, in the parish of the Lea.

Thomas Nourse . . . a new barn at Nockolles in the parish of Newland.

William Ridre . . . a new dwelling house in [Richard] Blast's ground near the Lea Bayly, in the parish of Newland.

William Thomas . . . a new dwelling house in [Richard] Blast's grounds near the Lea Bayly, in the parish of Newland.

John Baddam . . . a new barn and house near the Lea Bayly, in the parish of Newland.

Thomas Dobbs . . . a new dwelling house near the Lea Bayly, in the parish of the Lea.

Phillip Phillips . . . a new erection on the lands of William Phillips, near the Lea Bayly.

Thomas Dobbs . . . a new dwelling on the land of Mr. Feanes, near the Lea Bayly.

John Tengey . . . a new dwelling house on the land of Mr. Nourse near Michel Deane.

Edward Morse . . . a new dwelling house on the land of Duncomb Colchester, in the parish of Michel Deane.

Richard Collins . . . a new dwelling house on the land of Thomas Parke, gent. in the parish of Abinghall.

James Heynes . . . a new barn on his own land in fee in Abinghall parish, near adjoining unto the Common of the Forest, and making a way from the barn into the Forest.

William Peirce . . . a new dwelling house on the land of the heirs of Baynham Vaughan Esq, in the parish of Abinghall.

William Phelps . . . a new barn on the land of the heirs of Baynham Vaughan Esq, in the parish of Abinghall.

John Stibbs . . . a new dwelling house on the land of the heirs of Baynham Vaughan in the parish of Abinghall.

Roger Clarke . . . a new barn on his own land in the parish of Abinghall.

William Phelps . . . a dwelling house on the land of Baynham Vaughan in the parish of Abinghall.

Nicholas Marfail . . . a new dwelling house on the land of William Hoskins in the parish of Newland.

Thomas Skin . . . a dwelling house on the land of William Skinn in the parish of Newland.

Thomas Sibrance . . . a new dwelling house on the land of Richard Worgan in the parish of Newland.

Francis Reyne . . . a new dwelling house on the land of Jane Hoskins, widow, in the parish of Newland.

Edmund Jennis deceased . . . a new barn and a sheep-coate on his own land in the parish of Newland.

William Gilbert . . . two new dwelling houses and a barn on the land of William Yerrett in the parish of Newland.

John Morgan . . . a new dwelling house on the land of William Carpender of Coleford in the parish of Newland.

Sterly Kedgwin . . . a new dwelling house on the land of Jane Hoskins in the parish of Newland.

James Powell . . . a new dwelling house on the land of Jane Hoskins in the parish of Newland.

Thomas Caswill . . . a new dwelling house on the land of Jane Hoskins in the parish of Newland.

John Kear . . . a new dwelling house on his own land in the parish of Newland.

Mary Burtt, widow . . . a new dwelling house on the land of William Wyrrall Esq in the parish of Newland.

Edward Fryor . . . a new dwelling house on the land of William Wyrrall Esq in the parish of Newland.

John Reynolds . . . a new dwelling house on his own land in the parish of Newland.

William James . . . a new dwelling house on the land of Benedict Hall, Esq, near Coverham in the parish of Newland.

Roger Lewes . . . a new dwelling house on the land of Benedict Hall, Esq near Mailscott in the parish of Bicknour.

John Ambrey . . . a new barn on the land of Benedict Hall, Esq near Mailscott in the parish of Bicknour.

John Wheeler . . . a new dwelling house on the land of Richard Machen in the parish of Bicknour.

George Harris . . . two new dwelling houses on his own land in the parish of Ruerdeane.

Robert Welling . . . a new dwelling house on the land of John Vaughan Esq in the parish of Ruerdeane.

Ann Cruer . . . a new dwelling house on the land of [?] Olive Knight in the parish of Ruerdeane.

John Stephens . . . a new dwelling house in the parish of Ruerdeane.

George Harris . . . a new dwelling house in the parish of Ruerdeane.

John Knight . . . two new barns on the lands of Benedict Hall Esq in the parish of Ruerdeane.

William Roper gent. . . . . five new dwelling houses on his own land in the parish of Ruerdeane.

Widow Vaughan . . . a dwelling house on the land of Benedict Hall Esq near Hopes Well in the parish of Ruerdeane

John Horne . . . a new dwelling house on his own land in Michel Deane.

William Vaughan . . . a new house on the land of the heirs of Baynham Vaughan in the parish of Abinghall.

William Vaughan . . . a new barn on the land of William Wade in the parish of Abinghall.

Kettford Brayne . . . a new barn on his own land, in the parish of Little Deane.

Thomas Rock . . . a new dwelling house on the land of Henry Heane, clerk, in the parish of Little Deane.

Stephen Steele . . . a new dwelling house on the land of John Brayne gent, near Little Deane.

James Junn . . . a new dwelling house on the land of John Brayne gent, near Little Deane.

George Nash . . . a new dwelling house on the land of John Brayne, gent, near Little Deane.

Edward Collis . . . a new dwelling house on the land of John Brayne, gent near Little Deane.

Guy Yeates . . . a dwelling house on the land late of Sir John Wintour called Yorkely, in the parish of Newland.

Guy Yeates the younger . . . a new dwelling house on the land late of Sir John Wintour called Yorkely, in the parish of Newland.

Joane Ellis widow . . . a dwelling house on the land late of Sir John Wintour called Yorkely, in the parish of Newland.

Joane Ellis widow . . . a new barn on the land late of Sir John Wintour called Yorkely, in the parish of Newland.

William Davis . . . a new dwelling house on the land late of Sir John Wintour called Yorkely, in the parish of Newland.

William Stephens . . . a new dwelling house on the land late of Sir John Wintour called Yorkely, in the parish of Newland.

Henry Perke . . . a new dwelling house on the land late of Sir John Wintour called Yorkely, in the parish of Newland.

William James . . . a new dwelling house on the land late of Sir John Wintour called Yorkely, in the parish of Newland.

John Butler . . . a new dwelling house on his own land, in the parish of Awre.

Rodric [?] Leeke . . . a new dwelling house on the land of John Butler, in the parish of Awre adjoining the Cover.

John Pimmon alias Pray . . . a new dwelling house on the land of John Butler in the parish of Awre adjoining the Cover.

Thomas Hayward . . . a new barn on the land of Robert Young, in the parish of Awre.

Thomas Sallins . . . a new barn on his own land, in the parish of Awre.

Richard Heyward . . . a new dwelling house on his own land, in the parish of Awre adjoining the Cover.

John Robbins . . . a new dwelling house on the land of John Wintle in the parish of Awre adjoining the Cover.

William Evans . . . a dwelling house on his own land, in the parish of Awre adjoining the Cover.

John Wintle . . . a dwelling house on his own land, in the parish of Awre adjoining the Cover, and same built with Forest timber.

John Smith . . . a new dwelling house on the land of Thomas Dunning, in the parish of Awre adjoining the Cover.

William Hodges . . . a new dwelling house on the land of John Berrow, in the parish of Awre adjoining the Cover.

William March . . . a dwelling house on the land of Mr. Ofspring in the parish of Newland adjoining the Cover.

Thomas Bannister . . . a new dwelling house on the land of Mr. Sternece, in the parish of Newland.

Thomas Simons . . . a new barn on his own land, in the parish of Newland.

Thomas Kear senior . . . a new barn on the land of Baynham Throckmorton called Lords Lease, in the parish of Newland.

William Withenbury . . . a new dwelling house on his own land, in the parish of St. Briavills.

John Ford . . . a new dwelling house and barn on his own land, in the parish of St. Breavills.

Oliver Worgan . . . a new dwelling house and barn on his own land, in the parish of St. Breavills.

James Gough, gent. . . . a new barn, and part of his dwelling house on his own land, in the parish of Newland.

Richard Church . . . a dwelling house on the land of John Marshe in Breame in the parish of Newland.

Thomas Berrow . . . one room of house on the land of Richard Berkin, in the parish of St Breavills.

Capt John Giffard . . . a barn and wane house on the land of the heirs of John Berrow, gent. in the parish of Newland, being made and built with timber out of the Forest.

George Gough, gent., deceased . . . one room of a house, in the parish of Newland.

William Brown . . . a dwelling house on the land of Richard Hill gent. in the parish of Newnham adjoining the Cover.

Henry Bellamy . . . a dwelling house and outhouse on the land of Richard Hill gent., in the parish of Newnham adjoining the Cover.

Thomas Stayner a dwelling house on the lands of Richard Hill, gent, in the parish of Newnham adjoining the Cover.

Eustus Hardwick . . . a dwelling house on his own land, in the parish of Little Deane.

Roger Robins . . . a dwelling house on the lands of William Rowles gent, within the parish of [blank].

Person John Wilse . . . a dwelling house on the lands he then owned in fee but now in the fee of Eustus Hardwick gent, in the parish of Little Deane.

Capt. John Brayne . . . a room of a dwelling house in the parish of Little Deane.

Walter Thayer . . . one room of a dwelling house on the land of James Bovey near Little Deane.

John Chapman . . . a dwelling house on the land of James Bovey near Little Deane.

Thomas Francis . . . a dwelling house on the land of John Hawkins, gent, near Little Deane.

John Bond of Newnham . . . a barn on the land of Richard Hall gent, in the parish of Newnham.

Andrew Horne . . . a barn on his own land, in the parish of Awre.

John Dew . . . a Grist Mill on his own land in the parish of Newland.

Thomas Kear of Clowerwall . . . enlarged his dwelling house on his own land in the parish of Newland.

William Yerworth . . . a barn on his own land in the parish of Newland.

John Gray . . . a dwelling house on his own land in the parish of Ruerdeane.

William Bromage gent . . . enlarged his dwelling house on his own land in the parish of Newland.

*COPPICES CUT WITHOUT LICENCE:[12] WASTES IN GROVES* made and committed within the Perambulation but without the demesne woods of his Highness the Lord Protector within the Forest of Dean

First they say that Richard Harris hath within the space of three years last past felled and cut down one Coppice Grove called Retford Grove containing by estimate 4 acres, being the fee of the heirs of Baynham Vaughan Esq. in the parish of Ruardean.

Then follow similar presentments (the length of time varies):

James Palmer . . . of the parish of Weston . . . one Coppice Grove, 1 acre, being the fee of the heirs of Baynham Vaughan Esq of the parish of Ruerdeane.

George Harris . . . one Coppice Grove called [?] Calshere near Bishop wood furnace, in the parish of Ruerdeane.

The widow Fisher . . . one Coppice Grove, 2 acres, in the parish of Bicknor.

Thomas Reeves . . . one Coppice Grove, 1½ acres, in the parish of Ruerdeane.

Michell How . . . one Coppice Grove, 1½ acres, in the parish of Ruerdeane.

Benedict Hall of Heymeadow, gent, . . . one Coppice Grove called Stowfield Grove, 20 acres, being in his own fee in the parish of Bicknour.

George Wyrall Esq, deceased . . . one Coppice Grove, 10 acres, being in his own fee in the parish of Bicknour.

Benedict Hall Esq . . . one Coppice Grove called The Copes, 60 acres, being in his own fee in the parish of Bicknour.

Benedict Hall Esq . . . one Coppice Grove called Bungeps Grove, 40 acres, being in his own fee in the parish of Stanton.

Benedict Hall Esq., one Coppice Grove called the Upper Furnace Grove, 20 acres, being in his own fee in the parish of Stanton.

Capt. Griffantius Phillipps . . . one Coppice Grove called the Lower Furnace Grove, 20 acres, being in the fee of Benedict Hall esq, in the parish of Newland.

William Wyrall Esq . . . one Coppice Grove, 6 acres, being in his own fee, in the parish of Newland.

John Harris . . . one Coppice Grove, 4 acres, being in the fee of William Wyrrall gent, in the parish of Newland.

Arthur Ricketts deceased . . . three Coppice Groves, 16 acres, in his own fee in the parish of [blank].

Hugh Dixon deceased . . . one Coppice Grove, 10 acres, being in the fee of Warren Jane and Dorothy Packer, in the parish of Newland.

Hugh Dixon deceased . . . one Coppice Grove, 12 acres, being in the fee of Griffith Morgan and Dorothy Packer, in the parish of Newland.

Mary Perkins of Pilson in co. Monmouth and her son . . . two Coppice Groves, 14 acres, being in the fee of William Wyrrall esq. in the parish of Newland.

[12] Permission to cut groves was necessary even on privately owned land.

Edward Perkins of Pilson, gent., deceased . . . one Coppice Grove called The Great Grove, 20 acres, being in his own fee in the parish of Newland.

Edward Perkins of Pilson, gent., deceased . . . three Coppice Groves called Rickinghill, Wyshill and Fruce Grove, 30 acres, being in his fee in the parish of St Breavills.

Sir William Catchmay knight . . . three Coppice Groves, 20 acres, being in his own fee in the parish of St. Breavills.

Thomas James Esq . . . two Coppice Groves, 6 acres, being within his own fee in the parish of St. Breavills.

Capt. John Brayne . . . one Coppice Grove called Rodmore Grove, 30 acres, being in the fee of [blank] Woodruffe in the parish of St. Breavills.

Joyce Gough, widow . . . one Coppice Grove in the fee of the heirs of Richard Gough of Wilsbury, deceased.

Capt. Giffard . . . one Coppice Grove within Sir John Wintour's Park, 8 acres, being then in the fee of the said Sir John Wintour.

Capt. Giffard . . . one Coppice Grove called The Shraves, 10 acres, then in the fee of Sir John Wintour Kt. in the parish of Newland.

John White, gent. and partners, the late purchasers of Sir John Winter's estate . . . one Coppice Grove, 7 acres, in the parish of Newland.

Col. John Berrow . . . one Coppice Grove called the Hay Grove, 40 acres, being in the fee of the said Colonel, in the parish of Awre.

Giles Russell . . . one Coppice Grove, ½ acre, being in the fee of John Horne infant, in the parish of Awre.

Richard Hill, gent. . . . one Coppice Grove, 10 acres, being in his own fee in the parish of Newnham.

Tanner Morse . . . one Coppice Grove, 10 acres, being in the fee of Sir Gerrard (?) Kempe Kt in the parish of Flaxley.

Margaret Driver, widow . . . one Coppice Grove, 3 acres, being in the fee of William Cook Esq in the parish of Flaxley.

William Bovey and his partners . . . part of Flaxley Woods, 1000 acres, being in their own fee in the parish of Flaxley.

Katherine Kingston, widow . . . one Coppice Grove called Comly Grove, 8 acres, being in the fee of William Bovey and his partners, in the parish of Flaxley.

Elizabeth Vaughan, widow . . . one Coppice Grove called Abinghall Grove, 50 acres, being in the fee of the heirs of Baynham Vaughan Esq, in the parish of Abinghall.

Thomas Wade and Thomas [?] Cort . . . one Coppice Grove called Wilkwood, 6 acres, being in the fee of the heirs of Baynham Vaughan Esq, in the parish of Abinghall.

William Bridgman . . . one Coppice Grove, 5 acres, being in his fee, in the parish of Abinghall.

Elizabeth Aylway, widow . . . one Coppice Grove called Longhope, 20 acres, being in the fee of Duncomb Colchester, gent., in the parish of Abinghall.

Thomas Nourse . . . one Grove called Owley Grove, 10 acres, being in the fee of Mr. Farmour within the parish of [blank].

Edward Morse of Michel Deane, deceased . . . one Coppice Grove called Nockalls, 4 acres, being in the fee of Mr Forrester, in the parish of Michel Deane.

Henry Phillipson . . . one Coppice Grove, 3 acres, being in his own fee, in the parish of the Lea.

Thomas Adam . . . one Coppice Grove called Baker Land Grove, one acre, being in the fee of Edward Servient, gent, in the parish of Michel Deane.

Elizabeth Aylway, widow . . . one Coppice Grove called Harpe Grove, 7 acres, being in the fee of Duncomb Colchester, gent., in the parish of Michel Deane.

Edward Morse of Michel Dean, deceased . . . one Coppice Grove.

John Hawkins . . . one Coppice Grove called Sturns Grove, 10 acres, being in the fee of Duncomb Colchester in the parish of Michel Deane.

Thomas Waller . . . one Coppice Grove called Barn Hill Coppice, one acre, being in the fee of Duncomb Colchester, in the parish of Michel Deane.

Richard Blast of Machelshope [? Hopemansel] . . . one Coppice Grove, 8 acres, being in his own fee in the parish of Newland.

Sir Baynham Throckmorton Kt . . . Coppice wood, 10 acres, in his fee, in the parish of Newland.

Mr. Hoskins . . . one Coppice, 4 acres, being in his own fee, in the parish of Newland.

Benedict Hall Esq . . . one Coppice Grove called Ellens Reding, 5 acres, being in his own fee in the parish of Stanton.

Benedict Hall Esq . . . one Coppice Grove called Lords Land Grove, 5 acres, being in his own fee in the parish of Newland.

John Kear . . . one Coppice Grove in his own fee in the parish of Stanton.

Benedict Hall Esq . . . two Coppice Groves called [?] Winnell Grove and Blake Grove, 10 acres, both being in his own fee in the parish of Stanton.

William Jones Esq . . . one Coppice Grove, 3 acres, being in his own fee in the parish of Awre.

Richard Hooper . . . one Coppice Grove, 3 acres, being in his own fee in the parish of Awre.

Richard Driver . . . one Coppice Grove, 2 acres, being in his own fee in the parish of Awre.

Mr. Gawer . . . [blank].

Thomas Ayleway gent . . . two Coppice Groves, each one acre, being in the fee of Mr. Cox, in the parish of Awre.

Walter Thayer . . . one Coppice Grove, 6 acres, in the fee of the Lords of Flaxley near Little Deane.

Benedict Hall Esq . . . one Coppice Grove called Brookes Head, 5 acres, being in his own fee, in the parish of Bicknour.

Capt. John Brayne . . . one parcel of Coppice wood, 3 acres, lying in the Abbotts Wood near Suttons Mill.

George Bond, gent., . . . 16 small Coppice Groves, 73 acres, being in his own fee in the parishes of Newland, Stanton and St Briavills.

Benedict Hall Esq., George Bond and Richard Jones gent . . . one Coppice Grove, 20 acres, being in the fee of the said Hall and Bond in the parish of Newland.

William Teagey and William Tanner of Monmouth . . . one Coppice Grove, 8 acres, in the fee of Sir William Catchmay Knt., but now in the fee of George Bond gent., in the parish of Newland.

William Probin of Heymeadow . . . one Coppice Grove, 10 acres, being in the fee of Griffith Morgan and Dorothy Packer within the parish of Newland.

Joane Preest . . . 4 Coppice Groves, 8 acres, all being the fee of George Bond gent., in the parish of Newland.

Christopher Dowle . . . two Coppice Groves, 8 acres, in his own fee, in the parish of Newland.

Jane Elly, widow, and Richard Elly gent, her son, . . . 4 small Groves, 9 acres in all, being in the fee of the said Richard, in the parish of Newland.

Sir Baynham Throckmorton Knt . . . one Coppice Grove, 1½ acres, being then in his own fee in the parish of Newland.

William Worgan of Colford . . . one Coppice Grove, one acre, being in his fee, in the parish of Newland.

Lawrence Sled . . . one Coppice Grove, one acre, being in his own fee in the parish of Newland.

George Forster gent . . . one Coppice Grove, one acre, being in his own fee in the parish of Newland.

William Bramadger, gent . . . one Coppice Grove, 1½ acres, being in his own fee in the parish of Newland.

Thomas Simmons of Clowerwall . . . one Coppice Grove, one acre, being in his own fee, in the parish of Newland.

Capt. Griffantius Phillipps [ironmaster] . . . one Coppice Grove called Bircham, 8 acres, being in the fee of Benedict Hall Esq, in the parish of Newland.

John Witt of Breame . . . one Coppice Grove, 1½ acres, in his own fee, in the parish of Newland.

Edward Ricketts, gent . . . one Coppice grove, 1½ acres, being in his own fee, in the parish of Newland.

Benedict Hall Esq . . . two Coppice Groves called Dingle Grove and Ashtredge Grove, 5 acres, both being in his own fee, in the parish of Newland.

Christopher Worgan . . . one Coppice Grove, 1½ acres, being in the fee of Kedgwin Hoskins, in the parish of Newland.

Benedict Hall Esq . . . four Coppice Groves, 16 acres, all being in his own fee, in the parish of Bicknour.

Warren Jane . . . one Coppice Grove, 3 acres, being in the fee of George Bond, gent. in the parish of Newland.

Simon Dubberly . . . one Coppice Grove, 2 acres, being in the Lords of Flaxley, in the parish of Flaxley.

John Gonning [ironmaster] of Bristol Market . . . one Coppice Grove, 3 acres, being in his own fee in the parish of St. Breavills.

*PURPRESTURES* within his Highness the Lord Protector's wast soyle of the Forest of Deane:

First they say and present that Benedict Hall Esq. hath within the space of 6 years last past enclosed with a stone wall the Rudge and Nockolls containing by estimate 200 acres more or less being his Highness wast soyle of the said Forest of Deane.

Also . . . Sir John Wintour hath within the space of [blank] years last past enclosed with a stone wall the Sneed and Kidnels containing by estimate [blank] acres be it more or less, being his Highness wast soyle of the said Forest.

*Cabbiners*

Also . . . Edward Jenkin hath maintained a cottage or cabberne [cabin] on and thereto inclosed a garden ground of his Highness said wast soyle.

Then follow similar presentments (the length of time varies):

John Dubberly . . . a cabbin and garden
Margery Williams, widow . . . a cabberne and garden
George Cinderby . . . ¼ acre of land at Chestnutts
Widow Baddam . . . a cabberne
Mary Ap Thomas . . . a cabberne
John Floyd the elder, John Floyd the younger and Walter Floyd . . . a dwelling house and 3 acres
Thomas Proppit . . . a cabberne and garden
John Morris. . . a cabberne
Widow Nurse . . . a cabberne
Joane Lowes, widow, alias Tawgett . . . a cabberne, yard and garden
Edward Gaudy . . . a cabberne
Ann Woolrudge . . . a cabberne
John Baker . . . a cabberne
Joane Harris . . . a cabberne
Thomas Ralfe . . . a cabberne, in Kidnell
Anthony Hercott . . . a cabberne
Richard Haywood . . . a cabberne
John Bond . . . a cabberne
Joane Lewis . . . a cabberne

Edward Fryer . . . a cabberne
George Clerk . . . a cabberne
Jenkin Heures . . . a cabberne
James Parry . . . a cabberne
Ann Williams . . . a cabberne
Thomas Biby . . . a cabberne
Ann Biby . . . a cabberne
Edmund Phillip . . . a cabberne and $\frac{1}{2}$ acre
Widow Ford . . . a cabberne
Widow Webb . . . a cabberne
William Powell . . . a cabberne
William Hayward . . . a cabberne
William Hiler . . . a cabberne
Elizabeth Moreson . . . a cabberne
Thomas Fristin . . . a cabberne
William Drake . . . a cabberne
William Lea . . . a cabberne
Mary Arnold . . . [blank]
Edmund Long . . . a cabberne
Blanch Evans . . . a cabberne
John Procer . . . a cabberne
Reece Whitmore . . . a cabberne
John Whetson . . . a cabberne
Christopher Tatberer . . . a cabberne
John Baker . . . a cabberne
Elizabeth Hopkins . . . a cabberne
George Brayne . . . a cabberne
Thomas Moore . . . a cabberne
Edward Hart . . . a cabberne
Henery Dobes . . . a cabberne
Reece Williams . . . a cabberne
Thomas Barnes . . . a cabberne
Hughes Lawrence . . . a cabberne
Thomas Williams . . . a cabberne
Widow Lawrence . . . a cabberne
Peter Black . . . a cabberne
Francis Edwards . . . a cabberne
Simon Powell . . . a cabberne
John Morgan . . . a cabberne
James Web . . . a cabberne
Thomas Morgan . . . a cabberne
Widow Lewis . . . a cabberne
William Waite . . . a cabberne
Samuel Mason . . . a cabberne
George Jordan . . . a cabberne
Prudence Edward . . . a cabberne
Widow Barden . . . a cabberne
William Shearer . . . a cabberne
Widow Hawkins . . . a cabberne
Clement Nicholas . . . a cabberne
Roger Morritt . . . a cabberne, in the Woodwardship of Abinghall
Blanch Collier . . . a cabberne, in Ruerdeane Eves
Joane Morris. . . a cabberne
Robert Guilliam . . . a cabberne
Walter Warren . . . a cabberne and one acre

John Guilliam . . . a cottage, outhouse, garden, yard, $\frac{1}{2}$ acre
Henery Robins . . . a naile house
Thomas Jordan . . . a cabberne
Andrew Dollaway . . . a cabberne
Howell Jones . . . a cabberne
Edward Paine . . . a cabberne
Thomas Clarke . . . a cabberne
Susan Aston . . . a cabberne
Joane Watkins . . . a cabberne
Richard Tiler . . . a cabberne
Nicholas Page . . . a dwelling house and $\frac{1}{4}$ acre, in the Sneed
William Marshall . . . a cottage and $\frac{1}{4}$ acre, in Wawmore
John Goodcheepe . . . a cottage and $\frac{1}{4}$ acre
William Smith . . . a cottage, in the Lower Meene near St. Briavills
Widow Fines . . . a cottage, in the lower Meene near St. Breavills
Widow Ragnalls . . . a cottage and $\frac{1}{4}$ acre, in Hudnolls
Phillip Taylour . . . a cottage and $\frac{1}{2}$ acre, in Hudnolls
Thomas Grindall . . . a cottage and $\frac{1}{3}$ acre, in Hudnolls
Howell George . . . a garden, in Hudnolls
Richard Green . . . a shepcot and $\frac{1}{4}$ acre, in Hudnolls

*PURPRESTURES* upon and within his Highness the Lord Protector's wast soyle of the Forest of Deane:

First they say and present that Sir John Wintour Knt. has since the last Justice Seat [1634] inclosed with a stone wall a parcel of land called the Sneed and Kidnells containing by estimate 200 acres, being his Highness wast soyle of the Forest of Deane. [This is a repetition of an earlier presentation.]

Benedict Hall, Esq. hath since the last Justice Seat [1634] inclosed with a stone wall parcels of land called the Rudge and Nockolls containing by estimate 200 acres, being his Highness wast soyle of the said Forest. [This is a repetition of an earlier presentation.]

The said Sir John Wintour Knt. hath since the last Justice Seat [1634] raised and made a dam-head and thereby impounded the water called Bull Bollock Pond to the over-flowing and drownding of an acre of his Highness wast soyle of the said Forest.

Col. John Berrow hath within the space of 20 years last past raised and made a dam-head and thereby impounded the water called Black Poole to the over-flowing and drownding of $1\frac{1}{2}$ acres or thereabouts of his Highness waste soyle of the said Forest,and hath also made a ditch of near 3 foot broad, and a quarter of a mile long to carry the said water through the said soyle unto his Furnace.

Eleanour Hooper, widow, hath maintained a waine house upon his Highness wast soyle of the said Forest within the Woodwardship of Staunton.

Nicholas Mousall hath maintained a small beast house upon his Highness wast soil within the Woodwardship of Staunton, and hath encroached thereupon by putting his hedges 2 foot out and 26 foot long.

Richard Nash alias Gilbert hath inclosed with his hedge 3 foot broad and 10 foot long upon his Highness wast soyle, and hath also maintained a small Cott thereon in the Woodwardship of Staunton.

Jane White hath maintained a waine house upon his Highness wast soyle, within the woodwardship of Staunton.

Richard Palmer hath maintained an oxhouse upon his Highness wast soyle within the Woodwardship of Staunton.

William Carpender of Colford, gent., hath maintained a waine house upon his Highness wast soyle at Coverham within the Woodwardship of Staunton.

The said William Carpender, gent., hath maintained part of an outhouse being built 3 foot broad upon his Highness wast soyle within the Woodwardship of Staunton.

Benedict Hall, Esq., hath encroached with his ditch 20 yards long and 2 foot broad upon his Highness wast soyle at Coverham in the Woodwardship of Staunton.

Sir John Wintour Knt hath encroached with his ditch 20 yards long and 4 foot broad upon his Highness wast soyle at Coverham within the Woodwardship of Staunton.

John Reece tenant to Dowler Land hath maintained a small shed built against the house upon his Highness wast soyle within the Woodwardship of Staunton.

Hugh Jones hath maintained a small shed from his house on his Highness wast soil near Broad Stone.

Eleanour Thomas hath maintained a small Cot upon his Highness wast soyle, at Mailscott.

Richard Baughan hath maintained a waine house upon his Highness wast soyle.

Reece Higgin hath encroached by building his chimney upon his Highness wast soyle, in the Woodwardship of Ruerdeane.

Henry Oare hath maintained a sheep cott upon his Highness wast soyle within the Woodwardship of Bicknour.

Thomas Meeke hath inclosed with a stone wall 20 foot in length and 5 or 6 foot in breadth of his Highness wast soyle within the Woodwardship of Ruerdeane.

Thomas Hobbs hath built part of his barn upon, and inclosed a garden ground of his Highness wast soil within the Woodwardship of Ruerdeane.

William Reaper, gent., hath inclosed near ¼ acre of his Highness wast soyle, in the Woodwardship of Ruerdeane.

Widow Sterry, tenant to the land of the heirs of Baynham Vaughan hath inclosed ¼ acre within the Woodwardship of Ruerdeane.

Henery Edy hath inclosed about ½ a quarter of an acre and maintained 2 sheds within the Woodwardship of Ruerdeane.

John Gray hath made a fence encroachment, within the Woodwardship of Ruerdeane.

John Cradock, Clarke, hath maintained à shed within the Woodwardship of Ruerdeane.

James Smith of Walford hath built part of a small house within the Woodwardship of Ruerdeane.

Henry Baker hath maintained a small beast house, within the Woodwardship of Ruerdeane.

George Harris hath built a waine house and other outhouses, and inclosed a garden ground, within the Woodwardship of Ruerdeane.

Walter Meeke hath maintained a small cott, within the Woodwardship of Ruerdeane.

Richard Martin hath built a small barne, in the Woodwardship of Ruerdeane.

William Roger hath built part of a small cott, and inclosed a small outlett in the Woodwardship of Ruerdeane.

John Chapman hath inclosed 4 foot broad and 20 foot in length, in the Woodwardship of Ruerdeane.

John Adams hath maintained a sheep cott, and inclosed ³/₄ acre, in the Woodwardship of Ruardeane.

Thomas Daw hath maintained a barn, in the Woodwardship of Ruerdeane.

Simon Matthews hath built part of his house highway, in the Woodwardship of Ruerdeane.

Widow Vaughan hath inclosed a small garden, in the Woodwardship of Ruerdeane.

Robert Dowse tenant to Benedict Hall Esq for inclosing a watering place, part of a garden ground, and building a waine house, in the Woodwardship of Ruerdeane.

Reece Jones tenant to Nicholas Jordan, gent., hath kept inclosed in two places part of an acre, in the Woodwardship of the Lea Bayly.

Walter Partridge built a small cott, in the Woodwardship of the Lea Bayly.

John Ennis of the parish of Weston inclosed ¹/₂ acre, in the Woodwardship of the Lea Bayly.

Henry Dancock tenant to Mr. Bridgman inclosed 15 yards in length and 2 foot broad, in the Woodwardship of the Lea Bayly.

Morgan Pritchett built half his dwelling house, and inclosed about 5 yards in length and so much in breadth, in the Woodwardship of the Lea Bayly.

Richard Collins, deputy woodward there, inclosed one-eighth acre, in the Woodwardship of Lea Bayly.

John Evans inclosed 15 yards in length and 6 foot in breadth, in the Woodwardship of the Lea Bayly.

William Workeman inclosed with his hedge one yard in breadth and 40 yards in length, in the Woodwardship of Abinghall.

William Gibbins encroached upon 10 yards in length and one in breadth and maintained a shed, in the Woodwardship of Abinghall.

Richard Nelmes of the parish of Flaxley inclosed 15 yards in length and 5 in breadth, and built a waine house, in the Woodwardship of Abinghall.

Eleanour Osburne maintained half her house, within Chestnutts.

Joane Pope built a smiths shop in Chestnutts.

Thomas Asman maintained a cott in Badcocks Bayly.

Thomas Rock tenant to Kettford Brayne, gent, inclosed one-fifth acre, in the Woodwardship of Abinghall.

William Andrews inclosed a garden ground, in the Woodwardship of Abinghall.

Henery Adams maintained a Cott, in the Woodwardship of Abinghall.

John Pinnion [? Pimmon] alias Pray enclosed one-twelfth acre and maintained an outhouse in the Woodwardship of Blakeney.

Trustrome Vertue maintained part of a Cott, in the Woodwardship of Blakeney.

William Hodges inclosed 15 yards in length and 2 yards in breadth, in the Woodwardship of Blakeney.

Thomas Sibrance maintained half his barn, in the Woodwardship of Staunton.

Trustrum Treshard maintained 2 Cotts, in the Woodwardship of Staunton.

George Cinderby inclosed ¼ acre in Chestnutts.

Francis Mason maintained a stable and barn, in the Woodwardship of Staunton.

Walter Thayer maintained a waine house and inclosed with a stone wall near his dwelling house about one-sixth acre and thereon are built two outhouses being near Little Deane.

Richard or Thomas Birkin maintained a waine house.

Thomas Donning of Bristol kept inclosed unto his own land about one-fifth acre.

Widow Walmers erected a dwelling house upon the said land.

John Fox, Baker, built a bake house and sheep cott.

John Guilliam built a shed in the Woodwardship of [blank].

Thomas Knight enclosed one-twelfth acre in Wawmore.

Thomas Dray erected a piggs cott in Wawmore.

Edmund Crispe kept inclosed 6 acres of ground called New Moore (Wawmore), but by what warrant they know not.

Sir William Catchmay inclosed one acre in Hudnolls.

Richard Skinner, gent., within the space of 20 years last past maintained a dwelling house and thereto inclosed a garden ground.

Col. John Berrow, within the space of 10 years last past inclosed one-twelfth acre for a place to put his oare and cinders near his Furnace.

Thomas Godman, servant to the Farmers Sir Baynham Throckmorton and his partners since the last Justice Seat [1634] maintained a dwelling house and inclosed [blank] acres.

Thomas Foard, gent., within the space of 20 years last past maintained a dwelling house, and inclosed a garden ground adjoining, called Lumber Marsh containing 12 acres.

*WASTES* made in vert and timber within and upon his Highness wast soyle of the said Forest:

First they say and present that Francis Pace of Michell Deane hath within the space of 5 years last past felled and cut down one timber oak containing 3 tons of timber or thereabout, and converted the same to his own use.

Then follow similar presentments (the number of years varies):

Richard Nelmes of the parish of Flaxley cut down and converted to his own use near a cart load of young vert of the Forest. Presented by Major Wade.

John Hodges of Lidbrooke has been a very great spoiler and destroyer of the wood of the Forest. Presented by Henry Rudge.

William Marshall of Ruerdeane barked and stript divers timber oaks to the killing of them. Presented by Major Wade.

Capt. John Brayne took and converted to his own use 2 tons of timber to build Steeles house. Presented by Collis.

Capt. Evans took out 10 tons of timber and converted the same to his own use. Presented with Wicher the Carpenter who squared it.

Charles Ellis carpenter (1645) felled and cut down for the use of Col. Massy 20 timber oaks containing [blank] tons which the same Col. imployed for the repair of the Iron Works. Presented by the Preservators.

John Clarke of Colford, Richard Palmer, Lewis Dandford, Daniel Jones, Richard Worgan, Thomas Sibrance and Edmund Harris (1643) stript and felled 60 oaks. Presented by Richard Smith woodward.

Thomas Plomer and John [blank] both of Breeme (1645) barked and stript 12 oaks in the Woodwardship of Staunton and converted the bark thereof to their own use. Presented by Richard Smith woodward.

Anstelme Manning in Sneed and Kidnells felled and carried away 24 beeches and oaks, the least as big as the small of ones leg, and 13 hollies and beeches, and converted them to his own use. Presented by Thomas Preist.

Sir William Catchmay, Knight caused to be felled and cut down 4 or 5 oaks containing by estimation 20 cords of wood and converted them to charcole being burnt with other wood which he had in the Park of White Meade. Presented by John Matthews and John Hinder senior of Breeme.

Capt. John Brayne cut down divers timber oaks containing by estimation [blank] and sold the timber and converted the offal wood to charcole. Presented by [?] Golfe.

Thomas Baker, cabiner, cut divers crookes of oaks containing 40 horse loads and carried them to Newnham and sold them there. Presented by Collis.

Thomas Creed late Bowbearer of the Forest felled and cut down one timber oak and sold the same for £5. Presented by Collis.

Capt. John Brayne felled and cut down, in and about Crumpe Meadow and at Lidney neare 100 stript oaks and converted them to charcole, and also sold timber unto Thomas Pullin of Michell Deane. Presented by Richard [?] Golfe.

There hath been stript by Sir John Wintour's order in Kenslyes Edge since the last Justice Seat [1634] 500 oaks. Presented by Henry Rudge.

The Preservators viz. George Olfield, Christopher Worgan, Thomas Berrow, Andrew Horne, and Arthur Rowles, in 10 years, felled and cut down 500 beeches in Kenslyes Edge and converted them to charcole. Presented by Henry Rudge.

James Clement alias Soaper of Newland, stript or barked one oak in Oakewood. Presented by Daniel Morse.

Richard Nash of the parish of Newland carried bark which was stript of oaks in the Forest unto Bristol. Presented by Major Wade.

The Lord Maynard by his servants or agents caused to be cut and corded in Cannopps fellett, in the year 1649, 118 cords of 3 foot wood which Capt Griffantius Phillip took away and converted to his own use. Presented by Preservators.

Robert Monjoy hauled or drew out 12 tons of oak timber into his own land near Ruerdeane, worth £5.

Thomas Hall, now of Monmouth, farmer, by his workmen stript divers oaks in the Sallies. Presented by Collis.

Richard Jones of Ruerdeane cut down 4 oaks and converted them to make hurdles for Col. Kirle's use. Presented by Henry Rudge.

Col. Robert Kirle by his workman William Tiler of Birdwood within the Lea Bayly cut down 16 timber oaks which were carried to Walford for the use of the said Col. Presented by Henry Rudge.

William Collis of Little Deane carried out one oak containing 1½ tons of timber worth 15s. and converted it to his own use. Presented by John Heane of Little Deane.

The said William Collis cut down and carried away 2 loads of the Cover thereof. Presented by John Heane of Little Deane.

The said William Collis drew out about a ton of good timber in [?] sleetes worth 9s. and converted the same to his own use. Presented by Phillip Meeke.

Capt. John Brayne cut down by his workmen in Aywood one great oak to make an Hammer Beame.

Kettford Brayne cut down and stript oak containing 3 tons of timber worth 30s. and converted it to his own use. Presented by Phillip Meeke.

Col. Massy and Richard Skinner, gent., cut down by their workmen 200 short cords of wood worth £50. Presented by James Smith, corder.

Col. John Berrow sold unto cardbord makers as much timber as he had out of moriers and brouchers within the Woodwardship of Blakeney, as came to £10. Presented by George Guyes, deputy woodward.

The Preservators viz. George Olfield, Christopher Worgan, Thomas Berrow, Andrew Horne and Arthur Rowles, sold out of the Woodwardship of Stanton, unto William Bick of Colford as much timber in Hogshead and Barrell Staves as they required about £20 for. And as much timber as made a vessell of [blank] tons. Presented by Richard Smith, woodward.

Mr. John Beck drew out unto Flaxley's forge, one oak made into a Hammer Beam worth £8.

Anthony Clifford, Esq, drew out 7 tons of timber and converted it to his own use, worth £3.10s. Presented by William Howle, corder.

John Stephens cropt 4 small sallies and such like, growing before his house. He confessed it to the Regard.

*Major Wade* [see Section VIII] There hath been cut within the space of 3 years last past by the appointment of Major John Wade, 210 tons of timber which hath been spent in building the furnaces and forge, and the housings and buildings thereunto belonging, which were likewise built by the appointment of the said Major Wade for the use of the Common Wealth. Also there hath been cut and corded within the space of 3 years last past by the appointment of Major John Wade for the use of the said Iron Works:

|  |  | *Short cords* |
|---|---|---|
| Complement wood | – | 4,210 |
| Birch and Holly Wood | – | 340 |
| Stubbs, Bottomes and logs | – | 8,300 |
| Offal of timber | – | 1,550 |
| Stoggall Beeches | – | 8,937 |
| Stoggall Oaks and dead trees | – | 1,100 |
|  |  | 24,437 |

Also they say that Sir Sackfeild Crow [for Sackville Crow] and Sir Baynham Throckmorton, Knights, Capt. Taylour and John Gonning of Bristol Merchants, farmers to the late King [Chas. I] for his Iron Works within the Forest of Dean, have since the last Justice Seat [1634] by their workmen felled and cut down great numbers of trees, both of oak and beech, in divers places within his Highness wast soyle of the said Forest, and have cut yearly and charcoled the same, but how many they cut is impossible for them to know because the stubbs and bottomes thereof have been long since taken up, and what quantities of cord wood, or loads of charcole they have had, they cannot be informed of because many of the workmen who wrought for the same Farmers are dead and they that are yet alive, most of them being illiterate and not able to keep accompt thereof, cannot remember for so long time past.

But they say that Sir Sackfeild Crow, Sir Baynham Throckmorton, Capt. Taylour and John Gonning did maintain and keep going the said Iron Works, viz. three Furnaces, and three Double Forges, and one Single Forge, viz. Parke End Furnace, Cannop Furnace, and Soudlyes Furnace, Parke End Double Forge, Whitecroft Double Forge, Bradlyes Double

Forge, and Soudlyes Single Forge, with the charcole that they made of the wood within the said wast soyle only and with no other, but how long the said Furnaces and Forges did blow and go for the said Farmers they cannot be truly informed. Only this they say may be shown that for the time the said Furnaces and Forges did blow and go, the three Furnaces did not spend less than 24,000 short cords of wood in one year, and the three Double and one Single Forge 5,800 short cords. So that the whole quantity that the said Furnaces and Forges did spend was never less than 29,800 short cords of wood every year.

The said Farmers within the time aforesaid did dig up and spend of the Forest cinders 3,000 tons per annum worth £300, which the furnaces blew.

Major General Massy hath within the space of 15 years last past by his workmen cut and corded within his Highness wast soyle of the said Forest 6,000 long cords of log and stub wood worth £3,000 and converted it to his own use.

There hath been gotten within the wast soyle of the said Forest for the use of White Meade furnace within the space of three years last past at least [blank] thousand tons of Cinders worth [blank] by the appointment of Major John Wade.

There hath been burnt within the space of a year last past between 16 and 20 acres of his Highness wast soyle of the said Forest and thereupon 6 decayed oaks which were burnt by the accidental falling of a half load of [char]cole which one of Richard Matthews' horses did carry, but whether the said Richard or his boy was present when the cole fired they cannot truly be informed, but one of them was present.

Col. John Berrow hath within the space of 11 years last past sold out of the Woodwardship of Blakeney within his Highness wast soyle of the said Forest divers quantities of wood and charcole unto Capt. John Giffard, Capt. John Brayne, and other Iron Masters, the quantities thereof they cannot be truly informed of.

Richard Skinner gent hath within the space of 15 years last past, taken and converted to his own use the [?] utenses of iron from the works within his Highness wast soyle which Sir Sackfeild Crow, Sir Baynham Throckmorton, Capt. Taylour and John Gonning gent., farmers of the Late King [Chas. I]. Presented by Mr. Plant.

Capt. John Giffard hath within the space of 10 years last past by his workmen felled and cut down great numbers of oaks and beeches in divers places of the said Forest and converted the same (excepting what timber the Preservators preserved of it) into charcole, and therewith maintained (amongst other cole made of wood which he bought in the country) and kept going about 2 years, three Furnaces, viz. Parke End Furnace, Lidbrooke Furnace, and Lidneyes Furnace, and four Forges, viz. Bradlyes Forge, Lidbrooke Single Forge, Slitting Mill Single Forge and Lidneyes Pill Single Forge. But what number of trees were cut by his workmen they cannot certainly know because the stubbs and bottomes are taken up, and what quantities of wood were converted to charcole they cannot be informed of, but the quantities of wood that the said Works did spend in 2 years could not be less than 40,000 short cords, worth [blank].

Capt. John Giffard hath within the space of 10 years last past taken and carried out of his Highness wast soyle of the said Forest one Cole house and another house both made of timber and converted the same to his own use.

Col. Robert Kirle, Capt. John Brayne, Capt. Pury, and Capt. Griffantius Phillipps have felled and cut down by their workmen within the space of 10 years last past great numbers of oak in Ruerdeane Eves within his Highness wood a great part whereof were timber trees, and converted the same to charcole for their own use. But how many trees were by them felled and cut down they know not, because the stubs and bottomes are taken up and cannot be numbered or what quantity of wood they have converted into charcole they cannot be rightly informed of. Presented by Henry Rudge.

Thomas Bannister hath within the space of 10 years last past made divers loads of [char]cole within his Highness wood [at Cannop etc.] within the said Forest, and sold the same to Capt. John Giffard. Presented by William Stephens.

[Augustus] Aldridge Ship-Carpenter hath within the space of 4 years by his workmen fallen and cut down divers oaks, [blank] tons of timber, which are employed for the use of the Common Wealth.

Edward Gilson hath within the space of one year fished a Pool lately made by Col. Berrow [? in the Woodwardship of Blakeney] within his Highness wast soyle of the said Forest and caught trout and converted them to his own use.

Richard Nash of Michell Deane hath within the space of 3 years last past carried out of the Lea Bayly, within his Highness wast soyle of the said Forest, 2 tons of timber worth 20s and converted the same to his own use.

*PURPRESTURES* made upon his Highness Demayne Lands within the said Forest:

*White Meade*

First they say and present that there is a faire house, stable, barn and outhouse thereto belonging, formerly built by one Richard Hankinson upon his Highness Demayne Land within his said Forest, adjoining to the cover thereof, now in the possession of the widow Simons called White Meade, containing by estimation [blank] hundred acres which is assarted, and part thereof within those two years under [blank] corn, and the greater part of the rest mowed, and by colour of the same widower living there doth keep a great stock of cattle, swine, and sheep to the exile of his Highness wild beasts and the oppression of the inhabitants of the said Forest, and that the same widow doth keep upon the said Meade near 20 [?] kins, having no right of common.

Also . . . there are 6 other small dwelling houses on the said Meade in the possession of Henery Gibbins, John Jefferis, Humphry Plant, Richard Jones, Widow Mason, and her son Francis, by colour of whose said dwellings have and do keep great stocks of cattle, pigs, and sheep upon his Highness wast soyle of the said Forest adjoining to the cover thereof to the exile of his Highness wild beasts, and the surcharging of the common of the said Forest having no right of common as aforesaid.

Also . . . the said inhabitants on the said White Meade have also assarted the same land called White Meade by grubbing, and mooting up the ferns and underwood thereof, and have ploughed and sowed with winter corn, and other corn to the number of 30 acres and the rest to winter the beasts and cattle that are summered in the said wast soyle.

Also . . . Robert Cruse, gent. and fee farmers of the said Forest hath within the space of 10 years last past by his workmen dug up and broke the land called White Meade, being his demaine land within the said Forest, and hath gotten and sold the quantity of 80 tons of Cinders worth 2s per ton − £8.

Also . . . John Simons deceased being tenant for part of the Parke of White Meade hath within the space of 9 years last past built a mault house upon his Highness Demaine Land called the Parke of White Meade and there continued making mault some [blank] years with the wood of the said Forest, and also within the time aforesaid erected a Pig Cot (near his dwelling house) within his Highness wast soil of the said Forest.

*WASTES* made by digging and breaking up his Highness wast soyle of the said Forest:

First they say and present that Capt. John Giffard hath by his workmen within the space of 10 years last past dug and broke up his Highness wast soyle in divers places of the said Forest, and taken and carried away and converted to his own use as many Cinders as were spent at White Meade Furnace, Lidneyes Furnace and Lidbrookes Furnace containing in the whole near 6,000 tons, worth 2s each ton which makes [£600].

Also . . . Col. John Berrew and Mr. John Beck have within the space of 8 years last past by their workmen dug and broke up his Highness the Lord Protector's wast soyle of the said Forest for the getting of Cinders, and have gotten and carried away to their furnace near Blakeney at least 1,000 tons, each ton being worth 2s. which amounts unto £100.

*IRON WORKES* made within and upon his Highness wast soyle of the said Forest:

First they say and present that there hath been built by the appointment of Major John Wade, within the space of 3 years last past, upon his Highness wast soyle of the said Forest, one Furnace with Cole house and other buildings thereunto belonging, which is imployed for the use of the Common Wealth.

Also . . . there hath been built by the appointment of the said Major Wade within the space of 3 years last past, upon his Highness wast soyle of the said Forest, one Forge with Cole house, Store house and other buildings thereunto belonging which is imployed for the use of the Common Wealth.

### THE REGARDERS' PRESENTMENTS

### THE GOSHAWKS

They say and present that there hath not been any eyrie of goshawks in the Forest during the space of 23 years last past since the last Justice Seat [1634].

### PORTS UPON SEAVERNE

First they say and present that they have viewed the ports upon the River Seaverne, viz. the Ports of Gattcomb and Newnham, and they say there hath been built three barques at Newnham by William Jefferies and his partners, of the parish of Newnham.

Also . . . that there hath been built at Gattcomb since the last Justice Seat [1634] one barque of 50 tons, one boate of 19 tons, and one of 8 tons, built by John White of the parish of Awre.

### MINES OF IRON AND COLE

First they say and present that there are divers mines of Iron in Clowerwalle Meene within his Highness wast soyle of the Forest.

Also . . . that there are divers mines of Iron in the lands of Baynham Throckmorton, Esq., Benedict Hall, Esq., the lands late of Sir John Wintour, John Gonning, gent., Christopher Bond, Henery Hooper, Edward Worgan, Mr William Sternill.

*PURPRESTURES* by Iron Works made within and upon the uttermost bounds of the Perambulation but without his Highness wast soyle of the Forest of Deane.

First they say and present that Benedict Hall, Esq., hath within the space of 28 years last past built one Furnace at Redbrooke within the parish of Newland.

Also . . . the said Benedict Hall, Esq., hath within the space of 7 years last past built one iron Forge at Lidbrooke within the parish of Bicknour being on his own land in fee.

Colonel John Berrow hath within the space of 7 years last past built a Furnace upon his own land in fee near Blakeney within the parish of Awre.

William Bovey hath within the space of 7 years last past repaired one iron forge on his own land in fee in the parish of Flaxley.

The said William Bovey hath repaired another forge upon the uttermost bounds of the Perambulation of the said Forest upon his own land in fee in the parish of Flaxley.

Thomas Hanwell, Esq., hath within the space of 3 years last past built 2 half Forges, the one upon the uttermost bounds of the Forest and the other within the Perambulation.

The Farmer of the Forest hath taken tithe of geese in Wamoore as a due belonging unto him for their commoning there, when they are not commonable within a forest.

Col. John Berrow doth take of the Quarry men that get tile and sanding at Baddams feild quarry the tenth of their labour there, but by what warrant he doth receive it they know not.

Also . . . since the Country hath been restrained fetching firewood out of his Highness wast soyle of the said Forest, the Colliers beneath the wood [i.e. in the east of the Forest] have unreasonably and extraordinarily enhanced the prices of their [sea]cole, working upon the Country's necessity, because being for the generality thereof forced to burn cole they be compelled to give what rates they demand for the same, or else to go without it, to the great oppression and grief of the Country, and unless some speedy course be taken to prevent it, will undoubtedly cause the deaths of poor people that are not able to come to their rates, there being now little or no other recourse for firing to be had for them in the Country. All which they leave to the grand judgment of the honorable Bench.

*MASTIVES UNEXPEDITATED*

First they say and present that John Bellis doth keep a mastive unexpeditated living at Coverham adjoining to his Highness waste soyle of the said Forest.

Also . . . Simon Mathews doth keep a mastive unexpeditated living at Bullocks End adjoining to the cover of his Highness wast soil of the said Forest.

Thomas Kitten doth keep a mastive unexpeditated living near the cover of the said Forest.

Thomas Simmons doth keep a mastive unexpeditated.

Widow Simon of White Meade adjoining to the cover of the wast soyle of the said Forest doth keep a mastive unexpeditated.

Walter Thayer doth keep a mastive unexpeditated living near the wast of his Highness said Forest.

The Widow Winbury doth keep a mastive unexpeditated.

Humphry Plant living at White Mead adjoining to the cover of his Highness wast soyle of the Forest [blank].

*WASTES* made and committed in dwelling houses within the Perambulation, but without the wast soyle [blank].

*HOUNDS, GRAYHOUNDES AND GUNNES* [blank].

The foregoing lengthy records apparently relate only to the Swanimote Court, in which case there is no record of action by the Eyre itself; and no evidence of any fines have been found. It appears probable that the Eyre was started but not continued. Perhaps the political and social circumstances were not conducive to further proceedings. One possibility is that judicial proceedings were suspended because a parliament was about to meet; the elections for the second Protectorate Parliament were held during July and the Parliament itself met in mid-September. Another possible reason is that Major-General Disbrowe, as one of Cromwell's Councillors, had an important role to play in this Parliament. Furthermore, the government may have preferred to have no judicial proceedings of this nature continuing, particularly any over which Disbrowe was presiding, during a parliamentary session and one in which the role and position of the major-generals were likely to be discussed and debated.

In any case, on 9 June 1657 the government passed 'An Act for the mitigation of the rigour of the forest laws within the Forest of Dean and for the preservation of wood and timber in the said Forest.'[13] The reason given was that the 'forest laws have seemed to be grievous and burdensome to the good people of the Commonwealth inhabiting within the Forest of Dean, by reason of a rigorous execution thereof'. The Act granted many powers to freeholders, tenants and other inhabitants; restoring to them freedom in the management of their properties and the exercise of their privileges. Grants made previously to Sir John Winter and John Gibbons were declared void. The Lord Protector was empowered to enclose and encoppice up to one-third of Dean at any one time; enclosures were to be thrown open within twelve years. The Act may have saved from punishment many of the offenders presented at the Swanimote and Eyre of 1656, but it did not bring full order into the Forest.[14] Abuses continued; some of the enclosing was opposed. On 8 April 1659 John Wade wrote to the Admiralty:[15]

> It were well if a justice in Eyre were resolved upon and empowered; the time approaching for the keeping of it, according to law [three years] and never more needed, when horrid offenders can so impudently appear with petitions in their hands, calling that to be right which is against all law and justice. One of those petitioners has come down, making great brags of what great favour their petitions receive, and that all the inclosures shall be put open, and the whole rabble put in their cattle of all sorts; there are boasts of what great promises some members of the House have made, that all things shall be granted that is desired; out of the encouragement they receive by letters from London, they speak strangely, and act worse, for the Forest in the chief coppices has been set on fire in 20 places. The chief of these petitioners is named Stallard, and is now in London; he was heretofore a Cavalier, and for offences done in the prime part of the Forest was fined at the last Justice Seat [1656] nearly £300, but it was mercifully mitigated to £20. Lord Desborow knows him well and so does Sergeant Siese [They had officiated in 1656].

[13] Firth and Rait, *Acts and Ordinances of the Interregnum* (1911), II, pp. 114–15. Hart, *Royal Forest*, p. 148 and Appendix X, pp. 284–5.
[14] Ibid. p. 149.
[15] SP18/202, p. 328; Hart, *Royal Forest*, p. 149.

Some conference should be had about it, but if it be the Parliament's pleasure, or any others, that the Forest shall be left at the pleasure of the people, let me know it, and I shall as willingly turn my back upon it as ever I came from school. It were acting the part of a schoolboy to make complaints, but I have cause, as last Monday some of the officers were set upon in performance of their duty, one being knocked down; but the next day I sent some more, who met with no opposition.

Other of Wade's complaints are extant, as well as information on his resignation in April 1660[16] – see Section VIII of this Part Two.

Henceforth, forest law in Dean dwindled. The only semblance of it to continue was the holding of the Attachment Court (the Speech Court) and of a Swanimote Court in 1676 (see Section IX) and in 1713 (see Section X).

[16] Hart, *Royal Forest*, pp. 149–51.

# VIII. MAJOR JOHN WADE: ADMINISTRATOR OF DEAN: 1653–60

Major John Wade, at one time of Gloucester and later residing at Littledean, was administrator of the Forest of Dean for The Commonwealth from August 1653 to April 1660.

In the absence of easily accessible information it must be assumed that Wade rose entirely with the Civil Wars (1642–7) having played a noticeable role on the side of the Parliamentarians. It is possible that he was of a local family. In 1633 a Thomas Wade, Gent., held profits of land in Mitcheldean;[1] he may have been the father of John Wade. The latter appears to have arrived in Gloucester in 1648 (five years after its siege) in Sir William Constable's regiment, who had followed Col. Thomas Morgan as governor. Constable had come from Yorkshire. His second in command was Lt. Col. Grimes, and after Grimes's apparent disgrace in 1649, Wade took his place as major, and at least from 1650, seven years after the siege of Gloucester (1643), he became deputy governor.[2] Although working in Dean as one of the four 'Preservators' (appointed on 16 January 1650) and as sole administrator there from 27 April 1953 (residing in Littledean), Wade retained his commission in the regiment and continued to undertake service connected with it. In 1650 he dealt with regimental matters in Gloucester;[3] and in May 1651 was concerned with raising 400 foot soldiers in Gloucestershire for Ireland. In that year (1651)[4] Wade was directed by the Council of State to distribute £7 among the 14 companies of foot in Gloucester 'for their extraordinary labour in the fortification of the garrison for two days and two nights past'. In 1651 Wade among others was given power and instructions by the Council of State to preserve the peace.[5] It is possible that he was the John Wade, Gent., Gloucester City, who in 1651 was connected with properties relating to 'Cockshoote in or near Blythes Bayley' in the east of the Forest of Dean.[6] On 9 February 1653[7] the Council of State referred to a letter from Major Wade to the Lord General, with papers relating to the late garrison of Gloucester. On 23 April 1653[8] Wade informed the Navy Office: 'On your warrant to impress 200 seamen in cos. Gloucester and Worcester; I have made some progress, and send a list of men pressed; send some printed tickets and the money.' Wade also had some connection with troops sent from the county to Ireland;[9] he played some part in

---

[1] *I.P.M.*, Thomas Pyrke, Esq. of Mitcheldean, taken 29 April 1633. Thomas Wade was Thomas Pyrke's grandfather and guardian.

[2] Gloucester chamberlains' accounts for 1650, Glos. R.O., GBR F.4/5, f. 406; CSPD, Commonwealth, Vol. III, p. 110, 21 March 1651, p. 100; Howes, Russell, 'Gloucestershire Roundheads', *Gloucestershire History*, No. 7, 1993, pp. 4–7.

[3] SP18/153(15), p. 37, 28 Nov. 1655; Howes, Russell, *op. cit.*

[4] *Bibliotheca Gloucestrensis*, p. cxxi.

[5] Ibid. pp. 389, 398.

[6] Glos. R.O. D2957, pp. 1112, 215 (56).

[7] SP18/33, p. 156.

[8] Ibid. /35, p. 292.

[9] Ibid. /1.75/448, p. 451; SP28/229, 20 May 1651 (box of loose papers).

sending wheat and oats to Ireland via the Treasurer-at-War. In September 1653 Wade was in charge of partly dismantling the fortifications in Gloucester;[10] he had the guardhouse removed from the Wheatmarket in Southgate Street.

Following renewed Royalist threats to Gloucester during 1653–4, in 1654 Wade may have been involved in the 'readying of 400 men for the defence of the city but fortunately the crisis passed.'[11] On 24 March 1654[12] Cromwell wrote to Wade, Major Creed, the Mayor and Aldermen of the City of Gloucester expressing his thanks for their 'zeal and forwardness and their assistance'. By 1654 Wade was a Justice of the Peace for Gloucestershire.[13] On 14 March 1655[14] he wrote from Gloucester to General John Disbrowe:[15]

> Sir, I had a meeting yesterday with Captain Nicholas concerning the raising of forces for the defence of our county, to which I answered him, that there is no doubt, if authority be given for that purpose, and provision made for accommodation, force will be speedily raised; and therefore if you think it will be with any advantage to the public, no doubt by God's assistance, men of a sufficient number shall be forthwith raised for the safe keeping of Gloucester, whereby the horse here may be spared for service abroad. I came to Gloucester this day, being sent for by the mayor and aldermen of the city, and am a putting the well affected of the city in a posture of defence, which at present is four hundred men. I do think to go into the Forest [of Dean] again tomorrow, to put things in the best condition possible. What you conceive me fit or capable to do in order to the raising of men, let me have command and authority, and there shall be no want in me. I conceive it were not amiss, if there were a forbearance of raising of those for the present, money being a precious thing with you, and raw iron a vendible commodity. Your forge [at Whitecroft] is in work. Thus, desiring your answer to what you shall think fit, I rest your faithful servant, JOHN WADE.

Wade for a short period appears to have had some connection with the governorship of the Isle of Man. On 29 December 1655[16] Major-General Disbrowe wrote from Bristol to Oliver Cromwell:

> I understand that Lt. Col. Briscoe was to be made colonel, and Major Wade lieutenant colonel; but instead I hear that Major Wade is like to be put out of his government of the Isle of Man. I beg that nothing may be done to prejudice of poor Wade, who is a faithful person, and exceeding useful to your highness and the commonwealth in the county of Gloucester and the Forest of Dean.

The Manx Museum and National Trust at Douglas have been unable to locate any records relating to Major Wade apart from a minor entry in J.J. Kneen's *The Personal Names of the Isle of Man*, 1937, Oxford, p. 215, which refers to a Major Wade being

---

[10] Gloucester City Council minutes, 28 Sept. 1653, Glos. R.O., GBR B3/2, p. 753; Gloucester chamberlains' accounts, Glos. R.O., GBR F.4/6, f. 27.

[11] Atkin, M. and Laughlin, W., *Gloucester and the Civil War*, 1992, p. 130.

[12] *Bibliotheca Gloucestrensis*, p. 412.

[13] Bodleian, Rawl. MSS A261, f.29; Hart, *The Free Miners*, p. 201.

[14] *Bibliotheca Gloucestrensis*, Appendix, p. 414, being copy of Thurloe State Papers, III, p. 239.

[15] Major-Gen. Disbrowe [Desborough] on 24 April 1654 was appointed by Richard Cromwell constable of St Briavels Castle and keeper of the Forest of Dean, [Glouc. Liby., MS L.F.1.1, pp. 16–17; Bodleian Rawl. MS A328, pp. 31–2]. In 1656, he attended the Justice Seat in Eyre for the Forest of Dean (see Section VII).

[16] Thurloe State Papers, IV., pp. 359–60.

appointed 'Gov. of Mann' in 1653. This entry is contrary to all other references concerning the governorship of the Island: from 1652 to 1659 the governor was Mathew Cadwell, followed in 1659 by William Christian, and then by James Chaloner who continued under the restored rule of the Stanleys after the period of English suzerainty, 1652–60, had been overthrown. The issue is complicated by the fact that between October 1652 and January 1654 the then Lord of Mann, Lord Fairfax, appointed commissioners in place of governors, believing that the latter had become obsolete and that the former could serve just as well. In 1654 he was persuaded otherwise. It is therefore probable that Major Wade acted as commissioner, not governor, probably in a purely military capacity ('troubleshooter') and only for a very short period of time; hence his omission from the records.[17] Under an Act of 9 June 1657[18] he was named as one of the commissioners for the monthly assessment in Gloucestershire. On 23 June 1659[19] Wade was given a warrant from the Council of State for payment to him of £200 'for the militia troop under him in co. Gloucester on account for payment while in actual service.' On 22 July 1659[20] he was given a warrant of £75.16s. 'for his troop in co. Gloucester, for 28 days.' On the same day[21] he received a warrant of £314.13s. 'for the troops in the Isle of Man (from their arrears of £800)'. On 29 September 1659 he is referred to as Lt. Col. John Wade.[22]

It is unknown where John resided before, during and after he was appointed in 1650 as one of the four 'Preservators' of the Forest of Dean; nor after he was appointed in 1653 as sole administrator of the Forest. In any case, as a serving commissioned major, he was probably moving around. It is generally assumed that he resided at Dean Hall in Littledean: most of his extant letters were written from that village. After General Massey's Parliamentary troops attacked and took the Hall in May 1644,[23] the Roundheads or sympathizers with their cause may have occupied it from time to time. Wade himself may have occupied it during 1650 to 1657; certainly he occupied the Hall and other property in Littledean by 1659[24] –

[17] Following are comments which either refer to John Wade (of the Forest of Dean) or to some other (?) relative of the same name: (i) Aylmer, G.E. (ed.), *The Interregnum: The Quest for Settlement 1646–1660*, 1972, p. 180, mentions John Wade 1653–58 as being a military man loyal to the regime. (ii) Firth, Sir Charles, *The Regimental History of Cromwell's Army*, 1940, pp. 387, 557: Col. Horton (in Wales) praises the services of Major Wade and others, in his account of the victory at St. Fagans 8 May 1648; also mentions Wade's promotion to Lt. Col. in Mitchell's new regiment, July 1659. (iii) MacDonald-Wigfield, W., *The Monmouth Rebellion*, 1980, pp. 26, 27, 36, 38, 42, 44, 49, 50, 54, 56, 62, 63, 67, gives extensive references to Nathaniel Wade, mentioning his birth in 1646, the third son of the Ironside Major later Major-General John Wade; and contains the complete text of Nathaniel Wade's *Narrative*, 1685, pp. 76, 78, 119, 122, 123, 149, 171, dictated whilst a wounded prisoner. (iv) Ashley, Maurice, *Cromwell's Generals*, 1954, does not mention Major Wade.

[18] C.H. Firth and R.S. Rait, *Acts and Ordinances of the Interregnum*, 1642–60, ii, p. 1114.

[19] SP Interregnum, 107(20), p. 588.

[20] Ibid. (54), p. 578.

[21] Ibid. (51), p. 578.

[22] SP18/204(36), p. 216.

[23] During the Civil Wars, Dean Hall was attacked by a party of Massey's Horse on 7 May 1644, which captured 20 soldiers in the guardhouse. Inside the Hall were a few private soldiers and Colonel Congreve (governor of the Royalist garrison at Newnham) and Captain Wigmore (in charge of the garrison). They surrendered, but one of the soldiers fired and killed a Parliamentarian trooper. In the skirmish which followed, all the Royalists were killed including Congreve and Wigmore who died inside the Hall. [Nicholls, *Personalities . . .*, p. 97; information from D. Macer-Wright; Atkin, M. and Laughlin, W., *Gloucester and the Civil War*, 1992, p. 124.]

[24] "The house in which John Wade dwelleth" [Glos. R.O., D36, Colchester Documents].

two years after he purchased them for £400 from the owner, Charles Bridgman of Poultons Court[25] in the parish of Awre (*infra*). In 1662 Wade, two years after his resignation, resold to Bridgman for £600 (*infra*).

During the Civil Wars (1642–7) administration in the Forest of Dean was erratic, and the inhabitants and ironmasters suffered by the supporters of both Royalists and Parliamentarians. The inhabitants had no particular tendency to national causes either way and most local people probably tried to affect a neutrality for as long as possible. From the beginning, Charles I had in his Forest loyal and influential supporters in Sir John Winter of Lydney, Sir Baynham Throckmorton of Clearwell and Benedict Hall of Highmeadow, all of whom made use of many of the local furnaces and forges, and took trees for charcoaling to supply fuel.

However, with the Parliamentarians' success, rewards came to the faithful or at least to their friends. In 1644 the ironworks at Lydney, Whitecroft, Parkend and Cannop, all on the Newarne stream, were either wholly or partly destroyed.[26] Winter lost most of his property, and his ironworks at Lydney were leased in 1644 to his main opponent, Major-General Edward Massey (the successful defender of Gloucester) whose assign was Captain John Gifford. Lt.-Col. Robert Kyrle held the Bishopswood furnace. In the same year, Capt. John Braine of Littledean seized the Cannop furnace and the Lydbrook ironworks from William Dunning, assigning the latter to Thomas Pury and Griffantius Phillips. Braine, in partnership with Col. Robert Kyrle, also in 1645 had the furnace at Redbrook as well as that at Rodmore. Braine was also working Winter's furnace at Guns Mill, the king's forge at Bradley, and another forge at Lydbrook which had been leased by George Vaughan of Courtfield to Thomas Dunning. Massey along with his assignees and other Parliamentarians, enriched themselves at the expense of Dean's ironworks and trees; the quantity of the latter taken for charcoaling was immense.[27]

In 1649 Wade was on the jury of inquisition regarding the ironworks and timber.[28] At the beginning of The Commonwealth (1649) much of the economy of Dean was still based on the iron industry – mining, smelting and forging. Hundreds of the inhabitants (many were mere 'cabiners') eked out a livelihood by cutting, cording, charcoal-burning and carrying; also busy were the miners and carriers of iron-ore. The effect on the woodland cover was so disastrous that on 16 January 1650 Parliament ordered the four 'Preservators' to demolish the ironworks and to

---

[25] The history of the Bridgmans and Poulton Court has not been researched. However, it appears that the Court was held *c.* 1558 by William Bridgman [Sir R. Atkyns, *The Ancient and Present State of Gloucestershire*, 1712, Vol. I, p. 237; Samuel Rudder, *A New History of Gloucestershire*, 1779, p. 248] . At the Forest of Dean Eyre of 1634, Charles Bridgman [I] claimed rights of common in the Forest for his manor of Poulton Court and for his properties in Littledean; also for perquisites as one of the verderers of the Forest (an office he held until at least 1637). His will is dated 1639 [Glos. R.O. Wills Collection]. In 1642 Charles Bridgman [I or II] held lands in Littledean [Glos. R.O. D36, Colchester Documents M73]. In 1657, Charles Bridgman [III] sold Dean Hall and other properties in Littledean to John Wade for £400 [Glos. R.O., D4431, Phillipps Deeds No. 29116]; and repurchased them from Wade in 1662 for £600 [Glos. R.O., D4431, Phillipps Deeds Box 15/1]. The ancient Poulton Court as well as its chapel were demolished, but the water-filled moat remains. The present Poulton Court Farm House built nearby has an ancient stone edifice above the northwest doorway containing the Bridgman coat of arms and the initials 'C.B.'. The house, renovated during this century, is owned by the Crown Commissioners and occupied by the MacFarlane family.

[26] SP23/136; Hart, *The Industrial History of Dean*, p. 17.

[27] Hart, *Royal Forest*, pp. 131–3.

[28] SP25/63, p. 626, 16 Jan. 1650.

stay the felling and sale of trees unless directed.[29] How far this order was obeyed is not known; there is no record of ironmaking in Dean from 1650 to 1652, nor during most of 1653.[30]

## WADE'S ADMINISTRATION IN DEAN (I)

When Major John Wade was appointed by the Council of State on 16 January 1650 as one of their four 'Preservators' of the Forest of Dean, he merely joined a group of men of some slight local prominence, entrusted with the administration of the Forest and now ordered to demolish the ironworks because of their adverse effect on the trees.[31] He appears to have given satisfaction and shown initiative, because on 27 August 1653 the Council appointed him as sole administrator (under the Admiralty Commissioners) of the Forest of Dean.[32] Wade may partly have owed his appointment to the recommendation of his friend Colonel John Clerke, one of the Admiralty Commissioners.[33]

One of Wade's earliest actions in 1653 was to clear from the Forest countless goats and almost 400 cabins.[34]

He proved to be a capable and efficient administrator. In brief, he acted as supervisor of ironworks, timber merchant (especially as regards ship-timber) and silvicultural manager: he will be remembered as the person responsible in Dean for the first sowing and planting of forest trees. Learning about technique and organization as he went along, Wade turned the ironworks and the Forest into a sensibly complementary enterprise. Success in the iron industry, the encouragement of shipbuilding locally, and supplying immense quantities of timber to the dockyards, as well as attempting to 'replant' the Forest, enabled him to achieve the rational integration of the Forest as an economic asset despite many difficulties. Wade was no grammarian: his letters to the Admiralty and others consist of one breathless sequence, not always brief but generally to the point; he was no bookkeeper either.[35]

Wade was to resuscitate the ironworks, using only dotard trees and saving any timber fit for the Navy.[36] He was soon ordered to manufacture iron shot and ordnance, and for that purpose to erect a new furnace at Parkend and to repair that at Lydney lately belonging to Winter. He could draw upon a sum of £1,000. Within a fortnight Wade drafted his general proposals for the administration of the Forest: all trees were to be inspected by ship carpenters as soon as felled and any of timber quality in them were to be squared (axed) on site, so that the reject (offal) could be charcoaled; parts of the Forest were to be 'encoppiced' for future supplies of wood and timber.

[29] SP25/63, p. 139; SP18/5, p. 482.

[30] Ibid. p. 140.

[31] SP18/5, p. 482; Hart, *Royal Forest*, p. 139; SP25/63, p. 525; /87, p. 110; E178/6080, Pt I, Parliamentary Order, 1645–7; L.R.R.O. 5/7A.

[32] SP18/39, p. 107; Hart, *Royal Forest*, p. 140.

[33] SP18/66/38, 16 Feb. 1654; a letter from Wade to Clerke begins 'My Dear Friend' and appeals for his special support in a matter thought by Wade of public importance.

[34] Br. Liby., Harl. MS 6839, ff. 332, 337; *Cal. SP29*, Addenda, 1662, p. 142; Hart, *Royal Forest*, Appendix XI.

[35] Hammersley, G., *pers. comm.*

[36] SP18/38, p. 14.

At least one of Winter's furnaces at Lydney would have needed extensive repairs, if not rebuilding.[37] The new furnace at Parkend, probably of the same dimensions as that of 1612–13, stood on the Newerne stream a short distance downstream but still east of (the much later) York Lodge. Wade planned the supply of a greater volume of water 'to move the bellows', and averred that his new furnace 'will be one of the best watered furnaces in this nation'.[38] Costing £750 to build,[39] it was completed by 19 January 1654 and began to operate on 28 February.[40] Wade reported that the Lydney and Parkend furnaces were capable of casting 50 or 60 tons of pig-iron a week at £3 a ton, and 20 tons of shot at £4 a ton. Work began on 13 September 1653. He drew £400 on 1 December 1653.[41] (In just under six years Parkend furnace cast 4,450 tons of pig-iron or almost 18 tons 5 cwt a week, operating for 78 per cent of the time available between its first blowing and the eventual handover by Wade in 1660.) Wade probably had to learn most of the job from scratch – though his military service would have been of some use to him.

In 1654 Wade was given authority to erect lower down the same Newerne stream at Whitecroft a forge 'to convert the raw iron thrown in the making of shot, or it will be wasted or sold at a loss'.[42] In 1653 he had informed the Admiralty that the cost of the forge would be £100, not £200, 'and the ordnance can be bored here'. The forge began to work on 10 March 1655; instead of the estimated £100 to £200 it cost the immense sum of £835.[43] (In just over five years of working it produced 720 tons of bar iron plus a quantity of specialized naval forgings. Even an expensive forge could pay for its building.)

Wade pointed out that two furnaces could make little more than 20 tons of shot per week whereas their capacity for pig-iron might be in the region of 50 or 60 tons, and that the production of plain pig-iron was an inevitable incident in the casting of shot. (Evidently he had learnt much since being one of the 'Preservators' from 1650). Thus he requested authority to build a forge (at Whitecroft) to fine pig-iron into bar, mainly using the small charcoal or 'brazes' (breeze) which could not be used in smelting. Finally he proposed that a ship be built locally (alongside the Severn) from Dean timber, equipped with Dean ironwork and ballasted, for cheaper transport, with the shot cast in the Forest.[44] His general programme was slowly realized although the Admiralty Commissioners needed some persuasion, supplied by Wade in successive letters, until he gained approval.

Apparently Wade had offered to get the first furnace repaired by 1 November 1653; by 15 September he decided that Winter's old furnace (at Maple Hill, north of Lydney) would be less convenient than the new one begun on or near the old Parkend furnace, despite the delay entailed.[45] On 5 December he wrote that the new furnace would be finished by the end of the month; but it was 19 January 1654 before it was pre-heated and 28 February when it began to cast iron.[46] Meanwhile Wade had convinced the Admiralty that his new furnace at Parkend 'will be one of

[37] SP25/70, pp. 260, 288–90; SP18/40 p. 61, 73; E178/6080, Pt. I, mm. 18d–19d.
[38] SP Interregnum 62, f. 67.
[39] SP18/40 p. 73; /66 p. 38, i and ii; /130 p. 102.
[40] Ibid. /78. p. 165; /130 p. 102.
[41] Ibid. /42, p. 279.
[42] Hart, *The Industrial History of Dean*, p. 19; SP18/62 p. 93.
[43] SP18/62 p. 93; /130 p. 102.
[44] Ibid. /40/61, 10 Sept. 1653.
[45] Ibid. /40/73, 15 Sept. 1653.
[46] Ibid. /62/34, 5 Dec. 1653; /78/165; /130/120, p. 20.

the best watered furnaces in this nation', large enough to use up all the waste wood in Dean, and would produce as much shot as they could reasonably hope for. By 10 December 1653 he was given permission to install one furnace only, as he had always intended.

By 24 January 1654 Wade had 'lit the furnaces' and needed money, 'being much importuned by the poor people'.[47] (For six years his works supplied much ironwork for ships built on the Severn, and immense quantities of pig-iron, shot, spikes, hoops, bars and bolts to naval dockyard stores. An improvement in his manufacture was the admixture of scrap-iron to the charge; the proportion, however, was fairly small compared with the cinder added, e.g. 16 tons 4 cwt of scrap-iron and 701 tons of cinders to make 701 tons of pig-iron in 1656–7.)[48]

Wade continued reminding the Admiralty of the need for a forge. By 21 September 1653 he had obtained an estimate for it, at £100 (which sum was to turn out to be much below its costs).[49] On 13 December he obtained permission to build one. (It was not built until after September 1654, and began to operate on 10 March 1655.)[50]

All the while Wade agitated for ship carpenters to co-operate with his woodcutters so as to save naval timber.[51]

By the end of January 1654 Wade had used up his first £1,000, and had to ask for more money.[52] He thought that he would need about £50 per week to cast 15 tons of shot and 5 tons of pig-iron.[53] It took almost two months, in which Wade had to remind the Admiralty of the poverty of his employees (miners, woodcutters, charcoalburners, smelters, forgers, etc.) who could not live on credit, before he was paid another £1,000 through the navy agent at Bristol.[54] About the same time Wade began to enquire whether he should cast guns, but was not authorized until August 1654.[55] (Even so, there is no evidence of any gunfounding in Dean under the Commonwealth and the Protectorate.)

By August 1654 Wade was again short of money; by the end of October he suggested that he had cast enough shot for a while and that he would now prefer to sell pig-iron in order to generate some funds.[56] This was agreed to, and was proceeded with by 1655.[57] Meanwhile, some of the shot sent to the Portsmouth naval yards was not fully satisfactory.[58]

Gradually during 1655–6 production of pig-iron for sale replaced shot as the principal product; and the state ironworks made mainly commercial iron, either for sale as pig or as bar.[59] In November 1655 the iron tested by a naval purveyor in Dean for its use in bolts, hoops, spikes, crows and other general naval iron work,

[47] SP18/42, p. 565.
[48] Ibid. /62, f. 157B.
[49] Ibid. /401/103.
[50] Ibid. /130/102, pp. 9, 20.
[51] Ibid. /62/34, 5 Dec. 1653; /62/93, 13 Dec. 1653.
[52] Ibid. /78/165, 24 Jan. 1654.
[53] Ibid. /78/21, 6 Feb. 1654.
[54] Ibid. /80/55, 15 March 1654; /68/13, 20 March 1654.
[55] Ibid. /68/13; /87/77, 26 Aug. 1654.
[56] Ibid. /89/64, 21 Oct. 1654.
[57] Ibid. /106/120, 31 March 1655; /130/102, pp. 4, 6, 8, 20, 21.
[58] Ibid. /111/71, 16 July 1655.
[59] Ibid. /130/102, p. 20.

was found satisfactory.[60] Henceforth manufactured wrought iron was supplied to the naval yards from the Forest.[61]

As to shiptimber from Dean, several reminders from Wade were needed before the Admiralty Commissioners would arrange to organize its collection.[62] A purveyor of naval timber (Aldridge) was at last instructed on 2 December and formally appointed on 5 December 1654, when he was equipped with £450.[63] Slowly the unprecedented organization of a regular supply of naval timber from Dean got under way: but by 13 September 1655 only 100 tons of timber and 800 treenails had been put on board for Chatham.[64] Almost another year elapsed before the Council of State at last approved a recommendation from the Admiralty Commissioners to build two fifth-rate frigates near Dean with local timber and ironwork, and another month until a shipwright, Daniel Furzer, was appointed on 13 August 1656 to build the first of them.[65] Thus it had taken almost three years for Wade's first report to be wholly implemented.[66]

The shipwright Furzer had from the start been placed under Wade's authority;[67] in effect the timber purveyor Aldridge also acknowledged it, although both their instructions came sometimes directly from the Admiralty. But as the ship was being built, Furzer and Aldridge began to compete for the same timber and wood, also for the same manpower, even to the point of bidding against each other.[68] Wade, asked for his advice, suggested that Furzer should do both jobs;[69] Aldridge was recalled.[70] The work of both Furzer and Aldridge are detailed elsewhere.[71]

Thus by 30 May 1657 Dean was at last properly organized to use its resources to the full and to maintain it at its most productive. The ironworks did not merely supply some of the material needed for the ship built at Lydney but also helped to finance both it and the timber, treenails and ironwork sent to the naval yards.

Despite the delay over naval timber supplies and shipbuilding, it was evident that the state, unlike private landowners, was able, if it so wished, to regulate its exploitation of woodlands to balance all interests, short and long; therefore the achievement in Dean remained notable, even if it was completed very slowly.[72]

In 1656[73] Wade was helping to prepare for a Justice Seat in Eyre for Dean. At the (uncompleted) swanimote held at Mitcheldean on 9 June and the eyre on 26 August,[74] Wade's name occasionally appears as presenter of some offenders. Also recorded are some of his connections with the ironworks, for example, during 1653–6 his use of cinders for his 'White Meade furnace'; also the following information:

[60] SP18/117/69, 9 Nov. 1655.
[61] Ibid. /138/62, 9–25 April 1656.
[62] Ibid. /40/61, 10 Sept. 1653; /40/103, 21 Sept. 1653; /90/125, 23 Nov. 1654.
[63] Ibid. /91/8; /117/154.
[64] Ibid. /113/135, 13 Sept. 1655.
[65] SP25/77, p. 242, 10 July 1656; SP18/143/123.
[66] SP18/40/103.
[67] Ibid. /143/123.
[68] Ibid. /166/115, 15 May 1657.
[69] Ibid. /166/70; /167/6, 9 and 16 May 1657.
[70] Ibid. /167/94.
[71] Hart, *Royal Forest*, pp. 142–6.
[72] Hammersley, G., *pers. comm.*
[73] SP18 /143/28, p. 399, 4 Aug. 1656.
[74] Glos. R.O., D2026 Bond Papers, X.14.

There has been cut within the space of three years last past within his Highness's wast soil of the Forest of Dean by the appointment of Major John Wade, 210 tons of timber, which has been spent in building the furnaces and one forge, and the housings and buildings thereunto belonging which were likewise built by the appointment of the said Major Wade to the use of the Common Wealth. Also there has been cut and corded within the space of three years last past by the appointment of Major John Wade for the use of the said ironworks:

|  | Short cords |
|---|---|
| Complement wood | 4,210 |
| Birch and holly wood | 340 |
| Stubbs, bottomes and logs | 8,300 |
| Offal of timber | 1,550 |
| Stoggall beeches | 8,937 |
| Stoggall oaks and dead trees | 1,100 |
|  | 24,437 |

About the same time (1656), Wade was the sole signatory of a petition to Parliament of the gentry, freeholders and other inhabitants within the Forest of Dean, 'whose ancestors for some hundreds of years have enjoyed many rights and liberties there', for Oliver Cromwell to be appointed Constable of the Forest.[75]

In 1655 Wade informed the Admiralty that if sufficient shot had been made, he wished to 'turn the furnaces so as to cast pig-iron'.[76]

Wade, though occupied with ironmaking, was informing the Admiralty of other matters. On 21 September 1653 he reported that he had persuaded a Bristol person of the advantage of building a ship 'in the Forest': the waste wood could be charcoaled and the woodwork and ironwork would be cheaper and better.[77] The same month he informed the Admiralty:[78] 'A settlement of the Government of the Forest is of no small moment for its preservation, as hundreds live upon the spoil thereof.' By March 1654[79] the situation was no better: 'The spoil carried on daily in the Forest makes my blood boil'. The Admiralty, though instructed by the Council of State 21 February[80] to consider 'fit powers and instructions for better preservation of Dean's timber' seems only to have assigned Commander Peter Pett to visit the Forest regarding the making of 'second-rate ships'.[81] The Council told Wade[82] to fence Whitemead Park and to carry out instructions sent by Oliver Cromwell 'to enclose the common woods and to improve the Forest for the public service'.[83]

In May 1654 Wade was equipped with the ancient offices of 'gaveller (of mines), riding forester and aleconner' in the Forest, thus combining in his person the old and the new dispensations.[84] By the end of 1656 he was a verderer.[85] After his

[75] Glos. R.O., D2026 Bond Papers, X.17.
[76] SP18/98, p. 444.
[77] Ibid. p. 161.
[78] Ibid. /40, p. 151.
[79] Ibid. /61, p. 41.
[80] Ibid. /46, p. 410.
[81] Ibid. p. 519.
[82] Ibid. /77, p. 403, 30 Nov. 1654.
[83] Ibid. /46, p. 520; Bodleian, Rawl. MSS A261, f. 29.
[84] Bodleian, Rawl. MSS A328, pp. 31–2.
[85] SP18/130/102, p. 23.

administration had been carefully examined in 1656, his complete control of the Forest under the Admiralty Commission was explicitly re-affirmed.[86]

Large supplies of timber for naval shipbuilding were arranged under Wade by Augustus Aldridge residing in Lydney, from late 1653 to 1656,[87] but on 16 April 1656, Wade wrote:[88] 'The purveying of timber does not go well for want of money to pay the workmen.' On 4 August 1656[89] the Admiralty decided to build a fifth-rate frigate on the Severn at Lydney Pill, and Daniel Furzer, master shipwright, was appointed to supervise the work.[90] Wade was to supply money, timber, and ironwork. In 1657 Wade complained[91] against Aldridge's 'commission to fell and convert 400 tons of naval timber', and 'hoped to see no more orders'; 'the clashing of one against the other was destructive both to the State and to the workmen'. Both Furzer and Aldridge were honest as far as Wade knew, but he suggested that 'one should be chosen to do both, and the other not to meddle'. He could not say which of the two was the more fit to be retained;[92] Aldridge 'had carried himself like an honest man', while Furzer 'also carried himself very honestly and carefully in husbanding all things, and was young and able of body, and an able artist'. The commissioners were advised[93] that in future instead of delivering to Lydney Pill, where trows had to be sent up by the ships which lie at Hunger Road [near Avonmouth, Bristol] delivery should be made to Shirehampton on the [Bristol] Avon and a rebate of freight obtained. Wade had a '20 ton trow' built by Furzer 'out of waste'.

In January 1658[94] Wade informed the Navy Commissioners that Furzer had done good work, but needed money to pay his workmen 'as he did not know where to show his face'. On 8 July Wade welcomed the Admiralty's order for the building of 'another fourth or fifth-rate frigate', as 1,500 tons of timber in the Forest and in the yard by the waterside were 'spoiling through sun and wind'. He pointed out that to make iron without building ships, or vice versa, was a loss, 'as what is to become of the offal timber?' The selling of 100 or 200 tons 'would surfeit the whole country and yield but little money'. He was dismayed that 'there is not one tree in a thousand in the Forest which is not decaying'.

On 8 April 1659 Wade gave the Admiralty an account of 1,458 tons of timber and plank and 123,709 treenails, part sent from Lydney Pill to the naval stores and part used in repairing and building frigates from 27 September 1656 to 28 March 1659. There were 700 or 800 tons of timber still lying in the Forest awaiting carriage.[95]

In May 1659[96] Furzer the shipwright was having trouble with his workmen and carriers. Wade would do all he could 'but his hands and heart are full enough with the continued and frequent riots and insolences of an unruly generation of men, some of whom vented forth insufferable and disdainful language, and in action have not spared the Lea Bayley, the nursery of the Forest, but broken down the gates and turned in their cattle'.

[86] SP25/77, pp. 485–7, 16 Nov. 1656.
[87] Hart, *Royal Forest*, pp. 142–3.
[88] SP18/138, p. 534.
[89] Ibid. /143, p. 399.
[90] Ibid. p. 408.
[91] Ibid. /166, p. 562.
[92] Ibid. /167, p. 575.
[93] Ibid. /96, p. 56; ibid. /156, p. 56, 6 Aug. 1657.
[94] Ibid. /175, p. 516.
[95] Ibid. /210, p. 552.
[96] Ibid. /203, p. 361.

## WADE'S ADMINISTRATION IN DEAN (II)

Meanwhile in 1655 Wade's ironworks were shipping to naval stores pig-iron, spikes, hoops, bars and bolts.[97] On 26 June 1656[98] the Council of State ordered an audit of Wade's accounts and posed the questions what allowance should be paid to him for his services and 'should he be continued?' His accounts from 13 September 1653 to 2 August 1656[99] provide details of the payments and receipts of ironmaking, and give other information. Wade had expended £214.4s.5d. in wages 'for ditching and carrying of stones to make walls for enclosing about 6000 acres of coppices, and gates for the same'. He had also paid £1.6s. to six keepers,[100] 'for their extraordinary pains in watching and apprehending offenders', £5 each to three verderers, William Coke, Richard Machen, and himself, for a half year's fee to 25 March 1656, other officers 'by Letters Patent', £6.6s.8d. to each of twelve regarders[101] and £11.5s. to Humphrey Plant, 'clerk of the wood' for three-quarters of a year's wage to 15 July 1656. His receipts included £37.6s.5d. for timber for cardboard, £95 for small charcoal ('brazes'), £7.10s. for 7½ loads of bark, and 30s. for each of four cords of beech. He had done commendable work, and more was to follow.

On 11 November 1656[102] the Council of State confirmed Wade's appointment at £200 per annum to take charge and oversight of the woods, timber, and ironworks in Dean 'for their best preservation and improvement for the public service'. His instructions were 'to preserve the timber from waste and embezzlement, and improve its growth'; the ironworks were to use only wood unfit for the Navy. The pay of regarders and 'other officers in Dean' was approved by the Council 8 December 1657.[103] Wade was allowed £500 'for his pains for three years'.[104] His accounts were again audited in November 1657.[105] He supplied an account of 'shot, hoops, bolts, spikes, etc.', sent for the Navy to London and Bristol,[106] and requested money: £300 was due 'to all sorts of workmen'.[107] Since his last account about 850 tons of timber had been shipped,[108] and by 28 March 1659 1,158 tons had been used on building and repairing ships.[109]

On 15 April 1657 Wade purchased from Charles Bridgman [III] of Poultons Court in the Parish of Awre, the following property for £400; in effect it was Dean Hall in Littledean – the house and property which Wade had been occupying for some time:[110]

---

[97] SP18/149, p. 409; /117, p. 551.

[98] Ibid. /128, No. 20.

[99] Ibid. /130, pp. 102, 155; ibid. /130, pp. 155/6, 11 Nov. 1656.

[100] John Addams, Simon Margretts, Henry Chain, Richard Jelfe, Edward Roberts, and Thomas Barnst. Their salary was £10 annually.

[101] William Jones, George Bond, Richard Birkin, Edward Sargant, Thomas Hawkins, William Aylberton, Thomas Dunning, Thomas Pyrke, John Witt, Richard Hooper, John Browne, and George Barke.

[102] SP18/130, pp. 155–6.

[103] Ibid. /158, p. 206.

[104] Ibid. p. 172.

[105] Ibid. /157, p. 175.

[106] Ibid. /202, p. 328.

[107] Ibid. /223, p. 540.

[108] Ibid. /244/38; E178/6080; Glos. R.O., D3921, Hart Collection Item 27.

[109] Ibid. /210, p. 552.

[110] Glos. R.O., D4431, Phillipps Deeds, No. 29116.

Plate VI. Littledean Hall, during 1653–60 the residence of Major John Wade, administrator of the Forest of Dean for Cromwell and the Commonwealth. (Photograph by courtesy of Donald Macer-Wright, the present owner of the improved Hall, 1995)

"All that messuage or dwelling house [not named] with the appurtenances situate and being in Little Deane, and now in the tenure, holden or occupation of Katherine Bridgman the relict of Charles Bridgman deceased, grandfather unto Charles Bridgman [III] party to these presents, his assigns or assignees, undertenant or undertenants, and all houses, edifices, buildings, barns, stables, outhouses, courts, yards, backsides, gardens and courtyards, to the said messuage or dwelling house belonging to or in anywise appertaining or therewith used, or occupied, as part, parcel, or member thereof or belonging thereunto.

And also all that parcel of land, meadow or pasture called and known by the name of Deanes Hill meadow, set, lying and being in Little Deane aforesaid, between Paynes Lane on the south part, Dukes Meadow on the west part, Privie Lane on the north part, and the lane leading from Little Deane toward Newnham on the east part.

And all that other parcel of land, meadow or pasture called by the name of Privie Croft lying in Little Deane aforesaid between the Skynnes meadow on the north part, Privie Lane on the south part, and other lands now in possession or occupation of the said Katherine Bridgman or her assigns on the other parts thereof.

And all those parcels of land, meadow or pasture called by the names of Conningree, Tymbrells Croft, and one other parcel of land called Goughes meadow, and one other parcel called Goodesland, and one acre at the south end of the Ryefield which said last premises lie in Little Deane aforesaid, between certain land there called Overmore, the highway leading from Little Deane toward Newnham, the Ryefield aforesaid and the Comon on all or most parts thereof, And also those two parcels of land, meadow or pasture called Athertons Hills lying likewise in Little Deane aforesaid, between the aforesaid parcel called Goodesland, the land late of James Heane, gent., deceased, the Chantrie land, the Ryfield, Bassell Field, and a way there heretofore leading to Goodesland, on all or most parts thereof; together with one piece of ground without the Cunnygree Wall and the garden and cottage wherein Thomas Gosling heretofore dwelt;

And all other lands, tenements and hereditaments of him the said Charles Bridgman [III] party to these presents which by the last will and testament of the said Charles Bridgman [I] the grandfather were given, or meant, mentioned of expressed thereby to be given; after the decease of Charles Bridgman eldest son of the said Charles the Grandfather, to the said Charles his son, party to these presents and his heirs for ever, all which premises now are in the tenure or occupation of the said Katherine Bridgman her assignee or assigns, undertenant or undertenants, or of John Wade party to these presents; And all ways, waters, comons, easements, freedoms and profits whatsoever to the said premises or any part or parcel thereof belonging or in anywise appertaining, together with the remayne and remaynder, reversion or reversions, and the inheritance of all and singular the premises."

There is no signature of Charles Bridgman [III] nor of John Wade; but there are five witnesses, one of whom is Thomas Wade: this is the first information found of Wade having a family. (In 1662 he resold the property to Bridgman.)

The final set of Wade's audited accounts is that for the period 15 September 1657 to 28 July 1660.[111] He had received £161 for timber sold in the Lea Bailey to makers of cardboard, saddletrees, and trenchers; also £28 for coopers' timber sold to Richard Bridge, William Glew, and William Hope, and £6.8s.5d for 13,600 laths.

[111] E178/6080/Pt. 1, m. 1–43. Copy in Glos. R.O., D3291, Hart Collection.

He had delivered 1,300 laths to the ironworks and 2,500 to Furzer for his house in the shipyard at Lydney. Sales of twenty-two loads of bark at 17s.6d. a load to William Hopton, Thomas Howby and John Saunders amounted to £19.1s.4d., of 411 loads and eight sacks of small charcoal to £492.12s.6d., and of 200 kinderkin staves[112] to 15s.

Wade had paid the keepers,[113] Richard Powell the bowbearer at £9.2s.6d. a year, William Callowe and Henry Rudge the two rangers at £15 a year, three verderers (he was one of them) at £10 a year, William Cross the beadle at £15 a year, and himself as administrator at £200 per annum. Other payments were £140 to Mr. James for two and a half years' rent of Whitemead Park, £40 (twenty years' purchase at £2) to widow Cowles for the free farm rent of the Snead and Kidnalls coppices, and £1,500 to Lord Mainard for Cannop Fellett (Kanopp Vealett).[114] Workers employed to make 21,700 laths in the Lea Bailey had been paid at 3s.4d. a thousand, and to make 1,340 kinderkin staves at 2s. a hundred. £3,067 had been advanced to Furzer for the building of one ship from 15 September 1657 to 26 April 1660. Cutting and cording 24,884 cords had cost £3,091, about 2s.6d. a cord, carrying £2,030, and charcoaling £492, large charcoal at £2.5s. a load and small at £1.2s.6d.

Workmen had been employed in ditching, 'quicking' (planting quicks) and 'pasading' (palisading) the new enclosures. For the 'New Coppice from Milkwall to Bream and thence to the Whitecroft forge, the Furnace, and Cannop (Kanopp) Wall', 1,160 perches had been paid for at 10d. and 18 perches at 6d. At Cannop Coppice, John Ward was paid 9d. a perch for 56½ perches he ditched, 'quicked' and 'pasaded'; also 1s.6d. for erecting a gate. For the enclosure of part of Whitemead Park 'from the brook at Symons house to the style at the New Bay', Walter Pritchett and Francis Paine were paid 7d. a perch for ditching and hedging 65½ perches. Stone-walling by Henry Monning, mason, and William Board, around Cannop Coppice had cost 1s. for each of 175 perches and 1s.6d. for each of 596 perches. Wade expended about £477 on enclosures.

For the first time in Dean, acorns and beech-mast were collected and sown. For collecting 16 bushels and 3 pecks of acorns 'to sow the several enclosed coppices and waste grounds' Wade paid 1s. a bushel, total 16s.9d.; and for 207 bushels of beech-mast for the same purpose 2s. a bushel, total £20.14s. Again for the first time seedling oaks and beech, gathered from the Lea Bailey, were planted. William Cross, the beadle, was paid 9d. a thousand for lifting 23,400 oak and beech seedlings and carrying them 'to the rest of the officers to plant the waste ground of the Forest and the New Coppice'. Presumably the sowing by dibbling or placing under a turf, as well as the planting, were done by the keepers; no separate sum was claimed by Wade for this work.

Wade's stock on 26 April 1660 included 240 loads of charcoal at 2s. a load, 100 loads of small charcoal, £1 a load, 26,550 laths, 10s. a thousand, 8,000 short cords, 5s. a cord, 3,400 'coopers' timber', £3.15s. a thousand, and 2,000 kinderkin staves,

---

[112] Probably barrel staves.

[113] Henry Cainsford, Philip Jones, John Adams, Richard Jelfe, Henry Cheyne, Simon Margretts, Edward Roberts, and John Merrett. These keepers were paid at the rate of 4s. and 5s. a week. Philip Jones was one of the keepers of the Hudnalls, near St Briavels.

[114] Ordered by the Council of State 20 Aug. 1657 (SP18/156(16), p. 73) and on 31 Dec. 1657 (ibid./ 158(14), p. 39).

not valued. Wade invested £131.16s.2d. in a coalmine (see Appendix) and expended £435.1s.6s. on coalmining. He paid £88.8s. to stock the Forest with deer for the Lord Protector (Cromwell). His accounts were certified as correct by Sir William Throckmorton and Sir Baynham Throckmorton.

Following the 1656 Justice Seat in Eyre (uncompleted),[115] on 9 June 1657 the Council passed an Act[116] to mitigate forest law in Dean, and to provide enclosures for the growth of timber. The Act granted many powers to freeholders, tenants, and other inhabitants; never before had they legally had such freedom in the management of their properties and the exercise of their privileges. The Lord Protector was empowered to enclose and encoppice up to one-third of Dean at any one time; enclosures were to be thrown open within twelve years. But the Act did not bring full order into the Forest. Abuses, disorders, riots and destruction of enclosures continued; the enclosing was opposed. Wade begged the Admiralty Commissioners 8 April 1659:[117]

> It were well if a justice in Eyre were resolved upon and empowered, the time approaching for the keeping of it [three years], and never more needed, when horrid offenders can so impudently appear with petitions in their hands, calling that to be right which is against all law and justice. One of those petitioners has come down, making great brags of what great favour their petitions receive, and that all the inclosures shall be put open, and the whole rabble put in their cattle of all sorts; there are boasts of what great promises some members of the House have made, that all things shall be granted that is desired; out of the encouragement they receive by letters from London, they speak strangely, and act worse, for the Forest, in the chief coppices, has been set on fire in 20 places. The chief of these petitioners is named Stallard, and is now in London; he was heretofore a Cavalier, and for offences done in the prime part of the Forest was fined at the last Justice Seat nearly £300, but it was mercifully mitigated to £20. Lord Desborow knows him well and so does Sergeant Siese. Some conference should be had about it, but if it be the Parliament's pleasure, or any other's, that the Forest shall be left at the pleasure of the people, let me know it, and I shall as willingly turn by back upon it as ever I came from school. It were acting the part of a schoolboy to make complaints, but I have cause, as last Monday some of the officers were set upon in performance of their duty, one being knocked down; but the next day I sent some more, who met with no opposition.

On 11 May 1659[118] the Commons heard that 'upon the third day of this instant month, divers people in tumultuous way in Dean Forest did break down the fences and cut and carry away the gates of certain coppices enclosed for the preservation of timber, turned in their cattle, and set divers places of the Forest on fire, to the great destruction of the young growing wood'. The matter was ordered to be 'referred to the Sheriff and the Justices of the Peace for Gloucestershire to take special care to suppress and prevent all tumults and riotous meetings', and a committee of twenty-two members of the House was appointed 'to take care of the preservation of the timber and woods of the Commonwealth'. The outrages are referred to in a letter of 4 June[119] which states: 'There were risen in Dean 800 men at the first meeting who declared for nothing but their forest privileges, which they say have been extremely

---

[115] SP18/129, p. 2; ibid. 25/77, p. 246; Glos. R.O., D2026 Bond Papers, X.14.

[116] Firth and Rait, *op. cit.* ii, p. 1114; Hart, *Royal Forest*, p. 148, Appendix X, p. 284.

[117] SP18/202/70, p. 328; Hart, *Royal Forest*, p. 149 and *Coleford*, p. 126.

[118] *Gloucester Notes and Queries*, v. Pt. III, new series; Hart, *The Free Miners*, pp. 203, 204.

[119] *H.M.C.* Bath MSS, i, p. 132.

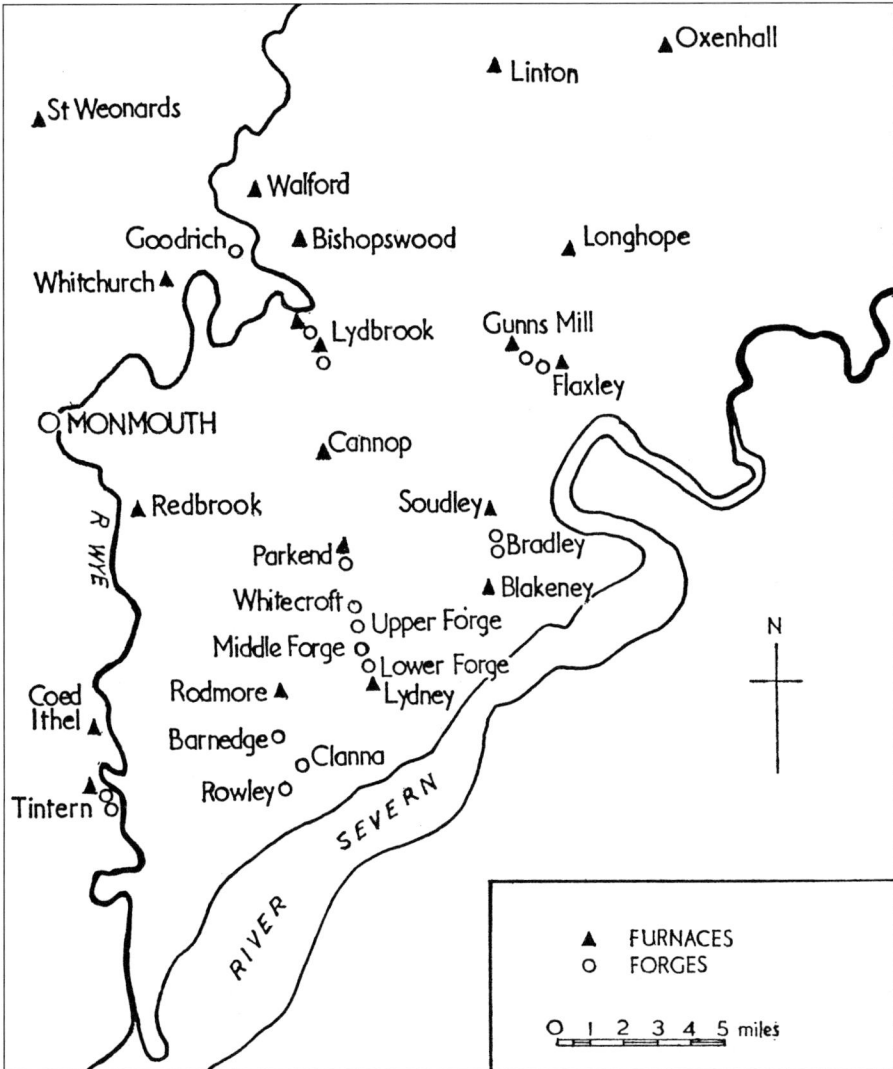

Map VII. Charcoal blast furnaces and forges in the Forest of Dean and its vicinity during the seventeenth and eighteenth centuries.

violated'. Another letter of 24 August the same year[120] mentions that 'Colonel
[John] Okey was sent down to suppress those that met'. An Order in Parliament 9
July 1659[121] instructed the Council 'to keep the peace of the Forest of Dean and
preserve the woods there as they were enclosed 7 May last'.

On 30 March 1660[122] Wade gave the Admiralty an account of pig, bar, and other
ironwork, made at the furnace and forge in Dean, from September 1657 to 30
March 1660; also of what money had been received and was owing for the same by
persons named. He had no money left, and there was upwards of £300 due to all
sorts of workmen. Wade found it impossible to obtain adequate help. Between
September 1657 and April 1660 (when he resigned) he sold some 1,200 tons of pig-
iron at prices ranging from £6.12s. to £7.5s., about 5 tons of chimney-backs and
baking-plates at £12, and between 300 and 400 tons of bar iron, usually at £17.10s.
Much of the bar iron was probably supplied to forge-masters in various parts of the
country. By 13 April 1660[123] he could no longer stand the conditions, and he wrote
to the Admiralty:

> I have already informed you of the throwing open of the enclosures and coppices, and of
> the horrid wastes and spoils committed, and by whom the people were instigated; all of
> which availing nothing, nor procuring any redress, it put a stop to my further troubling
> you in a business of such nature. The master-builder, seeing the horrid destruction that
> was committed by daily burning and cutting down of young and old trees, and carrying
> them away, together with such timber as he had prepared for building the frigate, as also
> that cut by the State for the use of the ironworks, made a journey to London to wait upon
> you therein: but I hear of no coercial power to punish what is already done, or to prevent
> further mischief. My humble entreaty is that my account be taken and I discharged, for it
> eats my very heart and mind to see the barbarous dealings that are done in this forlorn,
> disowned piece of ground so much talked of, and so little cared for in reality. It lies at such
> a pass now that it is dealt with by the inhabitants as if proclamation were made: 'let all the
> waste, spoil, and destruction be done and committed upon the Forest of Dean that the
> hearts of wicked people can invent or imagine to do'. It had been better that the State had
> given £10,000 and I dare say twice told, than that this same law [the Act of 1657] that
> preserved should have been forborne to be executed, which has been the cause of all the
> ruin that has followed.

He had been a commendable administrator and had done his best: he had
superintended the ironworks, acted as both forest-manager and timber-merchant,
and under great difficulties had accomplished much else. He will be remembered as
the person responsible in Dean for the first sowing and planting. No longer was
replenishment left wholly to nature, yet the inhabitants, finding their commons and
pannaging reduced, threw down enclosures and set fire to them. Local history had
repeated itself.

From 24 April 1660 Wade's work was taken over by commissioners appointed for
Charles II.[124] The accounts of the new superintendent of the ironworks, William
Carpender of Coleford, show that he continued to pay the keepers but no evidence
is found that he or they resumed the silviculture began by Wade, much of whose

[120] *H.M.C.* Bath MSS, i, p. 136.
[121] SP18/203 p. 14.
[122] Ibid. /223(151), p. 540.
[123] Ibid. /220, p. 413; Hart, *The Free Miners*, p. 204, *Royal Forest*, p. 150, and *Coleford*, p. 126.
[124] SP18/220(106), p. 42.

work was in vain. Wade would have been disgusted with the assertion made in later years[125] that Cromwell had 'reafforested the 18,000 acres, and so preserved the same by forest law, with all the wood and trees'. Such a statement disregarded the chaos in Dean during some years of the Commonwealth. Perhaps it was true that Wade under Cromwell 'had expelled near 400 cabins of beggarly people, living upon the waste and destruction of the wood and timber, and great numbers of goats, sheep, and swine that destroyed the young wood and soil thereof';[126] but there was much more that the Commonwealth could usefully have done. In any event, after the Restoration the animals began 'to invade the Forest as formerly'.[127] To the Commonwealth must go the credit of the first sowing and planting in Dean. It had too, through Wade, made good use of much iron, timber, and other woodland products. But beyond this there is little evidence to confirm that Cromwell's administration had been 'active and vigilant for the prevention of the waste and abuses in the Forest'.[128] Its efforts in replenishment were more commendable than the Tudors', but if Dean was to be 'a nursery of timber' more strenuous exertions would be necessary.

## WADE'S RESIGNATION AND RETIREMENT

The audited accounts of the whole of Wade's administration are available, covering three periods: 13 September 1653 to 2 August 1656,[129] 3 August 1656 to 15 September 1657,[130] and 16 September 1657 to 26 April 1660.[131] They contain a few errors and ambiguities, but are sufficient to provide a fair approximation of costs, revenues, debtors/creditors, and stocks – hence of profits. In terms of material achievement the success of the enterprises are evident. Some extraneous payments included: shipbuilding and buying in woods in the Cannop valley. The enterprises were not debited with any value of wood and timber used.

The more efficient administration of Dean, though it provided much employment, did not reconcile the whole population to its commercial use. Petitions and complaints about threats to the wellbeing of the commoners in particular, if not of the woods themselves, still appeared occasionally. In April 1659 riots and attacks on enclosures occurred, and mounted to a high in April 1660.[132] Wade used the riots as pretext for his resignation in April 1660.[133] On 25 April 1660 he formally handed over the ironworks.

Severe difficulties in Dean, particularly opposition from the commoners and other inhabitants, led to Wade's resignation in April 1660[134] about the time of the Restoration of the Monarchy (Charles II). From 24 April administration and overseeing were taken over by commissioners: the accounts of 3 October 1660 of

[125] 3rd Rept. of the Commissioners of 1788, p. 14.
[126] Ibid.
[127] Ibid.; Br. Liby., MSS 6839, f. 332; *Cal. SP*, Addenda, 1662, p. 42; Hart, *Royal Forest*, p. 289.
[128] 3rd Rept. of the Commissioners of 1788, p. 13.
[129] SP18/130/102.
[130] Ibid. /157B.
[131] E178/6080, pt. i, f. 25–50d.
[132] *Commons Journal*, VII, p. 648, 11 May 1659; p. 670, 1 June 1659; SP18/202/70, 8 April 1659; /203/29, 30 May 1659; /220/79, 13 April 1660.
[133] SP18/220/106, 25 April 1660.
[134] Hart, *Royal Forest*, pp. 148, 150.

the new superintendent of the ironworks, William Carpender, are extant.[135] Following the Restoration (May 1660), much of the Forest was regranted to Sir John Winter, but the ironworks were worked for the crown by Carpender, Philip Rod,[136] and George Wyrrall.[137]

In 1661 the Treasury authorized George Charnock, sergeant-at-arms, 'to pay off the workmen in Dean' and to meet Major Wade's claim out of the stock in Winter's hands.[138]

On 1 May 1662 Wade resold to Charles Bridgman (III) for £600 the house and property at Littledean. The deed included the following:[139]

> . . . and further, he the said John Wade and Anne his wife and the heirs of the said John Wade shall and will from time to time and at all times hereafter within the space of seven years next ensuing the date hereof, at the request, costs and charges of the said Charles Bridgman, his heirs and assigns, make and execute or cause and procure to be done and executed... [any legal documents which may be required, but in order to make the same] be not compelled to travel from the place or places of their several abodes for the doing thereof above the space of ten miles.

The deed is sealed and signed by 'Jo. Wade' and is witnessed by four persons. The mention of Anne Wade is the first information found of their marriage. The deed gives no indication as to where the Wades intended to reside.

In 1675 Sir Charles Harbord, surveyor-general of woods, in reporting on abuses, etc. in the Forest, urged that they 'ought to be totally suppressed, and would be so by a good officer, as Colonel Wade was in the times of the Usurpation'.[140] On 23 July 1679 Wade was included in another Commission which reported in 1680.[141]

Wade's subsequent life story is unknown. However, his knowledge and experience were sought and utilized by the crown. In February 1661 he was helping the surveyor-general of woods in Forest matters[142] and as late as 5 March 1662 it appears that he was willing and able to advise the crown on the best use of its assets in Dean.[143] In 1665 he was well 'recommended',[144] and in 1673 included in a Commission on Dean affairs.[145] In October 1696 a 'Major Wade of Gloucester' held, by mortgage, three meadows in Mitcheldean, noted at a Court Baron of Maynard Colchester, Lord of the Manor of Mitcheldean.[146]

The family of Wade was fairly widespread in the Gloucestershire and Bristol regions. Full information about it has not come to light. (There appears to have been several John Wades.) It is known that Major John Wade of Littledean married Anne; and there was a Thomas Wade, probably a son. The most researched member of the Wade family was the somewhat notorious Nathaniel

[135] Hart, *Royal Forest*, p. 150.
[136] Possibly John Roades, see Hart, *Royal Forest* , p. 153.
[137] Hart, *Royal Forest*, p. 153.
[138] *Cal. Treas. Bks.*, VII, Pt. I, p. 308; Pt. II, p. 1631.
[139] Glos. R.O., D4431, Phillipps Deeds, Box 15/1.
[140] 3rd Rept. of 1788, p. 18.
[141] Hart, *Royal Forest*, p. 300.
[142] SP25/77, pp. 458–9; Hart, *Coleford*, p. 126.
[143] E178/6080, Pt. I, ms. 10, 11.
[144] Hart, *Royal Forest*, p. 161.
[145] Ibid. p. 173, note 163.
[146] Glos. R.O., D36, Colchester Papers, M80.

Wade (1646–1718).[147] The *Dictionary of National Biography*, Vol. LVIII, p. 418, describes him as 'Conspirator, born probably about 1646, third son of John Wade of the Wick-house, Arlingham, Gloucestershire'. However, it further states that 'John Wade was a major in Cromwell's army and governor of the Isle of Man for a short period under the Protector; and the maiden name of his mother, who was buried in St. Stephen's Bristol, on 22 March 1678–9, was Lane.' Some confusion is likely, and some of the information may not relate to the Major John Wade 'of the Forest of Dean'.[148]

One day it may be discovered where John and Anne Wade retired to, in what year they died, and where they were laid to rest.

[147] Wade, Len, 'Nathaniel Wade (1646–1718), Traitor or Patriot?', *Bristol and Avon Family History Society Journal*, No. 56, June 1989, pp. 29, 30. Nathaniel Wade, his wife Ann (married 4 May 1687), and three daughters retired to Nailsea Court in 1695. A portrait of the parents hangs in the Court.

[148] The *D.N.B.* records also: 'The John Wade who is claimed as the founder of the family was Mayor of Bristol in 1576, and is described in the corporation records as a lollard. From 1560 the family resided at Filton, near Bristol.'

# APPENDIX

## John Wade's Connection with Coalmining in Dean, in particular with Aywood Surfe and Coalwork

Around 1656, John Wade on behalf of the Commonwealth opened 'a surfe and coalwork' at Aywood (Eywood) – modern Heywood north of Cinderford. He invested £131.10s.2d. for the State in the coalmine. John Chapman was his overseer of sale to take care of the coalworks. A 'surfe' (apparently a term derived from 'sought' – an adit for carrying off water), had been driven to the 'coalwork' – an early reference to dewatering.[149]

In 1656 two relevant coalpits are mentioned – Aywood and Crabtree – both 'owned' by the Lord Protector, Oliver Cromwell; also a private pit called Oake in Aywood 'near to the way from the meene to Ayllow Hill',[150] and another called Hopewell 'above the wood', i.e. in West Dean.[151] In the same year, it was recorded of Oak pit in Aywood that it was 'coaled and worked out . . . and their deep pit was sunk as deep as it could possibly be worked for water'.[152] Wade expended £435.1s.6d. for the state on coalmining.

On 6 February 1660[153] local commissioners (Nicholas Throckmorton and others) appointed John Witt of Bream and John Byrkin 'to set to work such persons as they shall think fit in and upon the surfe and coalwork lately begun in Eywood', to have necessary wood and timber, and 'to sell such coal as shall be raised at reasonable rates to the country people'. The appointments were confirmed by Sir Charles Harbord, surveyor-general of woods, on 14 February 1660; John Witt was to have £40 annual salary out of the profits of the coalwork.[154]

On 6 February 1661 Sir Charles Harbord informed Witt that because of continued interruption by the other colliers he had obtained a warrant from Lord Treasurer the Earl of Southampton to suppress them.[155] The warrant, dated 6 February 1661, addressed to Major Wade (although 'retired') and the verderers and regarders, empowered them to take action against Edmund, Thomas and Richard Haynes and other colliers who dig and sink coalpits near his Majesty's surfe and coalwork.[156] On 27 February 1660 the local commissioners informed Witt that whereas certain colliers now at work in Aywood 'take away his Majesty's benefit in his surfe and coalwork, and although forbidden, continue, you are to "put off and hinder" all such workers that you still find there'.[157]

---

[149] Hart, *The Industrial History of Dean*, p. 255.
[150] Hart, *The Free Miners*, p. 78.
[151] Ibid. p. 79.
[152] Hart, *The Industrial History of Dean*, p. 255.
[153] Glos. R.O., D2026 Bond Papers, X.20.
[154] Ibid.
[155] Ibid.
[156] Ibid. See also Glos. R.O., D3921, Hart Collection, 38; P.R.O. T51/7.
[157] Ibid.

In 1661 it was recorded that 'there had been used for the same works in timber the value of £1,000', also iron, and that the works may be carried on for the future with woad of oarle [alder], holly, birch and sally [willow].[158]

On 12 April 1662 commissioners reported that they had 'viewed the several coalworks and surfes, and although the ordinary pits be liable to water and the miners could only dig in summer, yet the surfe [Aywood] has made such a passage for the water as they dig the whole year and get a vast quantity of good coal'.[159]

'Major Wade's Surfe' was still referred to in the mid-1700s, but any future connection of it with subsequent coalmining is unknown. Haywood Coal Level worked the Coleford High Delf seam which dips westward at 20° to 40°. The mouth is 700 yards east-south-east of the old Steam-Mills Railway Halt.[160] Haywood Coal Pit worked the same seam, dipping westward at 30° to 40°; the coal was raised by two cross-cuts in the shaft at depths of 210 feet and 362 feet.[161]

[158] Glos. R.O., D2026 Bond Papers, X.20.
[159] Hart, *The Free Miners*, p. 206 and *The Industrial History of Dean*, pp. 257, 258.
[160] Trotter, F.M., and Rose, W.C.C. (1942, 1964), *Geology of the Forest of Dean Coal and Iron-ore Field*, p. 36.
[161] Ibid. p. 38.

# PART THREE

## IX. ATTEMPTS AT ENCLOSING AND PLANTING OF DEAN: 1660–87

By the mid-seventeenth century the stocks of timber-trees and coppices in Dean were much reduced – because, in particular, enormous numbers of trees had been felled: for building and repairing ships on the Severn; for timber despatched to naval dockyards; and for charcoal to fuel ironworks. Also there had occurred two great storms and several fires; miners and colliers had taken wood requirements; 'fee trees' had been taken by hereditary forest officials; and the inhabitants had taken estovers including firewood. Most of the uses were rational, and increment of trees had made good some of the loss. But relatively few large timber-trees of sound quality remained. The wooded cover, reduced in quantity and quality, and possibly in extent, called for new measures if it was to be replenished and enhanced.

During the century, Dean had contributed towards the support of government, and had been the great resource for gratifying the favourites of the monarchs, but the improvident and often ill-defined grants with the confused mixture of rights, privileges and customs created by them, had the worst possible effect on the woods. The lessees of coppices wished to prevent the growth of timber-trees by which their crop was diminished; whilst it was to the advantage of those to whom common had been allowed that as few trees as possible should grow up. The whole was 'a perpetual struggle of jarring interests, in which no party could improve his share without hurting that of another'.[1] There is no kind of property that requires the protection of laws more than timber, 'which may easily, and in very little time, be hurt or destroyed, but requires a century to come to perfection'.[2] Dean's need of protection was urgent.

### THE COMMISSION OF 1661–2

In March 1661[3] a commission was issued to the Marquis of Worcester, constable-warden, along with thirteen others to enquire into the state of the Forest, to recommend how to improve it, particularly to build up stores of timber for the Navy. They were specially to view 'those parts in grant to Sir John Winter, the late Earl of Pembroke, Sir Robert Bannister [Cannop valley woods], Lady Villiers [Mailscot], and others', and to certify 'as to the advantage to the Crown by purchase of them'. Furthermore, they were to view 'the timber, deer, and ironworks and to certify whether the latter were fit to be kept and, if so, how they might be best employed for his Majesty's benefit without prejudice to naval timber'. Sir Charles Harbord, surveyor-general of woods, on 28 December 1661 commented:[4]

---

[1] 3rd Rept. of the Commissioners of 1788, p. 6.
[2] Ibid.
[3] *Cal. Treas. Bks.*, VII, Pt. I, p. 58.
[4] 3rd Rept. of 1788, p. 14.

His Majesty has been pleased to be present with my Lord Chancellor and Lord Treasurer at
the hearing of this business of the Forest of Dean and has given order that a commission
enquire into the state of the Forest; intending upon the Return of the commission to
acquaint Parliament with the true state of the business, and to recommend it to their wisdom
to provide that the Forest may be restored to his Majesty's demesne and reafforested and
improved by inclosure for a future supply of wood, for a constant support of the ironworks
there, producing the best iron in Europe for many years, and for the production of timber for
the Navy and other uses in time to come, which might be of great use for the defence of this
nation, the old trees there standing being of above 300 years' growth,[5] and yet as good timber
as any in the world; and the ground so apt to produce and so strong to nourish and preserve
timber, especially oaks, that within a hundred years there may be sufficient provision there
found to maintain the Royal Navy for ever.

The commission's investigations took place around the time of a great storm which
on 18 February 1662[6] caused havoc in Dean's woods; 3,000 oaks and beeches were
'blown down or broken'. Pepys wrote 25 February: 'We have letters from the Forest
of Dean that above 1,000 oaks and as many beeches are blown in one Walk there'.[7]
   Meanwhile in the same year an important Memorial was presented to the
commissioners by the freeholders and inhabitants of the Forest. After setting out
their claims to commoning, pannage and estovers (as well as the right to dig iron-
ore and coal) they made the following constructive proposals:[8]

We whose names are underwritten, apprehending the gracious inclination of the Sacred
Majesty and his Parliament towards the preservation of wood and timber in the Forest of
Dean and in the sense of public advantage to his Majesty and the Kingdom, do humbly
offer and propose on behalf of ourselves and all other the freeholders in the Forest to bind
ourselves by any lawful act to forbear our claim and rights to wood and timber in the
Forest for so long time as his Majesty shall be graciously pleased to suspend the imploying
of his ironworks and cutting the woods of the Forest. Provided that our rights and claims
before-mentioned be secured to us after the time of forebearance as aforesaid, and that we
and all the inhabitants of the Forest may be freed from the power and exercise of the forest
laws upon any of our or their particular lands and tenements, and that we humbly desire
that the 18,000 acres may be reafforested and that the Letters Patent for the sale thereof to
Sir John Winter, Kt., be made void and that the forest law may be put in execution on the
waste soil of the Forest whereby the woods and timber may be the better preserved.

(The foregoing proposals were somewhat similar to those proffered five years later,
in 1667.)

THE REPORT OF 1662

The commissioners' Report to the Exchequer, made on 12 April 1662,[9] explained
the state and content of Dean's woods at that time. They had called to their

   [5] Perhaps the ancient trees were those that Winter had mentioned to Pepys as being left 'at a great fall
in Edward III's time, by the name of forbid-trees, which at this day are called "vorbid trees"' (Wheatley,
op. cit., II, p. 306).
   [6] Cal. SP 29/52, p. 296.
   [7] Wheatley, op. cit., II, p. 195.
   [8] F.20/1(17), p. 9, P.R.O.; Hart, Royal Forest, pp. 155–7 and The Free Miners, p. 205.
   [9] Br. Liby., Harl. MSS 6839, f. 332; Cal. SP 29, Addenda, 1662, p. 142; Hart, Royal Forest, pp. 154–7
and Appendix XI.

assistance 'several carpenters, corders, and other men of known experience in timber and wood' and then 'viewed all the waste grounds of the Forest containing about 22,000 acres, whereof 18,000 acres were improved for his Majesty's (Charles II) use, the residue (4,000 acres) being left in common to the inhabitants claiming right of common'. They also viewed and valued 'all and every the trees in the Forest and waste, as well good standing oaks and beeches fit for shiptimber and other timber, as stoggalls and other decaying trees only fit for cordwood. And by reason that so many trees of all sorts lay broken in pieces on the ground, blown down by the last great storm, by which we could sufficiently inform ourselves of the nature and quality of the timber and wood in its several and particular kinds, we thought not fit to put his Majesty to any unnecessary charge and therefore caused no more to be fallen, but put a stamp or mark on every of the said trees as follows: on a sound timber-tree, a broad arrow with a crown, and on such as had some timber and wood and yet decayed, a single broad arrow. And upon the best computation we can possibly make, having used as great exactness as we could, we find the ensuing number of trees containing these several parcels of oak and beech timber:

> Oak 25,929 ⎫ in all 30,233 trees [apparently
> Beech 4,304 ⎬ excluding the Lea Bailey]
>
> Whereof, standing in the 18,000 acres, 29,957 trees
> and blown down in the 18,000 acres, 276 trees
>
> Both which parcels contain 11,335 tons and 30 foot of shiptimber fit
> for the Navy.'[10]

'The lop and top of all the trees would amount to 60,786¾ long cords[11] besides the underwood, together with the coppices, which will amount to 12,000 long cords, the whole being 72,786¾ long cords'. As for the timber and cordwood in the 4,000 acres allotted for the commoners, 'it is inconsiderable, there being not above 50 trees on the whole which were also granted to Sir John Winter, and therefore we inserted them in the other quantities of timber and cordwood'. The commissioners further reported:

> (1) Although we cannot but see a great prejudice to the whole Forest by dismembering of any part thereof as also almost an impossibility exactly to answer this Article which commands us to set out 4,000 acres out of the 18,000 acres which in our judgments is fittest for pasture and meadow, the fittest places for that use lying here and there in small flats which if so appointed would destroy any inclosure for future timber and wood, yet in obedience to our Instructions we thought these following parcels the most proper and convenient for an inclosure (viz) Breams Eves, Okewood, Parkehill, Lumberchmarsh, Brumley, Winhall, Colverts Eves, Brickslade, Veterhill, Titenetreehill, Barnehill, Backingsole, Owleglade, Whimberly Slade, The Perch, Coverham, Hangerberry, Morenwood, Worrelhill, The Berry, Godmeadow, Rewerdens Eves, Harwood Eves, Aywood, Litemore, The Salleys, Santley Castle, Little and Great Santley, Middlerudge, Hollingturf, the old vellet, Newmans Rudge and to Yarkley wall, Wayenway, Whitecroft

---

[10] The quantities are confirmed in SP46/136/30 – 'The state of the Forest of Dean given in by Commander Pett'. There were also 117 tons of timber 'squared by Mr. Furzer lying in the Forest'.
[11] Ibid.

Poul, Bollock Hill, Shadowinghurst, Wettwood, Perryhay, Whitelay, Stone-edge, Kensley's Edge, Little Kensley, Rushey Lawe, Horse Lawe, Lowsey Oake, Crookedham, Cromp Meadow, Leonard's Hill, Westons Greene, Aglewey hill, Broademore, the Cole delves, Beathwood, Seyridge, Danwellmore, Great Kingley. The aforesaid parcels we compute to contain near 12,000 acres more or less and have nothing to prejudice an inclosure or ring to increase wood or timber for the future, but Canup which we find of an absolute necessity to be reduced into His Majesty's hands as being 1,100 acres of the best land within the Forest a great part whereof hath been lately fallen by Sir Baynham Throckmorton, junior, and Whitemead Park being a parcel of good land containing near 300 acres and hath a lodge on it much out of repair. This reinclosed would make a fair park and maintain as many deer as are now in the Forest which the keepers compute at 300. And although this parcel of land be within Sir John Winter's 18,000 acres yet is excepted out of his grant.

The circumference of this inclosure we compute may be near 17 miles, which if His Majesty should inclose with a wall of $4\frac{1}{2}$ foot copsing in height and 2 foot in breadth, at 4s. per perch and $16\frac{1}{2}$ foot to a perch and 320 perches to a mile, will amount unto £1,088, but to inclose it with ditch and double quicksett will cost 12d. per perch which will amount only unto £272 and £50 for gates and stiles, which if well looked to at first may be we conceive a sufficient fence to preserve the inclosure.

(2)    We also find that 14 years' growth is a sufficient term to cut the underwood, but by reason that several of the coppices are well grown already before the offal wood be spent many of them will be ready to succeed especially with the help of the offal wood in the Lea Bayley so that the barest places will be near 20 years' growth before His Majesty's ironworks will need them; by that time they will be, considering the extraordinary aptness of the soil, very good coppices of underwood; so that if His Majesty should fall every year only a thousand acres, which to compute moderately at six long cords per acre will yield each year 6,000 long cords, and that converted to iron with the help of his ironworks will produce yearly the ensuing revenue and advantages; and we further advise that 30 of the best and straightest young shoots of oak and beech be left as standards for timber in every acre and no more lest it prejudice the underwood.

(3)    Besides the parcels aforesaid to be inclosed for coppice, computed at 12,000 acres, there is a certain coppice of underwood called Hudnall lying on the south-west part of the Forest containing by estimation 700 acres more or less whereof two-thirds were assigned to Sir John Winter and the residue was set out as part of the 4,000 acres allotted to the commoners, so there remained 463 acres clear out of the said coppice. There is also some other coppices called the Copes, Bradley and Pigslade containing near 300 acres lying on the east side of the Forest, but if the 4,000 acres hereafter set out to be improved be so, these must be incoppiced by themselves when they fall in hand, the Lord Stanhope holding them by lease, 10 years whereof are unexpired.

And there are also these several and other following coppices and parcels of land fit to enclose for coppice by themselves and cannot (by reason of the 4,000 acres hereafter mentioned and set out to be improved for meadow and pasture although they could turn to better advantage if converted to wood) be joined and incoppiced within the main ring and inclosure, called Edgehills, Badcocks Bayley, Shapridge and Chestnuts lying on the east side of the Forest and containing by estimation 10,000 acres, but if so be the said 4,000 acres are so improved these parcels must have a particular inclosure there being only a small freehold of 4 acres lying within them.

(4)    The Article requiring us to set out 4,000 acres out of the 18,000 acres fittest for meadow and pasture, we must make use of the same answer to this as we did to the precedent Article that many small flats lying severally were fittest for meadow and pasture. But to have admitted of so many small improvements within the grand ring or inclosure would have been inconsistent with His Majesty's resolution to incoppice for future timber

and wood and infinitely prejudicial in our judgment to its thriving and preservation. Wherefore although the very dividing and severing these following 4,000 acres from the main body of the Forest be of great prejudice to a thriving nursery as aforesaid, yet we humbly conceive these parcels if any are fittest to be spared for such an improvement (viz) Little Stapledge, two-thirds of Walmore, Year Slawes, Phelps Mead, Great Stapledge, Moseleys Greene, Blackneys Bayley, Thorneyhill, Little and Great Bramson, Dead Man's Crosse, Blackneys End, Broomshill, Meseyhurst and Partridge. The premises aforesaid lie on the east side of the Forest and contain near 4,000 acres more or less, which if improved will admit of a survey and also an exception that all the trees growing thereon may be reserved for His Majesty's use and benefit and we estimate the said lands be worth one year with another 5s. an acre.

(5)   We enquired and observed what cabins have been built within these late years on the Forest and wastes, and were informed that in or about the year 1653 there were near 400 cabins and cottages then standing, but the person [Major John Wade] then entrusted with the supervisorship of the Forest and wastes ejected them by due course of law, and we find not above five now standing. As to what damage they occasion to the timber and wood, they erect their cabins and cottages with the King's timber, breed great store of swine, burn the offal wood, committing many other wastes, and the same course as formerly must be used to prevent their increase.

(6)   We were informed that the said supervisor at his first coming into that employment did find the Forest and waste full of goats but by his direction they were all driven away and now there are few or none remaining. We also ordered the keepers and other officers to make presentment to us of all persons who had offended by keeping hogs and sheep on the premises at undue seasons of the year and unrung, and other trespasses, but their presentments were so long that we rather chose to have them fair written out and kept till they may be proceeded against by the laws of the forest than to return them now by reason of their multiplicity; but the keepers having delivered them upon their oaths, if His Majesty's Counsel learned in the law shall think to proceed against them presently, the said presentments shall be ready upon demand.

(7)   We have endeavoured with all exactness to answer to the best of our judgement all the foregoing Articles of Instruction, and this latter commanding our opinion upon the whole state of the Forest together with our advice for its preservation thereof towards an increase of wood and timber, we humbly conceive it very necessary for His Majesty to reassume all grants and to take the whole into his own hands, giving such other satisfaction to the grantees as in His Majesty's gracious judgment may seem meet; or else in our opinion it will be almost impossible to preserve the whole for a future nursery by reason of the country's obstinacy and the inconveniences that will happen by a division; as also that present care be taken for encoppicing it, and that upon all falls some person very well experienced in ship-timber be always ready to attend whensoever any trees are cut down wherein there shall be any timber fit for the Navy, to be disposed of for His Majesty's best advantage. And forasmuch as former allowance of perquisites to the respective officers of the Forest did conduce much to the destruction of the timber and wood, we humbly conceive it necessary upon a reafforestation to retrench them and reduce them to moderate and certain salaries.

The commissioners supplied calculations showing the handsome profit that could be made if the king took the ironworks into his own hands. The whole Report was submitted 'to His Majesty's gracious will and pleasure'. However, appropriate action was not immediately forthcoming.

## THE SECOND GRANT TO WINTER (1662)

The commissioners' sound recommendations could not be followed unless a settlement was effected with Sir John Winter (who still held under his first grant). Samuel Pepys, Secretary to the Navy, took a hand, and on 18 June 1662[12] met Winter and perused his 'last contract with the King for the Forest of Dean whereof I took notes because of this new one that he is next making'. Pepys' part was perhaps no more than approving clauses relating to naval timber, ensuring that those parts of trees suitable for shipbuilding should be reserved for the Navy. The contents of this second grant to Winter, dated 30 July 1662, are suggested from a proposal made by Sir Baynham Throckmorton 7 July[13] 'to pay the £30,000 allowed to Sir John Winter by his Majesty for surrender of his grant of the Forest of Dean, thereby to obtain some advantage to the King, and satisfaction to himself, for his interest in the woods'. Winter on receipt of £30,000 was to relinquish his previous grants, retaining his manor of Lydney and the nearby woods of Snead and Kidnalls. His nominees, Francis Finch and Robert Clayton, were to have a grant for eleven years of the king's two remaining furnaces, at Lydbrook and Parkend, and necessary supplies of wood, ore and cinders.[14] Most serious was the licence under which Winter was to have the 30,133 timber-trees, reserving 11,335 tons of their content for the Navy or paying for it at 15s. a ton. He had given with one hand and taken with the other; and in addition might receive £30,000.

John Evelyn, a prominent figure in the public life of Restoration times, on 5 November 1662 was engaged with the Council of the Royal Society[15] in a discourse concerning planting of the Forest of Dean with oak, 'now so much exhausted of the choicest shiptimber in the world'. He may or may not have known that by 20 October Daniel Furzer, master shipwright and now a purveyor of timber to the Navy, had collected 100 bushels of acorns in Dean ('they begin to sprout and grow very much already')[16] and hoped to collect another 60 bushels. A severe storm in the previous month had thrown many trees.

Winter's second grant soon generated much trouble. The inhabitants, as could be expected, opposed his operations, and the grant 'was rapidly followed with consequences so destructive to the Forest, and so detrimental to the public, that complaints were very soon made to the House of Commons of the great waste done there'.[17] A committee was appointed to consider the whole matter, and on its behalf Sir Charles Harbord, surveyor-general of woods, reported to the House 13 April 1663[18] that Winter 'had 500 cutters of wood employed in Dean, and all the timber would be destroyed if care should not be speedily taken to prevent it'. The House made an Order to prohibit felling, and on 20 July[19] a Bill was brought in 'for settling the Forest and improving and preserving its trees', but Parliament was prorogued before the Bill could pass, and the House 13 May 1664 recommended to the Lord Treasurer and the Chancellor of the Exchequer to

[12] Wheatley, op. cit., II, p. 260.
[13] Cal. SP 29/57, p. 430.
[14] 3rd Rept. of 1788, p. 14.
[15] Bray, Evelyn's Sylva, 2nd edn., i, p. 354.
[16] SP 29/61/74.
[17] 3rd Rept. of 1788, p. 14.
[18] Ibid.
[19] Ibid. p. 15.

take care for the preservation and improvement of Dean. Winter and his nominees would not stop their operations, and Sir Baynham Throckmorton, who ostensibly had the well-being of the Forest at heart, and the inhabitants who wished to safeguard their customary benefits, would not agree to Dean's exploitation.

## THE THIRD GRANT TO WINTER (1667)

No relevant action appears till 17 July 1665[20] when a warrant was issued to George Charnock, sergeant-at-arms, and to Thomas Agar, one of the two surveyor-generals of woods, to view the 18,000 acres 'which the King had resolved to dispose of for the making of convenient nurseries for future growth of shiptimber to supply the great decay thereof in the Kingdom'. They were to report on the state of the trees, the best method of enclosure, and particularly to inform themselves, 'on conference with the freeholders of the several parishes, concerning discontent at the award made formerly by Sir Charles Harbord and others by way of composition for their pretended rights of common therein'. The raising of 'nurseries there for the future growth of shiptimber' and the 'prosecution of the King's rights therein' were to be committed to Sir John Winter,[21] news received with great disappointment and anxiety by the inhabitants and officials of the Forest. Under his third grant, 1667, Winter was to have 8,000 acres for his own use, and to manage the remaining 10,000 acres as a 'nursery of timber'; 4,000 acres were to be set aside for the inhabitants.[22]

Meanwhile Daniel Furzer continued to struggle under atrocious difficulties to build and repair ships and to despatch naval timber, felled and squared by Winter's men.[23] Much discontent continued over the grant and commission to Winter. A survey in December 1667[24] disclosed that of 30,133 timber-trees sold to him there remained only about 200. During his felling operations the Forest was a hive of industry, with the almost continuous sound of axes and falling trees, and with many teams of horses lugging timber to the sawpits or to the local pills and creeks.[25] The local populace, except those finding employment under Winter, looked on with disgust. Fortunately he had not been allowed to squander the fine timber-trees in the 1,000 acres of the Lea Bailey.

## PROPOSALS FOR 'SETTLING THE FOREST'

On 1 August 1667[26] another commission was appointed, comprising Harbord, Throckmorton and thirteen others. On 8 August[27] the following Order was given by Charles II: 'To our right trusty and entirely blood cousin Henry Lord Marquis of Worcester, constable of our Castle of St. Briavells and warden of our Forest of Dean, and to all others who it may concern':

[20] *Cal. Treas. Bks.*, I, p. 673.
[21] Ibid. p. 699.
[22] *Cal. SP* 29/146, p. 222; ibid. /211, pp. 300, 376; *Cal. Treas. Bks.*, II, pp. 23, 26, 64, 200.
[23] Hart, *Royal Forest*, pp. 162–4.
[24] *Cal. Treas. Bks.*, II, p. 149; Br. Liby., Harl. MSS 6839, f. 356.
[25] Hart, *Royal Forest*, p. 165.
[26] *Cal. Treas. Bks.*, II, pp. 169, 174.
[27] F20/1 (11).

Whereas by vertue of a commission under the Great Seal granted by our Royal Father [Charles I] to Sir Charles Harbord Kt. our surveyor-general [of woods] and others for improvement of part of the wasts of our Forest of Dean it was then agreed, amongst other things, between those commissioners and the freeholders and inhabitants of that Forest who claimed common therein, that the lands and tenements of such of them as did or should assent to the improvement of the said wasts then made should for ever after be exempt and discharged from the jurisdiction of the Forest law to which the same were otherwise liable in which consideration the Forest Courts usually kept there have for divers years been discontinued to the great damage of our Forest in destruction of the wood and timber there and the retardment of our nurseries for future growth of shiptimber which we intend to raise out of the wasts thereof.

Our will and pleasure therefor is, and we do hereby charge and command all our respective officers of that Forest, that the Court of Attachments commonly called the Speech Court and the Swanimote Court be duly and orderly kept, and that the Regard be made and ridden as ought to be done according to the Forest Law for the discovery and conviction of all purprestures and other offences against the same that have been committed or continued in or upon our said wasts that are not deafforested or any the lands and woods of other persons within the perambulation of the Forest since our gracious Act of General Pardon. And forasmuch as we are given to understand that many of the freeholders and inhabitants within this Forest do assent to the said improvement of the wasts abovesaid and have submitted thereunto upon the late Information of our attorney general in our Court of Exchequer, we do therefore further declare our Royal Will and pleasure to be that none of the said freeholders or inhabitants so assenting shall be proceeded against in any of the said Courts or Regard for any purpresture or offence against the Law and Assize of the Forest contrary to the abovesaid Agreement made by Sir Charles Harbord and the other commissioners which we are graciously pleased in all points to confirm and make good. Whereof the constable of our Castle of St Briavels and lord warden of the said Forest, and his deputies, and all verderers, regarders, keepers and all other officers and ministers thereof are to take special notice and according to their several charges to put into execution these our Royal Commands concerning the presents so given. Given under our Sign Manual at our Court at Whitehall, August 8th 1667.

By his Majesty's Command.              [Signed]              ARLINGTON

Subsequently, on 20 November 1667[28] the Marquis of Worcester, constable-warden, informed the Treasury:

My Lords may improve the business of timber and yet satisfy the country as to their right of common, for by Sir John Wintour's grant the King is to have but 10,000 acres, Wintour 8,000 acres and the commoners 4,000 acres, and the forest law at an end as to 18,000 acres. As to this, the country would be willing the forest law were set up again in the Forest, and would consent to what further is necessary for the common good. As to the great occasion of the destruction of wood (*viz.* the right of the commoners to 'estboot' or cutting of wood for their own use, and of pannage) these two the country are willing to part with, provided always one-third of the Forest shall be in enclosure, and as any of the wood opens then liberty to the King to enclose as much more. I believe the enclosure of a third of the Forest may be done for £1,000, but the commoners desire the forest laws may be taken off their own lands. I believe that the King may have presently £2,000 per annum out of the underwoods and £4,000 out of them after six years.

[28] *Cal. Treas. Bks.*, II, p. 131.

Thereafter, still in 1667, the Treasury considered complementary 'Proposals' similar to those made in 1662 by and on behalf of the freeholders, inhabitants, and commoners for the preservation and improvement of the growth of timber'[29] who had proposed:

That 11,000 acres of the waste soil in the Forest of Dean, whereof the Lea Bailey and Cannop [valley woods] to be part, may be enclosed by his Majesty, and discharged for ever from all manner of pasture, estovers and pannage; and if ever his Majesty or his successors, shall think fit to lay open any part of the said 11,000 acres, then to take in so much elsewhere, so as the whole enclosure exceed not at any one time 11,000 acres.

That all the wood or timber which shall hereafter grow upon the remaining 13,000 acres shall absolutely belong to his Majesty, discharged from all estovers for ever, and pannage for twenty years next ensuing. That the whole waste soil be reafforested and subject to the forest laws; but that the severity of the forest laws be taken off from the lands in several, belonging to the freeholders and inhabitants within the Forest, they themselves being contented to serve his Majesty, according to their several offices and places, as formerly, at the forest courts.

That the deer to be kept on the waste soil may not exceed 800 at any one time, and the fees which belong to the particular officers touching venison may be preserved to them as to venison only, and not to wood or trees. [There followed consent to the times of winter heyning and fence month.]

That all grants of any part of the waste soil of the Forest be reassumed and made void, and that no part of the waste or soil be aliened for ever from the Crown, or farmed to any particular person or persons, by lease or otherwise.

And that this may be settled by Act of Parliament.

[Signed]    Ben Hall       Dun. Colchester
            Wm. Probin    Jo. Witt

The prime consideration was the unpopularity of the grant and commission to Winter, particularly in view of the unsatisfactory way in which he had executed past commitments in Dean. The second was the endeavour of the inhabitants to safeguard their customary commoning and pannage, though willing to relinquish their taking of estovers. On 17 December 1667[30] 'the whole business of the Forest of Dean' was before Parliament. There was now an opportunity for a new attempt to 'settle the Forest', but Winter's grant must first be revoked. In the face of accusations during 1667–8 he went to great length to vindicate himself,[31] but to no avail. He was proved to be in great debt to the king,[32] but in the following year he was discharged of 'his covenants concerning the improvement of the waste soil in Dean, and of his recognisance of £2,000 entered into in pursuance of the same'.[33] Thus ended Winter's long and unfortunate connection with the Forest; he had been one of the chief causes of local discontent in Dean over several decades, during which the store of timber-trees and coppices was much reduced. Dean's need of protection and replenishment was now even more urgent. With the departure of Winter, and the commendable 'Proposals' made on behalf of the inhabitants, the government was enabled to proceed with 'the settlement of the Forest'.

[29] 3rd Rept. of 1788, p. 15; Hart, *Royal Forest*, p. 166.
[30] *Cal. Treas. Bks.*, II, p. 151.
[31] Br. Liby., MSS 726, c.i. (2), 8, 1667; Hart, *Royal Forest*, pp. 165–7.
[32] *Cal. Treas. Bks.*, II, pp. 288, 535.
[33] *Cal.* SP 29/1667–8, p. 466.

## THE DEAN FOREST (REAFFORESTATION) ACT 1668

On 9 May 1668 legislation was enacted for that purpose. The Dean Forest (Reafforestation) Act[34] was based in part upon the constructive 'Proposals' made by representatives of the inhabitants (*supra*). The preamble to the Act asserted that 'the wood and timber of the Crown, which of late years was of very great quantity and value, within the forest or late forest of Dean, is become totally destroyed, except what is standing within the Woodwardship of the Lea Bailey, whereby there is an apparent scarcity of timber there, as in other parts of the Kingdom, so that some course is necessary to be speedily taken to restore and preserve the growth of timber for the future supply of his Majesty's Royal Navy, and the maintenance of shipping for the trade of this nation'. In summary, the Act provided:

1.   That 10,000 acres, part of the waste lands of the Forest shall be inclosed and kept for the growth of timber; likewise the 1,000 acres in the Cannop valley (see Section VI). The whole crown Forest totalled 23,000 acres.

2.   The cost of the inclosures to be defrayed by sale of decayed trees of beech, birch, hawthorn, hazel and holly, and other like trees not being timber.

3.   The inclosures to be bounded by sufficient mounds and fences.

4.   When the 11,000 acres of inclosures were past danger of browsing by deer and cattle, and other prejudice, they should be thrown open; and other areas inclosed – provided that the total area inclosed never exceeded 11,000 acres.

5.   The 11,000 acres, as well as all other waste lands to be under forest law.

6.   There shall be no alienation of the lands, mines or quarries within the inclosures.

7.   The number of deer within the Forest shall not exceed 800.

8.   Felling on private land to be allowed without licence.

9.   Previous offences under forest law to be remitted and discharged.

10.   Existing privileges of commoning and pannage to be retained.

11.   Existing privileges in Hudnalls of the inhabitants of the parish of St. Briavels to be retained; and saving the rights and privileges of the miners.

12.   Saving to Sir John Wintour, Francis Finch and Robert Clayton of a grant, made under letters patent on 30 July 1662, for a certain term of years unexpired.

13.   Saving of lease of coppices (named) to Thomas Preston (now claimed by the Stanhope family).

14.   Saving of grant of land at Mayly Scot [Mailscot] to Sir Edward Villars; the land shall not be part of the 23,000 acres.

---

[34] 19 & 20 Chas. II, c.8; Hart, *Royal Forest*, Appendix XII.

15. £1,500 to be paid to Banistree Mainard, his heirs or assigns in lieu of the Cannop valley woods.

16. The metes and bounds of the Forest to be in accord with the perambulation of 20 James I [1622–23].

17. Saving of grant [to the Terringham family] of coalmines and quarries of grindstone (except those within the 11,000 acres to be inclosed.)

At last, for Dean there was legislation ostensibly acceptable to most interests, whereunder the sylvan cover could be enriched and enlarged, making Dean again a storehouse of timber. Much would depend on the energy and integrity of the officials. On 11 June 1668[35] the Treasury was to consult the Marquis of Worcester, constable-warden, as to the names of those who with him and his deputy Sir Baynham Throckmorton, were to be commissioners under the Act. Sir Charles Harbord, one of the two surveyor-generals of woods, and his son William, considered how best to use the new powers;[36] they advised the appointment of three verderers (Col. William Cooke, Edward Cooke and Duncombe Colchester), and twelve regarders (John Witt, William Ailburton, Thomas Pyrke, William Gough, George Bond, George Berrow, Christopher Woodward, Edward White, Thomas Worgan, William Carpender, John Birkin, Jeremiah Hiet, Edward Morse, Edward Machen, Richard Nash, Thomas Walter, Edward Skin and William Brown). In July[37] the Treasury approved instructions to the commissioners, and a warrant was issued to the King's Remembrancer in October for thirty-two persons to be appointed:[38] they are named in Appendix II to this Section IX. Articles of Instruction to be observed by them are also given in Appendix II.

Throckmorton took charge of the deer and attended to the keepers.[39] On 23 June 1668[40] he had been given £46.14s.3d. to repair the court-house at Kensley (the Speech House) and the prison in St. Briavels Castle. The division between his duties and those of the marquis, John May (supervisor), and the two surveyor-generals (Harbord and Agar) is not clear.

Concurrently the Navy Commissioners continued to rely chiefly on Daniel Furzer, their local purveyor, to keep them informed about shiptimber in Dean. The relatively few sound timber-trees (oaks and beeches) were conserved, but the Treasury 8 January 1669 authorized the felling of dotards.[41] On 7 July 1669[42] the Treasury instructed the Dean commissioners to sell coppice 'at the best price', sufficient to raise £1,500 to compensate Lord Mainard (for the Cannop valley woods taken from him), but Agar was not to sell wood in the Lea Bailey until instructed.[43] May sold £3,000 of wood on the Treasury's instruction, half to be paid to Mainard and half to be used for enclosures.[44] Until this was accounted for, no more sales of wood were to be made.

---

[35] *Cal. Treas. Bks.*, II, T29/2, p. 351.
[36] Ibid. pp. 352, 371, 375.
[37] Ibid. p. 382.
[38] Ibid. p. 629; Treasury Miscellanea Warrants Early, XXXVII, pp. 175–7 (T51/37, p. 629).
[39] *Cal. Treas. Bks.*, p. 1607.
[40] Ibid. p. 584.
[41] Ibid., III, Pt. I, p. 4.
[42] Ibid. p. 78.
[43] Ibid. p. 244.
[44] Ibid. pp. 112, 113.

May and the verderers were instructed in July 1669[45] and again in August[46] 'not to suffer any sheep to go into the Forest, nor the colliers to have any wood unless they buy it'. May was instructed 'to take special care of the woods, in particular the 11,000 acres, to keep out cattle, and to forbid miners and colliers to cut wood'.[47] The Treasury wrote to the verderers concerning 'the great spoils and destruction of young sprouts of oak and beech heretofore made contrary to law by sheep, hogs, and other uncommonable cattle, which have frustrated the King's intention of preserving a nursery of trees'.[48] They were to 'proceed effectually against the like offenders in future'.

The Treasury at their meeting 12 October 1669[49] considered a letter from May 'about planting acorns in Dean Forest', and a copy was sent to the commissioners, who were to 'do what is fit, and provide the money'. The marquis, with Col. Cooke of Highnam, a verderer, attended before the Treasury 13 December[50] and reported that the ground they had resolved to enclose 'is fit for wood, and agreed at a swanimote court'; it was 'that resolved on in Cromwell's time'. The same day,[51] Harbord was informed that the king 'has this afternoon approved the enclosing of the ground in Dean'.

During this year, 1669,[52] a perambulation of the Forest was made by nineteen regarders (see Appendix I to this Section IX). Opposition to the enclosure was soon evident: enclosure was abhorrent to most of the local populace, as it had been to their ancestors. On 7 March 1670 the marquis wrote to Col. Cooke:[53]

I have met with several complaints and particularly from Mr. Agar the King's Surveyor [-general of woods] about the spoils the cabbins and other purprestures still continue in the Forest of Deane. You all know how much we contended for the preservation of that Forest and with what difficulty we got it restored to the condition it now is in, but if after all this the several officers who are entrusted with the care of it be remiss in the performance of their duties and putting the same in as vigorous expression, we can hope for little benefit or improvement either in or without the inclosure but the expectation of his Majesty and the whole kingdom to be altogether . . . which will certainly be charged upon the misgovernment of the Forest and negligence of the officers.

Wherefore I do earnestly recommend to your serious consideration: First that you admit of none to be sworn deputies to the [hereditary] Foresters or Woodwards but such as are capable and fit to serve and that you require them strictly to bring in their presentments at every [Attachment] Court taking care that their Masters allow them such convenient salaries as may enable them wholly to intend the business of the Forest.

Secondly that the Regarders do with all convenient speed perambulate the Forest to reduce all purprestures and incroachments which should indeed have been done long before this.

And lastly that you [the verderers] do by your own view of two or more of you together with the Regarders and Keepers cause all the cabbins throughout the whole Forest to be

[45] *Cal. Treas. Bks.*, III, Pt. I, pp. 112, 113.
[46] Ibid. p. 262.
[47] Ibid.
[48] Ibid.
[49] Ibid. p. 145.
[50] Ibid. p. 170.
[51] Ibid. p. 313.
[52] F20/1 (12).
[53] Glos. R.O., D2026 Bond Papers, X.22. See proposals for an overseer to prevent abuses etc., in Glouc. Liby. LX10.3(3), after 1668.

utterly demolished and thrown down out of hand and to inflict the severity of the law upon such as shall presume to erect any more except such as are necessary and of present use for Mr Foley's colliers [charcoal burners], and those also to be taken away as soon as the wood is [char]coaled, that so the Forest may be cleared and left free from any thing that may hinder the growth and improvement . . . I hope you will take such effectual care of them and every thing else which may conduce to the benefit and advantage of the Forest as become persons so intrusted as you are and that I shall have just occasion to thank you who are Your affectionate friend and servant, [Signed] WORCESTER.

On 12 April 1670[54] the Treasury considered and passed to the Privy Council information from the marquis relating to abuses in Dean. On 21 June[55] the marquis with Throckmorton, his deputy, attended 'about pulling down hedges in Dean', whereupon the Treasury solicitor was ordered ' to prosecute the rioters in the King's behalf'.

The Dean commissioners were asked by the Treasury 18 April[56] to give account of enclosures made and what money had been expended. Agar was forthwith 'to draw an exact plot of the Forest,[57] to fell 40 tons of timber for building a new Speech Court,[58] and to sell at Bristol or elsewhere to the king's best benefit the many parcels of timber, some rough, some ready-squared, amounting in all to 1,200 tons or thereabouts, lying dispersed in Dean and especially in the new enclosures.[59] The timber was 'running in daily decay, being purloined and embezzled by the country, and will be of great damage to the enclosures if left to be drawn when the young shoots are up'. In July[60] the Treasury ordered a Mr Burlacy to stop grubbing-up roots under a right he claimed from Sir John Winter; his agents had grubbed up in the enclosure of Austons Bridge, lately sown with acorns 'for future King's timber'; grubbing-up would be 'a great destruction to that intended nursery'. His claim was to be heard.[61] About this time John Smith was commended by the Duke of York 'for his care in improvement of the Forest of Dean',[62] but what he had done is unknown.

In July 1671[63] Samuel Pepys, Secretary to the Navy, with Lord Brounker and J. Tippets, surveyed the Forest for three days,[64] and found no trees suitable for the Navy except in the Lea Bailey, about half beeches and half oaks. However, within the Forest they found:

Several parcels of well grown woods from 10 to 90 years growth containing in all per estimate 1,200 acres for the most part very thriving and well secured, wherein is no want for heirs or standells both of beech and oak, the ground seeming equally inclined to both; and were the underwood (which shares too much of the nourishment with what is fit to be preserved) taken away, these would thrive much the better, and would soon get the mastery thereof, and the underwood (as it is said) will yield, over and above the charge of

[54] *Cal. Treas. Bks.*, III, Pt. 1, p. 401.
[55] Ibid. p. 457.
[56] Ibid. pp. 406, 553.
[57] Ibid. p. 531.
[58] Ibid. p. 648.
[59] Ibid. p. 408, 19 April 1670.
[60] Ibid. p. 650.
[61] Ibid. p. 493.
[62] *Cal.* SP 29/1670, p. 560.
[63] Ibid. p. 463.
[64] Pepys' Liby. MSS Cambridge, 2265; Hart, *Royal Forest*, p. 172 and Appendix XIII.

cutting, from 5s. to 6s. the acre, which in case it be sold it is conceived necessary to fell it at his Majesty's charge, thereby to prevent the cutting down of what should be found fit to be preserved.

They further commented:

Of the 10,000 acres ordered, it is said that 8,486 acres are already planted [much of the replenishment had been effected by natural regeneration and coppice regrowth, but there had been some sowing of acorns and possibly of beech mast] and very well fenced either with stone walls or ditches with banks quick-sett [planted with quickthorn]; in divers places (especially where there are bushes) the oaks come up very well but not so in the bare places what is judged to be the greatest part thereof. The soil for the greater part is light sandy ground, here and there rocky, the timber much alike on both, which gives little encouragement to expect much thence for the support of the Navy in future ages, yet it was conceived that it would be convenient that which is fenced in should be preserved, the charge thereof being already over, and will require only the care of the officers, whose duty it is to look after it, but that no more charge be laid out in planting there, not only for that the timber is no better qualities, but in regard of the great charge of transporting the same to any of his Majesty's yards which is likely to be no less than the full price of as good (if not better) timber than this Forest affords.

Pepys and his colleagues did not think highly of the quality of Dean's oak because of its over-maturity, its heart-rot and stem-rot, and the shakes within it, probably from lack of shelter. But they misjudged the potential of the younger trees on the 1,000 acres of the Lea Bailey and those in the 8,000 or so acres of enclosures, chiefly of oak and beech, growing slowly but surely.

In April 1672[65] May reported that 'another fire occurred in the Forest'; he with the constable-warden were ordered by the Treasury to 'take an exact state of it'. On 15 January 1673[66] May was confirmed in his appointment as supervisor, with a salary of £100, and £20 to be paid to each of his two deputies. He was 'to preserve the standing woods and young woods that shall grow on the 11,000 acres and all the woods and underwoods on the wastes'. A warrant 2 January[67] had instructed him to 'keep off all uncommonable cattle and to forbid all colliers and miners to cut any beech, birch, ash, hazel, or other underwood upon the wastes other than rights saved to them by the Act of 20 Charles II [1668]'. He was to take special care that no fires were started, and to guard against spoils. Persons found cutting underwood or trees were to be apprehended and brought before the constable-warden or a justice of the peace, or before 'others enabled to inflict punishment thereon'.

On 10 July[68] the Treasury issued a warrant to May, Agar and the other surveyor-general, Charles Strode who had replaced Harbord, to mark sufficient trees for 120 tons of timber, half for rebuilding the Speech Court House and half for repairing St. Briavels Castle, as well as sufficient dotard trees to raise £200 for repairing the house and £200 for repairing the castle.[69]

The Treasury, finding that the commission on Dean was not 'fully perfected',[70] on 3 June 1673[71] asked the attorney-general for a commission to the marquis,

---

[65] *Cal. Treas. Bks.*, III, Pt. I, p. 1065.
[66] Ibid. IV, p. 1.
[67] Ibid. p. 48.
[68] Ibid. p. 369.
[69] The warrant was written over and dated 22 Sept. 1673 (ibid.).

Throckmorton, and ten others, Sir Thomas How, Sir George Probert, three verderers (William Cooke, Edward Cooke, Duncombe Colchester), John Smith, Thomas Agar, Henry Milburne, John May and John Wade. They were to call to their assistance Thomas Dunning of Purton, William Walter, William Taffe, John Witt, Kedgwin Hoskins, George Worrell, Thomas Perke and John Hawkins, 'gentlemen inhabiting those parts'.[72] The Articles of Instruction given to them are in Appendix IV to this Section IX. On 16 June[73] a Treasury warrant was given to Agar for £100 'to be obtained by felling dotard timber for charge of the commission and to do necessary repairs of the mounds and fences'.

## THE END OF THE 'KING'S IRONWORKS'

A major consideration in 1674 was whether to relet the 'King's Ironworks', and the effect of them on the reforestation.[74] Re-leasing was not wanted in Dean. The marquis, Throckmorton and Col. Cooke attended a Treasury meeting where it was minuted that 'the Lord Chief Baron is to be consulted about prosecution of those men that commit spoils in Dean' and 'to urge the King to remove the ironworks out of the Forest as they are conceived to be the destruction of the wood and timber'. Throckmorton was of the opinion that 'cutting down of the coppice was inconsistent with the raising of timber'. The sale of cordwood was considered. On 11 March[75] the Treasury announced the sale of the ironworks to Paul Foley (Herefordshire ironmaster) to be demolished before 1 May next and to be carried away before September. Thus ended the sixty-four years' story of the 'King's Ironworks'. Thereafter, only ironworks beyond Dean's sylvan cover were sustained by Dean's cordwood.[76] In March 1674 much cordwood was sold in the Lea Bailey to Messrs. Hanway and Forth.[77]

## KEEPERS' WALKS AND LODGES

On 10 March 1674[78] the Treasury proposed to appoint a new supervisor of Dean's woods at £100 per annum and six keepers at £20 per annum each; to spend annually £30 on repairs to fences and gaps; and to build six lodges for the keepers. On 18 April that year[79] the Treasury appointed Throckmorton conservator and supervisor of Dean; its officials were put in his charge. He was to admit no sheep, hogs, or other uncommonable cattle. On 23 May[80] he was allowed £400 to repair the enclosures. £300 was to be handed to William Wolseley for building lodges, and £100 to Throckmorton[81] who with Agar and Strode were to 'repair substantially

[70] *Cal. Treas. Bks.*, IV, p. 63; F20/1(14).
[71] Ibid. IV, p. 150.
[72] F20/1 (14); Hart, *Royal Forest*, p. 173.
[73] *Cal. Treas. Bks.*, IV, p. 167.
[74] Hart, *Royal Forest*, pp. 174–5.
[75] *Cal. Treas. Bks.*, IV, p. 489.
[76] Hart, *Royal Forest*, p. 175.
[77] Ibid. p. 174.
[78] *Cal. Treas. Bks.*, IV, p. 172. Copy of proposals in Glouc. Liby. LX10.3(2).
[79] Ibid. p. 508.
[80] Ibid. p. 244.
[81] Ibid. p. 529.

the banks, gates, and stiles of the enclosures, taking none but ready-cut timber for the work.[82] The same two surveyor-generals of woods were ordered 3 August[83] 'to sell to the best advantage 318 tons of timber cut and lying dispersed in Dean and 88 tons of timber saved out of the dotard trees in the Lea Bailey this summer'.

In September 1675[84] the Marquis of Worcester, still constable-warden, was reminded that 10,000 acres were enclosed under the Act of 1668 'but for want of proper view and care thereof the same are like to be of no effect, no particular part being under any man's distinct charge as in other of the King's forests where they are by walks or districts'. Treasurer Danby had thereupon 'caused the Forest to be divided into six walks and had built six lodges therein, with 30 acres of grazing land to each, and appointed six keepers'. The six lodges and land, part of the statutory 11,000 acres, were named, as well as their walks, 'The King's' or 'Charles II' or 'Speech House', 'York', 'Danby', 'Worcester', 'Latimer', and 'Herbert'.[85] Descriptions of the boundaries of the Speech House Walk and York Walk are extant.[86] The marquis, besides being constable-warden, was President of the Council of Wales, Governor of Chepstow, and later became Duke of Beaufort. For the management of Dean he had to rely substantially on Throckmorton, who resided alongside the Forest at Clearwell. The six Woodwardships (cf. Bailiwicks) were still in existence; their boundaries are given in Appendix III to this Section IX. On 9 June 1676 a Swanimote Court for the Forest was held at the Speech House – see Appendix V to this Section.

A document of c. 1677[87] restating that following the Act of 1668 a commission was issued out of the Court of Exchequer, and that '8,500 acres or thereabouts had been admeasured, set out and inclosed', confirmed that inclosing 'did for some years prove ineffective until about two years since [c. 1675], when the Forest had been divided into six walks, lodges built, and an increase of maintenance allowed for a supervisor and six keepers, and repair of fences'; but 'there yet remained some things to be done necessary for completing the work'. There remaining decayed trees sufficient to bear the charge, the Treasury were requested to direct the inclosing of 2,500 acres to make up 11,000 acres, and issued a new commission, directing that:

> The inclosures may be made of such lands as may be most apt and fit for the increase and growth of wood and timber.

> Inquiry be made of the fitness or unfitness of any parts of the former inclosures, and if any part of it be found unfit, or out of danger by cattle, the same be laid open and other parts more fit inclosed in lieu thereof according to the Act of 1668; and of what parts of the inclosures may be fit to be planted with young plants of oak and what best sown with acorns, and what the charges will be.

> Strict inquiry be made how the verderers, supervisor, foresters[-of-fee], woodwards, keepers, and all other officers do their duties in relation to this Act and the trust reposed in them, and that rules and directions be given them for that purpose.

[82] *Cal. Treas. Bks.*, IV, p. 543.
[83] Ibid. p. 562.
[84] Ibid. p. 822.
[85] Hart, *Royal Forest*, p. 177.
[86] Ibid.
[87] F20/1 (10).

Inquiry be made what persons dig coal or quarries of stone, and in what parts of the Forest, and with what prejudice to the inclosures and woods, and to inquire into the claims of the colliers and miners who pretend to take wood for their collieries and iron mines, and how destruction of wood by them may for the future be prevented.

Inquire by what right sheep are kept in the Forest, and how they may be restrained by law.

Inquire how fitly the districts [walks] are made, and the lodges situated and built, and what has been expended about St. Briavels Castle and the Speech House.

Inquire how the fences around inclosures are at present preserved, and how they may be better for the future; as also the young wood, and particularly in the Lea Bailey; and how the Forest has of late been damnified by firing the covert, and who have been responsible.

Inquire what quantity of fallen timber was left in the Forest belonging to the King when the Act of 1668 passed, and how and by whom disposed of, and what is less.

Inquire what trees and wood and of what sort have since that time been felled in the Forest, and by what authority, and how and by whom disposed of.

Inquire how the necessary [high]ways of the Forest are prejudiced by overhanging of boughs, and how the same may be remedied without prejudice to the growth of timber.

Mend and complete the map of the Forest [probably that of 1608] by setting down the names of each of the Inclosures and the contents of acres, to distinguish the bounds of each woodwardship and also of the several walks as now set out and how the lodges are situated, and what parts of the Forest are hilly and as they lie uphill or downhill, and what is lawn, and to distinguish all the brooks and rills of water.

## THE COMMISSION OF 1678

For 1678 there is a Return of Commissioners for Dean, made by Agar and others including: 'John Aram, Will. Dunning, Will. Walton, John Witt, Kedgwyn Hoskins, George Wyrrall, Thomas Pyrke, Jo. Hawkins, and Will. Aylburton, gent.':[88]

We have viewed and perambulated the several parts and places of the Forest as well inclosed and uninclosed . . . and we have considered the coppice woods now growing in the Forest which might be fit to be cut being generally of 20 years growth and upwards, and according to our best computation and the judgment of several experts and able corders do estimate the whole to amount to about 7,372 acres dispersedly over the Forest; and contain in short cords of wood about 61,643 cords, each cord being of 2ft. 2ins. in length of the billett, 4ft. 6ins. in height of the cord and 8ft. 4ins. in length of the cord on the ground, according to the usual Forest measure. Which to be cut in seven years, proportionately one year with another, will amount unto 8,860 cords by the year.
   The first year, the fellett to be made on the Vinyhill, Deadman's Crosse, Hardbrook, the Bayley, the old Fellett, Breams Eves and the Park Hill, being generally beech and some birch wood of 30 years growth containing about 600 acres and about 20 cords on an acre.
   The second year, on Darkhill, Bromly, Oakwood, Whinmill, Birchhill, the Cleeve, Quistslad, Fetterhill, Bicksheadslad and Barnehill, being generally beech and some birch

wood of 25 and 30 years growth containing about 400 acres and some 20, some 40, cords on an acre.

The third year, on Tiritryhill, Whimbereleyslad, The Perch, part of Cannop next to Coverham, under Fetterhill, under Barnihill from Bickshead to Owley Slad, Hangerbury and Wyrrall Hill, being generally birch of about 30 years growth containing about 320 acres, and between 20 and 30 cords on an acre.

The fourth year, on Newnhams Rudge, Bleekes Fellett, Brockweare Hill, Joymere Head, Wainway, Shadoweringhurst, Phelpes Meadow, Stonedge, the Wetwood, Little Kensley, Rushie Lawne and Brockweares Ditches to [?] faire mere, being most birch and some beech upwards of 20 years growth containing about 800 acres and about 12 cords on an acre.

The fifth year, at Meere Brook, Perryhay, Middle Rudge, Saintly, Saintly Brake Green, Little Staplege, Cudley, Mizyhurst, Blackenys Eves, Badgershurst, Great Kensleys Edge, and the Cole Delfs, being generally birch and some beech of 20 years growth and upwards growing dispersedly over a great quantity of ground.

The sixth year, at Danniel Moor, [?] Oxeling, Myzy, Beechenhurst, Handsley, the Moorewood, Godmeadow, Aywood, and Bliths Bayley, being most part beech upwards of 20 years growth containing about 800 acres and 12 cords on an acre.

The seventh year, at Edgehills, Chestnutts, Bradley, the Copes, and the Lineing Wood, being beech and hazel, some 12, some 20 years growth containing about 1,000 acres and 10 cords on an acre.

Which at 8,860 cords per annum amounts to £2,201.10s. in money.

The said [cord]wood cannot be well valued by the acre because it grows more dispersedly than usually coppice does, but might be cut and sold by the cord and we conceive may yield 5s. per cord, all charges of cutting and cording being deducted.

There are yet standing in the Lea Bailey some 10,984 trees of oak and beech which are generally old and decaying and very fit to be cut having little or no timber in them useful for shipping. But do contain in them, according to the best computation we could make, 1,449 tons of timber such as may be vended in the country at better rates than the cordwood, and also 33,694 short cords of wood, which to be cut in 7 years, proportionately one year with another, will amount to 4,813 cords by the year. And in certain quarters of the wood, for the benefit of the young spring [natural growth – seedlings and coppice regrowth]. And we do conceive the same may be worth to be sold 5s. the cord, all charges of cutting and cording being deducted. But we cannot tell certainly what quantity may be vended in the year, Chapmans [buyers] refusing to treat with us without certain price and that we had powers to treat or sell.

A good part of the coppice wood above certified is now standing and growing within his Majesty's inclosures, and in many parts of them there are hopeful young woods of oak and beech, and were very many more before this last year that the country people's cattle lay commonly in them, all which hath caused a very great destruction of the wood that was springing up. The mounds of the said inclosures are generally standing and very substantial, but many gaps in them and also in the stone walls; and the gates almost all thrown down, broke or stolen away and the hooks and eyes torn out and carried away, but they are done for the most part in the night, so that the offenders cannot be discovered. And by reason of these and the like misdemeanours the inclosures lie as common as any other parts of the Forest. If his Majesty will be pleased to cut only the old wood of the Lea Bayly for the present and let the other young woods of the Forest be respited for some years, and that the Iron Works be demolished and sold [as they had been], it would lend very much to the preservation of the Forest and the raising of timber again for the benefit of posterity according to the intent of the late Act of Parliament [1668].

No records of action on the above Return have been found.

## THE COMMISSION OF 1680

On 23 July 1679[89] the Treasury secretary asked Harbord to draw up instructions for preparing a new commission for Dean, and a warrant 26 August[90] was given to the King's Remembrancer for a commission to the marquis, Throckmorton, the two surveyor-generals of woods, the surveyor-general of crown lands, Charles Lord Herbert of Raglan, and thirteen others, namely: William Cooke, Henry Norwood, Tracy Catchmay, Herbert Westfaling, Robert Codrington, John Fitzherbert, William Morgan, William Paulett, William Wall, Abraham Clarke, William Wolseley, John Wade, and Col. Edward Cooke.[91] They were to 'view and perambulate Dean to observe the present state and condition thereof'.[92] They reported 23 April 1680[93] that the Forest was about 23,600 acres:

1.   Much of the better half, dispersedly over the Forest, is well-covered with young wood of oak, beech, birch, hawthorn, hazel and holly, in many places whereof are very hopeful young oaks and beeches of 40 years growth and particularly on Edge Hills, Hangerbury and the Moore Wood, Newhams Ridge, Ivymorehead, Brockweares Ditches, Bleekes Fellet, the Lineing Wood, Breems Eves, Parkehill, Nockeley, Oakewood, part of the Buckholt, Moyry Stocke, part of Cannoppe in Coverham, Queist Slade, Bickesheade Slade, Owlyslade, the lower part of Barnehill, and the lower side of the Great Inclosure between the hills and the Brook, all of which have been inclosed and are generally grown past danger of browsing of deer or cattle, and Bleythes Bayley, the lower side of Aywood, Bradley and the Copes, the lower part of Blakeneys Eves, Viney Hill, Deadman's Cross, Howbridgeslade, the Old Fellett, many parts of the Wetwood, of Blackpennywall and of Stone Edge, the Fence and part of the Great Boort next Moyry Stocke, which have not been inclosed of late years are in like manner well grown with oak, beech and birch past danger of cattle.

2.   The other parts of the Forest as well inclosed as uninclosed consist of hills bare of wood, and places called Lawnes in which nevertheless there are good store of bushes and cover convenient for the growth and shelter of young timber-trees, and where within the memory of man have been store of great oaks and as good timber as in other parts of the Forest and indeed all parts of it seem very apt and inclinable to the production of wood, but we do not find any considerable improvement from the late Inclosures those parts generally remaining still bare of wood within them, which were so before the Inclosures by reason that the fences have been very ill-kept and the gates wilfully broken and set open to let in cattle which have destroyed great quantities of young oaks in divers parts which had been sowed with acorns, so that we conceive Ruerdeane Inclosure and that of the Lea Bayley very fit to be kept inclosed and have accordingly taken care for the immediate repair of the gates and fences of them, they both containing by admeasureament 1,811 acres. That Edgehills and Hangerbury Inclosures may be thrown up and likewise the Great Inclosure except one part of it at Newnhams Ridge and Brockweares Ditches called Yorkley Inclosure containing about 800 acres, and that other Inclosures should be made in lesser quantities on the bare hills and Lawnes in places where no highway passes through them that there be no need of gates, as may be very fitly done on Blakeneys

[89] *Cal. Treas. Bks.*, VI, pp. 145, 196, 482.
[90] Ibid.
[91] Hart, *Royal Forest*, p. 178.
[92] *Cal. Treas. Bks.*, VI, p. 196.
[93] Glos. R.O., D.23/31, Probyn Papers; Hart, *Royal Forest*, pp. 178–9 and Appendix XIV; part in 3rd Rept. of 1788, p. 18.

Bayley, the Old Bayly, Misleyhurst, the Great Boort Hill, and in Daniel Moore, the two Kensleys, Covers Eves, and other such places which have formerly yielded large excellent timber-trees and may be so done at much less charge and far more easily kept and preserved to answer the end of their inclosing, and we conceive the charge thereof may be after the rate of 14d. by the perch.

3.    We do not find any considerable spoil done of late by cutting the young woods (except in Chestnuts and Edgehills lying upon the borders of the Forest near Severn) but the greatest mischief has been the firing of the gorse and young woods which has destroyed multitudes of hopeful young oaks and beeches. Neither do we know of any underwood fallen or sold within the Inclosures since they were made but what was cut to clear the keepers' 30 acres apiece in which the oak and beech were all left standing.

    The colliers and miners have had some birch and orle [alder] delivered to them for the support of their pits of the value of £6 or £7 per annum without paying for the same of late years which they pretend an ancient right to by prescription, and we humbly conceive the title ought to be tried with them whether they have such right or not.

    The keepers need very little browse for the deer in winter by reason the cover is so good, and when they do cut any it is chiefly holly of which there is plenty in the Forest, but they do cut hawthorn for the fences when they are repaired.

4.    We have viewed the Inclosure of the Lea Bayleywicke, wherein we find very hopeful thick spring of underwood growing in those parts which are out of the reach of the dropping of old trees and but little under them, and there are still remaining in the said Lea Bayleywicke 10,400 trees of oak and beech or near thereabouts which are generally windshaken and decayed especially the oak, and in which we fear will be found very little timber serviceable for shipping or worth the charge of carriage and transportation to His Majesty's yards, but by estimation of able carpenters and corders do contain in them 1,400 tons of timber useful for building and other ordinary uses in the country and may be sold at about 18s. a ton, and 30,000 short cords of 2-foot wood worth, as we conceive and as the price is according to the present contract with Alderman Forth and his assigns 5s. the cord clear of all charges, and we conceive it exceeding necessary for His Majesty's service and the benefit of the young spring that these old trees be felled and disposed of to His Majesty's best advantage and that the Inclosure be strictly and carefully maintained and looked to which in few years would produce an excellent Coppice and great store of young timber-trees for the service of future times.

5.    We know not of any persons that have been concerned since the said Act in receiving any money for wood in the Forest besides the surveyors of His Majesty's Woods and their agents, and one Mr. Davis of Clowerwall who received the money for the cordwood which was cut on the keepers' 30 acres apiece; and Mr. Rowles, steward of the Forest Courts, deposed before us that he has in his hands about £40 and no more for amercements imposed at the said Courts under the value of 4d. upon trespass in vert.

6.    There are still remaining about 30 cabins in several parts of the Forest, inhabited by about 100 poor people many of whom have been born in the Forest and never lived out of it and we have taken care to demolish the said cabbins and inclosures about them but that it will require some little longer time for the effectual removing and the legal settlement of them in other places.

7.    We have caused 340 old decayed oaks and beeches to be felled in the Lea Bayley (having been first viewed and allowed to be fallen by 2 Justices of the Peace as the said Act directs) to raise money for the several uses and services directed in and by

Plate VII. The Speech House in the centre of the Forest of Dean – venue of the Verderers' attachment court. (From a drawing by T. Pinnell, *c.* 1782)

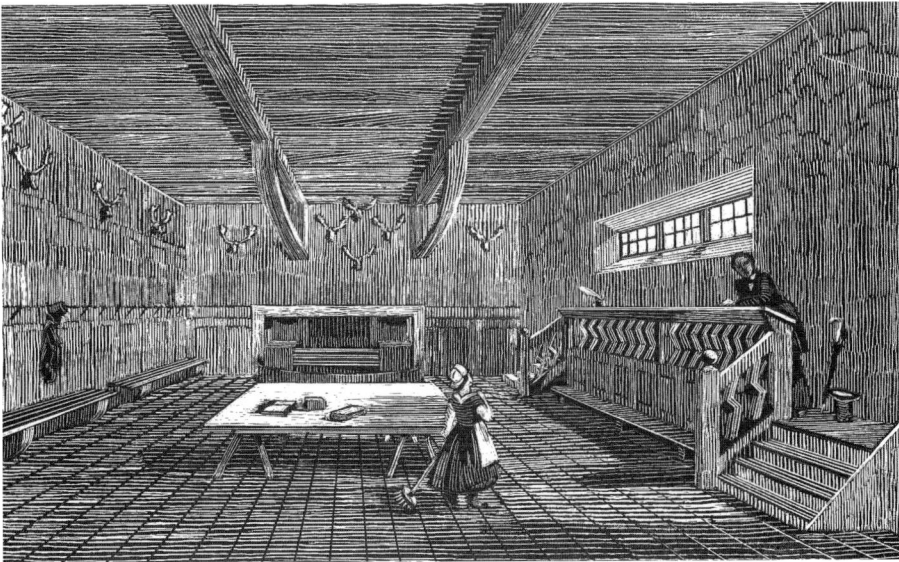

Plate VIII. The Speech House. The courtroom from an old lithograph.

the said Commission whereof Mr. Agar the surveyor of his Majesty's Woods is to render an accompt to his Majesty's Exchequer when the said trees are all cut down and the several services performed and done.

The commissioners also reported that St. Briavels Castle and the Speech House were being repaired and the lodges built (the keepers to keep them in repair out of their wages); that there was a need for a Justice Seat once a year for six or seven years to render the Forest Courts effective and to compel the Officers of Inheritance to be diligent and faithful in the discharge of their several duties; that cutting and clearing of the overhangings were necessary in the several highways leading through the Forest from Market to Market; and that the ironworks had been demolished by Paul Foley. Finally the commissioners reported that they had found 'in several places of the Lea Bayley where fires had lately been kindled among the thickest of the young trees to the destruction of many of them which will prove of fatal consequence to the rest of the Forest unless some remedy can be continued, because the Inclosures never so strictly kept up are no protection in this case'. The Report was signed by Baynham Throckmorton, Edward Cooke, Tracy Catchmay, William Wall, John Fitzherbert, Thomas Agar, Herbert Westfaling and John Wade.

The Treasury empowered the commissioners to raise money by sale of old decayed oaks and beeches sufficient to pay the warden and the keepers, to make a map of the Forest, to build pounds, to sow acorns (not exceeding £5) and to repair the Speech House and enclosures.[94] On 21 July 1680[95] the Treasury authorized Agar and Strode to raise from wood sales £210 for salaries of keepers and other officials for the year 1679; £40 for completing and finishing a proposed court-house over the market place in Coleford [this was not done, and no forest court was held there]; and the further sum necessary to make additional enclosures. The wood was to be sold to the assignees of John Forth under his unexpired contract for cordwood.

In the same year, as a result of the 1680 Report, the constable-warden, the Marquis of Worcester, issued to the keepers and other officers of the Forest firm instructions 'for the better preservation of the vert and venison thereof':[96]

First, you and every of you [sic] shall diligently and constantly both early and late perambulate within your respective walks for the discovery and apprehension of offenders in the vert and venison of the Forest and upon all occasions shall aid and assist one another in this service.

[Deer] That you do inform yourselves of and frequently search all suspected houses, outhouses and places adjoining to your walks for timber, wood, deerskins, guns, crossbows, nets &c and where you find them to seize them and apprehend the parties and bring them before a magistrate to find sureties to answer the offence and to kill or take away all greyhounds and other dogs that are dangerous and destructive to the game kept near the Forest by any persons whatsoever, and to apprehend all persons that shall be straying out of the highways of the Forest with guns or dogs. You are to have an especial regard to the gunsmiths and other smiths round the Forest and often to search their houses and shops, and take an account what kind of guns they make or mend and seize such as

[94] F20/1 (13); Hart, *Royal Forest*, p. 179.
[95] *Cal. Treas. Bks.*, VI, p. 641.
[96] F20/1 (13).

are unlawful and dangerous to the game, and make inquiry of the leather dressers round the Forest what deer skins are brought to them and by whom.

[*Vert*] You are to prevent all cutting of fern for ashes or other uses and furze, hollies, hawthorns and other vert whatsoever, it being found by experience that they do preserve the young trees at their first coming up.

[*Officers' duties*] And whereas heretofore the woodwards and foresters[-of-fee] of the Forest for want of a particular charge given them and their deputies, and for want of competent salary, have neglected to walk in the Forest for the preservation thereof as by the tenures of their lands are their duties they are obliged, it is now therefore thought most expedient for the more strict-looking to the same for the future that Sir Baynham Throckmorton's deputy forester and woodward of the Berse and Henry Worgan and Christopher Dowle, foresters, be especially assistant to John Byles keeper of York walk; and that Edward Hooper forester and the woodwards of the two woodwardships of Staunton and Bicknor be assistant to Ketford Bond, keeper of Worcester walk; and that Mr. John Vaughan's and Mr. Roper's deputy foresters and woodwards, and the woodwards of the Lea Bailey and Mitchel Deane be assistant to Thomas Creed gentleman, keeper of Herbert walk; and that Mr. Eustace Hardwick or his deputy forester Richard Hill gentleman and woodward of Blayes Bayley, William Brayne gentleman or his deputy forester and the woodward of Badcocks Bayly, be assistant to Richard Jelfe keeper of Latimer walk; and that Robert Wilmotts, William Ayres and Mr. Berrow's deputy woodward be assistant to Robert Belcher keeper of Danby walk; for the better preservation of the Forest. Which officers are required to meet and assist the keepers daily in their respective walks according as by the law they are bound to do; and if any of them shall refuse or neglect to do the same you are to give weekly notice thereof to the supervisor of the woods of the Forest or his deputy and make true presentments thereof to the verderers to the end they may be proceeded with as the law directs. And all the woodwards are to take notice that they and their woodwardships stand responsible for all spoil and destruction committed within their respective woodwardships.

[*Fishing*] You are to take care that the brooks and ponds of the Forest be kept and preserved from fishing and laving, and to apprehend all persons that shall presume to offend therein.

[*Fences and gates*] You are to go round the outbounds of your respective walks once every day to see what spoils are committed and diligently to perambulate the fences of the Inclosures, and if any part of them or the gates or stiles shall be broken down, cut or pulled up, you are to take care that the same may be made up and amended within 24 hours at the furthest, and that the gates be well hung with latches to such as shall require the same.

[*Impounding*] You are strictly to inquire after, and apprehend, and convey to the Castle of St. Briavels all persons that shall wilfully throw down any of the Inclosures or cut any gate or stile or that shall set open any gate on purpose to let cattle into the Inclosures, and to take notice of all persons that shall wilfully turn into the Inclosures, and especially in the night time any working horses or other cattle whatsoever, which you are from time to time to drive and to impound, and there in pound to keep them till the verderers shall give order for their release and then not to be discharged without paying a penny a foot for the first and second offences, and for the third offence you are to seize them and keep them till the next court and there present them as forfeit to his Majesty and to be sold by the verderers. That you do not permit any cattle of what nature soever to come and depasture within any of the Inclosures at any time of the year nor in any other part of the Forest during the Fence Month and Winter Heyning, but drive and impound them and cause the owners to pay as aforesaid.

[*Fires*] That you be very careful in the spring time and all other dry seasons of the year to hinder and prevent the firing of gorse and fern in the Forest and to apprehend the offenders. And the keeper of Worcester walk is to take especial care that the stowles [stools] of the trees therein lately cut be not cut up and conveyed away by the country.

[*Deer*] That you be aiding and assisting to the rangers of the Forest in the performance of their duties in the chacing and driving in the outlying deer and beating off of their hounds when the deer are come into the Forest. And that you take notice how the four men [of each township] and the reeve perform their duties all in making their presentments. And you are daily to fetch in the deer near the respective walks.

[*Impounding*] That all cattle taken in the Forest in King Charles the Second's walk [The Speech House walk] and in York, Worcester and Danby walks be brought to the new pound at Parkend and to no other place on any pretence whatsoever, and public notice given to the country thereof that so all people may resort thither when they miss their cattle, and that the pound keeper take a groat (and no more) for every man's cattle (be they more or less) according to the custom of the manor of St. Briavels and other places for his constant pains and attendance at the pound to receive them in and deliver them out.

[*Uncommonable animals*] That you suffer no sheep, hoggs, goats or other uncommonable cattle to go in the Forest at any time of the year, nor stone colts contrary to the Statute, nor maingy or other diseased horses. And if you find any pigs wilfully put into the Forest that you cannot conveniently drive you are to kill them and you are to give public notice to the country hereof that they may prevent it. That if any colts be found in the Fence Month or Winder Heyning within the Forest that cannot easily be taken up, and the owners after notice given there by public proclamation in the parish churches or market towns, shall not take them up and fetch them forth within 6 days, that you do kill them. It being formerly a custom that persons who have no right of common breed young colts and horses that are so wild that the keepers cannot take them though they almost ride their horses to death after them. That you take especial notice what cattle are put into the Forest by foreigners not having right of common there and give notice thereof to the fee-farmers and other officers of the Forest that they may be seized.

[*Strawberries and wimberries*] You are in the Fence Month (as much as in you lies) to hinder all persons from coming into the Forest to gather strawberries and wimberries; and to have a special regard to them in your several walks that they do not take up the young fawns.

[*Timber and wood*] That you suffer no timber or other wood of any kind to be carried out of your walks respectively without a good warrant for the same which is to be presented by you at the next Speech Court with the quantity and quality of wood or timber and by whom and when carried; and to that end every keeper is to take charge of all the timber and cordwood in his walk respectively and to stand responsible for the same.

[*Pitwood*] For preventing of abuses committed by the miners and colliers upon pretence of taking wood for their pits, you are to take especial care that every collier or miner shall presume to cut any oak or beech upon any pretence whatsoever be severely proceeded against as offenders; and the like for those that shall presume to cut any other wood before they first acquaint the verderers of their wants at the Speech Court and pray leave to have the same; or before the woodward of the woodwardship and keeper of the walk shall view their said wants, whether they be real or not, and thereupon to take notice how much and what sort of wood, and in what places they shall take the same for their said pits, and the value thereof, and make presentment of the same at the next Speech Court there to be recorded.

[*Cabins*] You are to take care that all cabbins upon the wast of the Forest be pulled down and none suffered to be erected for the future.

[*Gates*] You are to take care that colliers within Mosely gate do keep and secure that gate, otherwise you are not to suffer them to work there, and that the like care be taken for the gate upon the Bayhead in Lombard's Marsh.

[*Highways*] You are from time to time to give an account unto the deputy constable and to the supervisor of the Forest of the condition and want of repairs and overhanging of the common highways and of the bridges within your several walks to the end they may be timely amended to prevent greater charge.

[*Offenders*] You are likewise to give an account unto the deputy constable aforesaid of the names of persons that shall fly out of this country for any offence committed in the Forest to the end if they return again they may not be forgotten but apprehended and proceeded against.

[*Presentments*] That you be very exact in making your presentments at the courts of the Forest as to the person offending, of what place and condition he is, the true place and manner of his committing the offence, to what value the offence is, and with what instrument he committed the same being forfeited; and if the same offence be done with cattle as carrying wood or timber then you are to ascertain the number, quality and value of them with the value of the cart or waggon, to the end the King may be satisfied by and for the Forest thereof. You are to give speedy notice unto the supervisor of the Forest under the Lord Treasurer or in his absence to his deputy, of all spoils, trespasses and offences committed in the vert of the Forest and Inclosures thereof, and of neglect of officers touching the same, to the end the Lord High Treasurer may be acquainted therewith for the speedy and effectual redressing thereof. That for the better discharge of your duties you are to walk constantly armed with a gun, with a horn and doggline, and with a mastiffe and draught hound, and upon blowing the horn you are instantly to repair unto one another's assistance.

[*Attachments*] For the better understanding of making attachments you are to take notice that all persons taken in the manner by a forester or keeper for venison are immediately to be carried to St. Briavels Castle; and for wood or vert are presently to be attached and carried before a verderer to find sureties for his appearance at the next swanimote court to answer his offences, and to be imprisoned till he find such sureties in St. Briavels Castle. And if the party be not taken in the manner but discovered afterwards, or any wood, guns or skins &c. be found in or about his house, he is to be attached by his goods which you are to bring to the court and deliver to the verderers, and as forfeited to his Majesty as is aforesaid. And if any offender taken in the manner shall fly from you, you are to raise hue and cry, and pursue him as well out of the bounds of the Forest as within until you apprehend him so it be upon fresh suit.

[*Fines*] You are to keep an account of all moneys received by you for driving of cattle and of whom the same was received, and to present the same at the next Speech Court to be there recovered, and to keep the money till it be required of you by the Lord Chief Justice in Eyre, and to inquire after and present at the swanimote court which extortions have been committed by the officers of the Forest. That for very small offences and those committed by young or poor people, the party be rather proceeded against by the Statute Law, it proving a greater terror and punishment many times than the Forest Law. That when you have apprehended any offenders you be very careful that you suffer them not to escape from you but either carry them before a verderer or to the said gaol as the case requires; it being no small encouragement to offenders when they can so easily escape punishment as some have lately done though taken and committed.

[*Deer*] And because it is found by experience that in hunting time the keepers being employed to carry their deer warrant into remote parts out of the Forest do thereby neglect their duties in the Forest at a time when their being there is most necessary, therefore (unless it be by special command) you be very sparing to carry your deer warrant yourselves out of the Forest, but to deliver the same to the persons concerned or that comes for the same at your several lodges, you being not obliged by law to carry the same any further unless it be by any particular order, that so the concerns of the Forest may be the better taken care of by you. That in hunting time the keeper of the walk wherein the deer was rowsed with only one keeper, more to follow the hounds whilst the rest of the keepers within their walks attend their duties to prevent mischief, it being observed that whilst all the keepers are eagerly pursueing their chase in one part of the Forest, deer stealers and other offenders are busiest and securest in other parts thereof. That no warrants for the killing of winter deer for the present be observed till all the keepers have notice thereof to the end they may direct and assist each other therein, and that those warrants be served by turns by reason their number is few. That if you find any deer newly shot or mortally wounded that shall be in season and good, you are to carry the same to the Lord Warden of this Forest if he or his family be then in the country, and if not you are to carry the same and all other chance deer not killed in season (if the same be sweet) to his deputy living in or near the Forest equally, and all other deer killed you are to carry to the next Hospitall or Lazar House, the same being first viewed by a verderer or deputy constable if near the place.

That every of you do present every Speech Court what deer of any sort have been killed, hunted or rowsed in your walks respectively and by whomsoever and by what warrant soever killed. To the end the Lord Warden of the Forest may be satisfied therein and the King's Majesty be answered for all deer killed without lawful warrant. And that you all meet at the King's Lodge [The Speech House] within a week after Holyrood day, and there produce and compare your lists of all deer killed that season and the whole year past, and the same to deliver fairly written under your hands to Mr. David Drake, bowbearer, and to be presented to the Lord Chief Warden; and other part thereof you are to present at the next swanimote court there to be inrolled.

Lastly, you are carefully to observe all orders, commands and directions you shall from time to time receive from the Lord Chief Justice in Eyre or the Lord Warden of this Forest or any of his lordship's deputies, the Lord High Treasurer of England, the verderers, and the supervisor of the Forest, for the better preservation of the vert and venison thereof. And to put the Regard in mind that it is my desire that when they make their perambulation they would perambulate the bounds of the respective walks as they are set out and appointed by me.

[Signed]   [The Marquis of]   WORCESTER

The names of the officers of the Forest:

| Foresters(-of-fee, &c) | Woodwards |
| --- | --- |
| 1. Sir Baynham Throckmorton, Chief Forester-in-Fee (his bowbearer, David Drake, deputy) | 1. Sir Baynham Throckmorton for the Berse Woodwardship (Edward Monning deputy) |
| 2. William Roper Esq. (Thomas Mutloe deputy) | 2. Hon. Benedict Hall, Esq., for Staunton woodwardship (Symon Margats deputy). The same for Bicknor (William Pope deputy) |
| 3. The Mayor and Burgesses of Gloucester (Robert Wilmot deputy) | 3. Mr. Roper for Ruardeane (Thomas Reeve deputy) |

4.  Eustace Hardwick, gent

5.  William Brayne, gent

6.  Henry Worgan

7.  Christopher Dowle

8.  Edward Hooper

9.  William Ayres

4.  John Vaughan Esq. for Abbinghall
    (P. Hatton deputy)

5.  Thomas [?] for Badcocks Baily
    (William Powell deputy)

6.  Richard Hilegew for Blythes Baily

7.  Richard Farmer Esq. for the Lea
    (William Marshall deputy)

8.  Duncomb Colchester Esq. for
    Mitchel Deane (Jo. Philpot deputy)

9.  The heir of Jo. Berrow Esq. for
    Blakeny (William Packer deputy)

*The six keepers*
Charles the Second Walk:
   Daniel Drake gent.
York Walk: John Byles
Worcester Walk: Ketford Bond

Danby Walk: Robert Belcher
Herbert Walk: Thomas Creed gent.
Latimer Walk: Richard Jelfe

Agar raised in all £5,125.8s.9¼d. by the sale of cordwood and of timber 'that happened to arise out of the old oaks and beeches felled for cordwood and other uses', and of pitwood sold to colliers ['It appears that immediately after passing of the Act of 1668 the colliers . . . purchased their timber from the crown'[97]]. The money was expended in: 'buying in Cannop of Banistree Mainard, at £1,500; in setting up enclosures of 8,400 acres with gates and stiles, and some reparation of them; in employing a sworn surveyor to measure them; in building part of the Speech House'; in repairs at St. Briavels Castle; in the charge of executing two commissions; and in other services in the Forest.[98] The enclosures were:

|  | Acres |
|---|---|
| The Great Inclosure | 5,702 |
| Moorwood and Hangerbury | 256 |
| Ruardens Eaves | 672 |
| The Chestnuts and Edgehills | 688 |
| The Lea Bailey and Lyning Wood | <u>1,169</u> |
|  | <u>8,487</u> |

We are uninformed as to when the 2,513 acres were enclosed to complete the statutory 11,000 acres.[99] Some sowing of acorns had been done, but replenishment had chiefly relied on natural seedlings from the infrequent masts of acorns and beech-nuts; and on coppice regrowth.

[97] 3rd Rept. of 1788, p. 16.
[98] Ibid.
[99] The Commissioners of 1788 related: 'It is chiefly in those parts of the Forest which were then inclosed, that the timber with which the dockyards have been since furnished from this Forest has been felled, and in which any considerable quantity of timber is now to be found' (ibid. p. 17).

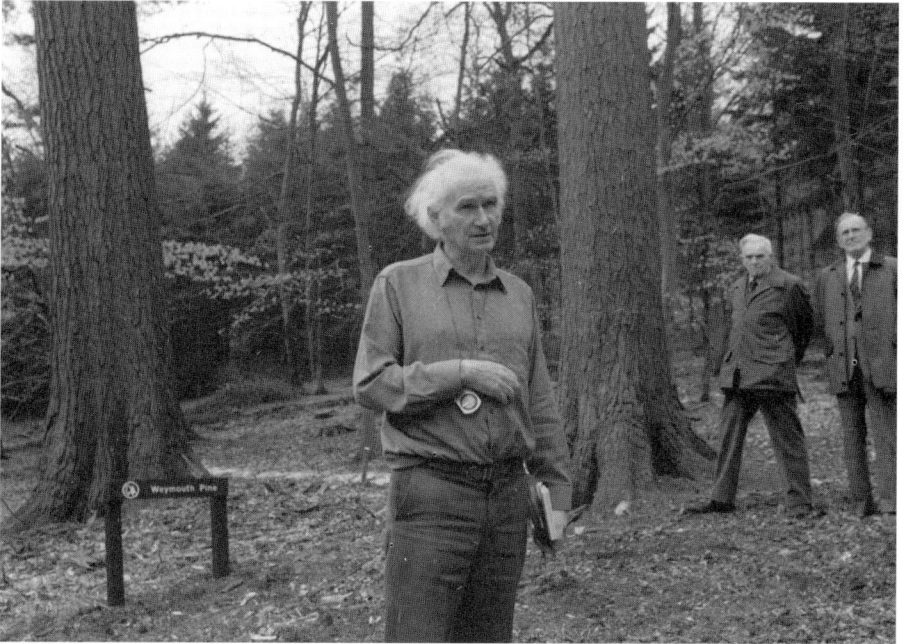

Plate IX. Weymouth pines in lower Sallow Vallet – the first conifers to be planted in the Forest of Dean (*c.* 1781). Some of the trees are now over 37 metres (121 feet) in height; one of them is the stoutest of the species in the British Isles. In the forefront is Alan Mitchell, distinguished dendrologist, now retired. (Photograph by the Forestry Commission, 24 April 1988)

On 24 October 1681[100] Throckmorton was succeeded by Sir John Ernle, junior, of Hom-House, Herefordshire, as 'conservator and supervisor for enclosures and springs of young oaks', with a salary of £100. Meanwhile the legal position of two large properties in Dean was being discussed. Benedict Hall of Highmeadow was challenged by the Treasury regarding his title to about 500 acres at Mailscot[101] and Abraham Clarke of Flaxley was 'praying for a survey' of Abbots Wood.[102] By 8 November 1681[103] '327 oaks and as many of the 128 beeches lately marked in the Lea Bailey as will make 50 loads of 4-inch plank' were reserved for frigates being built at Portsmouth. Agar and Strode were to fell old and decayed oaks and beeches to raise the usual £210 for salaries.[104] Agar averred that £2,000 would take two years to raise according to the best market he can make for wood. A new warrant for the purpose was given to him February 1683.[105]

[100] *Cal. Treas. Bks.*, VII, p. 279.
[101] Ibid. pp. 159, 165, 342.
[102] Ibid. p. 207.
[103] Ibid. p. 197.
[104] Ibid. p. 209.
[105] Ibid. Pt. II, p. 701.

## THE COMMISSION OF 1683

At this time the Forest contained, besides the young enclosures and a number of large oaks and beeches, much coppice and underwood. On 7 August 1682[106] Agar was asked to report on an offer received for 'the weeds of the Forest of Dean, meaning the orle [alder], holly, crooked beech, hawthorn, sally [willow] and hazel, the proposer to take as many thousand cords as will amount to £1,400 at 4s. a cord for 21 years, out of which his Majesty never yet made any advantages'. The crown, undecided what action to take, ordered a commission 26 November 1683[107] to consist of the constable-warden, the supervisor, the surveyor-general of crown lands, the surveyor-general of woods, and eight others (Sir Duncombe Colchester, William Cooke, Henry Hall, Tracy Catchmay, William Wolseley, Herbert Westfaling, John Kirle and William Wynter of Dymock). They were to report on what parts might be 'most fitly enclosed for a perpetual nursery of timber', waste and spoils during the last seven years, anything relating to 'the better government of the Forest and the increase of timber there', and a proposal by Ernle to raise a constant revenue out of the Forest by making iron.[108] They were to sell decayed oaks and beeches, not fit for the Navy, to defray their expenses. The commissioners found that 8,000 cords worth 8s. each could be cut annually from the underwood, 'it being in many places so thick and high as to hinder the growth of young oaks'. Computations showed that much profit would accrue to the crown if it built a large furnace and two forges at £1,000, and undertook the making of iron.[109] The proposal was not pursued; instead it was decided to sell the cordwood to ironworks in Herefordshire and Monmouthshire.

Instructions went out from the Treasury to Agar 30 November 1683 to fell £420 worth of decayed oaks and beeches for two years' salaries of verderers, regarders, and other officers;[110] and on 14 August 1684[111] to fell sufficient decayed trees in the Lea Bailey to raise £300. Felling of similar trees in the same wood was ordered 18 August.[112] The Lea Bailey was to supply still more; on 5 May 1685[113] Agar was instructed by the Treasury to fell and sell there sufficient old oaks and beeches, not suitable for shiptimber, to raise £2,000 per annum for three years.

The Chestnuts between Littledean and Flaxley was under review during the following year;[114] on 16 February 1686[115] the Treasury gave notice to the warden of an intended felling warrant 'if you have nothing against it'. The warrant 8 June[116] stated the area as about 350 acres, 'being only small hazel wood, though above 30 years' growth'; chestnut had almost disappeared through mismanagement. Agar was authorized to sell the underwood 'to the King's best advantage' and out of the

[106] Cal. Treas. Bks., VII, Pt. I, p. 359.
[107] Ibid. Pt. II, p. 962.
[108] Ibid. p. 845.
[109] Hart, Royal Forest, p. 181.
[110] Cal Treas. Bks., VII, Pt. II, p. 967; the Earl of Chesterfield, Chief Justice in Eyre south of Trent, was to be informed of the sale; a reference to him is in Glos. R.O., D.2026 Bond Papers, X.24.
[111] Cal. Treas. Bks., VII, Pt. II, p. 1289.
[112] Ibid. p. 1291.
[113] Ibid. p. 166.
[114] Ibid. p. 485.
[115] Ibid. p. 601.
[116] Ibid. p. 771.

proceeds to enclose the coppice 'with mounds and gates for future growth'; all young oaks and beeches were to be conserved.

The Fence, in the south-west towards St. Briavels, was another wood under review. Ernle was asked by the Treasury 8 June[117] whether the estimated 1,000 cords obtainable from the underwood, 'which is so cut and spoiled by the country people that it is in danger of being lost', can be cut for the king's use and the whole wood enclosed for future growth. It is not recorded to whom the underwood in the Chestnuts and The Fence was sold. Much cordwood in the Lea Bailey had been sold to Foley for his ironworks.[118]

For a while the Forest was without a supervisor: by 8 November 1686[119] Ernle was deceased, and his successor, Captain William Wolseley, was not appointed till 15 March 1687.[120] Strode, jointly surveyor-general of woods with Agar, had died by 4 January 1687.[121] By 18 October[122] Agar was deceased; Charles Morgan lately had been his deputy. Philip Ryley, sergeant-at-arms, took over some of their duties, along with Wolseley. Later, Ryley became surveyor-general of woods; and Henry, Duke of Beaufort was appointed constable-warden.

Despite good intentions following the Act of 1668, two decades of attempts at enclosing and replanting were still inadequate.

[117] Cal. Treas. Bks., VII, Pt. II, p. 770.
[118] Hart, Royal Forest, pp. 184–5.
[119] Cal. Treas. Bks., VIII, p. 983.
[120] Ibid. p. 1265.
[121] Ibid. p. 1135.
[122] Ibid. p. 1549.

# APPENDIX I

## THE PERAMBULATION OF THE FOREST OF DEAN, 1667[123]

It begins at Hopes Well in the Purlieu Green, and thence on the left hand between the counties of Gloucester and Hereford unto Bereley's Green, and thence descending between the said counties unto a certain stream called Bishop's Brook [south of Walford] following the ancient course thereof into the River of Wye, and so descending through the midst of Wye unto a certain place called Juttline, and thence leaving Wye and ascending a certain path or way called Slowpath unto a place where formerly a yew tree grew (below Symonds Yatt) being the bound between the counties aforesaid, and thence descending down over thwart those craggy rocks or hill unto Wye, and so descending through the midst thereof unto a little stream running down by Lady Park wall, and so up that stream unto the corner of Lady Park Grove, and thence ascending up that Grove unto an old oak called Bellman's Oak, and then turning short on the left hand up a certain meadow or pasture called the Reddings unto a certain ash, and from that ash thwarting that meadow or pasture ground unto a great beech on the south side of the Reddings' Barn, and from that beech ascending up a meer or ditch by a coppice wood or grove unto the end thereof, and then to the Scarrs (being an edge of rocks) unto a certain well called St John Baptist Well, and from thence to Stauntons Gate, and thence descending down the Highway unto a great stone called Broadstone, and thence to a well or water called Drybrook [? Tryebrook], and thence following the ancient course thereof into the River of Wye, and so descending through the midst of Wye unto a certain water called Brockwearsbrook, and so ascending that brook or stream which is the bound between the parishes of Hewelsfield and St. Breavills until it cometh to Meerwall alias Meeresmorewall, and thence turning short on the right hand by the upper end of the little moorish green unto the corner of a hedge adjoining to the Common there called Harthill, and so leaving Harthill on the right hand and the parish of St. Breavills on the left hand following the bound between the said parishes of Hewelsfield and St. Breavills unto Aylesmore Brook, and so descending that brook until it comes unto Conebrook, following the stream thereof unto Alvington's Woods, and thence by the bounds of Radmore Grove unto the lower corner thereof, and thence crossing the stream there called Woodward's Brook unto a certain old meer or mound, and so up that meer or mound to a place called Steadfast pound (being a heap of stones which formerly was a pound), and thence following that meer or mound through Sir John Wintour's park unto Chelfridge Well, and from that well up the aforesaid meer into the Highway heading from

---

[123] F20/1 (12); cf. Rudder, S., *Hist. of Glouc.* App. No. III, *c.* 1667 (with varying spellings); part likewise in Crawley-Boevey, A.W., *Flaxley Cartulary*, 1887, pp. 25–7. G.R.O. D1677 GG 1337 refers to a Perambulation made in 1634 by Warren Gough and other Regarders and returned in the Justice Seat of July 1634; only some of the northern perambulation is extant (see Section V, Appendix V).

Breem to Lidney called Marleway, and then leaving the wood called Warwicks Tuft on the right hand unto a little stream called Meerbrook, and down that brook by the ancient course thereof unto the lower corner of the Sneed, and thence ascending up a little stream called Sipmere unto Yorkeley Mead, and so directly up that Mead or pasture unto the place in the wall where anciently a hazel grew called Tachments Hazle, and thence crossing the Highway unto Soilwell, and so following the stream thereof unto Tachments Stream (being the next stream on the left hand), and thence up that stream unto the upper corner of the Haysgrounds, and thence leaving the Haysgrove on the left hand unto the Heyswell, and so descending the stream thereof which is called Launsbrook into the River of Severn (near Pirton's Village) and so ascending up through the midst of Severn unto a certain place called Fulemeadow Pill, and thence ascending that stream unto Chickwells Well, and thence to the Highway leading from Awre to Awreleford keeping the said way until it comes to Awreleyford, and thence ascending that brook unto a certain path called Shipway, and following that way unto a way called Rudgeway, and thence descending leaving the manor or lordship of Ruddle close on the right hand unto a certain watercourse arising in the Grove of Richard Hill gentleman, following the said watercourse unto the River Severn, and through the midst thereof unto Newnhams Pill, and thence ascending that stream unto a certain pasture formerly a Grove called Piper's alias Palmer's Grove, and thence up that stream unto the Highway leading from Newnham to Dean, ascending the said Highway unto Dean's Hill, and thence leaving the bounds of the manor of Rodley on the right hand and the Hundred of St Briavells on the left hand unto the Pool of Flaxleye's Forge, and thence to Blesdon alias Blaisons hedge and thence to Poulton's Hill and thence leaving the Hundred of Westbury on the right hand unto Bruiastones Yatt, and thence including the lands of the Grange of Walemore to the Highway leading towards Framulard, and thence to the Lawn of Walmore leaving the said Lawn on the left hand round about it, and so to a place called Whitecross, and thence to a certain way leading under the Park of the Ley, and from that way unto a grove called Birchinggrove, and from that grove unto Rareham, and from thence to the place where anciently was a mill called Seymour's Mill, and from that place to the brook of Blesdon alias Blaison, ascending that brook unto Gavellesgate alias Gawletts Yatt, and so ascending that brook unto a little stream called Tinbridge Sith, and so stretching up by the said stream between the woods late of the Abbott of Flaxley and the woods called Hopeswoods unto Hopes Shard, and thence to a path called Justy Path, and crossing that path and keeping straight forward unto the water that leadeth from Mitchell Deane to Hope, and so crossing over that water up under the edge of a coppice wood called Langrove, leaving it on the left hand unto the bounds of the parishes of Longhope and Mitchell Deane, and thence directly to Bradley Grove, leaving the grove on the right hand unto the little lane that leads from the Highway into the said grove, and so down that lane unto the Highway, and thence unto Bradley House, and thence athwart the meadow there unto Owley Grove, leaving the grove on the left hand unto a lane near the middle of the said grove, and thence turning up the said lane on the right hand and crossing the Highway leading from Mitchell Dean to the Lealine directly to Haungkins's Well, and thence athwart to the Highway leading from Gloucester towards Hereford by the Lealine Tree following the said way to the said Line Tree, and thence leaving a certain freedom of William Phillips on the left hand (being a cottage garden and about an acre of orchard) close adjoining to the said Line Tree, and thence to a lane called Batch Lane, and so up that lane unto a ditch and footpath in Owley Grove aforesaid (being at or near a place in the said grove where we came out a little before) leading down through the grove unto a piece of pasture ground called the Nockolls (being the ground under the grove), and thence leaving the hedge on the left hand directly to the mill called Clacerford Mill, leaving the said mill on the left hand, and then turning up a lane or Highway leading towards Cawnadge until it comes to the lane turning on the right hand towards the Lea Bayley unto the hither side of a piece of ground called Cudley Broom, and then entering into the said ground, and leaving the hedge on the right hand unto to the ground called the Noake, leaving it on the right hand and then crossing Noakham Lane unto a well called Gingerly Well, and so descending from that well unto an oak called Walton's Oak, and thence turning upon the left hand by a certain little watercourse unto the upper end or corner of a certain parcel of arable or pasture lane called Udnells, directly to the upper end of Poncell Lane, and from that lane unto the Yew tree in a certain parcel of pasture ground called Harthills, leaving a certain coppice grove on the right hand, and turning down under the Lea Baily hedge unto a stream called Megtrauces Stream (being the first stream running out of the Lea Bailey), and so down that stream unto Hope's Brook, and thence ascending by a certain meer or old hedge to the lower end of a piece of pasture or arable land formerly a grove called Hooper's Grove, and thence along by the lower side of that said pasture formerly a grove unto a certain yew tree in Blast's grounds unto the brook running down from Haseley, and so up that brook unto Hillam Lane, and so by the Bayley hedge unto the Lea Way, and thence turning on the left hand under the edge of the Lea Bayly unto the upper corner of the Lea Baily, and thence athwart leaving the Forest on the left hand and the Purlieu of the late Bishop of Gloucester on the right hand, unto a certain place where anciently an oak did grow called Silver Oak which was a mark between the counties of Gloucester and Hereford, in place whereof is a meer stone pitched, and thence to the bank near Blackwell Mead, following the same to the stream, and so down that stream unto Hopeswell.

The names of the Regarders of the Forest of Dean:

John Witt

William Ailburton

Thomas Pyrke

William Gough

George Bond

George Berrow

Christopher Woodward

Edward White

Thomas Worgan

William Carpender

John Byrkin

Jeremiah Hiett

Edward Morse

George Bond of Coleford

Edward Machen

Richard Nash

Thomas Walter

Edward Skin

William Brown

# APPENDIX II

## THE ORIGIN OF DEAN INCLOSURE COMMISSIONERS: 1668

The Dean Forest (Reafforestation) Act 1668 (19 & 20 Charles II, c.8) came into force on 9 May of that year. The Act is reprinted in *Royal Forest* (1966), Appendix XII, pp. 291–5. It was enacted for the 'settlement of the Forest', and was based partly upon the principles in the 'Proposals' made by the inhabitants in about 1667. Its preamble asserts that the wood and timber 'is become totally destroyed', except in the Lea Bailey, 'whereby there is an apparent scarcity of timber there'. Sir John Winter and other ironmasters had almost wholly depleted the Forest's stock of both medium-sized and mature trees. The crown was to enclose at any one time, by authorization of Inclosure Commissioners, not more than 11,000 acres of the 23,000 acres for the growth of timber, mainly for the Navy. The inclosures to be made were to be discharged of all rights of common and pannage till thrown open, taking of estovers (firebote, hedgebote, etc.) was no longer lawful, and deer were not to exceed 800. Forest law was again to apply to Dean, and verderers and regarders were to be elected. At last there was for Dean legislation ostensibly acceptable to most interests, and the powers under the Act could enrich the cover and make Dean once more a storehouse of timber, specifically for shipbuilding. Much would depend on the energy and integrity of the forest officials.

On 11 June 1668 the Treasury minuted that the Marquis of Worcester (constable of St. Briavels Castle and warden of the Forest) was to be spoke unto and acquainted with the names of such as are to be commissioners for Dean Forest.[124] On 15 June the Treasury minuted that Sir Charles Harbord (surveyor general of woods) was to go to the attorney general 'to advise what is fit to be done about settling the business of the Act for the Forest of Dean, and report'.[125] On 2 July, the Treasury minuted: 'The report from Sir Charles Harbord and his son about Dean Forest is to be considered tomorrow'.[126]

On 7 July the Treasury further minuted: 'The report from Sir Charles Harbord and his son Mr. Harbord read about the appointing of officers for Dean Forest. Warrant to the attorney general for a commission out of the Chancery for the country to choose three verderers. Mr. Harbord to draw this warrant and also to prepare a draft of instructions agreeable to the Act for the abuses in the Forest. The attorney general to advise the fittest way to choose the twelve regarders, viz. whether by royal letters patent or by the Justices in Eyre at the Justice Seats, or by the freeholders of the county at a County Court.'[127] The Treasury further minuted:

---

[124] *Cal. Treas. Bks.*, II, p. 351 (T29/2, p. 351).
[125] Ibid. p. 352 (T29/2, p. 352).
[126] Ibid. p. 371 (T29/2, p. 371).
[127] Ibid. p. 375 (T29/2, p. 375).

'Instructions for the commission for the Forest of Dean are brought in by Mr. Harbord; and read. A commission to be accordingly issued out.'[128]

On 27 October a Treasury warrant was issued to the King's Remembrancer 'for a Commission of 32 persons, detailed, for executing the articles of enclosure for Dean Forest as by the Act of Parliament passed 8 May 1668, for same; *prefixing* Articles of Instruction to be observed therein'.[129] The full minute reads:

> Let a Commission under the Seal of his Majesty's Court of Exchequer be directed to the persons hereunder or any three or more of them respectively according to the appointment, returnable 1671, and for so doing this shall be your Warrant.
>
> [dated at] Whitehall Treasury Chambers, October 1668
>
> [signed] Albemarle, Clifford, Duncombe.

To our Loving Friend, The Lord Viscount Fanshaw, his Majesty's Remembrancer of his Court of Exchequer.

The names of the Commissioners:

Henry, Marquis of Worcester
Richard, Earl of Carbery, President of [the Council of] Wales
Lionell, Earl of Middlesex
George, Lord Berkeley
Sir Wm Mortun Kt., one of the Justices of the King's Bench
Sir Job. Chasleton Kt., the King's Serjeant at Law and Chief Justice of Chester
Sir Baynham Throckmorton Kt. & Bt.
Sir Henry Frederick Thyn Bt.
Sir John How Bt.
Sir Robert Atkins Kt. of the Bath, the Queen's Solicitor
Sir Charles Harbord, the King's Surveyor General
Sir Thomas Overbury Kt.
Sir Thomas Stevens Kt.
Sir Thomas How Kt.
Evan Seys, Serjeant at Law
Sir George Charnock Kt.
Wm Morgan of Tredijar
John How Esq.
Thomas Mather Esq.
John Stevens Esq.
John Smyth Esq.
Richard Dowdiswell Esq.
Edward Cooke Esq.
Duncombe Colchester Esq.
Laurence Bathurst Esq.
John May Esq.
William Harbord Esq.
John Grabham How Esq.
Wm Cooke Esq.
John Maden Esq.
Thos. Agar Esq.
Wm Jones Esq.

---

[128] *Cal. Treas. Bks.*, II, p. 382 (T29/2, p. 382).
[129] Ibid. p. 629, Treasury Miscellanea Warrants Early, XXXVII, pp. 175–7 (T51/37, p. 629).

ARTICLES OF INSTRUCTION to be observed and executed by virtue of his Majesty's Commission hereunto annexed according to and in pursuance of an Act of the present Parliament passed on the 9th day of May 1668 in the 20th year of his now Majesty's reign, entitled an Act for the Increase and preservation of timber within the Forest of Deane.

1. The said Commissioners or any three or more of them are to go over and view all the parts and places of the wast lands of the Forest or the late Forest of Deane in the County of Gloucester, and to consider what part and places of the said wast lands are most convenient to be set out and enclosed for his Majesty's service, and to be most apt and meet to produce wood and timber for the future benefit of the Kingdom, and may be best spared from the use of the Commoners and Highways of the County. And forthwith to inclose, sever and improve within and out of the parts and places of the wast lands of the said Forest or late Forest of Deane (the whole containing by estimation about 23,000 acres) the full quantity of 10,000 acres of statute measure at 16½ foot to the perch, whereof the woodwardship of Lea Baily containing about 1,100 acres to be part, and also the grounds [in the Cannop valley] called by the several names of Cannop Fellett, Buckholt, Beachinghurst and Moyry Stock (containing about 1,000 acres heretofore granted to John Gibbon, John Mansill and Ambrose Babin, some or one of them, and now belonging or claimed by Bannistree Maynard Esq.), which added to the 10,000 acres shall make up the full quantity of 11,000 acres to be inclosed as aforesaid to be part.

2. The said Commissioners or any three or more of them are to consider of, nominate and appoint an able and sufficient person to be surveyor to whom the said Commissioners or any three or more of them are to administer an oath (viz.) that he shall well and truly without favour or affection admeasure such of the said wast lands of the said Forest of Deane at 16½ foot to the perch, as shall be set out and appointed by the said Commissioners or any three or more of them to be admeasured for the making up of the said 11,000 acres.

3. The said Commissioners or any three or more of them (after the same is so admeasured) shall set out and inclose, butt and bound the said 11,000 acres of wast lands, or cause the same to be set out, inclosed, butted and bounded with sufficient and notorious butts and boundaries, and the quantities, butts and boundaries thereof to be returned by the said Commissioners or any three or more of them into his Majesty's Court of Exchequer unto the Office of his Majesty's Remembrancer there to remain of Record for ever. And the said Inclosures so made and set out, butted and bounded as aforesaid to remain in severalty in the actual possession of the Crown for ever, freed and discharged of and from all manner of Right, Title and Pretence whatsoever (excepting of Fee Deer) and shall be made and reputed a Nursery for Wood and Timber only.

4. For defraying the charge of making and maintaining the said Inclosures so to be made as aforesaid, and also for the satisfaction of the claim or interest of the said Bannistree Maynard in the lands aforesaid which are to be made part of the said quantity of 11,000 acres as aforesaid, the said Commissioners or any six or more of them shall by the sale of the decayed trees of beech, birch, hawthorn, hazel and holly and other such like trees not being timber, or that can ever prove timber, now standing or growing in or upon the wasts within the said Forest or late Forest, raise monies for defraying the charge of making and maintaining the said Inclosures; and also for the satisfaction of the claim or interest of the said Bannistree Maynard Esq. in the lands aforesaid. But the said Commissioners are not to proceed to make any absolute contract for the absolute sale of any of the said wood or trees before they have certified the Lords Commissioners for the Treasury under their hands and seals the several natures, quantities and prices of the said wood and trees intended by the said Commissioners to be sold, and receive their directions thereupon.

5. The said Commissioners or any three or more of them are to see the said lands, so to be set forth as aforesaid, shall be fully and perfectly inclosed with sufficient mounds and fences by or before the Feast of St George, which shall be in the year of Our Lord 1671.

6. The said Commissioners or any six or more of them or some other person by their appointment, out of the monies to be raised by the sale of the decayed trees mentioned in the 4th Article shall pay or cause to be paid unto the said Bannistree Maynard Esq., his heirs or assigns, the sum of £1,500 in lieu of his estate in the lands called Cannop Fellett, Buckholt, Beachinghurst and Moyry Stock on or before the 24th day of June in the year of Our Lord 1669.

7. The said Commissioners or any three or more of them to enquire and inform themselves of all other matters and things which in the discretions and judgements they shall think fit to be further done for his Majesty's service in and concerning the premisses aforesaid in pursuance of the said Act of Parliament, and from time to time to certify the Lords Commissioners for the Treasury, the Lord Treasurer or Chancellor of the Exchequer for the time being thereof. And the said Commissioners or any three or more of them are to follow such directions and instructions as they shall from time to time receive from the same, for their better proceeding in the said works, so as the same may be fully finished by the time aforesaid.[130]

[130] Subsequent to all the foregoing, Inclosure Commissioners for Dean have been appointed from time to time by the Monarch's Remembrancer. The present seven commissioners are: Dr C.E. Hart, Dr W. Henry, Messrs M. Watts, R. Worgan, G. Morgan, B. Marfell, and R. Baber; their Clerk is Mr K. Griffin. Appointed and sworn in 1974, they can authorize the enclosure of up to 5,000 acres during their term of office (to date they have authorized 2,383 acres).

The main purpose of the commissioners, at their meetings with the Forestry Commission (through the deputy surveyor and his staff) is to note the intention of throwing open of enclosures when considered safe from damage, and to authorize other areas for reforesting, always ensuring that the statutory enclosure limit of 11,000 acres is never exceeded. The Statutory Forest does not include, for example, High Meadow and Tidenham Chase.

The Act of 1668 is now repealed, its legislation having been included in the Dean Forest (Timber) Act 1808 (48 George III, c. 72). This is reprinted in *Royal Forest* (1966), Appendix XVIII, pp. 315–17.

# APPENDIX III

## THE BOUNDS OF THE WOODWARDSHIPS (cf. BAILIWICKS) *c.* 1668[131]

*The woodwardship of Ruardeane*: Beginning at Lydbrookes upper Forge so up the brook to a stream that comes down between Hangerberry and Wyrrall Hill to the White Oak and from the White Oak along the road way to Pearche Pool, from the Pearch Pool along the road way to the head of Whimberleyes Slade, so down the Slade to a stream that runs down into Cannop Brook at a place called Stantons Ford, so from the said Ford up the brook to old Churchhay and from thence up a gutter to Bicknors gate, from thence along the green under Sheerridge to Josteeds Wayes and from thence down a little stream by Bryerleys Oares to Bryerleys Forde, from thence up the Forde to Tyle Hoocke, and from thence along the Lower Deanes way to Shooters Forde, from thence up the Brooke to Reavons Forde, and from thence up the Brooke to Morse, and from thence along by the Morse hedge in the parish of Ruardine to Diggins Lane end, and from thence along the hedge to Hopkin's Lane end, and from thence along the hedge to the Head of Newain, from thence along the hedge to Suicthwayes Lane end, and so along by the hedge to Highbeech Lane end, from thence down by the Reddings to Coldwell Lane end, and so along by the hedge to the New Invenions Lane end, and from thence along by the hedge between the Moorewood Coppice and lands of Richard Vaughan of Courtefielde, gentleman called by the name of Bilebursts Land in the parish of Ruardine to the Boxbush, from thence along by the hedge between the Moorewood Coppice and Lands of the Earles of Kent to a place called the Worlds End near Lydbrookes upper Forge aforesaid.

*The woodwardship of Staunton.* Beginning from the Corner of Yoarkley Wall down by the side of the wall to White Croft, from thence along by Brockhollons to Pastorrhill a place where one Mr. Gough lives, so along by the hedge by the lands of James Berrow gentleman to Breames Cross, from thence along by the lands of Sir Baynham Throckmorton Kt. and Bt. in the parish of Newland to Oakewoods Mill, from thence up a stream between Noxtone Park and Oakewood to the Blinde meene, from thence along by the hedge to Claypoole Lane end, from thence to Kites Stone [? Craddock Stone], from thence to Gattwell Fold, from thence to the Lane end at Perrygrove that leads to Coleford, from thence along by the hedge to Milkewalls, and from thence along the hedge to Colley Lane End, and from thence along the hedge to Poolway Lane End and from thence to a certain barn of Edward Hooper's in the parish of Newland at the head of Owleyes Slade, so down a Stream in Owleyes Slade to Newarnes Brooke, so down the brook to Meerebrook, so up Meerebrook between Blackpenny Wall and Whitelay to Blackpenny Wall's Well, so

---

[131] F20/1 (15); Glos. R.O., D421 Winter Papers, App. II, bdle. 1. The spellings vary.

from the Well along a way by Stone edge to Hinders Cabbin nere Blackpools Ford, so down Blackpoole Brook from the Forde to Mosley Bridge near the end of the Old Bayley, so up a stream between the Old Bayley and Moseley Vellett to Moseley Greene, from thence along a way through Bleeke's Vellett to the Corner of Yoarkley Wall.

*The woodwardship of Blakeney.* Beginning at Meerebrooke between Great Staple edge and Little Staple edge, and from the head of Meerebrooke across Light Moore to a way between St Ley and the Constables Toues that go down to Blackpooles Ford near Hinders Cabborne, so down along Blackpooles Brook between Middle Ridge and Phelps Meadow to Moseley Bridge near to the Old Bayley, from thence up a small Stream between the Old Bayley and Moseley Vallett to Moseley green, from thence along a way through Bleekes Vellett to the Corner of Yoarkeley Wall in the parish of Newland, from thence along by Yoarkeley Wall to Baddams Field, from thence to Sullawell, and from Sullawell down along by the lands of Mr. James to a little Stream that parts Purtons Purley and Deadmans Cross, so up that Stream to the end of the Hay Grove, so along by the Hay Grove to a place called Merryhole, so from thence to the Viney Lane end, and from thence to Blakeney Furnace in the parish of Awre, and so along between the parish of Awre and Blakeney's Eaves to Ayleaford, so up the Brook from Ayleaford to Broadley, so from Broadley up the Brook to Soudley Bridge, from Soudley Bridge up the Brook to Soudley Old Furnace between Great Staple edge and the Abbotts woods, so up Soudley to Meerebrooke between Great Staple edge and Little Staple edge.

*The woodwardship of Bicknor.* Beginning at Darkstiles Lane end [near Coleford], from thence to Darkstiles Pool, from thence along the Roadway to the Pearch Pool, from thence along the Roadway to the White Oakes, from thence down a Stream between Hangerbury and Wyrrall Hill to Howbrooke, so down the Brooke to Lydbrookes lower Forge, so from the Forge up the Hill between Hangerbury and a certain Grove of Henry Hall Esquire, from thence along the top of Hangerbury by certain lands of Edward Machen gentleman in the said parish of Bicknor to Espeech Lane end, from thence along by the hedge side to Whorrthornes, and from thence along by the hedge to Joyford, and from Joyford along by the hedge to Mailscott, so along the Ditch between Mailscott and Coverram to a Barn of John Reynolds near Shortstanding, from thence along by the hedge to the Bashes, and from thence to Berryhill Lane end, and from thence along the hedge to Mr. Carpender's Barn in the parish of Newland, from thence along the hedge to Darkstiles Lane end aforesaid near Coleford.

*The woodwardship of Blayes Bayley.* Beginning at the [Deanes Hill] Lane end, and leading along the top of the Hill between the Abbotts woods and Blayes Bayley along the way to a Grove of one Mr. Matthew Pumfreyes in the Lordship of Ruddle and the parish of Newnham, so along from Mr. Pumfreyes Grove along the hedge to a certain Lane leading down to Ruddle, and from that Lane end shooting down by the hedge to a certain Barn of Richard Hill gentleman in the parish of Newnham, from thence along the Ditch to a certain Lane end near the Cockshett, and from that Lane end ascending up the Hill by a certain hedge of the lands of Mr. Rowles to the end of the said Lane that comes from Deanes Hill.

# APPENDIX IV

## ARTICLES OF INSTRUCTION TO BE EXECUTED AND OBSERVED BY HIS MAJESTY'S COMMISSIONERS IN THE FOREST OF DEAN: 1673[132]

1. You or any three or more of you are to repair to the said Forest and there to view and perambulate the several parts and places thereof as well inclosed as uninclosed and to enquire and certify what coppice wood is now growing in the said Forest fit to be cut and of what growth, and where the same is situated, and what quantity may be cut for 7 years proportionably one year with another, and where and in what places those quantities may be cut in every of the said years, how many acres according to your best computation and judgment, and how many cords in each acre, and what the same may be sold for by the acre or cord, all charges of cutting and cording being deducted.

2. You or any three or more of you are to inquire and certify what the King's Ironworks may be worth by the year to be let apart from the woods, and what will be the charge of putting the said Ironworks and road bridges leading to the same in good and sufficient repair, and what quantity of timber must necessarily be allowed for the perfecting thereof, or, if the same should be pulled down, what the several materials would be worth to be sold. And moreover you are to inspect his Majesty's late lessee's grants of the said works, and to certify how far the said lessee or any claiming under him are bound by Covenants whereunder the same at the expiration of the said grants into his Majesty's hands should be in good repair.

3. You or any three or more of you are to inquire and certify the charges of supporting and maintaining his Majesty's Inclosures lately made within the said Forest in by and with all manner of needful reparation as well as the mounds and stonewalls, as of the gates, stiles and footbridges leading to the same; and also the charges of any other bridges necessarily required in any other part of the said Forest may annually amount unto for the 7 years now next ensuing.

4. You or any three or more of you are to certify what old or decayed woods and trees are yet standing in the Lea Bailey, parcel of the said Forest, how many cords they may contain in them besides timber to be cut in 7 years proportionably one year with another, and in certain places to prevent straggling and ramageing [sic] too much to the damage of the younger woods, and what the said woods may be sold at by the cord, all charges being deducted, and how many cords may be vended in the year to one or more chapmen in the country.

[132] F20/1 (14).

5. You are to inquire and certify what colepitts are taken in to his Majesty's Inclosures which might conveniently be left out without prejudice to the young woods, for the benefit of the country, and what the charge thereof may be.

6. You are to certify in what condition you find his Majesty's Inclosures as to the growth and product of them, and also the name and names of every such person or persons that shall commit any spoils or breaches either in the young woods or in the mounds and fences or to drive any cattle to depasture in the said Inclosures or wilfully break down or set open any other gates thereof, or shall dig any mine [ore], coal, tiles or cinders within the same contrary to law, that so a speedy order may be taken to bring every person so offending to condigne punishment and the like exorbitanars and mischiefs may be restrained and reclaimed for the future.

7. And lastly, you or any three or more of you are to call to your assistance John Aram, William Dunning of Pyrton, William Walter, William Goffe, John Witt, Kedgwin Hoskins, George Wyrrall, Thomas Pyrke, John Hawkins, William Rowles, William Aylberton gent. or any other able or knowing person inhabiting those parts for the better performance in all and every the particulars aforesaid for his Majesty's service therein or in any other matter relating to the said Forest, which you judge necessary to be inquired into. And you are to observe and execute all orders which from time to time you or any of you shall receive from the Right Honorable the Lord High Treasurer of England, or the Chancellor and under Treasurer of his Majesty's Exchequer now and for the time being for his Majesty's better service in this behalf.

To the Right Honourable   Henry Marquis of Worcester
                          Sir Baynham Throckmorton
                          Sir Thomas How
                          Sir George Probart
                          William Cooke
                          Edward Cooke
                          Duncomb Colchester
                          John Smith
                          Thomas Agar [surveyor-general of woods]
                          John May [supervisor]
                          John Wade
                          Henry Milbourne

# APPENDIX V

## SWANIMOTE COURT FOR THE FOREST OF DEAN HELD AT THE SPEECH HOUSE, 1676[133]

FOREST OF DEANE — Swanimote Court of the Lord King held for the aforesaid Forest at the King's House commonly called the King's Lodge 9 June 28 Charles II [1676] before Duncomb Colchester Kt. and William Cooke Esq., verderers of the said Forest.

Foresters

Baynham Throckmorton Kt. and Bt., chief forester-of-fee
    Thomas Davies gent. his deputy
William Brayne gent., forester-of-fee
William Rooper Esq., forester-of-fee
    Thomas Mutloe his deputy
The Mayor and Burgesses of the City of Gloucester, foresters-of-fee
    Robert Willmott their deputy
Eustace Hardwicke gent., forester-of-fee
Christopher Dowle, forester-of-fee
Edward Hooper, forester-of-fee
Robert Guning Esq., and Henry Worgan, foresters-of-fee
    Henry Worgan in person
William Ayres, forester-of-fee

Woodwards

Baynham Throckmorton Kt. and Bt., woodward of le Bearse
    Edward Monning his deputy
Henry Hall Esq., woodward of Bicknor Anglican' [English Bicknor]
    George Lewis his deputy
The same Henry woodward of the bailiwick of Staunton
    Simon Margetts his deputy
William Rooper Esq., woodward of the bailiwick of Ruardeane
    Thomas Reeve his deputy
John Vaughan Esq., woodward of the bailiwick of Abenhall
    Philip Hatton his deputy
The same John woodward of the bailiwick of Badcocks Bayley
    William Perrin his deputy

---

[133] Glos. R.O., D36 Colchester Papers, Q2. Some of the names are confirmed in Glouc. Liby. LX10.3(4), being a document signed at the Court.

Duncomb Colchester Kt., woodward of the bailiwick of
Deane Magna [Mitcheldean]
   Joshua Phelpott his deputy
Henry Farmer Esq., woodward of Lacu [Lea]
   William Marshall his deputy
Thomas Berrow gent., woodward of Blackney
   William Packer his deputy
Richard Hill gent., woodward of Bleyths [Blaize] Bayley

| | |
|---|---|
| Regarders | John Witt gent. |
| | William Aylburton gent. |
| | Thomas Pyrke gent. |
| | George Bond gent. |
| | William Carpender gent. |
| | William Gough gent. |
| | Richard Nash gent. |
| | William Browne gent. |
| | Jeremiah Hyett gent. |
| | John Berkin gent. |
| | Matthew Pumfrie gent. |
| | Edward Skinne gent. |

Names of the 'Custodi' (in English the Keepers)

| | |
|---|---|
| Daniel Dracke gent. | Robert Belcher |
|   John Tapp his deputy | |
| Thomas Creede gent. | John Boyles |
| Richard Jelfe gent. | John Knight |

Names of the Reeves and four men of every vill in the said Forest

| | | |
|---|---|---|
| Scus' Briavelli' [St Briavels] | Walter Preece reeve | |
| | Thomas Marten | |
| | Thomas Eavens | iiij men |
| | Edmund Bond | |
| | Thomas Oakley | |
| | | |
| Staunton | Arthur Smyth reeve | |
| | Richard Wysham | |
| | William Wisham | iiij men |
| | John Stephens | |
| | Thomas Griffith | |
| | | |
| Deane magna [Mitcheldean] | Richard James reeve | |
| | Thomas Osborne | |
| | John Matthews | iiij men |
| | Edward Hopkins | |
| | William Gough | |

| Awre | Josiah Robyns reeve<br>Thomas Wintle<br>John Robins<br>Richard Hineham<br>Warren James | iiij men |
| --- | --- | --- |
| Deane parva<br>[Littledean] | John Morgan reeve<br>Thomas Jones<br>John Rocke<br>Richard Knight<br>John Man | iiij men |
| Blackney | John Horne reeve<br>John A Deane<br>John Reeve<br>Charles Awre<br>Obadiah Stockes | iiij men |
| Newnham | Richard Layton reeve<br>Thomas Thynne<br>James Conklin<br>John Clarke<br>Walter Jones | iiij men |
| Breeme | Thomas Paddle reeve<br>Thomas Draper<br>Thomas Jones<br>John Pritchard<br>Robert Matthews | iiij men |
| Ruardeane | John Cradocke reeve<br>Michael How<br>John Harris<br>Henry Rudge<br>Thomas Long | iiij men |
| Bicknor Angli'<br>[English<br>Bicknor] | John A Deane reeve<br>John Cowmeadow<br>William Ambre<br>William Morse<br>Richard Phelps | iiij men |
| Colford | Sturley Kedgwin reeve<br>Philip Yerworth<br>Thomas Reeve<br>John Benfield<br>John Keare | iiij men |

| Lea | Richard Millard reeve | | |
| | William Hall | | |
| | John Palmer | } | iiij men |
| | Walter Floyde | | |
| | John Tippins | | |

| Flaxley | William Fletcher reeve | | |
| | Roger Howlder | | |
| | Isaac Williams | } | iiij men |
| | William Marten | | |
| | John Gwilliam | | |

| Abenhall | William Phelps reeve | | |
| | William Crosse | | |
| | William Gibbons | } | iiij men |
| | James Holleday | | |
| | John Meeke | | |

| Clowerwell [Clearwell] | Humphrey Vicke reeve | | |
| | Giles Symond | | |
| | Richard Keare | } | iiij men |
| | William Bond | | |
| | Nicholas Kedgwin | | |

| Northwood | Walter Yong reeve | | |
| | William Hart | | |
| | Philip Wathen | } | iiij men |
| | George Mann | | |
| | Roger Gwilford | | |

Names of the jurors sworn at this court

| William Callow gent. | Edmund Bond gent. |
| Richard Pyrke gent. | Thomas Worgan gent. |
| Richard Vaughan | Kedgwyn Hoskins gent. |
| Samuel White | John Berrow |
| Thomas Terrett | Thomas Berkin |
| John Dowle | William Withenburie |

It is presented by the foresters and twelve jurymen and convicted by the verderers that William Parklor of Bicknor Anglican' [English Bicknor] in the county of Gloucester yeoman on the thirtieth day of November 27 Charles II [1675] entered the aforesaid forest of the Lord King (vizt.) at the lord's wood called Coveram an enclosed 'hay' and felled diverse young beech trees growing there to the value of xij d. and took away six shillings' worth with a horse and cart to the destruction of the vert and to the detriment of the beasts of the chase of the Lord King.

It is presented by the foresters and twelve jurymen and convicted by the verderers that William Powell of Landiloe Pitholie in the county of Monmouth labourer on the fifth of April 28 Charles II [1676] entered the aforesaid forest (vizt.) in the lord's waste at the bailiwick of Abenhall and burnt heath growing there destroying the covert to the detriment of the beasts of the chase of the Lord King.

At this court William Powell of Landiloe Pitholie in the county of Monmouth labourer acknowledged that he owed the Lord King £10 and William Fletcher of Flaxley in the county of Gloucester yeoman and Henry Pyrke of Deane magna [Mitcheldean] in the county of Gloucester yeoman acknowledged that each of them owed the Lord King £5 to be levied on their goods and chattels land and tenements, on condition however that if William Powell appeared before the judges of the Lord King at the next eyre to be held before the aforesaid forest to do and suffer what the court should enjoin there and then, meanwhile being of good behaviour regarding the vert and the venison of the Lord King in the aforesaid forest, then the recognizance to be entirely void.

At this court William Parlor of Bicknor Angli' in the county of Gloucester yeoman acknowledged himself to owe the Lord King £20 and William Powell of Landiloe Pitholie in the county of Monmouth labourer and David Powell of Landiloe Pitholie aforesaid labourer acknowledged that each of them owe the Lord King £10 to be levied on their goods and chattels lands and tenements, on condition however that the aforesaid William Parlor did as above.

[Signed]

Dun. Colchester [verderer]

Will. Cooke [verderer]

# PART FOUR

## X. ATTEMPTS AT ENCLOSING AND PLANTING OF DEAN: 1688–1787

Throughout much of the seventeenth century, the commoners had played havoc with many of the enclosures. In 1688 the lodges Worcester and York had been 'pulled down by the rabble' and the Speech House 'defaced and spoiled'.[1] Henry, Duke of Beaufort, constable-warden, was unable on account of his other commitments to take his share of responsibilities in Dean. The Treasury secretary wrote to him 10 May 1688[2] expressing the Treasury lords' desire to speak with him 'when in town' concerning the state and condition in Dean. They were perturbed by a report from Philip Ryley (surveyor-general of woods) that only about 2,500 acres were enclosed at the moment out of 11,000 acres allowed, 'whereby the common is enlarged to the people and their stock of cattle thereupon increased proportionally, the underwood and young timber being exposed to the injury of both'. The good intentions of the Act of 1668 had been thwarted. Ryley urged the cutting of the underwood to relieve the young oaks and straight beeches; it could be converted to cordwood without overstocking the market; the underwood would never be timber or of a greater value 'but rather run more into decay by standing longer'. He continued:

> Were the underwoods cut and enclosures made and kept until the young timber should become past danger of browsing of deer, cattle, and other prejudice, such parts so deemed safe might then be laid open and other fresh parts cut and enclosed, thus improving the condition of the timber in a few years; furthermore, the cost of such enclosures will be small, many of the grounds having been formerly enclosed and others being bounded by the lands of the freeholders.

Ryley asserted that £800 net per annum could thereby be raised, and to this end he presented a schedule of woods and underwoods which might usefully be cut,[3] estimated to yield 50,000 short cords worth 4s. each, or £10,000:

> In Aywood: 3,000 short cords of holly, hawthorn, and crooked beech; needs not to be enclosed because of the thickness of the timber that will be left standing and because of the many highways through it.
> In Edgehills and Badcock's Bailey: 6,000 short cords of crooked beech, hazel, and holly: formerly enclosed and easily to be reinclosed.
> In Blyth's Bailey: 3,500 short cords of crooked beech; bounded by freeholders' lands and only wants two gates.
> In Moorwood: 2,000 short cords of crooked beech; formerly enclosed and easily to be reinclosed.

---

[1] *Cal. Treas. Bks.*, IX, p. 1495.
[2] Ibid. VIII, p. 1888.
[3] Ibid. p. 2002.

In Hangerberry: 4,000 short cords of crooked beech and birch; formerly enclosed and easily to be reinclosed.

In Bradley, the Copes and Bromehill: 5,000 short cords of beech, birch, holly, and hazel; bounded partly with a hedge and ditch and easily to be reinclosed.

About Worcester Lodge, Wimberley, the Buckhold and Cannop: 10,000 short cords of beech, some birch and hawthorn; fit to be enclosed.

From Mosely Gate down Blackpool Brook to Blackney Furnace and about Deadman's Cross: 10,000 short cords of beech and some hawthorn and birch; this being very full of trees that will be left standing for timber; will not need enclosing.

In The Fence: of stoggalls, 250 short cords of oaks that will never be timber; bounded round with lands of freeholders and only wants two gates and three perches of hedges to enclose it.

In the heart of the Forest from the brook betwixt Seridge and Daniel Moor to the Dam-brook and so to Sinderford Bridge and thence along Middle Ridge to Mosely Gate and thence along the way to the top of Stonedge to Seridge and at Missey Hurst: 6,250 short cords of old decaying hollies and of hawthorn and birch.

James II, consulted as to Ryley's proposals, approved the whole,[4] and 17 July 1688 a royal warrant was given to the Treasury for Ryley to 'cut away so much holly, hawthorn, crooked beech, birch, hazel, and stoggal oaks in places as will produce £800 per annum clear for so long as the same may conveniently be raised without prejudice to the state of the Forest'.[5] Out of the moneys so raised he was to repair the mounds and fences, 'to preserve them from the browsing of deer and cattle, and to build pounds in some convenient place in the Lea Bailey at a charge not exceeding £3'. It was a renewed attempt to halt the commoners' depredations.

Among the records of sales of trees is one of wood delivered in 1689 by Charles Morgan being cordwood from Moorwood 2,230½ cords, Sally Fellett 52 cords, and Hangerbury 5,394¼ cords.[6] In addition hundreds of minor sales were made from 21 November 1687 to 11 January 1690 of wood for such produce as hammer-helves, cardboard timber, bark, saddles, laths, stole legs, shovels, crooks and spokes.[7] The sales were from the Lea Bailey and totalled £746.16s.7d.

Ryley's attempts to overcome opposition to enclosure proved ineffective. On 21 April 1690 he wrote to the Treasury:[8]

There are not at present any trees that can be properly called principal timber for the Navy, such of them as lately were there having about 12 months since been felled and carried away by the country people with many thousands of young trees; and there are no enclosures for increase or preservation of timber as by the Statute in that behalf is directed, the same having been broken down and destroyed, likewise two of the lodges and the Speech House[9] pulled down to the ground at the time the former spoils and injuries were committed; but there are in the Forest near 100,000 young trees and saplings, some of them about 40 years' growth, which if carefully preserved may be of great use to the Navy. Also valuable quantities of holly, hawthorn, crooked beech, birch, hazel and stoggal oak that may be cut away and converted into cordwood; by their sale £1,000 per annum may

[4] Cal. Treas. Bks., VIII, p. 2001; Cal. Treas. Papers, I, p. 29, No. 54.

[5] Cal. Treas. Bks., VIII, p. 2001.

[6] Hart, Royal Forest, p. 185.

[7] Ibid. p. 186.

[8] Cal. Treas. Bks., IX, p. 586.

[9] On 9 July 1689 Ryley had been instructed by the Treasury to allow Daniel Drake, keeper of the Speech House Lodge, £3 towards its repair (ibid. p. 40).

be raised for many years without danger of overstocking the market by reason of the many furnaces and forges in those parts which want it, and the removal of which will be to the benefit of the young oaks.

Ryley further pointed out that, although the Act of 1668 authorized 11,000 acres, even when the enclosures of the Lea Bailey and the Chestnuts were repaired there would not be enclosed in the whole above 1,500 acres. Commoners extended their depredations everywhere. It would be to the king's advantage to make enclosures 'until the springs and saplings are beyond danger'. He was given permission 30 April 1690[10] to raise £235 from wood sales in order to repair the Speech House at a cost of £120, to rebuild two keepers' lodges at £45 each, and to enclose the Lea Bailey with new gates and posts at £10 and the Chestnuts at £15.

The previous month[11] the Treasury received a petition from Sir John Guise of Highnam Court asserting that 'the great timber of Dean has of late years been cut down, and the young springs of timber greatly injured and like to be destroyed, unless some extraordinary care be taken'. The best course was to enclose the Forest into '21 coppices, and to cut trees which were not of the kind to make timber, but usually called weeds of the forest'. He offered to do this at his own expense in return for those 'forest weeds' for twenty-one years, undertaking not to cut any oak, ash, or elm that are standards or 'ground trees' (as opposed to those arisen from stools). The Treasury 6 March 1691[12] asked Philip Ryley and William Harbord, the two surveyor-generals of woods, to report on a draft lease submitted to them. As part of the result the Treasury 18 May[13] appointed a new commission comprising Henry, Duke of Beaufort, constable-warden, Harbord, Ryley, Sir Duncomb Colchester, William Cooke, Reginald Pinder, Edward Cooke, William Boevy, Thomas Peck, John Viney and John Kirle.[14]

THE COMMISSION OF 1692

The commissioners reported to the Exchequer in 1692:[15]

> Firstly, we have repaired to the Forest of Dean and carefully viewed and perambulated the several parts and places thereof, as well as enclosed as unenclosed, and find there are great and valuable quantities of scrub beech and birch with some hazel, holly, and arle [alder] fit to be cut and disposed of. And provided due care be taken to preserve all oak whatsoever the straight beech with the principal shoots of such beech as grow upon old stools and sufficient shoots about them in all places, where either the thinest of their growth, or being exposed to weather shall make it necessary, we conceive it will be consistent with the Act 20 Charles II [1668] for increase and preservation of the timber in this Forest, the quantity and growth of the said woods fit to be cut, the places where situated, the number of acres, and quantity of cords on each acre, according to our best computation and judgment, together with the value for which the same may be sold by the cord, all charges of cutting and cording being deducted, and also the quantity of wood, besides oaks, that will be left standing on each acre after the Fellets proposed have been made, are:

---

[10] *Cal. Treas. Bks.*, IX, p. 606.
[11] Ibid. p. 901.
[12] Ibid. p. 1047.
[13] Ibid. p. 1156.
[14] 3rd Rept. of 1788, pp. 66–7; E178/6080.
[15] *Cal. Treas. Bks.*, IX, p. 1495; 3rd Rept. of 1788, p. 68, App. 8; Hart, *Royal Forest*, pp. 187–8 and App. XV.

| Places where situated | Acres | Years' growth | Cords on each | Total cords to be cut | Cords left standing |
|---|---|---|---|---|---|
| Aye Wood: scrubbed beech with some birch | 300 | 50 | 30 | 9,000 | 15,000 |
| Great and Little Bourt: forked beech | 50 | 40 | 20 | 1,000 | 1,000 |
| Ruardean Enclosure (the whole content | | | | | |
| 672 acres) whereof | 100 | 45 | 20 | 2,000 | 6,000 |
| Blaise Baily: most beech | 90 | 45 | 20 | 2,700 | 4,500 |
| Bradley and Copes: most beech & birch | 280 | 40 | 30 | 8,400 | 14,000 |
| Viney Hill: most beech | 80 | 40 | 30 | 2,400 | 4,000 |
| Blakeneys Eaves and Thorneyhill: | | | | | |
| most beech | 200 | 40 | 30 | 6,000 | 10,000 |
| Morewood and Hangerbury: not to be cut | 250 | 40 | – | – | 8,000 |
| Lea Bayly: beech & hazel | – | – | – | – | 3,000 |
| Deadman's Cross: most beech, very long | 250 | 45 | 40 | 10,000 | 12,000 |
| Blakeneys Bayly, Old Bayly, Moseley | | | | | |
| Green: beech & birch | 40 | 40 | 20 | 800 | 1,200 |
| Misleyhurst: most birch, well grown | 50 | 40 | 20 | 1,000 | 3,000 |
| Little Stapledge, Putnage and thereabouts | 150 | 40 | 20 | 3,000 | 6,000 |
| Edgehill and Badcocks Bailey: beech & | | | | | |
| hazel | 200 | 40 | 30 | 6,000 | 10,000 |
| Little Kensley, Kensley Edge, Rushy Lawn: | | | | | |
| most birch | 160 | 45 | 20 | 3,200 | 5,400 |
| Sturley Tufts: most birch | 100 | 45 | 20 | 2,000 | 6,000 |
| Perryhay Ditch, Middle Ridge, Saintley: | | | | | |
| beech & birch | 350 | 40 | 20 | 7,000 | 14,000 |
| Stonedge: most birch | 175 | 40 | 20 | 3,500 | 8,000 |
| Phelps Meadow: beech & birch | 80 | 40 | 20 | 1,600 | 2,400 |
| Old Vellet: most beech & birch | 60 | 40 | 20 | 1,200 | 2,000 |
| Brockwerehill and Brockwere Ditches: | | | | | |
| beech & birch | 200 | 45 | 20 | 4,000 | 9,000 |
| Wet Wood: most birch | 200 | 45 | 20 | 4,000 | 6,000 |
| Breams Eaves and Parkhill: beech & birch | 150 | 40 | 20 | 3,000 | 6,000 |
| Daniell Moore and Orlings Moores: | | | | | |
| birch & orle | 200 | 40 | 20 | 4,000 | 6,000 |
| About Fetters Hill, Stoney Stile and | | | | | |
| Wynnols, Quietslade, Cleve and | | | | | |
| Birch Hill: beech & birch | 340 | 40 | 20 | 6,800 | 13,500 |
| Tivey Tree Hill: beech | 70 | 45 | 20 | 1,400 | 3,000 |
| Darkhill, Churchill, Ivymoorhead, Little | | | | | |
| Faire Moore, Hunters Beech, | | | | | |
| Oakwood, Barnhill, Wimberley Slad, | | | | | |
| Cannop, Coverham and the rest of | | | | | |
| the Great Enclosure being besides | | | | | |
| waste: | 4,900 | 40 | 20 | 98,000 | 245,000 |
| | 9,025 | – | – | 192,000 | 413,500 |

To be cut: 192,000 short cords at 4s.10d. a cord clear
   of cutting and cording, amounts to the sum of     £46,000   0s 0d
To be left: 423,500 at the same value amounts to    £102,345  16s 8d

Total present stock besides oak: 615,500 short cords at    ————————
   4s. 10d. a cord                £148,745  16s 8d

Which woods being near of equal growth may be cut in the order that are aforesaid, and in such proportions as your Lordships shall think fit; but we are humbly of the opinion the quantity ought not to exceed 12,000 cords in any one year.

By the account aforesaid, if the underwood (certified as fit to be cut) which may be sold at 4s. 10d. a cord, clear of cutting and cording, be cut in 7 years, the same will yield the sum of £6,628.11s.5d. per annum during that term; and if the whole called underwood (oak excepted) be disposed of to any person, with liberty to cut the same in 21 years time, upon a covenant of repairing and keeping up the enclosures (as mentioned in the fifth article) the stock which such person may take off in that time (as appears by the account aforesaid) is worth at a moderate computation £148,745.16s.8d.; and it does not appear but that such a person may cut some part of the said wood twice within the said term of 21 years, by which the value will be proportionably augmented, though it cannot be ascertained by us; but we suppose the second fellet may amount unto the sum of £60,000 more or thereabouts. The repairs of the enclosures will be inconsiderable, and may be done for about £100 per annum.

It is very difficult to determine how mischievous and fatal the consequences of such agreement will be, not only in respect of this Forest but of the nation in general, especially not on the consumption of our naval timber is so very great, and our occasions for it not inconsiderable, doubtless besides the cutting down many thousands of straight beech that will be fit for their Majesty's naval service such agreement will utterly destroy the Forest which is now perhaps the best nursery for a Navy in the world, and has been of that esteem as to have justified the labour of our enemies for its destruction the care and endeavours of several Parliaments since the year 1660 for its preservation and for very tender of this Forest was the Parliament of 1663. That when agreement like what is now proposed had almost ruined it, that Honorable House thought it worthy their care to resine it, and reassumed many agreements that had been made to private persons and compounded for others at a great charge, and did then by a particular Act of Parliament [1668] for that purpose endeavour to prevent any lease or grant to be made of any part thereof or the woods growing therein to any person whatsoever as by the said statute does appear in the following words: [Here followed clause 6 of the Act of 1668].

In 1674 (as also in 1662) it was proposed that if his then Majesty would repair the old ironworks in this Forest and make an addition of one furnace and two forges (which might be done for £1,000) and cause the spareable woods to be cut and converted in these works, that then every 8,000 cords of long wood so converted should yield a profit over and above the value of 8d. per long cord and clear of all charges of the sum of £2,190. Yet upon consideration that the erecting of such works and supplying the same with the quantity of wood necessary for that purpose might endanger a great waste in this Forest, if not the destruction thereof, it was advised rather to pull down these ironworks than erect new, and the old ironworks were pulled down and the material sold accordingly. And the same reasons do still remain against any new works, and have this addition that their Majesty's woods are now sold for 8d. each long cord more than the same was at that time valued. It may be taken notice of also the great difficulty with which the many freeholders that had right of common and other privileges in this Forest were prevailed with in the year 1665 to submit the same to the Crown for enclosing the Forest according to the statute of 20 Charles II [1668]. Many of the same persons are yet living, and would doubtless be concerned to see the profit of it in any private hands, when they have freely parted with theirs for the public utility. And we are credibly informed that if any such grant pass, the freeholders intend to prefer a petition to be restored to the right of estovers enjoyed by them before the making of the statute. And although we certify that some woods maintained in the foregoing particulars may be cut, yet considering the great care and caution that has hitherto been taken to make this Forest useful for the Navy and the flourishing conditions it has now reached, and add to this how natural it is and certain for any person who can obtain such a grant to consult his own advantage, not the preservation of the Forest, and that experience acquaints every woodman that it is hard to preserve in coppice wood what ought and is intended to be left by those who design an increase of timber, we can by no means (if the Act would permit thereof) think it advisable to make a grant so certainly destructive to the Forest as this proposal, nor that the making of the Forest should be entrusted in any other hands than the present officers who have in those places given sufficient testimony of their care in observing the rules afore-prescribed for making the Forest, and preserving everything fit to be left for the increase and preservation of timber according to the statute in that behalf made.

The Lea Bailey is now a spring of oak and beech of 4, 5, and 6 years' growth, but much cropped and spoiled by cattle, by the inclosures made for the preservation thereof being in the night several times pulled down and destroyed by persons unknown. The other places particularly mentioned in the Act as part of the 11,000 acres are generally very well grown with oak and beech of 50, 40, and 30 years' growth and under; many thousands of them being 40 feet long and upwards without a bough to hurt them, but their numbers cannot well be known by reason of the thickness of their growth and of great quantity of other sorts of wood that will never be fit for the Navy and is proposed to be cut, in part as aforesaid.

Secondly, we have also enquired what the charge of supplying and maintaining the inclosures heretofore and lately made withall needful and necessary reparations may amount unto, and find that the fences necessary to be repaired are only those of the Lea Bailey, Chestnut Coppice, Edgehills and Badcocks Bayley, Ruardean Inclosure and The Fence, which contain about 2,400 acres and may be repaired for the sum of £137.10s. The other part and places formerly enclosed are not necessary to be repaired, being past danger of prejudice from deer or cattle, and the fences of the said 2,400 acres when repaired may be so kept by the annual allowance of £30 made to the keepers for that purpose, unless some accident of pulling down by the rabble, as hath been sometimes done.

Thirdly, there are but six coalpits within all or any of their Majesties' inclosures, and of those places the inclosures being generally down and not necessary to be repaired the wood there being past danger the country are not incommoded or prejudiced in that respect.

Fourthly, the salary of the conservator and six keepers amount to the sum of £210 and are usually paid at their Majesties' Exchequer out of the moneys arising by wood sales in this Forest. The Castle of St. Briavels has been a very great and ancient building but the greatest part is ruined and fallen down, and only some part kept up for a place to keep the Court in for the King's Manor and Hundred of St. Briavels, and also for debtors attached by process out of the Court, and for offenders and trespassers within the Forest; the same is very necessary to be repaired, and will for mending the roof and tiling and in glazing, plastering and repairing the prison building and new pound cost £10. 14s. 2d. There are two Keepers' Lodges, namely Worcester Lodge and York Lodge, that were pulled down by the rabble in 1688, and absolutely necessary to be rebuilt, and will cost £90 besides 12 tons of timber which we advise should rather be bought than cut in the Forest and will cost £18 more brought to the several Lodges. The Speech House (the place where the Courts are held for the Forest and being the principal lodge also) having been much defaced and spoiled by the rabble at the same time, will over and above the moneys already laid out for repairs of the roof cost £109 besides 2 tons of timber and carriage £2. 12s.

Fifthly, we have taken an account upon oath from Charles Morgan, deputy to the surveyor[-general] of the wood, of what quantity of wood has been cut in this Forest pursuant to their Majesties' Letters of Privy Seal of 28 April 1690, and find the same to be 6,186 cords of wood sold to Paul Foley [of Stoke Edith], at the rate of 6s. a cord clear of cording, which rate is equal to, if not exceeding, the value of like wood sold in the county of Gloucester. And we have also viewed the places where the cordwood was cut and find there is very great stock left on the ground for timber, and all imaginable care taken by the officers employed in making the said Fellet and preserving all the stores and saplings with the principal shoots of such beech as grows upon old stools and well sheltered by other wood for the improvement thereof. We have also enquired what offences have been committed in the Forest since 13 February 1688 and having taken upon oath the presentments of several woodwards, keepers and other officers of the Forest concerning the same have returned to your Lordships the particulars thereof as follows: [The presentments are of typical vert offences.]

We humbly observe to your Lordships that if some of the principal offenders are not made examples to others, we have great reason to believe that whatever inclosures are made or repaired or lodges erected the same will be demolished as have those formerly made. We also hold ourselves obliged to represent also that the colliers of this Forest have time out of mind had an allowance of wood for support of their pits, usually made by order of the verderers and taken by view of a woodward or keeper, but the allowance having been stopped for some time upon a question of their right thereunto, they have taken the same without such order or view, by which great wastes are daily committed. For prevention whereof, and that the colliers may be duly supplied, as we are humbly of opinion they ought, we propose it as expedient that the allowances may be made to them by the order of the verderers at the Attachment or Swanimote Court and taken by view of a woodward or keeper as formerly.

Sixthly, we have enquired how duly the Forest Courts have been kept and humbly certify the same are regularly held, but by reason that the Attachment and Swanimote Courts can only convict but not punish, the proceedings in either of them are ineffectual to the preservation of the Forest without a Justice Seat. And the great negligence of several of the 'foresters and woodwards-in-fee' contribute much to the spoils committed. How far the lands which are held and enjoyed by the several 'foresters and woodwards-of-fee' for the exercise of those offices are inseparable from them or forfeitable upon such neglect of their duties is humbly submitted to your Lordships. We are informed by Mr. Rowles, steward of the said Courts, that the moneys paid at the Forest Courts by trespassers since their Majesties' happy accession to the Crown do not exceed the sum of 5s.

Seventhly, we have endeavoured with all exactness according to the best of our judgment to answer all the foregoing Articles of Instructions and have consulted such persons as we thought by any advice or information might conduce to their Majesties' service therein. And to this last Article, commanding our opinion upon the whole state of this Forest for the better governing thereof according to the Act of 20 Charles II [1668], we do further humbly certify that the most likely way to render the Forest Courts effective for the punishment of offenders, which for want thereof have grown numerous and insolent, and to oblige the 'officers of inheritance' to be diligent and faithful in the discharge of their several duties for the preservation of the Forest, is to procure a Justice Seat once a year for 6 or 7 years to be held in the long vacation, or not very far remote from it, which might be done by deputation from the Lord Chief Justice in Eyre to some of their Majesties' Justices of Assize going in their ordinary circuits from Gloucester to Monmouth, by which means all the diligent officers will be encouraged in their endeavours, the negligent reproved, the vain hopes that some persons have given the many and daring offenders about this Forest that the same shall be made a free chace and consequently destroyed and they exempted from punishment, will be utterly defeated and disappointed.

| [Signed] | Wm. Cooke | J. Viney | Reginald Pyndar |
|---|---|---|---|
| | Jo. Kyrle | Wm. Boevey | Phil. Ryley |

During the investigation by the commissioners in 1692 and the preparation of their Report (supra), Ryley was authorized 'to fell old hawthorns and other sparable underwood sufficient to raise £1,604.4s.10d.' for expenditure outside the Forest. He was in the Treasury's favour for being successful in selling large quantities of cinders for re-smelting, which had heretofore been taken without payment, and he was given a reward of £1,110[16] for his diligence in apprehending clippers, that is, fraudulent debasers of coinage. He was connected with the proceedings against ten people convicted and outlawed for 'a pound breach and riot' in May 1696.[17]

The grant of the constableship and wardenship 'of the deer and woods' to the Duke of Beaufort becoming void by reason of his 'failing to sign the Association',[18] a warrant was issued 11 May 1697[19] for a grant of the offices to Charles, Viscount Dursley. He was 'to hold in as full and ample a manner as Henry Herbert, now Duke of Beaufort, held the same under Letters Patent of 18 June 12 Charles II', and to receive, 'without account, in consideration of good and faithful service', £6,000 which Ryley was authorized 28 May 1697[20] to raise within seven years from 25 December 1697 from the sale of 'scrubbed beech, birch, hazel, thorns, and alder in places where the same can be most conveniently taken or spared'. Almost at the same time another grant was mentioned, of £14,000 over seven years, to Henry Segar, lately Lord Dursley, making a total of £20,000 over seven years, the amount which the commissioners had reported in 1692 could be raised.[21] On 8 June 1697[22] a minute of the proceedings of the lords justices reads: 'A bill was offered for Lord Dursely's being constable of Dean; their Excellencies, informed that Lord Wharton had made some enquiries about that office, forebore signing the bill until they heard from him'. Again, proceedings in the House of Commons on 16 February 1698[23] indicated an objection to 'a grant to a Mr. Montague, in a borrowed name, of £2,000 per annum for seven years to be raised out of the woods in Dean'. The appointment of Charles, Viscount Dursley held.

Wolseley the supervisor of the Forest died 26 December 1697,[24] and on 11 January 1698[25] the office was given to Harry Mordaunt; his duty was to see to 'the inclosures of nursery timber under the Act of 1668, and to six other springs of young wood elsewhere in Dean'. All the officials were strictly to perform their duties. Ryley was to assist in choosing regarders; the verderers had certified to the Treasury that eight regarders were required in place of those dead or unqualified.[26] But Mordaunt's main occupation with Dean was in raising money from wood sales. If the greater part of the money had been applied to improving the cover, and more firm steps taken against the commoners, the aims of the Act of 1668 would have been more nearly achieved.

## CORDWOOD FOR THE IRON INDUSTRY

By the start of the eighteenth century the trees on the Forest's open lands, and the estimated 100,000 immature oaks with some beeches on its statutory 11,000 acres

[16] *Cal. Treas. Bks.*, XI, p. 93.

[17] Ibid. p. 150. The offenders, reported as being 'very poor', were: John and Mary Vaughan, William and Elizabeth Harry, Richard Morefield, Henry Roberts, John Chapman, John Ward, Thomas Walden, and Joseph Monjoy.

[18] SP34/1702/3, p. 630.

[19] SP32/1694–6, p. 150.

[20] *Cal. Treas. Bks.*, IX, p. 128.

[21] Ibid. p. 129.

[22] SP32/1698, p. 190.

[23] Ibid. p. 94.

[24] *Cal. Treas. Bks.*, XV, p. 288.

[25] Ibid. XIII, p. 216.

[26] Ibid. XIV, pp. 61, 284.

were in jeopardy; so too were its fences, hedges, walls, and gates. The commoners were still obstructive. The Treasury 17 August 1700[27] permitted a few of the large and sound timber-trees to be felled for the Navy; 40 oaks, and 60 beeches, sawn into 4-inch plank, were sent from Newnham-on-Severn to Plymouth.[28] Edward Wilcox, the new surveyor-general of woods, began June 1703[29] to complete the contract with Wheeler and Avenant, of which 26,756¼ cords were as yet undelivered. He was also contracting with Mrs. Boevey for 852 cords for her ironworks at Flaxley.[30] On 6 December[31] he was instructed to sell many hundreds of trees blown down in a severe storm.

There was much competition for cordwood. Paul Foley of Stoke Edith petitioned 7 December 1704[32] for a new contract for 6,000 short cords each year at 5s.10d. for best wood and 5s.4d. for 'thorny' (chiefly hawthorn and blackthorn). Wilcox advised that, at these prices, sales would decrease by £800 per annum.[33] Furthermore, Mrs. Boevey, Lady Wintour, and a Mr. White with ironworks near the Forest should not be excluded; 'if it all fell into the hands of one person the price would be deteriorated'.[34] Wilcox in January 1705[35] reported that the woods were 'very full of young trees, two-thirds whereof were beeches, which overtopped the oaks, and would prevent them from ever growing up to be ship-timber'. He advised that the statutory 11,000 acres should be in sixteen sections of about 700 acres. One section should be cut annually, leaving sufficient standards of oak or beech, and then enclosed; £3,500 would thus be raised annually for ever, and 'room would be given for the standards to grow and come to perfection'.[36] In effect he recommended a cutting-cycle and coppice-rotation of sixteen years and valued the crop, excluding standards, at £5 an acre. He agreed 7 February[37] that Foley should have 8,000 short cords annually for six years at 6s. for 'thorny' and 6s.6d. for better wood, and two-thirds of any surplus above 12,000 cords cut in any year. To fulfil this contract Wilcox was allowed to cut and then to enclose 700 acres annually for six years.[38] This was almost the last large sale to ironworks.

## ABUSES BY INHABITANTS

The Forest officials were still having trouble with some of the local populace. A report from Wilcox 6 June 1704[39] was passed to Mr. How, paymaster general of guards and garrisons, relating to a 'riot and destruction of timber'. Each attempt to enclose was opposed by the commoners; they petitioned the Treasury 14 January 1706,[40] asserting that enclosing would harm their interests, growth of underwood

---

[27] Cal. Treas. Bks., III, Pt. I, p. 923.
[28] Cal. SP 29, 1671, pp. 465, 493, 512.
[29] Cal. Treas. Bks., XVIII, pp. 306, 313.
[30] Ibid.
[31] Cal. Treas. Papers, p. 212, No. 7.
[32] Cal. Treas. Bks., III, p. 392.
[33] Ibid. p. 397.
[34] Ibid. p. 408.
[35] 3rd Rept. of 1788, p. 19.
[36] Cal. Treas. Bks., III, p. 392.
[37] Ibid. p. 412.
[38] Ibid. p. 402.
[39] Ibid. p. 263.
[40] 3rd Rept. of 1788, p. 19.

would lessen pasture, and enclosure would deprive swine of acorns and beech-mast. An opposing petition 10 February[41] from employees of neighbouring ironmasters 'prayed that the plan of enclosure might be persisted in for the increase of underwood, by the cutting of which they gained their livelihood'. The attorney-general, Sir Simon Harcourt, consulted 4 July 1707,[42] gave his opinion 'that no claim or right of common of estovers, herbage, or pannage could prevent the enclosing, keeping in severalty, or improving the 11,000 acres as her Majesty should direct, and preserving the same enclosed for ever as a nursery of wood and timber only'. Wilcox informed the Treasury 27 September[43] that certain inhabitants had stripped of bark twenty oaks of 3 or 4 feet above ground and others near the ground to kill them so that they might be taken as dead trees. He asked for a warrant to fell these trees and any others so found, in the hope that 'when disappointed the culprits would not take the pains to do the mischief'. The Treasury concurred, and gave a warrant for felling 'such other trees, not of use to the Navy, for making gates, stiles, and fences'; the remainder were to be sold, the money applied to her Majesty's service and annually accounted for to the auditor of the Exchequer.[44]

On 25 June 1708[45] a royal warrant for £2,500 from wood sales was given to Charles, Earl of Berkeley, then constable-warden; this was the balance of a royal bounty of £6,000 granted by William III, by felling 'scrub beech, birch, holly, hazel, thorn, and oak in seven years from 25 December 1697'.[46] The same 25 June[47] another warrant for £7,000 for sales was given to Henry Segar. Elizabeth, Dowager Countess of Berkeley, in 1711[48] claimed £1,750 due to her husband, Charles, from sales. Foley obtained a renewed contract for cordwood 'so long as any remains to be cut'.[49] Francis Wyndham, a verderer, persuaded the Treasury to agree to his distributing to the 'under-keepers' the fines received for offences.[50]

In 1711[51] a Bill filed in the Exchequer by the attorney-general against the colliers for cutting trees and wood, followed from the following report:[52]

Report by the attorney-general, Sir Edward Northey Kt, to the Lord Treasurer, Chancellor and Under Treasurer of the Court of Exchequer, the Lord Chief Baron of the same Court, and the rest of the Barons there:

Her present Majesty [Queen Anne] now is and ever since her accession to the throne hath been seized and possessed in right of her Crown of and in the Forest of Dean. And by virtue or in pursuance of an Act of Parliament 20 Charles II [1668] intitled An Act for the increase and preservation of timber within the Forest of Dean, great part of the wast lands of the said Forest, that is to say 11,000 acres or thereabouts, were about 30 years ago or upwards inclosed and kept in severalty and have ever since remained and been kept inclosed and in severalty for the growth and preservation of timber within the said Forest,

[41] 3rd Rept. of 1788, p. 19.
[42] Ibid.
[43] Cal. Treas. Papers, III, p. 537, No. 140.
[44] 3rd Rept. of 1788, p. 20.
[45] Cal. Treas. Bks., XXII, p. 285.
[46] Ibid.
[47] Ibid. p. 286.
[48] Cal. Treas. Papers, IV, p. 259.
[49] Ibid. pp. 305, 353.
[50] Ibid. p. 186; Cal. Treas. Bks., XX, pp. 3, 689.
[51] 3rd Rept. of 1788, p. 20.
[52] F20/1 (23).

which said inclosures were by the said Act freed and discharged of and from all manner of estovers and all other right, title and pretence whatsoever excepting of Fee Deer.

And that it was enacted and declared by the said Act that whensoever any wood or timber should at any time or times then after be directed to be fallen in any part of the wast of the said Forest, inclosed or not inclosed, the same should be viewed and allowed to be fallen by two or more of the Justices of the Peace unconcerned in the premises and should not be cut or fallen until the same should be viewed and allowed by such two or more Justices as fit and convenient to be cut and fallen and that the said Justices should have marked with a broad arrow and crown that it might remain to be seen so many and such trees as should be most fit to be preserved for growth of timber upon every one intended to be fallen and also should have certified under to the Lord Treasurer or Lords Commissioners of the Treasury for the time being the names of the places and number of trees so viewed and allowed to be fallen and so marked to be preserved as aforesaid; and it was also thereby enacted and declared for further preservation of the said Timber then growing or to grow upon the premises that no officer or other person or persons whatsoever should at any time then after have or claim any Fee trees out of the said Forest upon any pretence whatsoever as in and by the said Act to which the attorney-general refers amongst other things it doth and may more fully appear.

And that there is a very great quantity of wast lands within the said Forest not inclosed, that is to say 12,000 acres or thereabouts and that as well upon and within the said Inclosures as upon the said wasts not inclosed there have usually been and very lately were very many timber trees and great quantities of wood standing and growing from which great advantages have accrued and were likely to accrue to her Majesty and whereby the vert and venison of the said Forest were very much profited and increased.

That notwithstanding the premises, William Parry of Yorkley in the parish of Newland, collier, Richard Reynolds, collier, John Reynolds, Thomas Reynolds and William Smith of the same place, colliers; William Whetson of Little Dean, yeoman, William Haynes of Ruar Deane, stone collier, Nicholas Whetson of Little Dean, stone collier, James Morgan of Little Dean, yeoman, Moses Vobes of Mitchell Dean, wheelwright, Andrew Jones of Newland, yeoman, George Mason of Newland, yeoman, George Withorne alias James of Yorkley, yeoman, Nathaniel James of Lidney, yeoman, Sturley Kedgin of Coleford, yeoman, combining and confederating with divers other persons, at present to the said attorney-general unknown, whose names when discovered the said attorney-general prays may be herein inserted as parties hereunto with apt words to charge them to wast, spoil and destroy her Majesty's said Forest and the timber and wood growing and being as well within the said Inclosures as without the same, they [the aforementioned persons and their confederates] at divers days and times within the space of 3 years last past without any manner of title, licence or authority for so doing have cut down, felled and destroyed and converted to their own use great numbers of oak, ashes, elms, beech and other timber-trees and divers young trees and saplings which were likely to be timber and great quantity of wood lately standing and growing at several parts and places of as well within the said inclosed grounds as in other places within the said Forest, viz. at or near the several parts or places called Dead Mans Cross, Symones Way, Ayloe hill in Aywood, the Delves, Sally Vellet Wall, Edge hill, Wainway and Winnell and at divers other places which are parcel of or situate within the said Forest.

That the said confederates do absolutely refuse to discover the number, kinds and quantity of such trees and wood or to answer for the profits or value thereof to her Majesty to whom the same of right do belong, and do severally set up claim and insist upon some right, title or authority in themselves some or one of them to fell, cut down, sell, convert or otherwise dispose of to their own private use all or any of the timber, saplings and wood growing within the said Forest, of great quantities thereof as well within the said Inclosures as without, but do all refuse to discover by what right, title or authority they or any of them do so claim the same to the great prejudice of her Majesty's Right and the apparent damage of the vert and venison of the said Forest, and in contempt of the said Statute and of divers other laws of this Realm. All which acting and

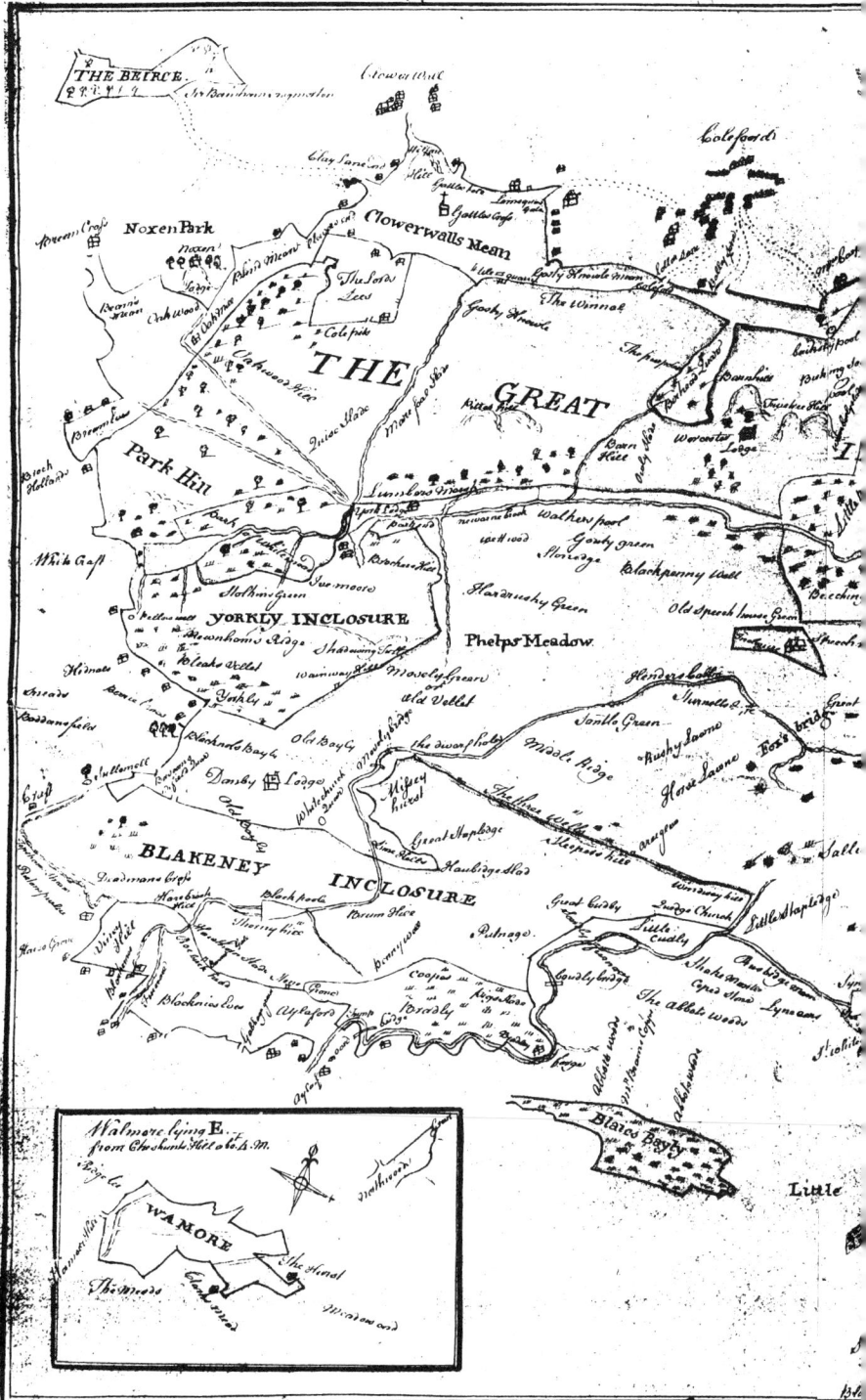

Map VIII. A map of *c.* 1710 of the Forest of Dean. (P.R.O. ref. F17/7)

A Description of the Forest of DEANE as it lyes in sev.ᵗˡ parcels wᵗʰ the Inclosures

doing of the said confederates are contrary to Equity and good Conscience and are a great violation to and usurpation upon her Majesty's Right and prerogative within the said Forest of Dean.

In tender consideration whereof and for that the said confederates do still continue and persist to fell, cut down and destroy the timber, wood, saplings and young trees likely to become timber within the said Forest and insist on their having good right and title so to do without discovering or showing forth the same, and for as much as it is proper before your Lordships in this Honorable Court for the preservation of her Majesty's Rights and Revenue, and for the preservation of the growth of timber pursuant to the Act of Parliament to have a full discovery of the right, title or authority which they the said confederates any or either of them have or claim to have in or to any of the timber, trees, saplings and trees likely to become timber or wood in the said Forest or in any walk, precinct, purlieu or place within the same (her Majesty's attorney-general on her Majesty's behalf hereby waving all penalties and forfeitures which may be had against them any or either of them for or in respect of the premises) to the interest therefore that [the aforementioned persons and their confederates when discovered] may upon their Corporal Oathes true and perfect answer make to all and singular the premises as is here again particularly repeated and interrogated and may set forth and discover what right, title or authority they any or either of them have or claim to have in or unto or to cut or fell any timber trees, saplings and trees likely to become timber or any wood standing.

That your Lordships grant her Majesty's most gracious Writs of Subpena to be directed to your Lordships unto [the aforementioned persons and their confederates when discovered] requiring them and every one of them to appear before your Lordships in the Honorable Court at a certain day and under a certain pain otherwise to be mentioned to answer your Lordships and to stand to perform and abide such order and decree therein as to your Lordships shall seem meet.

The protracted suit, following the Bill filed in 1711, was discontinued by the death of Queen Anne in 1714.

In 1712 Sir Robert Atkyns, having for long been chief baron of the Court of Exchequer, wrote:[53] 'The six lodges built for the keepers are the only houses within the present Forest, containing 23,000 acres, all extra-parochial.' Thereafter 'all care of the Forest appears to have ceased'.[54] The management during several decades before 1712 was inadequate to overcome opposition from the commoners and miners. The crown was in part to blame: there was no vigorous policy, courts were discontinued and only a small proportion of money raised from wood sales was reinvested in Dean. Officials' salaries were too low, and often in arrears, leading to dishonest practices and reliance on perquisites and poundages.

On 22 August 1713 a Swanimote Court for the Forest of Dean was convened to be held at Mitcheldean on 14 September of that year.[55] It was to be convened by the four verderers and the beadle of the Forest – see Appendix to this Section X. No records of the proceedings and presentments of offences have been found; but the list of the officials concerned is impressive.

John Orde, supervisor of the Forest in 1712, was succeeded two years later by Roynon Jones.[56] The constable-warden, James, Earl of Berkeley, petitioned the Treasury in 1717[57] for repairs to be done to five lodges (The King's, York, Herbert,

[53] *Ancient and Present State of Gloucestershire* (1712).
[54] 3rd Rept. of 1788, p. 20.
[55] National Liby. of Wales, Dunraven MS 330.
[56] *Cal. Treas. Bks.*, XXIX, Pt. II, p. 150.
[57] Ibid. XXXI, Pt. II, p. 161.

Latimer, and Danby) also to their stables and pounds. Not until 1721[58] was a warrant given to the surveyor-general of woods, Edward Young, to fell timber to raise £389.11s.6d. to repair the lodges; two were uninhabitable, 'inasmuch as the keepers are not able to prevent the great damage done to timber-trees of which there are very good stores'. Later evidence suggests that the repairs were not done. In 1718[59] Young informed the Treasury of persons who destroyed the fences round part of the Lea Bailey, and he pressed for powers to prosecute; 'for want of vigorous prosecutions on these occasions there are great damages done to the vert and venison in most of his Majesty's forests'. No help for Dean was forthcoming, yet later in the year[60] Young received orders to fell in Dean dotard trees to raise £64.19s.8d. to pay for repairs in Windsor Little Park.

On 15 September 1721[61] Viscount Gage of Highmeadow, a verderer, an office then sought for local prestige and authority, informed the Treasury that the roads in Dean were impassable and dangerous. As the Forest was extra-parochial the crown was liable for repairs, and in the past the surveyor-general of woods had done the work by direction of the Treasury. The matter was taken up with the new surveyor-general of woods, Charles Wither, who did not immediately comment on the roads, but informed the Treasury 25 February 1722:[62]

> The Forest of Dean contains 23,600 acres of which 11,000 of the best were enclosed pursuant to the Act of 1668. For several years after the enclosures were made, great care was taken in preserving them, insomuch that they produced a considerable annual revenue, but of late years they have all been slighted and thrown common, and when any part has been felled it has not been fenced and secured from cattle, so that the spring thereof has been cropped and spoiled. The soil is naturally so kind for wood and timber that the enclosures might easily be restored to a flourishing condition by being cut in orderly and reasonable proportions, and kept carefully fenced from the injuries of cattle. An annual warrant is proposed for cutting and fencing.

On 25 May 1725[63] Wither confirmed that as the Forest was extra-parochial the roads were not in the care of any particular parish, and had hitherto been repaired at the crown's expense. Officials and gentlemen of the county who had viewed the highways estimated the cost would be at least £854.10s. Ruardean lodge was in need of repair; its situation was so exposed that he recommended a more sheltered site. Five other lodges needed repair, at a cost of £207.10s. The roads, narrow and overhung with trees, should be widened to 30 feet 'in the clear', and the removed trees sold to defray the expense. The Treasury agreed and issued a warrant, followed by others during the next few years:

8 May 1730:[64] £561. 5s. and £247. 3s. 6d. to be raised by wood sales.
10 August 1731:[65] For removing 'Littledean Lodge' and repairing the lodges at the Speech House and Ruardean.

[58] *Cal. Treas. Bks.*, XXXI, Pt. II, p. 377.
[59] Ibid. p. 437.
[60] Ibid. pp. 161, 577.
[61] *Cal. Treas. Papers*, VI, p. 81.
[62] Ibid. p. 121.
[63] Ibid. p. 330.
[64] *Cal. Treas. Bks. & Papers*, I, p. 365.
[65] Ibid. II, p. 138.

28 June 1732:[66] £733. 12s. 6d. to be raised out of wood sales for repairing roads.
29 November 1732:[67] £871. 2s. 6d. for the same.

Some improvement in administration appeared for a time. The constable-warden was regularly given warrants for £52.10s. each quarter to pay the salaries of the supervisor and keepers.[68] Roynon Jones was succeeded as supervisor in 1730 by Christopher Bond.[69] However, depredations continued. Francis Whitworth, the new surveyor-general of woods, reported thefts of timber, resulting in orders to prosecute the offenders being given to the Treasury solicitor.[70] In 1735 there were renewed outrages by the inhabitants when pounds were broken into and lodges despoiled.[71] In the same year[72] the surveyor-general of woods explained that the colliers made a practice of boring holes in trees that they might have them when decayed. On 18 March[73] a warrant was issued to prevent 'such pernicious practices'; bored trees appearing to be dead and spoiled were to be felled, taking care that none of use to the Navy be cut down. Nothing is said about discovering and punishing the offenders, or recommending to the officials more attention and care. The slight attention then paid by the government to this matter is clear. It is apparent, too, that colliers did not think themselves entitled to any trees not dotard or decayed. In 1736 Christopher Bond, supervisor, drew attention to abuses in a Memorial to the Treasury:[74]

> After the Act 20 Charles II [1668], 11,000 acres had been enclosed. The officers were duly elected, forest courts held, and offenders prosecuted and punished, by which means were raised a great quantity of timber-trees; but within the last 30 years these elections had been neglected, the courts discontinued, and offenders left unpunished. The 'Officers of Inheritance', and others, were grown remiss and negligent; so that a few enclosures, and those of a few acres only, of the 11,000 acres were kept up, and these not carefully repaired. A great number of cottages were erected upon the borders of the Forest, the inhabitants whereof lived by rapine and theft. There were besides many other offences committed such as intercommoning of foreigners, surcharges of commons, trespasses in the Fence month and Winter Haining, and in the enclosures; keeping hogs, sheep, goats, and geese, being uncommonable animals, in the Forest; cutting and burning the nether-vert, furze, and fern; gathering and taking away crab-apples, acorns, and mast; other purprestures and offences; and carrying away such timber-trees as were covertly cut down in the night. By which practices several hundred fine oaks were yearly destroyed, and the growth of others prevented. It is feared that some of the inferior officers of the Forest, finding offenders to go on with impunity, were not only grown negligent, but also connived at, if not partook in, the spoil daily committed.[75]

---

[66] *Cal. Treas. Bks. & Papers*, II, pp. 238, 258, 289.

[67] Ibid. p. 302.

[68] *Cal. Treas. Bks. & Papers*, I, pp. 276, 289, 554, 584, 594; II, pp. 155, 170, 182, 327, 337, 347, 474, 487, 497, 509, 652, 663, 673; III, pp. 15, 75, 106, 117, 128, 141.

[69] Ibid. II, pp. 358, 538, No. 29.

[70] Ibid. p. 228, Nos. 66, 285.

[71] *Glos. Notes & Queries*, III, pp. 372, 1312.

[72] 3rd Rept. of 1788, p. 22.

[73] Ibid.

[74] Ibid.

[75] 'Up to 1736 the government had sold the oaks felled in Dean to a local dealer, who squared them up roughly and sold them again at a great profit for the use of the Royal Docks. At length in 1736 the government realized the meaning of this ingenious transaction, and put a stop to it. The disappointed dealer then sold the three ships with which he had carried on the trade.' (*Victoria County History, Glos.*, II, p. 200).

On 27 January 1736[76] the Treasury considered the Memorial together with proposals 'for a new law for remedy thereof'. The opinions of the solicitor-general, Sir Dudley Ryder, and of the attorney-general, Sir John Willens, were that 'the offences were chiefly due to the neglect of putting the Act of 1668 into execution'. They recommended that vacant offices should be filled, that the courts should be regularly held, and that the officials should be strictly enjoined to do their duty. All this should be explored before considering a new law. The Treasury solicitor was given renewed orders to prosecute offenders.[77]

The Treasury considered whether the lodges should be repaired and what should be done about their adjacent enclosures.[78] They also considered the repair of roads, which the verderers said would cost £645, and of Parkend Bridge, 'the parish of Newland being unable to bear the expense'.[79] The surveyor-general of woods was given a warrant to undertake the repairs.[80] He sold 1,600 cords to Thomas Crawley-Boevey of Flaxley at 5s.6d. a cord, and paid 2s. a cord for felling and cording;[81] he claimed a poundage of 20s. on each 1,000 cords, 'being the ancient and usual allowance'. The balance he expended on rebuilding Littledean Lodge and on repairing the lodges named Parkend, Speech House, Worcester and Ruardean.

Christopher Bond, junior, succeeded his father as supervisor 21 September 1736.[82] The following April[83] Augustus, Earl of Berkeley, was appointed constable-warden 'with £40 per annum to be distributed at his discretion among the keepers, and with all fees, wages, rewards, etc. out of the royal revenue of Dean Forest and the lordship and manor of Newland'; Thomas James of Lydney his gamekeeper, with the earl's steward, William James of Soilwell, were to have the sole rights over the game.[84] The earl appointed the keepers and regularly received the money warrants for their salaries.[85] He, with Lord Ducie, Sir John Dutton, and others supported a grant to the inhabitants of Coleford to repair their chapel.[86] Viscount Gage, Lord of the Manor of Staunton, asserted that the repair would be 'prejudicial to his ownership of the ground on which the chapel was built'.[87] In spite of this a warrant was issued to fell trees to provide £150.[88] Gage continued to oppose the earl and his supporters;[89] a complex lawsuit of uncertain issue followed.[90]

Additional serious trouble followed with Gage, who had relinquished his appointment as a verderer in favour of John Probyn of Newland. On 29 December 1743[91] he was accused of illegally taking beeches worth about £100 from 60 acres

[76] Cal. Treas. Bks. & Papers, III, p. 159.
[77] Ibid. II, p. 359.
[78] Ibid. pp. 206, 213.
[79] Ibid. pp. 298, 363.
[80] Ibid. p. 532.
[81] L.R. 4/3/59.
[82] Cal. Treas. Bks. & Papers, V, pp. 18, 231.
[83] Ibid. p. 453.
[84] The Deed of Appointment was dated 8 Jan. 1738 (MS. penes me).
[85] Cal. Treas. Bks. & Papers, IV, pp. 146, 167, 180, 362, 387, 401, 415, 573, 591, 662; V, pp. 161, 177, 191, 204, 397, 414, 430.
[86] Cal. Treas. Bks. & Papers, IV, p. 131. Hart, Coleford, p. 174.
[87] Cal. Treas. Bks. & Papers, IV, p. 215. Hart, Coleford, p. 174.
[88] Cal. Treas. Bks. & Papers, IV, pp. 291, 516.
[89] Ibid. V, pp. 70, 88, 149.
[90] Ibid. pp. 237, 243. Much correspondence is to be found in Glos. R.O., D.23 Probyn Papers; and in Gage MSS.
[91] Cal. Treas. Bks. & Papers, V, p. 338.

of the 200-acre Hangerberry Wood, east of English Bicknor. He claimed the 60 acres as his property; all 6,000 trees upon it were 'stunted and withered wood except 200 small oaks containing about 850 tons'. Gage also claimed under ancient custom wind-throws, with bark, lop and top, and roots of trees felled in his woodwardships of Staunton and English Bicknor, but not 'brushwood and twigs for the King's deer to feed on'. The whole matter was considered by the solicitor-general; in consequence of his report and on the advice of the attorney-general, Gage 24 April 1753 conveyed Hangerberry Wood to the crown.[92] In the long dispute many insinuations were made against Gage and his witnesses.[93] His chief accusers were two verderers, Maynard Colchester and Thomas Pyrke, also the new supervisor William Jones, and the deputy surveyor Tomkins Machen.

During the troubles with Gage the verderers made strong representations that miners of iron-ore and coal should be allowed timber for their works;[94] it was alleged that 'thousands must inevitably starve if timber cannot be found for their pits, of which the whole body of miners are already apprehensive and at which they express great uneasiness'.

On 12 April 1743[95] a warrant for £516.3s.10d. was given to Henry Legg, surveyor-general of woods, to be raised in Dean from sales of wood and damaged trees other than those fit for the Navy. The money was to be spent in repairing lodges in Bere Forest, Hampshire. It would have been more fitting if this money and the huge bounties given to the Berkeleys had been used to improve Dean, badly in need of rehabilitation and tending. But the Forest had few influential friends. No evidence of care is found until in 1758[96] John Pitt, surveyor-general of woods, proposed that 2,000 acres should be re-enclosed. The Treasury gave the necessary order.[97] In 1763 Pitt was removed from office in favour of Sir Edmund Thomas, whose deputy was Joseph Mabbot. From a survey of timber made in 1764[98] it was computed that 27,302 loads were fit for the Navy, 16,851 of about sixty years' growth, and 20,066 of dotard or decaying condition. Pitt, reinstated in 1767, reported in 1770 that in Dean he found much spoil and great quantities of wood and timber cut without warrant by his predecessor to the value of £3,235.[99] In 1771[100] he obtained permission to enclose another 2,000 acres; a warrant was given to him to fund its cost of £2,077.18s.10d. by wood sales. Between 1771 and 1786 he made representations to the Treasury regarding abuses by miners, colliers, timber stealers, and others, and tried means to prevent them, introducing checks on the delivery of timber to mines and paying rewards on the conviction of offenders. He was opposed by officials of both the old and the new regime, some of whom by taking perquisites were no better than the inhabitants who preyed upon the cover. The small success following Pitt's well-intended measures show how useless it was to attempt improvement while resident officers gained by continuance of abuses.[101]

[92] Glos. R.O., D.23 Probyn Papers, f. 478; Gage MSS 1082/7; *Cal. Treas. Bks. & Papers*, V, pp. 529, 662, 689.

[93] Ibid. pp. 448, 469.

[94] Glos. R.O., D.23 Probyn Papers, f. 478, 20 March 1743.

[95] Ibid. f. 463.

[96] 3rd Rept. of 1788, p. 23.

[97] See maps of Enclosures, 1758, in F.17/2 and 3.

[98] 3rd Rept. of 1788, p. 24.

[99] Ibid. p. 23.

[100] Ibid.

[101] Ibid. App. 38.

The supervisors during much of Pitt's term of office, Roynon Jones, senior and junior,[102] were paid a salary of £100 but are not recorded as forwarding the conservation of the cover. Neither are the constable-wardens, namely, John, Lord Chedworth, appointed 9 October 1761,[103] Norborne Berkeley, 21 May 1762,[104] and Frederick Augustus, Earl of Berkeley, 26 June 1766.[105] Many of the officials under them, and others over whom they had no jurisdiction, appear to have been concerned more with perquisites than duties. The deputy surveyor and his assistant made efforts to conserve the Forest and to prevent abuses, but they too took customary perquisites. They had at least ensured that much naval timber had been sent to Plymouth dockyard. But enclosures made on Pitt's recommendations 'were soon suffered to go to ruin'.[106] Letters tell part of the sorry story of the period.[107] These relate chiefly to naval timber which had become extremely scarce in England. A document of 9 August 1768[108] records that Dean 'still contained much useful timber in maturity, and numbers of trees in progressive states of growth, but there are wastes of vast extent, uninclosed, which produce no trees, though the soil is of a nature very fit for their cultivation'. A letter dated 15 May 1769 to the Navy Board[109] said that the miners each year took 700 to 1,000 oaks instead of inferior kinds. The woods were spoiled by animals and people. If proper care were exercised the Forest could supply much of the naval timber for Plymouth. Another letter 30 May[110] deplored the abuses in Dean 'which is one of the finest nurseries in the Kingdom, and has for these 16 or 18 years afforded for the service of Plymouth yard a great supply of the largest and most useful sort for naval purposes'. Some of this timber may have come from the enclosures made under the Act of 1668.

In 1774[111] Mr. Andrews, purveyor of naval timber in Dean, reported that cattle continued to spoil the young woods, and that the burning of gorse had ruined 10,000 oaks in one night. The only two enclosures made were ineffectively maintained, and acorns sown for raising transplants had been eaten by mice. There were no decayed timber-trees in the Forest; the oldest, none over 120 years, 'were put in [by Major John Wade] under Oliver Cromwell'. The abuses in Dean were so great that he knew of no better preventative than 'a troop or two of Light Horse to patrol the Forest day and night'.

A letter 30 April 1777[112] asserts that Dean was 'going to wreck and ruin: the depredations made therein by the colliers and country people are incredible'. Another, 28 February 1780,[113] from Benjamin Slade to the Navy Board, says that trees were stolen in the night and cut into coopers' ware. Other trees were shipped

---

[102] Appointed 12 May 1761; Home Office Papers 1760–5, p. 94.

[103] Ibid. p. 119.

[104] Ibid. p. 235.

[105] Ibid. 1766–9, p. 127.

[106] 3rd Rept. of 1788, p. 24. As an example, the Rev. William Crawley wrote 10 Dec. 1770: 'There is a hill of 3 or 400 acres called Chestnuts with no trees on it, but close by at Flaxley are some fine chestnuts'.

[107] *Eighteenth Century Documents relating to the Royal Forests, &c.* (selected from the Shelburne MSS. in the William L. Clements Library), by A.L. Cross (Macmillan, New York, 1928).

[108] Ibid. p. 102.

[109] Ibid. p. 103.

[110] Ibid. p. 105.

[111] Ibid. p. 134.

[112] Ibid. p. 141; Robert Gregson to Lord Shelburne.

[113] Ibid. p. 110.

to Bristol every spring tide; on one day at Gatcombe on the Severn there were five or six teams [of horses] with timber, plank, and knees, among which were several useful pieces for ships of 50 and 64 guns. Unless some method was found to prevent the depredations 'in a few years the whole Forest must be destroyed'. Slade himself had surveyed and marked timber in Dean last spring, the great part of which was fit for 'thickstuff and plank', likewise other timber which will be tendered for by Henry Mills, a contractor to the Navy.[114]

The letters and reports which the Navy Board received in and around the 1770s had little effect. Matters were still the same in 1780[115] when 29 May[116] the Treasury received from their solicitor a report on the abuses, advising the offering of rewards of £20 or £50 for information leading to the conviction of offenders. Thereafter some action is apparent, for during the seven years to Michaelmas 1787 no less than 247 persons were convicted of stealing timber, and of other offences, fines amounting to £729.9s.6d. were imposed and £540 was paid out as rewards by the deputy surveyor.[117] Much enclosing had been done during 1772–83,[118] but the only known planting was that of acorns and oak plants,[119] and of a few Weymouth pine, the first introduction of conifers, c. 1781.[120] In any event, 'the fences of most of the enclosures were destroyed soon after they were made, and such parts of them as consisted of pales, posts, and rails were carried away publicly by the country people in carts and waggons; none of them had contributed in any degree to the increase of timber, or advantage of the Forest'.[121]

In 1783 a new survey of Dean's timber, made by order of the House of Commons, showed 90,382 oaks, computed to contain 95,043 loads, and 17,982 beeches, 16,492 loads, 'both of square measure'.[122] The greater number of the trees ranged from 90 to 110 years; many were nearing their prime and were being felled for the Navy and other useful purposes, yet much of the Forest, through neglect, was 'a barren waste and heath'.[123]

In 1786[124] warrants were issued for raising £2,000 from timber sales in Dean towards the cost of building a gaol and certain houses of correction at Gloucester, for which purpose Joseph Pyrke and Thomas Crawley-Boevey, verderers, viewed 1,768 marked oaks and beeches. At this time Thomas Blunt, who resided at Abenhall, was deputy surveyor, and Miles Hartland his assistant.

## SALES OF TIMBER

In spite of abuses and maladministration Dean had supplied much timber for shipping, mining, and other uses. During seven years to Michaelmas 1787 the now combined court of attachment and swanimote had issued to the miners 2,930

---

[114] Mills was a timber merchant from Rotherhithe (2nd Rept. of 1816, p. 141).
[115] *Eighteenth Century Documents . . ., op. cit.*, p. 109.
[116] 3rd Rept. of 1788, App. 37.
[117] Ibid. App. 38.
[118] Hart, *Royal Forest*, App. XVI (A) and (B).
[119] 3rd Rept. of 1788, App. 32.
[120] Ibid. p. 113; F.16/31.
[121] 3rd Rept. of 1788, p. 37.
[122] Ibid. p. 24.
[123] Ibid. p. 78.
[124] Ibid. App. 35.

warrants for mining-timber,[125] under which taken without payment had been 7,486 oaks, 494 beeches and 2,369 various trees, a total of 10,349, a yearly average of 1,478, some the best in the Forest.[126] During twenty-six years from 1761 to 1786 the nation had benefited by huge quantities felled for the Navy:[127]

|  | £. | s. | d. |
|---|---|---|---|
| Oak: 16,573 loads, 34 feet[128] | 30,814 | 14 | 4 |
| Beech: 871 loads, 41 feet | 908 | 13 | 7 |
| Cordwood from the above: 22,430 cords | 6,953 | 7 | 1 |
| Stakes sold in 1786 | 12 | 3 | 10½ |
| Bark: about 1,510 tons | 2,650 | 1 | 5 |
|  | 41,339 | 0 | 3½ |

| Disbursements | £. | s. | d. | | | |
|---|---|---|---|---|---|---|
| Viewing, setting out and felling timber | 3,334 | 9 | 4¾ | | | |
| Allowances and poundages of the surveyor-general, and his deputies, besides costs of warrants, audits, etc. | 7,422 | 14 | 4 | | | |
| Discounts and brokerage of Navy Bills | 762 | 9 | 7 | | | |
| Repair of lodges and the Lea Bailey pound | 14 | 19 | 1 | | | |
| Repair of roads | 103 | 10 | 0 | | | |
| Repair of enclosures, sowing acorns and transplanting young oaks | 330 | 5 | 7½ | | | |
| Keepers looking after the timber and enclosures | 723 | 10 | 0 | | | |
| Keepers and other persons watching the Forest by night | 280 | 0 | 0 | | | |
| Expenses of prosecutions and rewards on conviction | 647 | 15 | 7 | 13,619 | 13 | 7¼ |
| Credit balance of Navy Timber Account | | | | 27,719 | 6 | 8¼ |

[125] 3rd Rept. of 1788, App. 10.
[126] Ibid. p. 22.
[127] Ibid. App. 32. Blunt since 1783 to 31 Aug. 1787 had delivered 2,025 loads to Plymouth and 2,783 to Deptford and Woolwich; and Henry Mills, contractor for the Navy, had taken about 1,000 loads in 1781–2 (ibid. App. 23).
[128] The price was £1. 18s. a load or ton, excluding delivery (3rd Rept. of 1788, p. 24).

During the same twenty-six years the following wood sales had been made:[129]

|  | £. | s. | d. |
|---|---|---|---|
| Oak and beech timber | 16,226 | 9 | 5½ |
| Cordwood from the same | 10,244 | 18 | 1¾ |
| Bark[130] | 1,263 | 16 | 3½ |
|  | 27,715 | 3 | 10¾ |

| Disbursements | £. | s. | d. |  |  |  |
|---|---|---|---|---|---|---|
| Viewing, setting out felling timber | 4,838 | 2 | 3¾ |  |  |  |
| Allowances and poundages of the surveyor-general, and his deputies, besides costs of warrants, audits, etc. | 2,892 | 10 | 8 |  |  |  |
| Discounts and brokerage of Navy Bills | 249 | 12 | 3 |  |  |  |
| Repair of lodges, etc. | 764 | 16 | 5 |  |  |  |
| Building a watch house in 1782 | 144 | 8 | 7 |  |  |  |
| Making and repairing roads | 11,221 | 11 | 10 |  |  |  |
| Building and repairing bridges | 306 | 2 | 0 |  |  |  |
| Repairing of old and making new enclosures | 3,676 | 5 | 6½ |  |  |  |
| Survey of timber in 1783 | 298 | 6 | 8 | 24,391 | 16 | 3¼ |
| Credit balance of Wood Sales Account |  |  |  | 3,323 | 7 | 7½ |

The credit balance of the two accounts totalled £31,042.14s.3¾d., of which £829.18s.5d. was expended in 1764 on repairs at Hampton Court House Park, £816.0s.5¼d. on repairs at Richmond New Park, and £2,000 on the buildings at Gloucester already noted. The rest remained in the hands of John Pitt, the surveyor-general of woods. Dean in spite of being robbed, exploited, and largely neglected, had thus proved an immense national asset. The enclosing during the

---

[129] 3rd Rept. of 1788, App. 33.

[130] Immense quantities of oak bark from Dean were shipped from Chepstow *c.* 1781 (I. Waters, *About Chepstow* (1952), p. 25); also from Newnham in the 1770s (*Trans. B.&G.A.S.*, 18, p. 12). As to local shipbuilding, some of Dean's timber may have been used for one or more of the three ships built at Newnham in 1776, 1778, and 1779 (ibid. p. 13). Other ships were built at Broadoak, Brockweir, Gatcombe, Lydbrook, and Newnham (G.E. Farr, *Chepstow Ships*, 1954).

Commonwealth and following the Act of 1668, and the efforts to encourage natural regeneration and coppicing together with some sowing and planting of beech and oak, despite obstructions, had been worthwhile.

However, in 1786 commissioners were appointed to 'enquire into the state and condition of the woods, forests, and land revenues of the crown', and to 'suggest plans for redressing any abuses in the management of them, and for the protection, increase, and supply of the Royal Navy'. Significant attention was given to the Forest of Dean, as explained in Part Five, Section XI.

# APPENDIX

## Forest of Dean

Maynard Colchester, Frances Wyndham, Nathanial Pyrke and Roynon Jones, Esquires, verderers of the said Forest of Dean.
To John Sladen, Beadle[132] of the said Forest.

These are in her Majesty's [Queen Anne] name to will and require you forthwith to make proclamations and to give publick notice in all market Towns and other places usual, That the Court of Swanimote for the said Forest will be holden at the house of Joan Voice widow in Mitcheldean upon Monday the 14th day of September next by 10 of the clock in the forenoon. At which time and place all Regarders, Foresters [-of-fee], Woodwards, Keepers, the four men and the Reeve of every Vill within the said Forest are to appear and give their attendance and on further to do as to their respective offices doth appertain. To which end you are to give them personal notice or by a note in writing left at their respective habitations. And you are to summon and warn 24 good and lawful men of the several Townships within the bounds of the said Forest to appear at the time and place aforesaid to inquire on behalf of our Sovereign Lady the Queen of all such articles, matters and things as shall then and there be given in charge to them. And further to hear and try such presentments as shall then be exhibited to them of offences already committed within the said Forest. And you yourself are to be then and there present with the names of the said four and twenty persons by you summoned as aforesaid and further to do and perform what to your said office doth belong. And hereof you are not to fail. Given under our hands and seals the 22nd day of August 1713.

| Regarders | Foresters-in-fee |
|---|---|
| Geo. Bond, Esq. | Francis Wyndham, Esq., or Tho. Ames, Deputy |
| Tho. Waller, Esq. | Charles Hyett, Gent., or Hen. Jelf, Deputy |
| Wm. Skin, Gent. | Mayor &c. of Gloucester, or James Hyett, Deputy |
| Kedgwyn Hoskin, Gent. | Tho. Folery, Esq., or Phillip Hatton, Deputy |
| Wm. Denning, Gent. | Edward Williams, or Hen. Stephens, Deputy |
| Richd. Birkin, Gent. | James Coster senior, or James Coster junior |
| Nathel. Rudge, Gent. | John Ayres |
| Wm. Probyn junior, Gent. | Lady Ann North |

---

[131] National Liby. of Wales, Dunraven MS 330.

[132] A minor office holder who at times acted as clerk to the Swanimote Court (see Hart, *Royal Forest*, pp. 69, 78, 80, 147, 148).

Ralph Gearen, Gent.            Eustace Hardwick, Esq., or Wm. Sadler, Deputy
John Brown, Gent.
Wm. Gardner, Gent.

<u>Under-keepers</u>                      <u>Woodwards</u>

Richd. Barrow snr, Gent.       Benedict Hall, Esq., or two Deputies
Wm. Waller                     Maynard Colchester Esq., or two Deputies
Giles Creed                    Tho. Vaughan Esq.
Rich. Trigg                    Tho. Barrow, Gent., or Geo. Bullock, Deputy
Richard Barrow senior          Chas. Hyett, Gent., or Josiah Chapman, Deputy
                               John Vaughan, Esq., or Rich. Holliday, Deputy
                               Gilbert Hearne, Gent.

<u>The 4 men and the Reeve of the Townships of the said Forest</u>

| | | | |
|---|---|---|---|
| Newnham | Abinghall | Bicknor | Breem |
| Awre | Mitchel Dean | Staunton | St. Briavells |
| Blackney | The Lea | Newland & Redbrook | Brockweare |
| Little Dean | Ruardean | Clowerwell | Lea Bayley Hamlett |
| Flaxley | Lidbrook | Coleford | Northwood |

# PART FIVE

## XI. ENCLOSING AND PLANTING OF DEAN: 1788–1818: WILLIAM BILLINGTON AND EDWARD MACHEN

In 1787 commissioners were appointed by the government to examine the state and condition of the woods and forests belonging to the crown (and managed by the Office of Woods and Forests), to suggest plans for reducing abuses in the management of them, and for the protection, increase, and supply of timber for the use of the Navy. Significant attention was given to the Forest of Dean,[1] where throughout much of the first three-quarters of the eighteenth century, the unsatisfactory state of its woods, particularly as a continuing resource of shiptimber, caused grave national concern. Depredations by the inhabitants, and inadequate management by the crown officials, were among the main reasons.[2]

In that year Abraham and William Driver, surveyors, of Kent-road, near London, were requested by the commissioners to undertake a survey of the woods, by walks, of the Forest of Dean (see Appendix I of this Section XI). They were also to estimate the expenditure and income over a hundred years if 18,000 acres of the Forest of Dean were enclosed and planted in six sections.[3] The planting was to be of oak, to produce shiptimber, no apparent thought being given to conifers. Messrs Driver estimated that fencing would cost £4,950 and planting acorns £4,500. They recommended 'planting' (with a dibber) one or two acorns in sods dug 3 feet apart and turned upside down; and early thinning or respacing (removing) every other oak at the end of ten years.[4] No immediate action appears to have been taken on these and other relevant recommendations.[5]

On 15 May 1788 Miles Hartland, assistant to Thomas Blunt the deputy surveyor (then aged 51, he had known the Forest from boyhood) deposed that when he was appointed in 1782 'the state of the Forest, with respect to Inclosures', was:

> Before his appointment there had been several inclosures made in the Forest, namely, the Buckholt, which was made many years before his remembrance; the Great Inclosure, Stone Edge, Coverham, the Perch, Serridge, East Haywood, and West Haywood, which were made within his remembrance, and since the commencement of his present Majesty's reign [1760] all these inclosures were open at the time of his appointment [1782]. The Buckholt Inclosure was repaired soon afterwards, has ever since been kept in repair, and is now well stocked with young oak and beech, but chiefly the latter, which require thinning, and would produce great quantities of cordwood, besides leaving a full stock of growing timber. The fences of most of the other inclosures were broke and destroyed soon after they were made; and such parts of them as consisted of pales, posts, and rails, were

---

[1] 3rd Rept. of the Commissioners of 1788.
[2] Hart, *Royal Forest*, pp. 198, 199.
[3] Ibid. p. 205. P.R.O. F16/31, /47(M415); /59; F17/5, /6 (All in 1787).
[4] Ibid. p. 206. P.R.O. F16/31, /47 (M415); /59, F17/5, /6 (All in 1787).
[5] Ibid. p. 205.

carried away publicly by the country people, in carts and waggons. They have not since been repaired; and he believes that none of the inclosures he has mentioned, except the Buckholt, has contributed in any degree to the increase of timber, or advantage to the Forest.

There have been three inclosures made since he has held his present employment [1782]; viz. Stapleage Inclosure, and a small inclosure near the Speech House [? The Acorn Patch], both of which were part of the Great Inclosure, and Birch Wood Inclosure, which was part of Serridge Inclosure before mentioned. All these were made in one season, about five or six years ago, and set with acorns; and there are a great number of young oak plants now growing in them, many of which are in a thriving condition; but the small inclosure by the Speech House having been ploughed, the ground lying hollow, harbours mice and other vermin, which eat the acorns, and destroy the young plants.

Hartland reported that 'the parts of the Forest now bare of timber, which he thinks fittest to be inclosed for the growth of timber, are the following':

In John Brett's Walk [Littledean], Hazle Hill, and Edge Hills (including Tanner's Hill, Green Bottom, and Green Hill) which lie together, and might be made one inclosure; Badcock's Bailey, and the Chesnutts, which, if inclosed must be separate, as there is a road between them; East Haywood and West Haywood, between which is also a road from Little Dean and other places to the Fire Engine Coal Works [in the bottom between Nailbridge and Cinderford Bridge].

In William Stephen's Walk [Blakeney], that part of Great Stapleage which is not already inclosed; Meezeyhurst, Howbeach, and Putmage – all these might come into one inclosure; Buckhall Moor, Bradley Hill, and several parcels near them, might be included in another inclosure.

In Robert East's Walk [Parkend], Birchen Dingles and Mason's Tump, which lie together; Blakes Vellet, separate; Breame's Eves and Howell Hill, together.

In Richard Bennett's Walk [Worcester], the Perch and Coverham, between which runs the main road [from Mitcheldean] to Coleford; and Great and Little Bourts, which lie together.

In Richard Bradley's Walk [Ruardean], the Lea Bailey, Bailey Hill, and Lining Wood, which might be laid together; Great and Little Berry together; and Plud's and Smether's Tump together.

In Thomas Harvey's Walk [Speech House], Blackthorn Turf and Serridge together; Salley's separate; Kensley's Ridge separate; Daniel Moor and Beechenhurst together. These places are now very bare of timber, but are of a very proper soil, and would produce great store of good timber, if inclosed and taken care of.

The kinds of fencing which he thinks best adapted for inclosures in the Forest, are a ditch about three feet deep, and about three feet and a half wide, with a quick[thorn] hedge planted upon a bank, and fenced with a dead hedge until the quick becomes a sufficient fence. He cannot recommend posts, rails, or pales in any case, as they consume a great deal of timber, and are liable to be soon stolen. Where the rock lies near the surface, the fence must be made of stone, which may be dug on the spot, and the wall built up batterywise, so as to leave a ditch on the outside.

He conceives the most likely method to produce timber in the inclosures is, to sow acorns, beech mast, and hawberries, hazel nuts, holly berries, and the seeds of most other kinds of wood at once, as they thrive best together, destroy the fern, and produce the quickest crop of underwood, which trains up and protects the oaks, and would in time amply pay the expense of fencing, by producing stuff for cordwood, etc of which the Buckholt is an example. But if oak only is to be produced, the best way of planting the acorn is either by turning up a turf and putting an acorn or two under it, or making a hole with a sharp instrument to put in the acorn. He thinks that the young oaks would be out of the reach of cropping by cattle in about 25 years; but the timber, even when grown to a good size, as well as the succession of young wood, would at all times thrive better if kept continually inclosed, and protected from cattle of all sorts.

The foregoing comments by Hartland indicate the huge task of reafforestation, and is further emphasized by the following statement made by Messrs. Driver in 1787:[6]

The inclosures which have been made for the cultivation of timber, and their present condition [1787]:

|  | A | R | P |
|---|---|---|---|
| The Great Inclosure, was begun to be made about 12 years ago [c. 1775] with post and rails, but before the whole was completed, a great part was taken away, and nothing now remains but the banks; there are no young trees of any kind. | 743 | 0 | 25 |
| Stonedge Inclosure was made about 12 years ago [c. 1775], and was fenced with a dry stone wall, which is for the most part destroyed; there are a great many thorns and hollies, with some very fine large oak, but no young timber of any kind coming up. | 125 | 1 | 10 |
| Coverham Inclosure was made about 15 years ago [c. 1773], part with dry stone wall, and part post and rails; nothing now remains of this inclosure but the bank, notwithstanding which there is a great quantity of young timber, for the most part beech, with a few oaks. | 350 | 2 | 34 |
| The Perch Inclosure was also made about 15 years ago [c. 1773], part with dry stone wall, and part post and rails; nothing but the bank now remains. There was a great quantity of young timber, particularly beech, in this inclosure, which is nearly all destroyed in consequence of the fences being pulled down. | 198 | 2 | 26 |
| Serridge Inclosure was made about 12 years ago [c. 1775] and was fenced with a dry stone wall, of which but little remains, being quite open in many parts; there are no young trees of any sort, and but few old trees. | 409 | 3 | 20 |
| Heywood Inclosure was made about 10 years ago [c. 1777], part with a dry stone wall, and part pales, very few traces of which now remain, and in some parts none at all. We have been informed that great part of the wall was pulled down, or fell, before the whole was completed, and the pales carried away by waggons, etc soon after they were put up, and from its present appearance, it is evident no advantage has been derived from this inclosure, as there are no young trees in any part of it. | 715 | 3 | 38 |
|  | 2543 | 2 | 3 |

The three following inclosure are all that remain inclosed and in good repair (except the Buckholt enclosure after-mentioned):

|  | A | R | P |
|---|---|---|---|
| Stapleage Inclosure was made about 5 years ago [c. 1783], part with dry stone wall, and part dead hedge; in general in good repair. In some parts of it there are some small oak and beech plants, and also a few large oaks and beeches. | 183 | 1 | 3 |
| Speech House Inclosure [? Acorn Patch] was made about 4 years ago [c.1784] by the Deputy Surveyor, and planted with acorns, which have produced some young oaks. | 5 | 0 | 6 |

[6] 3rd Rept. of 1788, pp. 36, 113; Hart, *Royal Forest*, pp. 306–7, App. XVI(A).

Birch Wood Inclosure was made about 5 years ago [*c.* 1783], part with
dead hedge, and part dry stone wall, which in general is in good repair;
there are but few young oaks coming up.

|       |   |    |
|-------|---|----|
| 135   | 0 | 24 |
| 323   | 1 | 33 |

Buckholt Inclosure was made about 80 years ago [*c.* 1708], the greatest
part with a stone wall, the rest hedge and ditch. The fences have of late
years been kept in good repair. There are some very fine large oaks in it,
but in general it contains a great quantity of fine young beech. There
are also some oak trees of about 10 or 15 years' growth, and young oaks
are coming up from acorns which have been set in vacant places. A few
Weymouth pines have also been planted in this enclosure, which grow very
well.[7]

|       |   |    |
|-------|---|----|
| 352   | 3 | 20 |
| 676   | 1 | 13 |

The extent of the two categories of inclosures, totalling 3,219A 3R 15P, plus the
Lea Bailey, indicate that there were over 7,000 further acres requiring reafforesting
in order to achieve about 11,000 acres. A full survey by Messrs. Driver in 1787 is
given in Appendix I of this Part Five. No action was taken following the survey.

The Napoleonic Wars drew further attention to England's dire need of
shiptimber. Nelson visited Dean in 1802 and was perturbed that much therein
appeared to be unsatisfactory: there were fewer oaks than the Forest might grow. His
Memorandum written about 1803[8] indicated deficiencies and suggested remedies.
He asserted that less than 3,500 loads of shiptimber were available, 'and none
coming forward'; the Forest, if developed, would grow 920,000 oaks and produce
9,200 loads yearly. He proposed strong measures, including the appointment of a
'guardian of the support of our Navy', and submitted thoughts 'on encouraging the
growth of timber'. However, Nelson underestimated the amount of suitable timber
in Dean.[9]

In 1803 the government appointed Lord Glenbervie as surveyor-general of woods
and forests. In the same year, James Davies was appointed deputy surveyor of Dean.

---

[7] Some of the Weymouth pine, planted *c.* 1781 are still growing. The area is now called Sallow Vallet.
Photograph in Hart, *Royal Forest*, Plate V. Also herein, Plate IX.

[8] 30th Rept. of the Commissioners, 1853, App. 16, p. 223; Hart, *Royal Forest*, p. 207, App. XVII.

[9] Notes written in 1818 by Edward Machen, deputy surveyor (see Appendix III). 'The quantities of oak
timber delivered from this Forest for the service of the Navy from the year 1809 to 1817 were:

|      | Trees cut | Loads: feet (1 Load = 50 ft) |
|------|-----------|------------------------------|
| 1809 | 3079      | 4430:12                      |
| 1810 | 1835      | 1829:34                      |
| 1811 | 763       | 844:39                       |
| 1812 | 1216      | 1481:31                      |
| 1813 | 1401      | 1868:48                      |
| 1814 | 1711      | 1220:24                      |
| 1815 | 752       | 853:46                       |
| 1816 | 264       | 652:35                       |
| 1817 | 301       | 484:29                       |
|      | 11,322    | 13,666:48                    |

And there have been rejected by the purveyor of the Navy Board and sold or used for repairs, etc. 2,108
of the above trees containing about 2,500 loads of timber. There have also been cut for sale by Auction:
[*cont. on p. 225*]

Plate X. Edward Machen, deputy surveyor from 1808 to 1854. He died at Eastbach Court near English Bicknor in October 1862, aged 79. (Photograph in the office of Forest Enterprise, Coleford)

| [cont. from p. 224] | | Trees cut | Loads:feet (1 Load = 50 ft) |
|---|---|---|---|
| | 1809 | 713 | 203:32 |
| | 1810 | 460 | 133:44 |
| | 1811 | 403 | 98: 5 |
| | 1812 | 531 | 167:33 |
| | 1813 | 281 | 99: |
| | 1814 | 444 | 150: |
| | 1815 | 106 | 27: |
| | | 2,938 | 878:14 |

This makes altogether 14,260 oak timber trees containing 14,545:12 loads and there have been in the same time about 50 trees containing about 50 loads of timber blown down, stolen, etc.'

In May 1807 Glenbervie was authorized by the Treasury to thin trees 'where so
thick as to impede each others growth', to give room for the improvement of those
likely to become fit for naval purposes.[10] He was anxious to replant Dean, and gave
much thought as to how the Navy's requirements could be met.

In February 1808 a new deputy surveyor, Edward Tomkins Davies (later the
surname was changed to Machen), replaced his father James Davies under whom he
had worked for two or three years. He was in time to undertake important work
authorized by the Dean Forest (Timber) Act of 1808,[11] which confirmed much of
the Dean Forest (Reafforestation) Act of 1668.[12] The new Act provided the powers
necessary to complete the enclosure of 11,000 acres (at this time only 676 acres at
Stapledge, Acorn Patch, Birch Wood, and Buckholt were enclosed).[13]

In 1808 Messrs. Driver were employed to survey and report on the oak timber
standing in the Forest 'by which it appeared that there were 34,827 oak trees
containing 22,883 loads of 50 cubic feet each', but according to Machen 'The Report
was not exact and is supposed to be much under the real quantity'. Appendix II
provides many details of the Survey. In summary the count was:[14]

| Walk | Oaks | Content in 'round measure' cu. ft. |
|------|------|------|
| Ruardean | 10,171 | 222,705 |
| Latimer | 422 | 6,455 |
| Worcester | 3,794 | 146,855 |
| Parkend | 5,593 | 226,165 |
| Speech House | 10,505 | 431,910 |
| Blakeney | 4,342 | 110,055 |
| | 34,827 | 1,144,145   or 22,883 loads of 50 cu. feet. |

Also 9,500 tellers or young standards 'exclusive of those before-mentioned in this report'.

Glenbervie could not at once make full use of his powers, chiefly because of lack of
funds. To help overcome this he sought to make miners pay for their pitwood, and

---

[10] L.R.5/11, p. 48.
[11] Act 48 Geo. III, c. 72, 1808.
[12] Act 19 & 20 Chas. II, c. 8, 1668.
[13] By 1808 the enclosures were:

| | A | R | P | |
|---|---|---|---|---|
| Buckholt (1707) | 352 | 3 | 20 | [includes a few Weymouth pine] |
| Stapledge (1782) | 183 | 1 | 3 | |
| Birchwood (1782) | 135 | 0 | 24 | |
| Acorn Patch (1783) | 5 | 0 | 6 | |
| | 676 | | 13 | |

'The Buckholt contained principally beech, Stapledge was thinly stocked with oak except the north
and called Little Stapledge on which there was plenty, and Birchwood had some clusters of natural young
oaks scattered about it; the Acorn patch was well filled with thriving young oaks about 25 years old.'
(Machen Notes, 1818).
[14] P.R.O. F20/3. Photocopy in Glos. R.O., D3921, Hart Collection.

Plate XI. Whitemead Park House, Parkend – office and residence of the deputy surveyor of the Forest of Dean from 1816 to 1968; demolished in 1970. Edward Machen resided here from August 1816 to 1853.

also to obtain revenue from entrepreneurs seeking permission to lay industrial tramroads through the Forest. In 1810 an Act[15] united the office of surveyor-general of woods and forests with that of surveyor-general of land revenues to form the new office known as 'the Commissioners of Woods, Forests, and Land Revenues of the Crown' ('The Office of Woods'). Glenbervie having decided on an extensive programme of enclosure, planting began in the autumn of 1808 at Whitemead Park (which the constable-warden, Frederick Augustus, Earl of Berkeley, had surrendered on 7 April 1807 – about 240 acres in all – so that it could be a 'nursery of timber').

## WILLIAM BILLINGTON: SUPERINTENDENT OF PLANTING, 1810–18

As the crown had few direct employees in Dean, the operations of clearing, fencing, draining and planting had to be undertaken by contract. This was entrusted in 1808 to Messrs Driver, land and timber surveyors, whose immediate agent was Amos Sleed. The work commenced in 1809. The main object was the raising of oak timber for naval purposes.

The local 'superintendent' from 1810, appointed by Glenbervie, was William Billington (from 1800 he had been 'gardener', much interested in trees, to Lord

---

[15] Act 50 Geo. III, c.65, 1810.

Yarborough of Brocklesby in Lincolnshire and the Earl of Haddington).[16] He was probably born between 1760 and 1790. His appointment in 1810 was 'to superintend the enclosing, fencing, draining and planting' of about 11,000 acres in the Forest of Dean. He was thus employed by the Commissioners of Woods and Forests, not by Messrs. Driver. He appears to have resided at Parkend: his eldest son, William Moreton, was born there in 1813; later followed two more sons and two girls. In October 1825 (having moved from the Forest to Chopwell Woods in 1818), Billington described his eight years of work in Dean, the difficulties he surmounted, the failures and successes he experienced, and the lessons he learned.[17] The following are his most relevant descriptions and comments:

## CLEARING AND FENCING

As the fencing and clearing of the ground for planting were the first objects, I shall endeavour to be as brief and clear as possible on those heads. The ground at first was cleared of most of the oak timber trees, and all other trees of different kinds. Many parts of the Forest were thickly covered with the most beautiful hollies which had originally, it is supposed, been planted for the support of the deer in severe winters, when the preservation of them was judged of more consequence than the value of the timber. Great quantities of thorn and crab trees were also cut down and cleared, for the better holing and planting according to the contract; but, towards the conclusion, it was considered an error to make it so bare, and in consequence more of the hollies remained for shelter, and upwards of 1,000 acres were left to nature, where a considerable quantity of oak timber trees were standing.

None of the undergrowth was cut down at first, but the spaces were to be filled up with oaks and Spanish chestnuts, if it should appear such places were not likely to be stocked from the acorns in a natural way, or by trying the experiment again with acorns on some of the largest bare spaces, and that were more clear from growing trees; which again failing, the vacancies were filled up with large plants of oaks and Spanish chestnuts, and some ash for the moist ground. The young oaks, that were making their appearance in the brakes of undergrowth after it was enclosed and the cattle, &c. kept out, were cleared by cutting it away from the plants.

We found a good deal of difficulty in bringing the fencing to answer the purpose of keeping out sheep, cattle, horses, mules, &c. that depastured on the uninclosed parts of the Forest; and, when their range became curtailed and the pasture scanty, hunger made them very keen for a better pasture, which they were sure to find if they could get over the fences into their former haunts.

We had upwards of 100 miles of new 'fences' about 25 miles of which were stone walls where the materials could be had convenient and cheap without the expence of hauling with teams, or wheeling too great a distance; upwards of 70 miles of earthen banks, and the rest of hedge and ditch, according to local circumstances; besides several miles of old fences, part walls, which had to be repaired and rebuilt.

The contract specified the earthen banks to be made 4 feet 6 inches wide at the bottom, 5 feet high, and 2 feet wide at the top; and a ditch 18 inches deep on the outside, with an offset 1 foot wide between the ditch and the foot of the bank; a row of furze or

[16] When in 1810 Lord Glenbervie was 'in search of persons properly qualified for the important duties of forest culture, he applied directly to the first nurserymen of that time (Mr. Lee and Mr. Kennedy, of Kensington), to find two persons of ability and experience'; they recommended Billington for the Forest of Dean and a Mr. Clayton for the New Forest. [Billington, 1854, p. 4].

[17] Billington, W., *A Series of Facts, Hints, Observations and Experiments on the Different Modes of raising young plantations of oaks for future navies, & c. 1825* (Plate XIII herein), pp. 1–72. The remainder of his book relates to general arboricultural and forestry matters.

Plate XII. Type of bank (made of turf, soil, stones and gorse) formed to enclose areas of woodland crops against sheep, cattle and deer. (Drawing by Martin Latham following a sketch by William Billington, superintendent of planting in the Forest of Dean, 1810–18)

whins [gorse] to be sown along the top of the banks, and another at the outside foot of the banks on the offsets, also at the foot of the walls on the outsides. The furze or whin to be used is what grows in the north of England, very different from the variety growing in the Forest and the south of England, being much stronger and more prickly, at least much stronger spines, and of a more quick and gigantic growth, which makes it much more destructive to young plantations than the other sort. The north of England variety flowers in the spring months whereas the other flowers towards the end of summer or autumn.

In general the earthen banks stood very well on all the wet or moory soils, and the dry thin soils on the high grounds where the turf was full of small roots of heath, furze, rushes, grass, &c; and care was taken to build them entirely of turf, cut thin, from three to four or five inches thick, according to the nature of the turf, placing the grass-side downwards, and no loose soil put in the middle, except the two or three first layers, well trodden down. But over the soils of a loamy nature, inclining to clay or marl, or where the ground had been formerly disturbed by old coal works, or wherever the land was of such a nature that the air, water, or frosts caused it to expand or pulverise, we had the utmost difficulty in getting them to stand. The sheep and cattle, by grazing on the outsides of the banks in such soils, pulled up the grass that grew between the layers of turf by the roots, which caused them to crumble down like clay, marl, or lime, and which occasioned a great extra expence in facing the banks with fresh turf, the grass-side outwards, or with stones, according to local circumstances, the contiguity of materials, and the kind of stock that frequented such parts.

When the banks entirely gave way, it occasioned gaps or breaks on the top of the whin hedge, which looked very unsightly. Sometimes only the outside turf slipped down, and did not in the least disturb the live hedge of whins. But the greatest difficulties were encountered after the banks were made, the whins sown, and prospering very well. The young whins, sown for the fence, were so tempting to the sheep and other cattle, that the sheep could get upon the banks in most places, particularly where they sloped towards the enclosures, which frequently happened on the first made banks from the middle having been filled with the loose soil. The other cattle also could reach to crop the young whins and grass that grew upon the tops of the banks which kept the fence from getting up, so that we could not keep the sheep out of the enclosures.

Well, what was to be done? The woodmen were complaining that the sheep were continually trespassing and injuring the young plants as well as the fences; and, as 'necessity is the mother of invention', after various trials of laying loose branches of thorns, hollies, crabs, &c. against the banks, which were soon found to do more harm than good; for the grass grew so strong when protected and sheltered by the branches, as to encourage the moles and short-tailed field mice to burrow and render them quite hollow and loose near the surface, which nearly ruined some of the first-made banks, and, when the cattle could get to graze upon them, soil and grass came away together.

At last, however, we hit upon a cheap method and which perfectly succeeded. By cutting some of the strong branches of the hollies, thorns, and crabs (or other wood, where these could not be had conveniently) into 2 feet to 2½ feet lengths, leaving the lateral or side shoots on, shortened a little on the part that would appear out of the ground, allowing a foot or 15 inches to drive in the bank, and about a foot or 15 inches out of the bank, according to the height of it; for, if left much longer, a heavy snow would be apt to break it down. The branches, or *sprags*, as we termed them, must be stuck in the bank at the outside edge of the uppermost turf projecting outwards. We had a dead hedge of stronger materials, drove in at the bottom of the banks, similar to the one at the top, to keep off the sheep and cattle from grazing the banks; but this was found of little use, and abandoned, nor was the ditch at the outsides of the banks found to be of much service, but in some cases prejudicial, as it caused the foundations of the banks to give way in wet ground inclining to clay, and the banks slipped down; but still we preserved the form of the ditch to carry off the water in the wet ground, and to add to the height of the bank when necessary, but seldom the full depth. The rows of whins, ordered to be sown at the outside foot of the banks and walls, were also abandoned as of no use; in fact, we could not raise them there without incurring a great unnecessary expence.

By experience we found that the banks stood and answered the purpose as well by reducing the dimensions to 4 feet wide at the bottom, 4 feet 6 inches high, and to about 18 inches wide at the top, putting one entire good thick turf at the top, or rounding it a little with good soil to keep the wet out of the inside in moist situations, to sow the seeds in, and to prevent them falling too deep between the turfs.

The walls were made of as flat stones as could be procured, without mortar, 5 feet high, with a good turf laid along the top to keep out the wet and hold them together. Both the banks and walls generally gave way, under the shock of heavy and long-continued rains, except where the stones were of a very durable quality and well put together. The earthen banks with the whin hedge answered better, as we found much disappointment and great extra expence from stone that appeared quite hard and good when dug out of the quarry, but, when it came to be exposed to the action of the atmosphere for some time, it crumbled away very fast, and occasioned such breaches in the walls as could not be repaired without dragging stones from a great distance, or substituting some other kind of fence. But, to secure a good and permanent fence in the Forest, and to guard against all unforeseen circumstances, were planted a row of quicks [quickthorn] on a raised bank, about 18 inches high, in the insides of the worst parts of the bank and walls, and afterwards extended it to the greater part of the banks, and where the stones appeared of a bad quality in the walls; in short, nothing was left undone that appeared necessary to insure the raising up of a new forest of oaks.

The workmen's prices, for making the earthen banks in the Forest, were from 2s.6d. to 3s. per rod; and the cutting, preparing, and making the dead hedge to protect the whins, 1s. per rod. The walls were generally made for 8s. per rod, including every thing, such as getting the stones, and wheeling, if necessary, a reasonable distance. The prices the 'fences' were contracted for were, the walls at 9s. per rod of 18 feet, the earthen banks at 4s. per rod, statute measure, 16½ feet, and to be kept in repair for three years, except in cases of wilful damage.

*DRAINAGE*

The drains were at first made only 15 inches wide at top, 12 inches deep, and very numerous; but this method was soon found not to answer, as most of the drains (except the main or carrying drains, which had a good descent) soon choked up, and did more harm than good, owing to the grass so soon growing in them, and by the soil thrown into them by the moles in crossing them. The great expence incurred in looking over and cleaning them out, induced me to think of a cheaper and more effectual method. Accordingly, we had them made both deeper and wider, from 2 feet 6 inches to 3 feet 6 inches wide at the top, and from 15 inches to 2 feet and 2½ feet deep, and about 10 inches or the breadth of a spade wide at the bottom. By enlarging the dimensions, fewer became necessary; consequently they could be sooner gone over, and cleaned out at a great deal less expence.

## PLANTING

The original contract with Messrs Driver was to have the land holed at 4 feet apart each way, the holes to be 15 inches square and 9 inches deep, turning the soil upside down previously to paring off the turf, and laying it to one side; except every tenth hole, which was to be 18 inches square with the turf taken off, and 12 inches deep; to plant in every tenth hole a strong five-year-old oak, and in every hundredth hole a five-year-old Spanish chestnut; the rest of the holes to be planted with a sound perfect acorn, except on such parts as should be deemed unfit for the growth of oak; these places to be planted with ash, elm, beech, or sycamore, with the fir and pine tribes [Norway spruce, European larch, Scots pine]. But, preferring the four first specified sorts to the fir and pine, where the ground should be thought fit for the growth of such trees, each vacancy [failure] that may happen to be made good for three years after it was first planted, with a plant of the respective kinds.

Plants and acorns were accordingly provided and planted, and the holes made agreeable to the contract; but after three years trial, we were obliged to desist, and substitute one year's seedling oaks. After counting the plants from the acorns (the first year after planting them) in 9,000 holes in various places in the different enclosures, we never found more than 40 plants in 100 holes from the acorns, and in some only 3 or 4 plants in 100 holes. On an average of those planted there appeared about 24 in every 100 holes, or little more than one fifth, though the greatest care was taken to plant and mend over each hole with a sound good acorn; but the acorns were taken out by the short-tailed field mouse, rooks, and other vermin. After being mended over with fresh acorns a season or two, it was no better; the plants still went off, from various causes which I shall hereafter describe; and, in some of the holes where the water lodged, the acorns rotted.

After we had ceased planting acorns, we continued to plant one year's seedling oaks in lieu of acorns, the large plants in every tenth hole the first time over, and to mend over the second year with two years' seedling oaks; in some cases we missed one year, and made good all failures with a strong three-year-old oak the last time over. In some parts of the enclosure, where the plants from the acorns and seedlings had so failed, and the furze, grass, &c. had become so strong before they were finally mended over, and finding it of no use to do so with seedlings, it was agreed to mend all over for the last time with strong four-year-old oaks, about 150 to an acre, to plant that quantity according to the number of acres such enclosure contained, but to plant them on the barest places, as some parts were sufficiently stocked with what had been planted and what came naturally, this quantity being considered quite sufficient to stock the enclosure according to the spirit of Mr Driver's contract.

On finding how fast the fern, furze, grass, and such shrubs as birch, broom, &c. increased after the enclosures were shut in, and the impossibility of procuring five-year-old plants so fast as they were wanted to plant such vast tracts of land so soon as it was got ready, rather than defer such a duty a year or two till the plants arrived at that age and size (because size was a material object) it was agreed to plant strong and good three and four-year-old oaks, instead of the five-year oaks, in every tenth hole, while the holes could be distinguished, or we must have planted it with seedlings, and left the tenth hole unplanted for a year or two, which could not have been so regularly filled up with large plants afterwards.

The Forest of Dean is a hilly district, some of the hills of considerable elevation, with flat and low grounds between them. On some parts of the most lofty hills we planted fir, ash, elm, sycamore, with oak and Spanish chestnut interspersed amongst them, which succeeded very well indeed on the dry ground; but where the soil was wet they did not succeed at first, although the ground was drained; but as the turf was taken off about an inch or an inch and a half thick with the mattock or holing instrument, it left the hole when the soil had settled that depth below the surface of the unstirred ground; when of a retentive nature, the holes were full of water all the winter, and when we came to plant in the spring with the mixture of plants, we could not fasten them, as the soil was like a puddle, and the first high wind that came would loosen the plants.

When the dry weather set in, the soil would become hard and crack, and expose the roots to the dry cutting frosty winds that generally prevail at that season of the year; if planted in the early part of the season it was worse, as the frost in that case would heave them out of the ground, and expose the roots to the sun and winds; of course, what were not killed made but little progress, nay, were scarcely kept alive. This was the case in all the wet ground planted with nothing but oak, as well as those planted with the mixture of trees. The wind had not so much effect upon the oak and other deciduous kinds, as it had upon the evergreen firs [Norway spruce and Scots pine]; but the seedlings, that were planted in the early part of the season, were thrown out by thousands in all the wet parts of the ground.

Something however must be done to obviate this and other difficulties, or all the labour and expence would be thrown away, besides the disagreeable feeling arising from the failure of attempts so earnestly made. On this principle I suggested to the Commissioners the idea of raising the holes for the plants above the original surface, to throw off the wet from the roots; a plan of which they approved, and which they ordered to be done, by taking a spade-full of good earth from the dry ground to each hole; but this I soon found to be both tedious and expensive, and not affording soil sufficient to answer the purpose. I then suggested another method, which was instantly adopted, which answered a two-fold purpose, and succeeded beyond my most sanguine expectations, being of much importance in all wet land, particularly where the fir and pine tribes were planted.

Instead of holing the ground where it had not been previously holed, the lines were laid down, as usual, at 4 feet apart, a good turf 16 or 18 inches square, as thick as the soil would admit, from 7 to 9 inches, laid with the grass-side downwards, at 4 feet apart each way where the holes would have been made. The turfs were cut in rows, to communicate with the drains; one row thus cut will raise the holes for about three rows of plants, which, if properly done, will carry off the water into the drains; some of them may be made into drains at a trifling expence. Thus the raising of the holes and draining the ground were done at nearly one expence, and by this method the ground is left a great deal drier, no water being capable of settling about the roots of the plants, affording at the same time a stratum of soil as thick again as the original; and, by being laid down a few months before planting, the two swards rot, and the sod becomes firmly fixed, so that they can be planted with the greatest ease without disturbing the sod; part of the roots will also be just within the original surface, and the rich soil, produced by the rotting of the two swards, affords a fine pabulum for the roots of the plants during the two first years, when they stand in so much need of it, preventing also their being loosened and thrown out of the ground by the frosts or winds, as the soil about the roots is always dry and kindly, the same as if planted in the driest soils.

Mr Driver's men holed the soil in the common way, only not so deep as before laying on the sods; but I do not think this mode necessary, as it is attended with more trouble and expence, and robs the plant of part of the rich soil, by removing the turf where the hole and plant are to be. I had several acres done in the way I have recommended for large five-year-old oaks, which was attended with the greatest success, without the loss of scarce a plant, the whole taking to the soil, and thriving in an extraordinary degree. Before we fell upon this plan, the plants where it had been planted on such cold wet lands, particularly where the fir tribe were planted, had failed, and we raised all such holes with a large square turf, planting it over again, and the effects were astonishing. Another benefit attending it was, the plants were not so soon encroached upon by the grass, &c.

## MICE

I have before stated, that the short-tailed or field mouse,[18] the rooks, and various vermin, took the acorns out of the holes, and caused a great deficiency in the plants at first coming up; but of the destructive ravages of that little animal, the field mouse, I was not so well aware till two years after I had been in the Forest, and the third from the commencement of planting it with acorns. In making my survey of the state of the enclosures and plants for the information of the Commissioners, I had frequently observed great quantities of the small oak plants from the acorn having been barked and bitten off, particularly where the grass was thick; and nearly all the ash that had been planted in the wet and moist grounds (for some ash had been planted in those situations) were barked all round the stem in the same manner as the oaks, only more so, as they seemed to be fonder of the ash than the oak bark. We all thought it was the hares that did the mischief, although at that time there were very few hares in the plantations; but still we found vast quantities barked and bitten off, and always so near to the ground, about 5 or 6 inches high.

In the Autumn of 1812 that circumstance struck me forcibly, so much so, that I was induced to examine more minutely; when I was not a little surprised to find, at almost every plant so barked or nibbled, great quantities of very small dung, much less than hare's dung, but something similar in its appearance; I thought of course it must be the field mouse, which we soon found too true. Having before observed, where the grass and other herbage were thick and rank the plants were chiefly barked, but where the stem of the plant stood clear of herbage of any kind, the plants were scarce ever touched; this is worthy of remark, and very natural, for without shelter they would have been more exposed to their natural enemies the hawk, owl, &c. and, like most other mischief, it must be done in the dark. Some of the small seedlings were barked all round the stem, as high as the mice could reach; others only in part, but much nibbled, and great quantities bitten off; and as the plants were destitute of leaves, and the rank grass getting above them and excluding the light, the greater part were soon killed, wherever the grass or other herbage was rank. Before the Autumn of 1813 the mice had become so numerous, that we could pick up four or five plants of the larger or five-year-old oaks on a very small space of ground, all bitten off, just within the ground, between the roots and the stem; and not only were the oak and ash injured, but the elm, sycamore, and Spanish chestnut, of which the mice are not so fond as of the two former.

Of the hollies that had been cut down, great quantities of young shoots had sprung from the stools, were looking very well, and making a fine shelter, as we thought at the time, perhaps thirty or forty shoots from a stool or old root; these were nearly all destroyed in one winter, by the mice barking them in the very same manner as the oak and ash; nor did the crabs, [Sallow] willows, nor even the strong shoots of the furze, escape their ravages; they appeared to feed very much on the young shoots of the furze or whin; and I have seen hollies, as thick as a man's leg, barked all round, and as high in the bush as 4 or 5 feet from the ground. This was in some thick bushes, where were plenty of leaves and old stumps to shelter them when at their mischievous work. The willows were barked every branch, to the height of 3 or 4 feet from the ground, when they grew in thick shelter of any kind. In fact the grass, in some of the small encroachments from the Forest in the occupation of the inhabitants, was very much destroyed by them, particularly the seeds or artificial grasses, and the people were frequently remarking how their crops of hay suffered from the depredations of the mice. Indeed, if I had not seen it, I should not have thought it possible. The long grass in the enclosures, when it got laid after completing its Summer's growth, in which state it smothered, and helped, with the mice, to destroy the plants, looked like a riddle, comparatively speaking.

---

[18] Probably *Microtus agrostis*, a species which occasionally increase to 'plague' numbers.

The mice had now become so numerous and destructive that, when Lord Glenbervie was in the Forest in the Autumn of 1813, he became so alarmed about the final success of raising a forest, that he soon after wrote a letter to the deputy surveyor [Edward Machen], instructing him to pursue every means we could think of, by cats, dogs, owls, poison, traps, or any method that could be devised, even to cutting up all the grass and fog (the old dead grass is termed fog in the Forest) by the roots, offering a reward at the same time to any one that could find out the most effectual way of destroying them. No expence was to be an obstacle, even if the cost was more than had been expended on the enclosing, holing, and planting; so anxious was his Lordship for the success of the undertaking!

Operations were immediately commenced, with traps, baits of various kinds, with poison, and with dogs and cats, but all with little success, so extensive are the plantations. At length a person hit upon a very simple and, eventually, a very efficacious mode. Having, in digging a hole in the ground some time previous, observed that a mouse or mice had got in and could not get out again, the idea was suggested to him, that, by digging holes of a similar form, he might succeed. He tried accordingly, and found it to answer. The holes for catching the mice were made from 18 inches to 2 feet long, 16 to 18 inches deep, about 10 inches or the breadth of a spade at the top, 14 or 15 inches wide at the bottom, and 3 or 4 inches longer at the bottom than the top. If the ground was firm, the better; some holes were made in a circular form, but this was only a work of fancy, which cost more trouble than the oblong holes, as either sort answered, provided they were well made, the sides firm and even, and 3 or 4 inches wider every way at the bottom than at the top, otherwise the mice would run up the sides and get out again, if they could find any footing. But, if well made, when they were once in they could not get out again; and, what is very extraordinary, they would really eat each other when left long in the holes!

Most of the mice were caught in the latter end of the year, and, what is rather singular, in the course of a wet or stormy night we always caught the greatest quantity; on the contrary, in calm, dry, or frosty nights, very few entered the holes; but, generally, most were caught when the holes were fresh made. Baits of various kinds were put in the holes to draw them, but without any visible effect, as the holes without the baits caught full as many; what attracted them in we could never tell, whether the smell of the fresh earth, or what other cause, we could only conjecture. We have taken 15 in a hole in one night. Sometimes the holes were made in the drains, where there was not a constant run of water, as the mice appeared to run along the drains, and a great many were caught in those holes.

The people who made the holes of course looked after the mice, and were paid for them by the dozen. They were obliged to attend to the holes, to take them out very early in the mornings, otherwise the crows, magpies, hawks, owls, weasels, and other vermin, attended very regularly, and made the first seizure. Several of these depredators were caught in the fact, the men dropping on them so suddenly, that great quantities were taken out and never accounted for. We soon caught upwards of thirty thousand, that were paid for by number, as a person or two were appointed to take an account of them and see them buried, or made away with, to prevent imposition.

The holes for the mice were made at 20 yards apart each way, over a surface of about 3,200 acres. In the beginning of 1814, was a heavy fall of snow, which, it is very probable, must have destroyed great quantities of them; for, with what were caught and killed by the different ways, added to the severe and long-continued storm, but little damage was done by them for two or three years afterwards.

*ANTS*

Ants I also found very destructive enemies to plants wherever they abounded which they unfortunately did on many parts of that old uncultivated land in the Forest; for the ant hillocks, on some parts, were very numerous, and on such parts the plants were sure to be killed, or never throve or made any growth. The roots, when examined, appeared cankered and unhealthy, and to the smell were something like fetid fungus. To destroy the ants, we opened their hillocks in the depth of winter; and throwing all the inside of those hillocks about in the frost and snow, appeared to me the cheapest and surest way to destroy them. Great quantities of plants were lost by the ravages of these insects.

## FROST

Another cause of such small plants being destroyed was by the frosts heaving them out in all the wet and clayey ground; even the five-year-old oaks and chestnuts were thrown out, and I was under the necessity of having some turf put round each large plant in such wet holes at the time of planting them (before we adopted the plan of raising the holes) which proved a great preventative of the plants being so thrown out by the frost. But as the seedlings were planted by the dibble or setting stick, we were obliged to leave them to their fate; such ground, however, we generally left till towards March, and planted all the dry ground in the early part of the season; but even this was attended with an extra expence to the contractor, by having to go over part of the ground, and to the same places, twice; but, after the plan of raising the holes was adopted, we could plant all kinds of land at any season. Great quantities often died, owing to the frosts that so frequently happen in the spring and summer months. After the plants come into leaf, being so low and on a level, or rather below the level, of the grass and the fog; the frost has such an effect upon the plants below the level of that fog, that frequently the young shoots and leaves of the small plants have been killed by it, when the plants of 3 or 4 feet high, and that stood above it, have not been injured at all, except in the lower branches among the fern, grass, &c.

In the nurseries in the same enclosures, and on the same elevation, which were kept clean from grass and weeds, the small plants were not injured at all by the same frosts that killed the young shoots and leaves of the plants among the fog and grass. If any plant should escape the first year, the next spring the remaining plants will make fresh efforts to produce leaves and branches, but the same effects ensue with increased means, as the grass, fern, &c. get stronger and taller every year; and the plants weaker, till they finally die. This became so serious in the Forest, that we were obliged to have the grass cleared from the plants for several years, and a sum of upwards of £1,900 was paid to Mr Driver, during his contract, for clearing the grass from the small plants, to prevent them being smothered.

## BRACKEN

Very large sums were also expended for cutting the fern [bracken] in the enclosures; for after he had fulfilled his contract, the sum of upwards of £264 was paid in one season for cutting fern, to save the plants from being killed by it. What was paid in other seasons I cannot tell, as I have not the accounts; but it must have been considerable, as it was obliged to be followed up for several years. Fern gathers strength very fast, if it is neglected to be cut; and it will soon get, where it is sheltered, to 6 or 7 feet high; and when such a mass falls down upon small plants, what chance have they to get up again, if it is not cut from them? Cutting it in July or August weakens it very much, or after it has got out of the curl, that is when all the lobes of the leaves are fully expanded, and before or about the time it has done growing, as it is then in a succulent state and bleeds, which perhaps weakens it; if it is cut too soon, it will require going over again the same season, which occasions a greater expence, and does not appear to weaken it more than that which was cut in July; and if it is left till late in the season, it will not weaken it for another.

## FAILURES IN PLANTING

In four of the enclosures, which contained about 1,700 acres, we estimated that 200,000 of the five-year-old oaks that were planted had been destroyed by the mice, besides the immense quantities from the acorns and seedlings. Mr Driver charged for 300,000 plants destroyed by mice in those four enclosures, besides what were destroyed from the same cause in others where no estimate or charge was made.

From the foregoing facts it will appear, that the experiment of raising a forest of oak from acorns, planted where they were intended to remain to become timber without being transplanted, was fairly tried, upon an extensive scale, and has completely failed. Nearly the same failing, I understand, occurred in the New Forest as in Dean Forest, and about the same time.

On all the slopes or steeps of the hills in the Forest the oaks did not appear to require any shelter, as they grew very well with the natural shelter of the hill and what under-growth there was; but in the plains and on the tops of the hills they required shelter, and the fir tribe seems best adapted of any for that purpose, if properly managed and taken out in time, otherwise they are the worst enemies. The growth of oaks is astonishing when sheltered a little in their infancy, and till they are large enough to shelter each other. In the lower or moist situations shelter for the oaks is equally necessary, and perhaps more so, to protect them from the frosts that injure them in the spring and autumn while in a growing state, when their shoots are extremely tender. I have frequently seen the young shoots, in such situations, killed three or four times through the spring and autumn months, although some tall fine trees were never touched, that were above the fog, as the damp atmosphere which rises in such situations mounts only to certain heights, and which causes the frost to act so upon the tender vegetables or young shoots of trees. In one low damp situation, planted in 1809 with oak and Spanish chestnuts, and where the land was very good, we were, in 1818, under the necessity of planting firs in all the open parts to nurse them up, as the plants were continually kept in a stunted shrubby state, from the frequent frosts that happened while the plants were making their young shoots. In the open parts, where there was no shelter, the plants were only from about 3 to 4 or 5 feet high in all that time; whereas, just above the level of that damp atmosphere on the rising grounds, the plants were 10 or 12 feet high, as were also some in the same level where they happened to be sheltered by alders or other undergrowth.

I have had opportunities of observing the beneficial effects arising from the shelter afforded by the firs to the oaks and chestnuts, in two or three low and wet places in one of the enclosures, where some firs had been planted among the oaks, before we adopted the plan of filling up with firs the low ground I have been speaking of.

To show more fully the difficulties that occurred in planting the Forest, from the failure of plants by the various causes before enumerated, I should have stated that, after Mr Driver had finally completed his contract by planting and mending over all failures for three years in each enclosure, we had provided, in the different nurseries in the Forest, to fill up such vacancies as might afterwards occur, and to plant some more land that had been purchased and attached to the Forest for growing navy timber. In the year 1818 there were growing, in the different nurseries for the aforesaid purposes, 4,039,000 oaks, and 888,000 plants of other kinds, viz. firs of sorts, ash, elm, Spanish chestnut, &c. making a total of 4,927,000 plants; and by a statement made to the Commissioners in October 1821, the vacancies were at that time very extensive, as the plants wanted to complete the enclosures in Dean Forest were 2,985,000; to complete the enclosures, not to plant fresh ones, 2,000,000 of which were planted the following season, and the rest as soon as the plants arrived at a proper size. This was four years after the last of the enclosures had been completed according to the contract.

## PLANTING LARGE OAKS AFTER FORMATIVE PRUNING

It may not be amiss to state an experiment that had been tried in the Forest and which was attended with great success. In planting out large oaks or other trees, if care is taken to get them up with good roots, replant them with care, and to thin out some of the branches and cut the others in, if the plants should have many branches, or to cut off their tops at from 10 to 12 or 13 feet from the ground, according to the height and strength of the plant to be removed, they will generally succeed very well. This method might be very desirable, and useful in many cases, where oaks are too crowded, by taking some out, and planting them in such places, where small plants would be smothered or injured by the causes before pointed out.

An experiment of this kind had been tried in the Forest some years ago. About five acres of land had been enclosed and sown with acorns [the Acorn Patch]; and at various times since, when the plants were from 12 to 14 or 16 feet high, and so strong as to support their own weight and stand upright, many have been taken out and planted in the open or uninclosed parts of the Forest, over about fifty acres, and fenced round with rough thorns to protect them from cattle. These have succeeded amazingly well, and are now in as healthy and vigorous state as can be imagined or wished. Of those that had been planted out the first, some appeared to have had their heads or tops cut off at from 10 to 15 feet high, and others to have been left with their heads or tops on. Part of those with their heads left on, look very well, and are making side branches; but, in general, those that have had their tops cut off at their removal, are by far the best plants, and are more disposed to throw out strong branches, to form crooks, knees &c than the others, and they begin to grow much sooner; because large plants when removed, if they are not well cut in, pruned, or divested of a great part of their branches, are much longer before they make fresh shoots, if ever they do; as probably the bark, sap, and air vessels get hide-bound and contracted for want of their usual supply and circulation of nutrient, and will remain in a weak and sickly state for years, or till it kills them, if they are not relieved by cutting all or part of the branches off; when they will soon make fresh and vigorous shoots, if that operation has not been too long delayed.

## TWO SPECIES OF OAK[19]

Some Botanists describe the two species of oaks – *Quercus pedunculata* [*Q. robur*] having petioles at the base of the acorn, and *Quercus sessiliflora* [*Q. petraea*] without petioles, others apply the term *Robur*, which means strength generally to the species *Q. pedunculata* and others again to the *Q.sessiliflora*, and some to the oak in general, which appears to me the most proper application, so that there appears nothing but confusion on that head among scientific writers.

Now, I well recollect that when I was in the Forest of Dean, the *Q. sessiliflora* was designated by the old experienced wood-cutters as 'the knot acorn oak', from the acorns growing in clusters close to the stalk, as being much better timber than the other kind; and I got so accustomed to observe it that I knew the trees, if of a large size, at a considerable distance, by the manner of their growth, and have often proved it by forming in my mind which species they were of, and have gone to see if I was right by examining the acorn, and was almost always correct in my previous judgment by my sight, – the trees are remarkably different in their appearance from the *Q. pedunculata*. As well as I can recollect, the leaves have a darker hue and more glossy appearance, with more numerous branches subdivided into a greater number of smaller ones, diverging from the stem in a more horizontal direction, whereas the branches of the other species diverge with more acute angles in a more upright position, and do not produce so many small branches, nor such closed heads. Might not the 'knot acorn oak', from its more numerous and smaller limbs and branches, with more annual buds and young shoots, whereby the tree is increased in substance, tend to give it a firmer, tougher, and harder texture than the other species, similar to what the Billingtonian system of pruning would effect, by increasing more numerous but smaller branches, with more annual buds and leaves?

The wood-cutters used to tell me *Q. sessiliflora* was by far the hardest, closest, and finest timber, and that they could tell whether it was the 'knot acorn oak' as soon as they applied

---

[19] Billington, pp. 57–60 of his pamphlet written in 1830 (*infra*). For current relevant information on the two species, see Oliver Rackham, *Ancient Woodland*, 1980, pp. 299–304. From 1790 to 1840 the species planted in Dean was mainly Sessile.

their axe in to cut it. This is a subject, I presume, worthy of the greatest consideration and enquiry, although now suggested publicly by William Billington.

Billington during his term in Dean (1810–18) gave umbridge to 'certain parties in authority'; he later asserted:[20] 'Mr. Machen, the deputy surveyor, and the gentlemen sportsmen adjoining the Forest – by my reports on the extensive damage done to young plantations from the depredations of the deer, hares and rabbits, which were then increasing very fast, and encouraged in the Forest, but which Lord Glenbervie very properly ordered to be destroyed; but then was a grave offence to Mr. Machen and the neighbouring sporting gentlemen, which was never forgiven. They combined to maintain a pack of harriers to keep down the hares, by hunting and galloping among the young plantations, a very pleasant and notable expedient certainly, for effecting the purpose, the preservation and success of the young oak being of course quite a secondary consideration. My reports on this subject, I have every reason to believe, were the ultimate cause of my removal to Chopwell, in 1819'.

William Billington moved from Dean, after eight years supervision, in 1818, and in Autumn 1819 started work for the same Commissioners of Woods and Forests at Chopwell Wood (about 900 acres) in co. Durham. In 1826 he was given a 'superannuation allowance'.[21] His appointment had ended by 1829, he having 'fallen out' with Alexander Milne and Mr. Cryer.[22]

At Chopwell in October 1825 Billington wrote his book noted earlier, entitled *A Series of Facts, Hints, Observations and Experiments on the Different Modes of raising young plantations of oak for future navies from the Acorn, Seedling, and Larger Plants, showing the Difficulties and Objections that have occurred in the Practical Part, &c.*[23] (see plate XIII). This book, relating chiefly to his work in the Forest of Dean, was written 'in vindication of his character and the correctness of his system of management of young plantations'; it 'caused considerable discussion among planters on the mode adopted by the Commissioners of His Majesty's Woods and Forests'. Some of his methods of raising seedlings, planting and formative pruning were criticized in parts of the forestry world, particularly by William Withers (an attorney at Holt in Norfolk) in 1826,[24] 1828,[25] and 1829.[26] Interested contemporaries were Sir Henry Steuart, Bart. in 1828,[27] and Sir Walter Scott, Bart. in 1828.[28]

---

[20] Billington, pp. 5, 36 of his letter written in 1854 (*infra*).

[21] Ibid. p. 6.

[22] Ibid. p. 7.

[23] 330 pp. Printed by Preston & Heaton, Newcastle upon Tyne.

[24] Withers, William, Junr. (1826). A Memoir, addressed to The Society for the Encouragement of Arts, Manufactures, and Commerce, on the planting and rearing of forest-trees. Printed by James Shalders, Holt, Norfolk. (2nd Edn. in 1827.)

[25] Withers, William (1828). A Letter to Sir Walter Scott, Bart., exposing certain fundamental errors in his late essay on planting, and containing observations on the pruning and thinning of woods, and mazims for profitable planting. London. Printed by James Shalders, Holt, Norfolk.

[26] Withers, William (1829). A Letter to Sir Henry Steuart, Bart., on the improvement in the quality of timber, to be effected by the high cultivation and quick growth of forest-trees in reply to certain passages in his *Planter's Guide* (*infra*). Printed by James Shalders, Holt, Norfolk.

[27] Steuart, Sir Henry, Bart. (1828). *The Planter's Guide; or A Practical Essay on the best method of giving immediate effect to wood, by the removal of large trees and underwood.* 1st Edn. Published by John Murray, Edinburgh. (2nd Edn. in 1828, 3rd Edn. in 1848.) See also footnote 17, *supra*.

[28] Scott, Sir Walter, Bart. (1828), see footnote 19, *supra*.

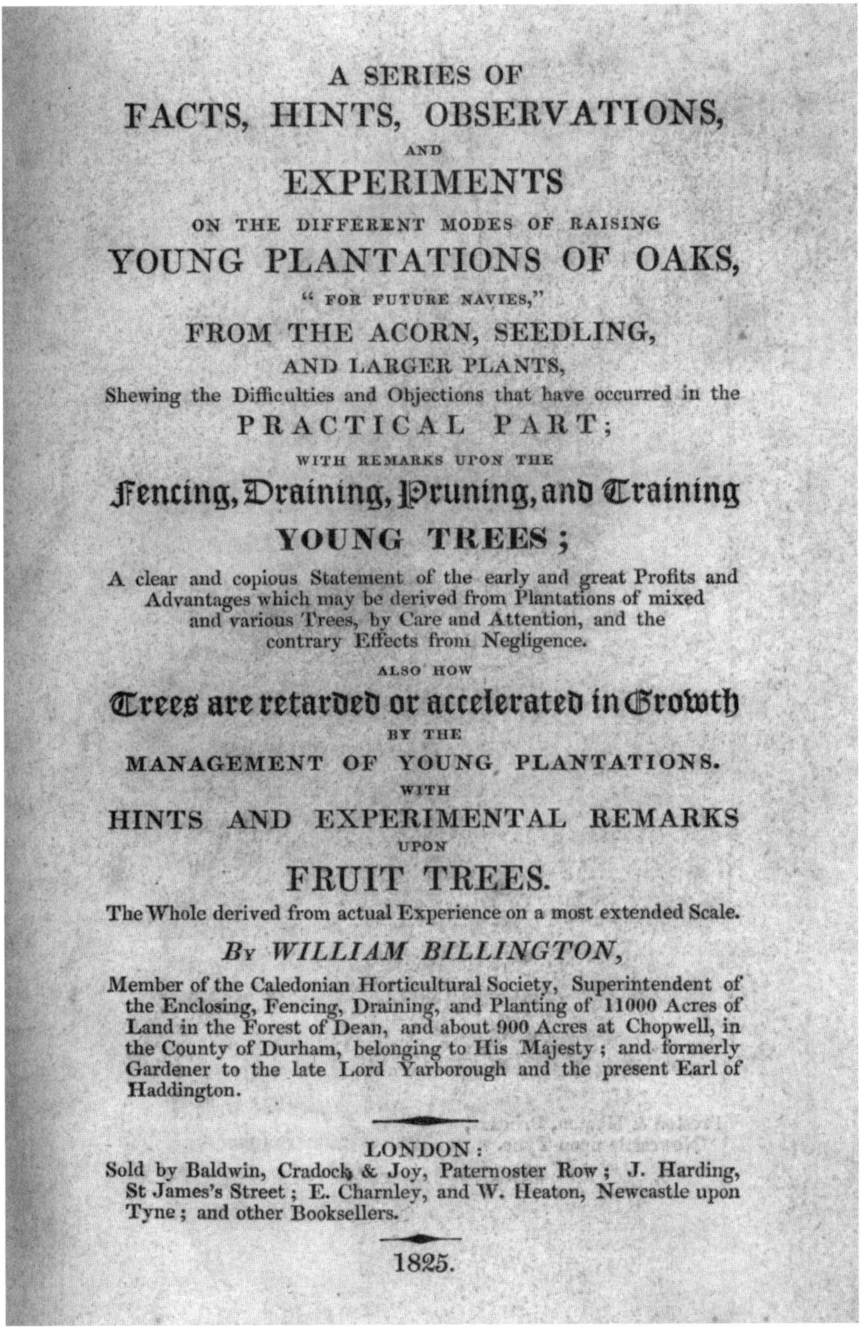

# A SERIES OF
# FACTS, HINTS, OBSERVATIONS,
AND
# EXPERIMENTS
ON THE DIFFERENT MODES OF RAISING
# YOUNG PLANTATIONS OF OAKS,
" FOR FUTURE NAVIES,"
## FROM THE ACORN, SEEDLING,
AND LARGER PLANTS,

Shewing the Difficulties and Objections that have occurred in the
### PRACTICAL PART;
WITH REMARKS UPON THE
## Fencing, Draining, Pruning, and Training
## YOUNG TREES ;

A clear and copious Statement of the early and great Profits and
Advantages which may be derived from Plantations of mixed
and various Trees, by Care and Attention, and the
contrary Effects from Negligence.

ALSO HOW
## Trees are retarded or accelerated in Growth
BY THE
## MANAGEMENT OF YOUNG PLANTATIONS.
WITH
## HINTS AND EXPERIMENTAL REMARKS
UPON
## FRUIT TREES.

The Whole derived from actual Experience on a most extended Scale.

## BY WILLIAM BILLINGTON,

Member of the Caledonian Horticultural Society, Superintendent of
the Enclosing, Fencing, Draining, and Planting of 11000 Acres of
Land in the Forest of Dean, and about 900 Acres at Chopwell, in
the County of Durham, belonging to His Majesty ; and formerly
Gardener to the late Lord Yarborough and the present Earl of
Haddington.

LONDON:
Sold by Baldwin, Cradock & Joy, Paternoster Row ; J. Harding,
St James's Street ; E. Charnley, and W. Heaton, Newcastle upon
Tyne ; and other Booksellers.

1825.

Plate XIII. The title page of William Billington's book of 1825.

# FACTS, OBSERVATIONS, &c.

BEING AN

## EXPOSURE OF THE MISREPRESENTATIONS

OF THE AUTHOR'S

## TREATISE ON PLANTING,

CONTAINED IN

### MR. WITHERS'S LETTERS TO SIR WALTER SCOTT, BARONET,

AND TO

### SIR HENRY STEUART, BARONET;

## WITH REMARKS

ON

### SIR WALTER SCOTT'S ESSAY ON PLANTING,

AND ON CERTAIN PARTS OF

### SIR HENRY STEUART'S PLANTER'S GUIDE;

ALSO,

**OBSERVATIONS ON THE MODE ADOPTED IN THE ROYAL FORESTS OF RAISING TIMBER FOR FUTURE NAVIES,**

AND ON THE

## QUALITY OF THE TIMBER,

AS AFFECTED BY THE TRENCHING AND MANURING SYSTEM, OR THE MORE COMMON METHOD;

WITH SOME

## ADDITIONAL INFORMATION, HINTS, &c.

# BY WILLIAM BILLINGTON,

Author of a Series of Facts, Hints, Observations, and Experiments, on the different modes of Raising, Pruning, and Training, Young Trees in Plantations; Superintendant of the Planting of the Forest of Dean, and the Chopwell Woods, belonging to His Majesty.

---

SHREWSBURY:

PUBLISHED BY CHARLES HULBERT; AND SOLD BY LONGMAN, REES, ORME, BROWN, AND GREEN, RIDGWAY, AND WRIGHTS, *LONDON;* CHARNLEY, AND HEATON, *NEWCASTLE UPON TYNE;* AND ALL OTHER BOOKSELLERS.

1830.

Plate XIV. The title page of William Billington's pamphlet of 1830.

Withers (1826, 1828 and 1829) disagreed with Billington's mode of raising seedlings in nurseries, planting and formative pruning of oaks. In an unkindly way, he asserted that Billington was the surveyor-general, when of course it was Lord Glenbervie! He urged the case for technical foresters to be the superintendents and not persons who he terms 'gardeners'. In some of the foregoing he could not persuade Sir Walter Scott (1828). Steuart (1828) urged the commissioners in future to employ 'Superintendents who are not mere Gardeners, like Mr. Billington and others'. However, in referring to 'the Art of Planting' on scientific principles, Steuart averred (1828) that 'a better example cannot be given than that, in 1825, Mr. William Billington published an account of his own, and Messrs. Driver's bungling operations in planting the Forest of Dean'. Yet Steuart continued, 'The reader . . . will find in the more homely and unpretending production of honest William Billington, probably the *best Instructions* for conducting . . . the Pruning and [formative] Thinning of Trees, that exist in the language, together with much good sense, and judicious practice, in several other departments'.

In 1830 Billington, when residing at Harmer Hill near Shrewsbury, wrote a pamphlet *Facts, Observations, &c being an exposure of the Misrepresentations of the Author's Treatise on Planting contained in Mr. Wither's Letters to Sir Walter Scott, Baronet, and to Sir Henry Steuart, Baronet, &c*[29] (see Plate XIV). The pamphlet was written to refute criticisms where some of his statements had been 'misunderstood, misrepresented, and others wilfully omitted' by Mr. Withers. Withers had particularly criticized Billington's comments on two modes of planting and Billington's pamphlet was 'to serve certain purposes, whereby the blame, where it may be deserving, is endeavoured to be fixed upon me, who was a subordinate officer'. Later, Withers presented one of his own books to Billington, requesting him to write a review of it for the *Gardener's Chronicle* or the *Gardener's Magazine*, which Billington asserted 'proved he had no mean opinion of my judgement'.[30] Billington hoped he would be reappointed in some capacity by the commissioners, but this did not occur.

Billington at some time after 1830 resided at Underhill near Oswestry. He and his wife, along with their three sons and two daughters, moved to Roy, Belmullet, co. Mayo, Ireland, sometime between 1844 and 1854 (he wrote from there on 25 March 1854). The family drained and reclaimed extensive bog land around Blacksod Bay leased from Lord Bingham of Roy Towers. The prime operator was William Billington junior (who had been headmaster of Tarven Grammar School, Chester); presumably he had learnt his reclamation skills from his father. He drained, ditched, fenced, roaded and developed the land, and built a large house, employing much local labour. Some of the land produced hay and potatoes. When the lease was up, Lord Bingham would not renew. William junior took him to court in an effort to reclaim some of the investment – £4,945 according to a valuation made 30 September 1871. (The last members of the family returned to England in 1935.[31])

On 25 March 1854 Billington wrote and had printed a 43-page letter (see Plate XV) from his residence at 'Roy, Belmullet, Mayo, Ireland' to Alexander Milne (lately one of the commissioners of woods and forests) headed 'How the Royal

---

[29] 76 pp. Published by Charles Hulbert, Shrewsbury.

[30] Billington, letter of 1854, p. 17.

[31] Personal communication from John Billington, Head of English, Repton School, a great-great grandson of William Billington.

# HOW THE ROYAL FORESTS HAVE BEEN RUINED:

# A LETTER,

TO

## ALEXANDER MILNE, ESQ.,

LATE COMMISSIONER OF HER MAJESTY'S WOODS AND FORESTS,

### ON THE SYSTEM PURSUED IN THE FOREST OF DEAN AND THE CHOPWELL WOODS.

## *BY WILLIAM BILLINGTON,*

SOMETIME SUPERINTENDENT OF THOSE FORESTS, AND AUTHOR OF A
TREATISE ON THE MANAGEMENT OF YOUNG PLANTATIONS
AND *TRAINING* FOREST TREES FOR TIMBER.

" Thrice is he arm'd that hath his quarrel just."

### LONDON:

LONGMAN AND CO., AND RIDGWAY.

1854.

Plate XV. The first page of William Billington's 43-page letter to Alexander Milne, 1854.
(Br. Liby. 8226.b.9)

Forests have been ruined: a Letter . . . on the system pursued in the Forest of Dean and the Chopwell Woods'.[32] Milne had been secretary to the commissioners from the time of Lord Glenbervie, and following the latter's retirement he 'had almost the sole control and management of the crown woods under every succeeding change of commissioners'.

Billington used his letter to criticize the way in which Milne (in particular) had managed the Royal Forests in general; and commented on future management. He confessed that his 'enthusiastic study' of the subject had been to him 'a hobby'. Since leaving Dean in 1818, Billington had become a rather embittered man, with a detestation of the actions and management of Milne and some of his associates. It is likely that there were some faults and attributes on both sides.

Billington's pamphlet of 1830 and his letter of 1854 indicate a man displaying a tone of outraged virtue – a man of probity in a corrupt forestry world driven to defend himself after having been wrong-footed by those more cunning in the ways of the world. On the first page of his pamphlet he quotes: 'Truth is great and will prevail'; also: 'When a rich man speaketh, every man holdeth his tongue, and look what he saith; they extol it to the clouds. But if a poor man speak, they say what fellow is this; and if he stumble they will help to overthrow him'. On the title page of his letter of 1854 he quotes: 'Thrice is he arm'd that hath his quarrel just'.

Included in Billington's letter was a nostalgic comment: 'I have always felt a hankering desire to visit Dean Forest, to see what progress they have made in forty years; but I apprehend my wishes will never be granted'. If he had found an opportunity to visit the Forest it is likely, despite his apprehensions, he would have been pleased with the condition of most of the plantations he had helped to establish. They proved of great utility during the subsequent two world wars; and the final stands of some of them remain to this day.

Billington, a knowledgeable and interesting man, was still residing in co. Mayo, Ireland in 1854. One day it may be discovered in what year he died, and where he was laid to rest.

## EDWARD MACHEN'S NOTES, 1818

Edward Machen, when appointed deputy surveyor in February 1808, found 'the Forest practically in the hands of the commoners, and the encroachments extended into the very centre of the forest'.[33] In 1818 he recorded much information confirming or complementing Billington's descriptions:[34]

> Mr Driver contracted to plant these Enclosures on a plan which he recommended, being to dig holes 4 feet apart or 2722 on an acre, and to plant an acorn in every hole but the tenth – in which an oak tree of 5 years old was to be planted. The six first mentioned enclosures [i.e. Barnhill, Serridge, Beechenhurst, Haywood, Holly Hill and Crabtree-hill] were planted in this manner, but from the exuberance of weeds etc. of all kinds and the quantity of mice etc. this method failed. Three-fourths of the acorns never appeared and many of those that did come up were too weak and unequal to make their way through the quantities of other more luxuriant growth that overwhelmed and choked them. The

[32] Printed copy in The British Library, London, Ref. 8226.b.9., 54 pp. (Plate XV herein).

[33] Observations on the 31st Rept. of the Commissioners of Woods, Forests, etc., 1 Feb. 1854, p. 1. Printed by John James Hough, Bookseller and Stationer, Coleford.

[34] Machen Notes, 1818 (see Bibliography).

remaining enclosures were therefore planted with seedling oaks instead of acorns and these by means of clearing the holes once or twice have succeeded much better but there is not doubt that the best plan is to leave the trees in the nursery until 3 or 4 years old when they are more likely to succeed if planted in uncultivated ground.

Mr Driver was to dig the holes for acorns and seedlings 15 inches square and 9 inches deep for 12s.6d. per 1,000, and for 5 years old trees 18 inches square and 12 inches deep at 18s. per 1,000. His prices of trees per 1,000 were:

| | | | | | |
|---|---|---|---|---|---|
| 5 years old oaks – 3 years transplanted | | | | – | 70s |
| 3 " " " – 2 years transplanted | | | | – | 40s |
| 5 " " Spanish Chestnuts | | | | – | 60s |
| 3 " " Spanish Chestnuts | | | | – | 40s |
| | | of which 1 in 100 was planted | | | |
| | | over the whole Forest | | | |
| 4 " " Larch | | | | – | 40s |
| 4 " " Scotch [Scots pine] | | | | – | 30s |
| 2 " " Pinus Pinaster [Maritime pine] | | | | – | 35s |
| 3 " " Sycamore | | | | – | 60s |
| 4 " " Ash | | | | – | 30s |
| 4 " " Elm | | | | – | 80s |
| 3 " " Alder | | | | – | 40s |
| 2 " " Black poplar | | | | – | 60s |
| 2 " " Norway spruce | | | | – | 40s |
| 1 " " seedling oaks | | | | – | 12s |

Acorns – 8s. per 1,000.

The planting therefore with acorns cost about £3.15. per acre, and with seedlings about £4.5s. per acre, and for this Mr. Driver agreed to mend over or keep good the plants for three years.

The fence was to consist of a bank at first 5 feet high but afterwards changed to 4ft 6 ins high with a row of French Furze [gorse] at the top and bottom; that at the bottom has been found useless, and short stakes driven in near the top of the bank to make the fence secure until the Furze grew up; the price 5s per rod of 16½ feet. In parts where a bank was impracticable a dry wall 5 ft high was made at 9s. per rod of 18 feet. This bank in most parts appeared to succeed very well and the Furze grew very luxuriantly; but in some places and those where the bank is composed of mould that has accumulated by being washed there in floods, the banks are mouldering and in the last two years Hawthorn-Quick has been planted in those parts and now looks very flourishing.

By 1816, 9,389 acres had been enclosed and planted;[35] the balance to make up 11,000 acres had been partly fenced and would be planted that year. Nurseries of 20 acres were now raising oak and other transplants. Expenditure on the plantations to date had been £59,172.5s.10d., about £6.6s.8d. an acre.

In 1818 Messrs Driver, at great expense to the crown, completed their contract for 10,324 acres.[36] Much silviculture remained to be done; failures not attributable to the contractors had to be made good. The same year, Billington having quitted

[35] 2nd Rept. of Commissioners, 1816, p. 22; Hart, *Royal Forest*, pp. 210, 211.
[36] A list of the inclosures with acreages and dates of planting is given in Machen Notes, 1818, and in the Rept. of a Select Committee, 1849. See Appendix II of this Section.

Plate XVI. 'The Machen Oak', a venerable tree designated in 1969 by the present author in commemoration of Edward Machen, deputy surveyor of the Forest of Dean from 1808 to 1854. Machen frequently passed this oak when travelling on horseback between Whitemead Park House, Parkend and Eastbach Court, near English Bicknor. (Photograph by N.D.G. James, 1991)

Dean, Machen was left with the care of the 11,000 acres of enclosed plantations wherein the young trees were looking 'remarkably well' but in places required enrichment of the stocking. A good mast year of acorns, the first since 1809, helped to fill gaps in the cover, and in 1819 the plantations were said to be 'in a flourishing condition'.[37] Of the 676 acres of enclosures made under the Act of 1668[38] and still intact in 1808, Machen observed in 1818:[39]

> In the Buckholt, the large timber has been cut, and parts of it planted with young oaks obtained from places where they had sprung up spontaneously, but it is still imperfectly stocked. Stapledge has been filled up by transplanting from the thick parts, and is tolerably well stocked on the whole. Birchwood has been planted in the vacant parts, and is fully stocked and very flourishing. From the Acorn Patch a large quantity of young oaks have been transplanted into the open parts of the Forest and the upper part of Russell's Enclosure. The trees drawn out are thriving, and many of them grow faster than the trees remaining in the Acorn Patch. There is a great quantity of holly and other underwood scattered on the parts where the trees are planted, and which serves for shelter and protection, and the soil is very good. The trees, though never transplanted before, came up with bunches of fibrous roots; and though of so large a size, being from 10 to 25ft high, scarcely any of them failed. Several experiments were tried as to pruning closely, pruning a little, and not at all; and it appears that those pruned sufficiently to prevent the wind from loosening the roots answer best, although many of those which were reduced to bare poles, and had their heads cut off, are now sending up vigorous leading shoots, and have every appearance of becoming fine timber; those unpruned did not succeed at all.

Alluding to the earthen banks, with which the plantations were mostly surrounded, Machen observed that 'in most parts they appear to succeed very well, and the furze on the top of them grows luxuriantly; but in some places, and those where the bank of mould has accumulated by being washed there in floods, the banks are mouldering, and in the last two years hawthorn-quick has been planted in those parts, and now looks very flourishing.' Machen added [1818]:

> There has not been a good year of acorns, that is, where a quantity have ripened in the Forest, since the commencement of the plantations [1810] until the present, and the trees are now loaded, and with every prospect of ripening.
> The young trees in the new enclosures are looking remarkably well this year, and some of them have made shoots so long that they more resemble willows than oaks.
> The six first-named enclosures, in addition to the acorns and five years old oaks, have had the same quantity of five years oaks planted in addition, in lieu of the mending over, viz. 270 on an acre; but there are parts of all these, and almost the whole of Crab-tree Hill and Haywood (which suffered not only from the failure of the acorns, but [in 1813 and 1814] from the ravages made by the mice) that will require to be filled up as soon as there is a stock of plants sufficient for the purpose.
> Russell's Enclosure is left to nature: only 10,000 Spanish chestnuts have been planted in it, and some young oaks from the Acorn Patch at the north end. There is a good deal of large timber over the whole, particularly the south and centre parts, and a vast quantity of natural young oaks sprung up in the neighbourhood of the large trees. The fern has been cut to relieve and encourage them for the last three years.
> The Lea Bailey Copse (north) consists of young copsewood well stored with oaks, growing on their own butts [i.e. 'maidens'], The Lea Bailey Copse (south) has more large

---

[37] 3rd Rept. of Commissioners, 1819, p. 20; Hart, *Royal Forest,* p. 211.
[38] Act 19 and 20 Charles II, c. 8, 1668.
[39] Machen Notes, 1818; Nicholls, *The Forest of Dean,* 1858, pp. 100–102; Hart, *Royal Forest,* p. 211.

timber in it; this has not been regularly planted, and some trees have been transplanted from the thick parts of the north copse, and from the woodmen's nurseries. The lower Lea Bailey Enclosure has a considerable quantity of young timber on it, and a large quantity of young oaks springing up. No planting has been done here. The fencing round these consists of a large ditch and bank, and a dead hedge at top, with hawthorn-quick planted within. The hedge having stood three years is decayed, and another will be required this year, which it is expected will last until the quick becomes a fence.

The addition to the Buckholt of about 15 acres was planted [in 1812] with 3 years old oaks from the woodmen's nurseries, and looks very thriving.

All the other enclosures were planted with seedlings and tenth trees, according to the second agreement with Mr. Driver, in 1812, 13, 14, and 15, and are this year looking very well. Parts of all the enclosures will require mending over, but I should think more than half are sufficiently stocked with oaks well established, and that will require no further attention until they want thinning.

On the high land of Haywood, Edge Hills, and Ruardean Hill, firs and a mixture of other trees have been planted, and are thriving and growing fast, particularly on Ruardean Hill, where the scotch and larch take the lead. Firs, etc. have also been planted in the wet and bad parts of most of the other enclosures, and succeed.

The plants in Whitemead Park [240 acres planted in 1809] are thriving very well in all parts which are situated at a distance from [the Cannop] brook, but near to it they are very thin, stunted, and unhealthy, and are constantly killed down by the spring frosts. Ash and fir trees have been planted amongst them, but with little success at present.

The principal part of the large timber now in the Forest is about Parkend, on Church Hill, Ivy More Head, Russell's Enclosure, Parkend Lodge Hill, and at the Lea Bailey. That at the Lea Bailey appears younger, and some of it shook by frost, and rather drawn up by standing too thick. The timber about Parkend is very fine, and I should suppose from 150 to 200 years old. There is a considerable quantity of young oak, from 15 to 40 years growth, about Tanner's Hill, etc., near Gun's Mills, on the outside of Edge Hill Enclosure, and some within it in the lower part. Chestnuts Enclosure is covered with hazel, that was cut down when the oak was planted, and is now growing up with the young oaks and chestnuts, both of which are more rapidly growing in this enclosure than in any other; a double quantity of chestnuts are planted in this enclosure.

There are scarcely any natural trees in the Forest but oak and beech; birch springs up spontaneously in every enclosure, and overruns the whole Forest. The few ash now growing look scrubbed and unthrifty.

In 1819 Machen recorded that on 29 May 'the frost was so severe that the verdure throughout all the low parts of the Forest, was entirely destroyed. There was not a green leaf left on any oak or beech, large or small, and all the shoots of the year were altogether withered. The spruce and silver fir were all injured; in short all trees but some Scotch fir [pine] and poplar suffered severely.' However, by 10 August 'the plantations had recovered from the effects of the frost – the oak more effectually than the beech, and had made more vigorous and thriving shoots than I ever saw. Shutcastle in the upper part, and the eastern part of Serridge, were looking best of all the new plantations, though all are looking in a very thriving state this year.'

Confirmation, up to 1816, of some of the comments by Billington and Machen is provided by the Commissioners of Woods:[40]

The general principle of the plan adopted for the plantations first set out in Dean was to plant in intermixture of acorns and oak plants, with a very small proportion of Spanish

[40] 2nd Rept. of Commissioners of Woods, 1816, pp. 28, 29; Hart, *Royal Forest*, p. 211.

chestnuts, so that if either the acorns or plants should succeed, a sufficient number of young oaks might be expected; and to plant no trees of any other sort, except in spots where it should be thought that oaks would not grow, and which it might be necessary to include, in order to avoid the expense of circuitous fencing, or for shelter in high and exposed situations. For the first two seasons the new plantations were commenced, no material deviation from this plan took place; but it was found, on frequent inspection of the Inclosures planted in this manner, that either from the destruction by birds and vermin, or from their being overgrown by the surrounding high grass and fern, or other causes, nearly the whole of the acorns which were planted, failed; although in many places they had sprung up and looked very favourable during the first year. In the second, their general appearance was less healthy; and after that period, very few were found to have survived. Seedling oaks of one or two years growth were afterwards substituted for the acorns; and in those places where the soil consists for the most part of loam, this plan has been attended with much better success than the planting with acorns; but in the strong tenacious clay, a species of soil well adapted to the growth of oak, and of which the soil of a great part of our plantations consists, the seedling plants have also, in many instances failed. In all cases, however, where plants which have been previously transplanted from the seed bed, and kept in the nursery from three to four years, have been made use of, a more complete success has attended our operations; and has fully justified us in recommending this mode, in preference to other methods which have hitherto been tried.

Much good work had been accomplished by Billington and Machen. In one respect it could be criticized: their objective was to grow oak for shipbuilding, but they carried this to the extreme. The upper slopes and crests of the ridges, a prominent feature, are in general too much exposed and the soils often too shallow for the satisfactory growth of oak; and there are considerable stretches of low-lying land in the middle of the Forest which are subject to late frosts and unsuitable to oak unless special measures are taken, for example by using a 'nurse' crop. The planting after the Act of 1808 did not sufficiently take into account these factors, and the result was not apparent till many years afterwards.[41] The dates of enclosing are given in Appendix III.

## EDWARD MACHEN'S AFTER-MANAGEMENT: 1819–54

While Billington had supervised the establishing of plantations, Machen and his assistant, John Dudgeon, had supplied 9,214 oaks to the naval dockyards; 2,108 oaks were sold by auction, as well as huge quantities of oak bark; and much pitwood to miners.[42] Many of the plantings following the 1668 Act had fulfilled their purpose, and Dean had been of great national value, particularly during the Napoleonic Wars of 1793 to 1815.

Machen and his staff carefully tended Dean's 11,000 acres of plantations and ensured that sheep and cattle were kept out of enclosures. From 1818 to 1822 nurseries were retained, and almost two million trees, over one-fifth of them European larch and Scots pine chiefly to nurse the oak, were used for enrichment and additional planting. By 1823 the plantations, between five and fifteen years, were fully stocked; although the Commissioners of Woods intimated[43] disappointment at the little growth of them, 'they were doing well, and slowness of growth was inseparable from their nature, particularly at that age'. Mrs. C. Arbuthnot, wife of

[41] Hart, *Royal Forest*, p. 212.
[42] Ibid., pp. 212, 213, 216.
[43] 4th Rept. of Commissioners of Woods, 6 March 1823.

one of the commissioners, wrote on 1 September 1823:[44] 'the Forest, which 50 years hence will be a *real* Forest; at present it consists of about 11,000 acres of young plantations six or seven years old, but where the oaks are growing luxuriously'. Young plantations of oak are an unimposing sight; rarely are the stems of the trees more than 1, 2 or 3 inches in diameter and their height would be from 5 to 20 feet. Machen had to ensure that such plantations came to perfection. The oaks in general suffered almost every year from the oak-leaf roller moth, the caterpillars of which feed greedily on oak foliage; the oaks recover. The enclosures in Dean had been made with little opposition from the local populace, most of whom looked upon Machen with mixed respect and awe, but in 1831 the commoners, aggrieved that the enclosures were not thrown open, rioted and destroyed many of the fences, gates, stiles, walls, mounds and hedges. They drove in their sheep and cattle; but were made to remove them and repair the enclosures; no trees had been damaged.[45] By that time, the natural birch had been cut to relieve the oak. Thinning of oak and conifers in the enclosures took place in 1831; those of the oak, as usual small and often crooked, were stripped while standing of their bark for tanneries, and felled a few months later as cordwood or small pitwood.

Machen's subsequent management is described elsewhere.[46] John Clutton, a surveyor, in 1848[47] found the Forest's trees in general to be extremely fine, some of the old oaks being the largest he had ever seen. Where oaks stood close, as on Church Hill, there were 25 to 40 an acre; he never saw longer timber, some trunks being 50 feet. The condition of the plantations proved they had been judiciously selected and planted: he had never seen plantations better thinned or drained, and they could not be better managed. This was indeed a tribute to Machen and his staff.

However, other views were later expressed. In 1852 T.F. Kennedy, Chief Commissioner of Woods, Forests and Land Revenues of the Crown, began an investigation of the Forest of Dean and Highmeadow Woods, in his care. Being doubtful of some of the management under Machen, he obtained the advice of a consultant forester (and author of *The Forester*, 1847 and 1851), James Brown, of Arniston in Mid-Lothian.[48] Brown's six reports increased Kennedy's disagreement with Machen on several matters.[49] The reports most relevant are Brown's descriptions of the then condition of the plantations, largely established by Billington and Machen 1810–18, and thereafter managed by Machen: (A) inclosures thrown open to commoners, and (B) inclosures remaining enclosed. They are recorded in Appendix IV of this Section; so too are: (C) Machen's statements on some of Brown's criticisms.[50]

In 1897 H.C. Hill, conservator of forests in India (on furlough), made a report on the Forest of Dean.[51] His description of the composition and condition of the

[44] *The Journal of Mrs. Arbuthnot 1820–1832*, ed. Francis Bamford and the Duke of Wellington, 1950, I, p. 253.

[45] Hart, *Royal Forest*, p. 214.

[46] Ibid., pp. 213–18.

[47] Rept. of Select Committee, 1848; Hart, *Royal Forest*, pp. 216–17.

[48] 31st Rept. of Commissioners of Woods, etc., 1853, L.R.R.O. 9/14, pp. 134 *et seq.*

[49] Hart, *Royal Forest*, pp. 219–23; Brown, James, *The Forester*, 3rd edn. 1861, pp. 30–1.

[50] Statement by Edward Machen, retired deputy surveyor, 1 Feb. 1854, printed by J.J. Hough, Coleford.

[51] Hill, H.C., *Report on the Forest of Dean with Suggestions for its Management*, 19 July 1897, H.M.S.O. See also information regarding some of the 1810–18 plantings in *Royal Scottish Arboricultural Society*: Excursion to the Forest of Dean, 3–5 August 1898, *Journal* of the Society, 1898, pp. 4–32.

Plate XVII. A so-called 'Charles II oak' which until it was felled *c.* 1965, witnessed many of the events described in this book. Its age was around 300 years, and its girth at base 31 feet. Growing in the oak's crown were five small seeded trees: hazel, beech, holly, ash and elder. Its butt was sound, but its crown was deteriorating and potentially dangerous. The tree stood opposite the Parkend Primary School. (Photo by the present author, 1961)

enclosures is included hereunder as Appendix V, recording how the 1808–18 plantings had progressed. Appendix VI records comments and criticisms of the after-management of the 1808–18 plantations, and includes some mitigation of the criticisms.

Significantly, the need to ensure supplies of oak for the navy, was ended somewhat abruptly from the 1830s onwards, and particularly from the 1860s, through the replacement of timber by iron (and subsequently steel) for ships of the Royal Navy. Previously, much of the oak was overthinned to produce large crowns and heavy branchwood for shiptimber rather than straight stemwood (boles). The need for change led to a new type of silviculture in which aims for broadleaved trees were straight, long boles of good quality; also, conifers were needed in increasing numbers.

Rewardingly, many of the broadleaved and coniferous trees planted by Billington and Machen during 1810–18 proved of great utility throughout subsequent decades of the nineteenth century and during this twentieth century.

# APPENDIX I

## DRIVER'S SURVEY OF 1787[52]

### (a. = acres)

SPEECH HOUSE WALK

Gorsy Green Inclosure (5 a.): Enclosed 4 years; half planted with acorns; remainder in tillage.

Beechenhurst Hill (202 a.): Formerly covered with good oaks but only a few now and few beech; but many thorns.

Nelmes Vallet, Serridge Green, &c. (162 a.): Full of old pits; a few scrubby beech and some thorns.

Serridge Inclosure (410 a.): Enclosed 12 years with a dry stone wall of which little remains; mainly open; covered with thorn; very few trees.

Daniel Moor (332 a.): Generally open with a few straggling beech and oaks.

Great Kemsley Green, Crump Meadow, Barreth Green, Sally Greens, &c. (937 a.): Interspersed with a few oak, beech, and birch, and some thorns; a great quantity of fine timber has formerly been cut down here.

Little Stapleage: see Bailey Walk (29 a.).

The Great Inclosure (743 a.): Begun to be enclosed 12 years ago with posts and rails but all soon destroyed and only the bank remains. Interspersed with many fine oaks, some hollies and thorns.

Phelps' Meadow (270 a.): Some good oaks with a few birch. A fall was made here for Gloucester Gaol. The timber towards Stonedge Inclosure is very good.

Stonedge Inclosure (125 a.): Enclosed about 12 years with a dry stone wall, now mostly destroyed. Many thorns and hollies, with some very fine large oaks, but nothing coming up.

The Russells (245 a.): A hanging hill under the Stonedge Inclosure. Some very fine thriving large timber of great height, with a few thorns.

Far Moor Lawn, Wetwood, &c. (442 a.): Very fine feeding land interspersed with a good sprinkling of very fine oaks, with some hollies and thorns.

---

[52] P.R.O., F16/31 (Book in manuscript). Photocopy in Glos. R.O., D3921, Hart Collection (Plate XVIII herein).

Foxberry, Blackpenny Wall, &c. (273 a.): Interspersed with a good sprinkling of fine oaks, with some hollies and thorns.

Little Kelmesley Green and Horse Lawn (176 a.): In general open, interspersed with a few good oaks, birch, hollies and thorns.

## WORCESTER WALK

Barn Hill, Howlers Slade, and Bixhead Slade (368 a.): A good sprinkling of very fine oaks; formerly very thick.

Lodge Hill (137 a.): Generally covered with very fine oaks; towards Winberry Bottom there are a great number of fine thriving beech.

Coleford Meend (312 a.): In general open except towards Barn Hill and Lodge Hill where there are some fine beech. In the past covered with very fine timber. Would grow firs well.

The Perch (199 a.): Inclosed about 15 years with part dry stone wall, and part post and rail; only the bank remains. There has been a lot of young growth but much injured by fences being pulled down. Still some fine young beech. A fall was made here for Gloucester Gaol. The timber is very sound and hard.

Coverham (351 a.): Inclosed about 15 years as for the Perch. Mostly now full of fine young beech and a few oaks. Nearly all the fence is gone, chiefly destroyed because it enclosed the Meend.

Berry Hill, Shortstanding, and Joyford (298 a.): Very open. Formerly covered with very fine timber, particularly beech, and would answer well for firs.

Eastbatch Meend (112 a.): Formerly good oaks and beech. Now very open.

Hangerbury, Worrall Hill, and the Moorwood (442 a.): Some beech underwood. Many old coal pits.

Great Bourt and Little Bourt (182 a.): Rather open and interspersed with a few good oaks, some small beech and thorns.

Sally Vellets, Middle Rudge and Rudhall Marsh (367 a.): A few good oaks and beech. Formerly has produced a great quantity of very fine timber.

Buckholt Inclosure (353 a.): Enclosed about 50 years; the greatest part with a stone wall, the rest with hedge and ditch. Fences in general are in good repair. Some very fine large oak and a lot of fine young beech, and in some of the vacant places young oaks are coming up from the acorns which have been set; there are also some oaks of about 10 or 15 years growth. The Deputy Surveyor has planted a few Weymouth Pines in this Inclosure, which grow very well.[53]

---

[53] Some of these Weymouth pines, planted *c.* 1781, are still growing. The area is now called Sallow Vallet (Plate IX herein).

PARTICULARS

OF A

SURVEY

OF THE

Foreſt OF Dean,

IN THE

COUNTY of GLOUCESTER;

Taken by Order of the

COMMISSIONERS

—— OF THE ——

LAND REVENUE,

by Ab.ᵐ &W.ᵐ Driver, Surveyors

1787.

Plate XVIII. The first page of the survey of the Forest of Dean made by Messrs Driver in 1787. (P.R.O., F16/31)

## RUARDEAN WALK

The Lea Bailey (1,155 a.): Is extremely thick with oak and beech, some large and a great quantity of saplings and underwood which require thinning. Lining Wood is also well covered with young timber and a few large, with a great quantity of underwood. Wigpool Green is open.

Michel Deane Meend (428 a.): Very open and poor.

Pump Hill and Dockings Hill (395 a.): Are very rough and stony, mostly covered with holly and thorns. Merring Meend, Holly Bush Hill, and Quarry Hill are in general sprinkled with holly and thorns, and a few scrubby oak and beech.

Ruerdean Hill (615 a.): Very open. A few beech and oaks about Beechin Hill.

Birchwood Inclosure (135 a.): Enclosed about 5 years, part dead hedge and part stone wall, in general in good repair. A few large oaks and some beech, but very few young oaks. Also a few hollies and thorns.

Dam Green (402 a.): Is rather open with a few bushes and a few oak. Lamor quog is a bog. The Delves is mostly covered with beech and bushes, also a few oak. Serridge is open with a few bushes.

Greatberry Hill (371 a.): Has some good beech and a few oak. God Meadow also has a few oak and beech, with bushes. Aston Bridge Hill has a good many scrubby oak and a few beech.

Barn Edge Hill (436 a.): Good many beech and a few good oaks, some bushes. Horsley Hill, a few scrubby oak, birch and beech, also some thorns and hollies. The Pluds has some young oak and beech and a few thorns.

## LITTLEDEAN WALK

Heywood Inclosure (716 a.): Enclosed about 10 years; part with a dry stone wall and part with pales, very little traces of which remain. No young timber is coming up. A few scrubby beech towards Stockwell Green. Some single trees with bushes interspersed. Very good timber has been grown here in the past.

Oiley Hill, &c. (175 a.): Low and wet, except a little higher near Oiley Hill; a few bushes and single trees, mostly beeches.

Little Dean Meend (274 a.): Chiefly heath.

Edge Hills (597 a.): In general very thick with underwood and a considerable number of young oaks and beech; also some good oak and beech. Includes Shapridge and White Hill.

Chestnut Hill (214 a.): Extremely thick underwood, and many young oaks in a thriving state.

Popes Hill and Hangman's Hill (140 a.): Very open; many encroachments.

Abbotts Wood (873 a.): Mostly covered with underwood and young timber, also some oak and beech of about 30 years growth. Ruspatched Meend and Soudley Green are open. The timber and underwood is claimed by Mr. Crawley.

Blaize Bailey (154 a.): Mostly open with some bushes.

## BLAKENEY OR BAILEY WALK

The Bailey and Winberry Hills (648 a.): Generally covered very thick with beech and some good oak, also some birch, thorns, and hollies.

Old Croft (174 a.): Mostly covered with thorns and hollies, with a few scrubby oak and beech.

New Years Hill (514 a.): Thinly covered with beech, and a few scrubby oak. Viney Hill is partly covered with thick underwood mostly of small beech.

The Copes (211 a.): Contain a considerable number of large oaks fit for the Navy, also some large beech with thorns and holly.

Blakeney Hill (114 a.): Very open poor land.

Broom Hill (316 a.): In general full of cover and a considerable number of fine oaks and beech, also some hollies and thorns.

Bradley Hill (279 a.): A few oak and beech, also some thorns.

Puttenage Inclosure (179 a.): Has produced a great quantity of timber; there remains some fine oaks and beech and is well covered with underwood. Some traces of the bank still remain.

Stapleage Inclosure (183 a.): Enclosed about 5 years; part dry stone wall and part dead hedge, in general in good repair; in some parts oak, beech, and birch are coming up. There are also a few large oak and beech, with some hollies and thorns.

Stapleage Hill (565 a.): An old inclosure; some bank is still to be seen. A few good oaks and beeches and some thorns. The part towards the east is open.

Middle Rudge and Awers Glow (347 a.): Mostly open. Low and wet.

Moseley Green (355 a.): Mostly open with a few single trees. Towards the old vallet the ground is higher and better and covered with oaks.

## PARKEND WALK

The Birches (174 a.): Formerly a great quantity of Navy timber but at present only a few small birch, beech, and hollies. Two years ago a fall was made here for Gloucester Gaol.

The Delves (461 a.): Rough through coalpits. 12 years ago it was covered with very fine Navy timber; now very little cover of any kind. Rudge Hill: good sprinkling of hollies, some few birch and beech and a few oaks. Used to be very fine timber. At Yorkley, only a few hollies and beech, previously very fine Navy timber.

Park Hill (344 a.): Now covered as far as the end of White Mead Park with very fine large oaks, and beech; a few years ago they were very thick; Bremes Eves was also covered with very fine Navy timber, now only a few hollies and pollards of beech. Towards Paster Hill is rather poor and uneven.

Breemes Meend (191 a.): Mostly wet. Towards Horwell Hill it is rocky and covered with furze.

Knockley Tump, Shutcastle Hill, Oakwood Hill, &c. (362 a.): All formerly well covered with timber. On Shutcastle and Oakwood there are a few good oaks and beech and a good sprinkling of small birch with some hollies and furze. Towards Drybrook the oaks are rather more numerous.

Ellwood Eves, Bromley Hill, &c. (478 a.): A good sprinkling of very good oak in most parts except towards Ellwood Eves where they are not so numerous. Also a few hollies and birch. Formerly covered with fine timber.

Clearwall Meend (376 a.): Generally covered with furze.

Coleford Meend (370 a.): Generally covered with furze.

Lodge Hill, Birch Hill, Slade Hill, &c. (677 a.): A good sprinkling of fine oaks. Also some good beech and birch. Formerly well covered with fine Navy timber.

Church Hill, Ivey Moor Head, &c. (287 a.): Good sprinkling of very fine oaks. About 7 years ago a great fall was made.

Whitemead Park (234 a.): Few birch, beech, and hollies.

The Bearce (101 a.): Full of thorns, hollies and hazel, with a few young oak, and some oak and underwood, which is always cropped by the cattle.

Mawkins Hazles (8 a.): Very rocky and covered in general with birch, oak and hazel underwood, of very little value.

The Fence (33 a.): Covered very thick with fine thrifty young oak which would succeed very well if not cut down by the cottagers and others for firewood &c.

The Glydon (23 a.): On the side of a very steep rocky hill, covered very thick with bramble, thorns, and a few hollies, which are continually cut by the inhabitants of the parish of Newland.

# APPENDIX II

## DRIVER'S OAK SURVEY OF 1808[54]

| RUARDEAN WALK | Trees | Content (cu. ft.) |
|---|---|---|
| The Damms and Serridge Green | 364 | 10,245 |
| Birch Wood | 4 | 60 |
| Holly Hill and Gosbrook | 281 | 4,065 |
| Hassen Bridge and the Plugs | 953 | 16,260 |
| High Beech | 921 | 14,895 |
| Great and Little Bury and Barn Edge | 603 | 11,470 |
| Ruardean Lodge and Briarlar | 427 | 7,865 |
| Bailey Hill and Wigpool | 1,073 | 23,295 |
| Lee Baily | 5,068 | 129,550 |
| Linings Wood | 477 | 5,000 |
| | 10,171 | 222,705 |

Tellers:    2,000 in Birch Wood, and 60 in The Stenders.

| LATTIMER WALK | | |
|---|---|---|
| North and South Haywood | 129 | 1,640 |
| Pipley and Edge Hills | 55 | 755 |
| Tanners and Middle Hill | 19 | 220 |
| Blaize Bailey | 146 | 3,230 |
| The Chestnuts and Popes Hill | 73 | 610 |
| | 422 | 6,455 |

In Bradcocks Bailey 6 trees of 4th class.
Tellers:    Full along the Bottom by Little Dean Road, but few upon the Hill.
About 40 acres full of Tellers and the rest nearly full in Tanners and
Middle Hill.
Collyfield Hill tolerably full of Tellers, Chapperidge 10 Tellers.

| WORCESTER WALK | | |
|---|---|---|
| Buckholt Inclosure | 542 | 28,830 |
| The Pearts, Lodge Hill and Vellets | 796 | 34,425 |
| Aspeage Meane and Coveram | 79 | 2,025 |
| Barren Hill | 1,488 | 45,720 |
| Treasures Mill | 51 | 2,575 |
| Sally Vellet | 531 | 25,575 |
| Moor Wood | 14 | 255 |
| The Boorts | 293 | 7,450 |
| | 3,794 | 146,855 |

[54] P.R.O., F20/3 (Plate XIX herein).

| Park End Walk | Trees | Content (cu. ft.) |
|---|---|---|
| Skinner's Garden | 86 | 3,215 |
| Church Hill | 1,830 | 77,595 |
| Shading Tuft | 251 | 12,855 |
| Ivymoor Head | 488 | 20,645 |
| Lodge Hill | 1,022 | 48,715 |
| Fetter Hill | 531 | 17,735 |
| Nags Head Hill | 500 | 18,290 |
| Wonnow | 17 | 340 |
| Bigshead Slade | 27 | 1,375 |
| Birch Hill | 52 | 920 |
| Little Cross Hill | 189 | 7,170 |
| Bromley Hill | 180 | 5,145 |
| Thirty Acres | 123 | 5,010 |
| Park Hill | 57 | 940 |
| Masons Tump | 37 | 815 |
| The Scrawles | 63 | 2,275 |
| Oaken Hill and Bleak Vellet | 140 | 3,125 |
| | 5,593 | 226,165 |

## SPEECH HOUSE WALK

| | Trees | Content (cu. ft.) |
|---|---|---|
| The Sallies | 615 | 19,055 |
| Kensley Ridge and Green | 265 | 10,555 |
| Daniel Moor | 591 | 12,955 |
| Buchenhurst | 517 | 23,810 |
| Blackpenny Wall | 388 | 19,890 |
| Foxberry | 866 | 46,230 |
| Serridge | 221 | 7,370 |
| White Leys | 994 | 46,440 |
| Russells | 1,071 | 57,510 |
| Fair Moor | 1,531 | 74,090 |
| Stonage | 644 | 27,420 |
| Hard Rushy Green | 245 | 8,085 |
| The Island | 98 | 3,105 |
| Phelps Meadow | 375 | 8,135 |
| Middle Ridge | 566 | 12,265 |
| Saint Low | 228 | 5,945 |
| Turner's Tump | 31 | 1,235 |
| Rushy Lawn | 42 | 1,790 |
| Yew Tree Brake | 155 | 5,055 |
| Gosty Tump or Green | 283 | 7,750 |
| Old Woman's Tump | 65 | 2,895 |
| Wet Wood | 714 | 30,305 |
| | 10,505 | 431,910 |

A
Survey
OF THE OAK TIMBER
situate and standing
in the
FOREST of DEAN;
in the
COUNTY of GLOUCESTER:
belonging to
His Majesty.
(Including the Account before delivered.)
Made in pursuance of
a Warrant and Instructions
from the
Right Hon.ble Lord Glenbervie
Surveyor General of all the Woods, Forests, Parks, & Chaces
belonging to the CROWN.
By A. W. & E. DRIVER.
1808.

Rec.d 16th Sept.r 1808.

Copy hereof sent to Mr. Davies
14th Nov.r 1808.

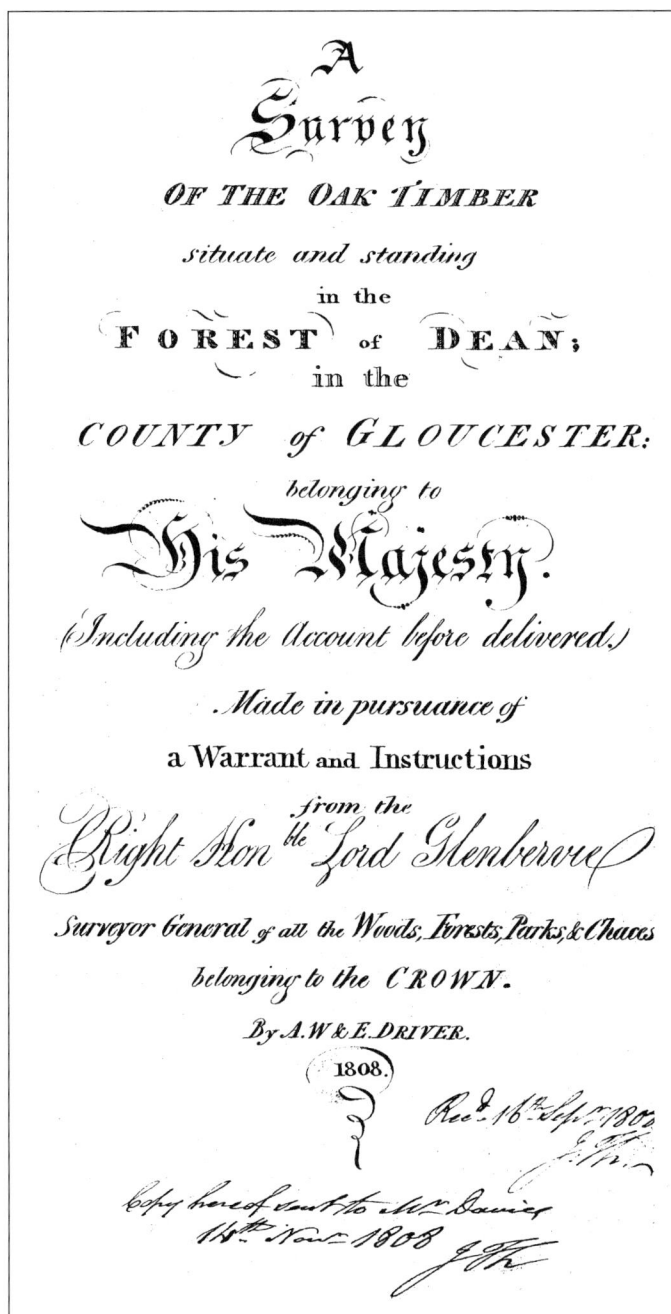

Plate XIX. The first page of the survey of oak timber in the Forest of Dean undertaken by Messrs Driver in 1808. (P.R.O., F20/3)

| Blakeney Walk | Trees | Content (cu. ft.) |
|---|---|---|
| Yorkley Bailey and Deadmans Cross | 249 | 5,570 |
| Newens Hill and Thorn Hils | 176 | 4,140 |
| The Copes | 83 | 1,800 |
| Bradley | 91 | 1,685 |
| Broom Hill | 96 | 3,005 |
| Lodge Hill | 691 | 18,815 |
| Yorkley Baily (Part of) | 217 | 6,065 |
| The Island, Old Vellet and Mosley Green | 556 | 15,995 |
| Middle Ridge | 525 | 11,950 |
| Muzen Hurst and Stapleage Hill | 532 | 13,230 |
| Awres Glow | 408 | 10,580 |
| Puttenage | 538 | 12,755 |
| Stapleage Inclosure | 180 | 4,465 |
| | 4,342 | 110,055 |

## ABSTRACT OF THE TOTALS

| Walk | Trees | Content (cu. ft.) |
|---|---|---|
| Ruardean | 10,171 | 222,705 |
| Lattimore | 422 | 6,455 |
| Worcester | 3,794 | 146,855 |
| Park End | 5,593 | 226,165 |
| Speech House | 10,505 | 431,910 |
| Blakeney | 4,342 | 110,055 |
| | 34,827 | 1,144,145 |

There are in the whole about 9,500 Tellers exclusive of those before mentioned in this survey.

[Signed] A.W. & E. DRIVER
Kent Road, Sept.16, 1808.

*Note*
The number of trees and their content are categorized in the survey as:
1st Class – Decayed trees fit for the Navy.
2ndClass – Trees not improving and not decaying.
3rd Class – Decayed trees unfit for the Navy.
4th Class – Residue.

# APPENDIX III

## The Sequence of Planting,[55] besides Whitemead Park planted 1809, 240 acres

| | | A | R | P | | A | R | P |
|---|---|---|---|---|---|---|---|---|
| 1810: | Barnhill | 353 | 2 | 3 | | | | |
| | Serridge | 387 | 3 | 24 | | | | |
| | Beechen Hurst | 308 | 2 | 36 | | | | |
| | Haywood | 407 | 1 | 34 | | | | |
| | Holly Hill | 41 | 0 | 38 | | 1,498 | 3 | 15 |
| 1811 | Crab-tree Hill | 372 | 2 | 34 | | 372 | 2 | 34 |
| 1812 | Shutcastle | 158 | 3 | 35 | | | | |
| | Bromley | 258 | 3 | 13 | | | | |
| | Chestnuts | 163 | 2 | 13 | | | | |
| | Sallow Vallets | 397 | 2 | 33 | | | | |
| | Ruardean Hill | 313 | 3 | 19 | | | | |
| | Addition to Buckholt | 14 | 3 | 29 | | 1,307 | 3 | 22 |
| 1813 | Oaken Hill | 477 | 2 | 11 | | | | |
| | Park Hill | 141 | 0 | 26 | | | | |
| | Blakeney Hill (N & S) | 816 | 1 | 0 | | 1,434 | 3 | 37 |
| 1814 | Stapledge | 943 | 2 | 17 | | | | |
| | Nag's Head Hill | 809 | 2 | 4 | | | | |
| | Russell's | 990 | 0 | 16 | | 2,743 | 0 | 37 |
| 1815 | Leonard's Hill | 66 | 0 | 32 | | | | |
| | Edge Hills | 494 | 1 | 36 | | | | |
| | Cockshoot | 598 | 0 | 22 | | | | |
| | Yew-tree Brake | 183 | 0 | 0 | | 1,341 | 3 | 10 |
| 1816 | Perch | 386 | 1 | 15 | | | | |
| | Astonbridge | 475 | 0 | 4 | | | | |
| | Kensley Ridge | 356 | 1 | 27 | | 1,217 | 3 | 6 |
| | | | | | Sub-total | 9,917 | 1 | 1 |

[55] (a) Because of the failures in planting due to mice and other agencies during the early years, the planting years should be seen as merely the years of enclosing, the years of effective full establishment being 5 to 7 years later.

(b) The extent of the enclosures, and the year of their (i) enclosing and (ii) planting (which often were not the same) differ somewhat in various surveys and reports.

|  |  |  |  |  | A | R | P |
|---|---|---|---|---|---|---|---|
|  |  |  |  | Sub-total | 9,917 | 1 | 1 |

Old Inclosures:

| | | | | | | | |
|---|---|---|---|---|---|---|---|
| Buckholt (1707) | 352 | 3 | 20 | | | | |
| Stapledge (1782) | 183 | 1 | 3 | | | | |
| Birchwood (1782) | 135 | 0 | 24 | | | | |
| Acorn Patch (1783) | 5 | 0 | 6 | | 676 | 1 | 13 |

Later additions [according to Edward Machen]:

| | | | | | | | |
|---|---|---|---|---|---|---|---|
| 1831 | Lea Bailey Copse North (mainly natural regeneration) | 86 | 2 | 0 | | | |
| 1837 | Lea Bailey Copse South (mainly natural regeneration) | 92 | 1 | 0 | | | |
| | Lower Lea Bailey | 168 | 3 | 29 | 347 | 2 | 29 |

Additions to:

| | | | | | | | |
|---|---|---|---|---|---|---|---|
| Acorn Patch (1842) | 35 | 1 | 39 | | | | |
| Birchwood | 2 | 2 | 0 | | | | |
| Ellwood | 4 | 1 | 23 | | | | |
| Bourts Nursery | 16 | 2 | 0 | | 58 | 3 | 22 |

|  |  |  |  |
|---|---|---|---|
| Total | 11,000 | 0 | 25 |

# APPENDIX IV

## Reports on Plantations by James Brown, 1852 (A, B)[56] and Statement Thereon by Edward Machen, 1854 (C)[57]

### (A) INCLOSURES THROWN OPEN TO COMMONERS

With a view to informing myself thoroughly regarding the subject, I examined very minutely (with the exception of Little Stapledge and part of Edge Hills, which, in point of size, are unimportant). The inclosures are all under a crop of oak of about 40 years' standing; and I propose, in the first place, to advert to the present condition of each, and at the same time to give a few suggestions for the improvement of any, as the nature of the case may require.

*Bromley* (258 acres) P. 1812. There is a full and regular crop of trees: they are in a fair state of health, and have not in the least been injured either by the commoners or their cattle, although they have had free access to the Inclosure for a period of nearly six years. The soil of this district is good and deep, naturally dry, and well adapted to the rearing of oak trees to valuable dimensions. I calculated the number of trees growing upon an acre on various parts of the Inclosure, and found the average 190; an average distance of about 15 feet between each tree, a space very proper for the healthy growth of oak trees of their age (nearly 40 years). I also measured a number of these trees at 6 feet from the ground, and found the average diameter nearly 7½ inches; this diameter I consider much under what they ought to have attained at their age, especially in so favourable a soil and climate for the growth of the oak. The average diameter ought to have been at least 11 inches; and therefore although there is at present a regular and full crop of trees on the ground, I cannot say that these have been hitherto well managed, for, had they been so, they would now undoubtedly have been much larger, and consequently more valuable.

As to the cause of the comparative inferiority of these trees, I propose to give my opinion after I shall have adverted to the present condition of all the Inclosures, which will also embrace my opinion as to the management of the Forest generally.

*Shutcastle* (158 acres) P. 1812. Crop very crowded and much in need of thinning. Average 290 trees/acre. Average diameter at 6 feet, about 6 ins., very small for trees of 40 years on such a fair soil. Crop in consequence of the good and naturally dry soil, is generally in a healthy and growing state. No damage to the trees by being thrown open.

*Crabtree Hill* (372 acres) P. 1811. Crop in a fair healthy state. On average 220 trees/acre, 7½ ins. at 6 feet. Considerable portion of the land is in a naturally damp state, rushes and rough grass growing upon it, requiring open drains 45 feet apart, 2½ feet deep. On the north corner, the lower branches of a few trees have been broken and gnawed by horses; elsewhere no damage by the commoners.

---

[56] 31st Rept. of Commissioners of Woods, etc., 1853, L.R.R.O. 9/14, pp. 297–305.
[57] Statement by Edward Machen, retired deputy surveyor, 1 Feb. 1854, printed by J.J. Hough, Coleford.

*Part of Stapledge* (258 acres) mainly P. 1814. Much overthinned of late. Average 150 trees/acre (should be 200/acre); average diameter 7½ ins. at 6 feet. One-half of the land is extremely wet, hence some trees unhealthy. The old open drains now nearly filled up and useless (need clearing and made 2½ feet deep; also more drains required). No damage by being thrown open.

*Blakeney Hill, South* (316 acres) P. 1813. Crop generally in a healthy and promising state, and comparatively well managed. Average 200 trees/acre; average diameter 9 ins. at 6 feet. On northern part very extensive damage has been and is still being done to the crop by the commoners opening stone quarries among the trees; otherwise no injury. Crop promises to become first-rate timber.

*Blakeney Hill, North* (500 acres) P. 1813. Crop promises to become first-rate timber. No damage of any description.

*Beechenhurst* (308 acres) P. 1810. Trees vary very much both as regards size and health. About 250 acres are dry, with the crop in a fair state of health; the remaining 58 acres are damp, with the crop in a very inferior condition. On the dry portion the trees average 200/acre; average diameter 7½ ins. at 6 feet. On the damp portion the trees average 260/acre; average diameter only 5 ins. at 6 feet (drainage is required). No damage from being thrown open.

*Birchwood* (137 acres) mainly *c*.P. 1787. Crop very severely thinned. Average only 130 trees/acre (which is 70 too few); average diameter nearly 8 ins. at 6 feet. Trees forming large branchy tops, and not growing proportionally to timber in the boles (overthinning is nearly as objectionable as neglect of thinning). A few acres of damp land which should be drained. Damage has been done by throwing open to the commoners, on about 3 acres.

*Holly Hill* (41 acres) P. 1810. Crop very severely thinned. Average stocking and size as for Birchwood (*supra*). A few acres damaged by cattle.

*Lea Bailey Copse, South* (92 acres) P. 1816. Crop generally healthy, but the trees very irregularly disposed. Some parts overthinned, and are too far apart; other parts underthinned, and much too close, and consequently drawn up. Judicious thinning required of the overclose crops.

In general, the throwing open of Inclosures has been done at a very proper time for the trees, that is, when they were 35 years of age.

## (B) INCLOSURES RETAINED

During my survey, I found that the limited time I had on hand would not admit of my inspecting minutely every one of the older Inclosures that are retained; the following are those I selected and examined.

*Edge Hills* (484 acres) mainly P. 1815. Stands at an elevation considerably above any other part of the Forest. All the land on the east side of the road in the southern point of this Inclosure situated betwixt Latimer Lodge and the Woodman's Lodge, altogether extending to about 80 acres, is of a very inferior quality, and in an extremely damp state; so much so, that the crop, which consists of oak, larch, Scots pine and spruce, is in a very sickly condition, and is now so much diseased, in consequence of dampness, that it will not recover. (I advise to cut down and clear off the whole crop, drain the land, and replant with larch alone at 4 feet apart.) The land on the west side of the road leading through the southern part of the Inclosure, about 50 acres, is under a crop of oak of eight years' standing, planted at 6 feet apart, with Scots pine and larch of the same age as nurses. The drainage is inadequate. On some parts whins [gorse] have grown up very strong among the young trees, and are doing much injury; all should be cleared off. The remainder of the land consists of dry sloping banks, which hang towards the north and north-east, and the crop on these consists of oak (40 years old) very closely mixed up with hazel, ash and beech underwood, all of a very strong growth. On the greater part, the crop is excessively close and much drawn up and should have been thinned at least three years ago. About 300 trees/acre; average diameter 6 ins. at 6 feet. The crop on the banks should be thinned in Spring 1853.

*Haywood* (407 acres) mainly P. 1810. Elevation and character very much like Edge Hills (*supra*). On the south-east side, the soil of about 40 acres is of poor and wet nature. The crop, chiefly oak 40 years old, is diseased and dying because of dampness. It should all be cut down and cleared; then drained and planted with larch. The remainder of the crop is in a comparatively fair state but has been overthinned, leaving only 170 trees/acre instead of 200/acre.

*Ruardean Hill* (313 acres) P. 1812. Crop comparatively healthy and in promising condition; but overthinned: only 160 trees/acre, and average diameter only 7½ ins. at 6 feet. The land is good dry quality well adapted for oak.

*Aston Bridge Hill* (475 acres) P. 1816. Land generally good and dry, but crop is very irregular in quality. On parts, due to underthinning, the trees are much drawn up, and weak, induced by excessive underwood. On the parts where there is no underwood, the crop has been overthinned, and the trees are of too branchy a character. Elsewhere on nearly one-third of the area the crop is in a very good state, and the trees in a promising state.

*Kensley Ridge* (356 acres) P. 1816. The oak stores are in a very crowded state, and generally much injured by the large quantity of beech, hazel and thorn underwood. Crop 250 trees/acre; average diameter only 6 ins. at 6 feet. Underwood should be cut, and the stores thinned to 200/acre. On almost 40 acres, the trees are in a sickly state, and many dying, because of damp soil; drainage is required. Elsewhere the land is of a good dry nature and well adapted for oak. The stores, although much drawn up, are generally healthy.

*Serridge* (378 acres) P. 1810. Crop much overthinned: 140 trees/acre; average diameter 8 ins. at 6 feet, of a branchy character and not growing so much to bole as they ought. Land dry and well adapted for oak. The crop despite its faults is generally healthy and progressing.

*Sally Vallets* (482 acres) mainly P. 1812. The method of thinning – stripping the bark off the trees to be felled and then leaving them for cutting later – was unsound and lost a year's benefit of space to the stores. While awaiting felling the crop averaged 300 trees/acre. The land is generally of excellent dry character and well fitted to rear valuable oak timber. On some of the flat strong land the trees are very good indeed, but, in general the crop is, due to underthinning, inferior for its age (40 years), and the average diameter is only 6 ins. at 6 feet. The considerable quantity of underwood should be cut away, as it both impedes the free passage of air, and tends very much to draw up the trees to an undue height in a weakly state.

*Buck Holt* (367 acres) mainly *c*.P. 1787. The crop of oak is to a considerable extent much injured by old full-grown beech among it; most standing in groups along the higher part of the hill, and a considerable number also growing singly on the slopes and lower ground; all of which, because of their large and branchy tops spreading widely over the surrounding ground, are injurious to the healthy development of the oak crop near them. The crop of oak is in portions of various ages, from 40 years down to 10; and each portion appears to have been planted as a clearing of old beech had been made. The soil is very variable in quality. On the low parts, and on the slopes of the hill, where the soil is good and deep, the trees are doing well; but on the higher parts, where the soil is very poor, and the rock protruding in many places, the young oak trees are progressing very slowly indeed, and will never become valuable as timber. On these high parts the oak crop has been planted without any nurses; this is an error in forest management. The greater part of the trees have suffered from underthinning; but on the slopes and lower ground, the soil being good and dry, there may, under future good management as to thinning, be reared to timber of first-rate value.

*The Perch* (386 acres) P. 1816. The crop is in good healthy condition, and generally under better management than any other in the Forest. The crop averages 196 trees/acre; and the diameter almost 10 ins. at 6 feet. The soil is generally very good and dry. However, on the higher portions the crop has been overthinned; here the trees are much exposed to winds, hence should be thinned more sparingly than on the low sheltered land. On the lower grounds there is a considerable quantity of underwood, which should be removed.

*Barn Hill* (353 acres) P. 1810. This Inclosure is in many respects very much like The Perch (*supra*), and the remarks made upon it are equally applicable here. On the higher portions the trees have been overthinned, and are much exposed to wind. On the lower grounds there is a considerable quantity of underwood.

*Nags Head* (809 acres) P. 1814. The 200 acres of land on the high and exposed parts is very poor and stoney, and the oak crop on it is not healthy or in promising condition. There are 260 trees/acre; average diameter only 5 ins. at 6 feet, although 40 years of age. There will never be oak timber of any considerable value. The 609 acres on the slopes of the hill, and in the hollows, is of an excellent deep rich nature, well adapted for the oak crop. The crop averages 170 trees/acre; the diameter is 8 ins. at 6 feet. However, great irregularities exist, as in some considerable parts there is over 200 trees/acre, hence much drawn up and weakly; while on other considerable parts there are little more than 100/acre, and the trees short in bole, and branchy. All the land is of a dry nature, and the 600 acres on the slopes and hollows are excellently adapted, under good management, to rear valuable oak timber.

*Park Hill* (141 acres) P. 1813 and *Whitemead* (240 acres) P. 1809. The trees in general are in a healthy condition, but very much retarded in their growth by the great quantity of underwood. The crop is very close; it should be thinned and the underwood cut and sold as cordwood. The land on the low flat part along the east side [alongside the Newerne brook] is very damp and needs draining.

*Oaken Hill* (477 acres) P. 1813. This Inclosure embraces very great variety, both of soil and crop. On the high-lying portions there have been coal workings [Bell pits] previous to planting, the oaks are extremely stunted in growth, and small for their age. The crop will never succeed; it should be cleared and replanted with larch. On the slopes below, the ground is generally good and the present crop of oak will become timber of secondary class. On the lower parts of the slopes, and on the flats and hollows, the land is excellent and will produce timber of first-rate size and value. The crop on the better land in general is too crowded, and much injury is being done by the large quantity of birch, beech and hazel underwood among the stores. Thinning should be undertaken and the underwood removed. On the flat hollow parts are a few acres in a damp state; the open drains should be attended to.

*Cockshot* (628 acres) mainly P. 1815. Here the soil and crop are in every respect of the same character as Serridge Inclosure (*supra*).

*Yew Tree Brake* (183 acres) P. 1815. The crop is very close and should have been thinned two years ago. The average is 280 trees/acre; the diameter 7 ins. at 6 feet. The soil being good, the trees have not as yet suffered much in health, although considerably drawn up; they should be thinned during Spring 1853.

*Stapledge, in part* (842 acres) mainly P. 1814. Here the soil, situation, and the stocking and diameter of the trees are very much the same as in Serridge Inclosure (*supra*); and the remarks equally applicable.

*Russells* (990 acres) mainly P. 1814. The crop is of various ages, between 40 and 20 years; planted at different periods successively, as the crop of old oak timber was removed. All the land is an excellent heavy loam, and well adapted to the rearing of oak timber to large and valuable dimensions; but a considerable portion of it, particularly on the west side, is damp, and should be drained, to secure a more rapid and healthy growth of the trees. That portion of the crop which has attained the age of 40 years is in a fair state of health, although the trees are by no means so large at the age as I expected to find them on land of so good a quality. The average is 240 trees/acre; the average diameter 7 ins. at 6 feet. The stocking is too many by 40, and is in a great measure the cause of the small diameter of the trees. Those portions of the crop which are under 40 years of age are generally in an extremely close state, and the trees much drawn up and weakly: in illustration of this, on some places of considerable extent, where the trees appeared to be 25 years of age, I found them only from 4 to 5 feet apart, and much drawn up and injured by a close mass of underwood. The latter should be cleared; and then the trees judiciously thinned (i.e. not overthinned). A large number of full grown oak trees, which grew interspersed among the younger part of the crop referred to above, have this season been cut down for the Navy.

Brown then gave his opinion as to the general management of the Inclosures:

I would not say that the crop on all the Inclosures have hitherto been well managed, because the trees are comparatively small for their age. The crop on all these Inclosures are oak (with the exception of a very few chestnut trees intermixed) of about 40 years of age; the greater part of the soil is excellently adapted to their growth; yet they are of small dimensions compared with trees in other plantations of the same age, much less favourably circumstanced as regards both soil and climate. The present average diameter of the trees in Dean Forest, of 40 years of age, scarcely comes up to 8 ins. at 6 feet, while in well-managed plantations in the North, where the soil and situation are very inferior to those of Dean Forest, the average diameter of oak trees of the same age is fully 9 ins. at the same height. [Brown had not taken account of the fact that many of the crops he adjudged as 40 years of age were in effect only 33 to 34 years due to early failures.] Before I visited this Forest, I expected to find the trees much larger at a given age; but when I inspected it, and saw the system of management that had been followed, I did not wonder that the trees are small; and the inference my inspection has compelled me to draw is that the inferiority in size of the trees in Dean Forest is entirely attributable to the defective system of management. The principal points of this system of management to which I would draw attention are:

1. The Inclosures have been thinned at intervals of from six to eight years. [Brown advocated more frequent thinnings.]
2. When an Inclosure is to be thinned, a number of woodmen are employed at the same time, to mark together the trees which are to be taken out. [Brown advocated that only one man should mark the trees – thus securing a uniformity and consistency of method from first to last.]
3. The trees taken out as a course of thinning are stripped of bark in their growing state, and not cut down for a period of about six months afterwards. [Brown deplored this method; and advocated stacking of bark instead of lying it on the ground.]

4. A great quantity of underwood is allowed to grow up among the young trees, until it is considered fit for cordwood. [Brown asserted that this practice was extremely injurious to the healthy growth of the crop.]
5. On all the different situations of the Inclosures the crop is left over the ground, after a thinning has been performed, at nearly the same distance from tree to tree. [Brown asserted that the desired spacing should vary according to situation, exposure, soil, and age.]

Brown then proffered his advice as to how the whole Forest should be managed, the number of woodmen to be employed, and the extent of their responsibilities; and recommended the introduction of sawing machinery.

## (C) STATEMENT BY EDWARD MACHEN, 1 FEB. 1854

As the observations by Mr. Brown on each Enclosure apply more or less to the whole, I would remark that I do not agree with any of his recommendations, except that as to the drainage, which applies to a very small proportion of the ground.

The conclusion Mr. Brown has come to in respect to the trees being larger if they had been under good management is altogether fallacious. He assumes that because the Enclosures are 40 years old the trees are of that age; but the fact is that for the first 6 or 7 years the planting entirely failed: one cause was an enormous increase of mice, which so completely destroyed the trees that the Enclosures were replanted. The average age of the trees cannot fairly be said to be more than 33 years. Two million trees were planted in 1820–21, and many much later, and taking this into consideration I think no plantations in England have grown faster. The premises therefore being wrong the conclusions must be so likewise. Furthermore, the growth of the trees had been checked by a blight which first appeared in 1830, and has continued more or less in every succeeding year, no doubt not peculiar to this neighbourhood, but which either from the large masses of wood together, or other local causes, has visited the Forest with peculiar severity.

It is recommended to thin a part of each Enclosure every year instead of thinning the whole of some. This would have the effect of keeping the Enclosures always open, because trespass cannot be excluded when the produce is remaining in them, and on the whole would be a less convenient arrangement for purchases.

The times of thinning recommended are identical with ours. Five or six years has been the usual interval between each thinning. The Enclosures of Edgehills and Kensley are exceptions to the rule, and were delayed only on account of the large quantity of old timber trees felled, all the workmen being required for that service.

Cutting away all the underwood, would I think be a great sacrifice of revenue without any adequate increased growth in the standard trees.

My opinion of the comparative merits or demerits of many of the Enclosures entirely differs from Mr. Brown's. The cutting down of 200 acres of Nagshead Hill Enclosure as he recommends, would I think be a great loss: the soil and exposure are just similar to Ruardean Hill which is pointed out as likely to produce large timber, the difference being that in Nagshead no nurses were planted at first, but there is no doubt in time they will produce good Navy timber.

The Sallow Vallets is said to have suffered from over confinement. I would point the attention of anyone conversant with oak woods to the state of this Enclosure; no part of it is in the least weak or drawn up, and £8,000 worth of produce has been taken from it in the last 25 years. From the whole Forest the total amount of thinnings in the same period is £135,000.

# APPENDIX V

## HILL'S DESCRIPTION OF THE ENCLOSURES IN 1897[58]

### ENCLOSURES

| Name of Block; Situation and Soil | Area in Acres | Description of the Wood |
|---|---|---|
| ACORN PATCH | 812 | Includes Acorn Patch proper, Middle Ridge and St. Low, three blocks separately described below. |
| ACORN PATCH Flat. Loamy soil over rubble stone and grey sandstone. Surface covered with grass, fern and brambles. | 122 | *a.* 14 acres. 110 years old oak. Some fifty stems to the acre. Cover very incomplete. Fair length of stem, but trees much branched. The best girth 5 feet, and a few 5 feet 10 inches and 6 feet. *b.* 35 acres. 5–55 years old. Oak with low branching crowns. The best stems are about 20 feet long and girth 3 feet. Heavily thinned 5 years ago, and prior to that, 14 to 18 years ago. Poor growth. *c.* 73 acres. 50 years old oak, with some ash and underwood of briars, birch and a little beech in the east portion, where soil is stiffer than elsewhere. Less heavily thinned than *b,* and growth more promising. A few larch and spruce remain. *a, b,* and *c* require underplanting, the trees in the overwood being trimmed of epicormic and low branches not forming part of the crown proper. *d.* 27 acres of old nursery planted and allowed to grow up for some 40 years. Contains oak, larch, spruce, chestnut and birch. The feature of the wood is the natural growth of beech and chestnut appearing generally. There is a small patch of spruce almost pure, but not complete. Also a small patch of chestnut complete, showing good growth, 4 feet to 4 feet 6 inches in girth and 55 feet total height, with underwood of the same species from stools. May be allowed to grow on and complete itself naturally. The dominant trees of the best species may be helped by thinning later on, say 10 years hence, all underwood being preserved. |

[58] Hill, H.C., *Report on the Forest of Dean with Suggestions for its Management,* 19 July 1897, pp. ii–xvii. H.M.S.O. Relevant correspondence between Hill, Baylis and Schlich is in P.R.O., F3/327.

This area does not appear to be included in the 109 acres enclosed on the stone, and it makes the total area 149 instead of 122 acres as recorded in the register.

SAINT LOW                    217
Same soil as Acorn Patch
block, except in low
lying parts, where clay
appears below a thin
covering of loam.

The whole is stocked with oak 54 years old, the dominant stems girthing 2 feet 3 inches to 2 feet 6 inches.

*a.* Contains a few beech and chestnut, and some self-sown beech underwood is making its appearance.

*b.* Contains less underwood than *a.* Some birch appearing. A belt a chain wide cleared for tram-line and allowed to grow up. Since heavily thinned and turned into coppice with standards. Calls for no special treatment; should not be thinned again nor underwood cut.

*c.* Underwood of beech and birch is coming up naturally. In south, spruce or Scotch pine most suitable.

Requires underplanting, but more urgently in *b* than in *a* and *c* (except south part where spruce would do well).

MIDDLE RIDGE                    473
Same as Acorn Patch.
Loam with tendency to
stiffness, and clay in parts.

Planted with oak, said to be 50 years old.

*a.* West of Railway and also east between it and central line contains oaks almost pure, less heavily thinned than in Acorn Patch. Fair growth, especially if, as is probable, trees are younger than is stated. Can be undersown with beech.

*b.* North of central railway line and south of spruce ride. In south-west corner a few acres (possibly old nursery) furnish example of oak under good conditions with spruce underwood. Generally oak with a few larch and scattered spruce. More open than *a.* Would have to be underplanted owing to fern and brambles.

*c.* West of spruce ride and south of ride from corner of Yewtree Brake. Oak, larch, and a few chestnuts. Some spruce in underwood, chestnut, and a little beech. Much low-lying ground on which spruce would thrive better than beech. Needs underplanting, but not urgently.

*d.* Oak and larch. Poor growth and open. Some undergrowth of oak, chestnut, and beech coming up. Would be the better for underplanting to fill up, but may be allowed to go on.

BARNHILL (NEW)                    20
Loam over rubble and
sandstone, somewhat
shallow.

Oaks 35 years old, with a few larch and spruce, the latter mostly suppressed. Good growth, the dominant stems measuring 1 foot 9 inches in girth. Lightly thinned in 1891–92. Complete. May be undersown with beech nuts at any time, wall being strengthened with a strand of wire to keep out sheep.

**BIRCH HILL**
Loam over rubble
sandstone.

27

53 years old oak and larch. Open poor growth of
oak, good growth of larch. Looks as if oaks had
been suppressed by nurses.
It is a narrow belt much exposed to the west.
Undersow with beech.

**BLAIZE BAILEY**
On slopes, with general
aspect east and north.
Deep rich loam,
generally sandy, but
with bands of clay and
marl, over old red
sandstone.

120

a. 24 acres planted in 1847 (50 years old) very
much thinned. Open crop of oaks with fine
growth, almost incredible for the age, as many
girth 4 feet, and exceptionally, some 4 feet
6 inches in girth are found. Soil covered with
growth of grass, brambles, and fern. Underplant
with beech.
b. 96 acres planted in 1871–72, therefore 25 and
26 years old. Very fine growth of oak, with some
larches, and also chestnuts in north-east. Oaks
measure 20–25 inches in girth, and larches and
chestnuts 2 feet 6 inches in girth. Thinned two
years ago and cover much interrupted. Brambles,
grass, and fern have appeared on soil. Requires
underplanting with beech, which, when
established, will allow of removal of all but very
best larches and of the oaks without promise.

**BLIND MEEND**
Easterly aspect. Loam
of coal measures.

5

53 years old oak, thinned in 1892. Very open, but
surface of soil fairly clean owing to fern having
been cut.
Undersow with beech.

**BOURTS**
On slopes, with a
generally northern
aspect, north-east and
north-west. Rich loam.

126

a. About 20 acres, divided in two halves by the
road. Oaks of 50–55 years old with a few larch.
Originally planted with chestnuts in alternate
lines. Thinned in 1893–94 when all chestnuts
were cut out indiscriminately, and many holes
made in the cover. Chestnut stools now
coppicing, giving the appearance of coppice with
excess of standards. The oaks have fine straight
clean stems, and a total height of 40 feet.
Let coppice of chestnuts and other underwood, of
which there is a little beech, grow up and repair
bad effect of heavy thinning by completing the
overwood.
b. About 15 acres pure chestnut clean cut in 1893
–94 and now growing up as simple coppice. Larch
have been interplanted, and it should not again be
cut over but left to grow into such high forest as it
will form, together with the rest of the block.
c. 77 acres of 50–55 years old oak of very fine
growth, but somewhat overthinned in 1893–94,
and urgently calling for underplanting or sowing
with beech. Some 10 acres in the north-west part
are younger and contain beech in the overwood,
much of which has been wrongly cut out with
the idea that oaks which have been long
suppressed would retake vigour. The beech

should be accepted in the overwood, either where no oaks exist, or such as may exist, give no longer any promise. The whole should grow up with a complete overwood, the canopy of which should not again be broken into.

*d.* 14 acres of 85 years old oak, grown up on the site of old nursery. Requires underplanting or sowing with beech.

The whole block should be tended on to maturity as high forest, which it will attain in 70 or 80 years.

| BREAMS TUFTS (Two enclosures) Slopes with north-east aspect. Sandy soil. | 29 | 27 years old wood of oak, larch, and some chestnut. Very much damaged by fires. Repaired with larch and Austrian pine, the latter doing well. Birch growing naturally. Complete with Austrian or Scotch pine, and undersow best parts with beech. |
|---|---|---|
| BREAMS EAVES Loam of coal measures. | 31 | 53 years old oaks of good growth. Heavily thinned, and crop of seedlings appearing. Undersow with beech. |
| BRAINS GREEN Slope with easterly aspect. Deep sandy loam over old red sandstone. | 8 | 36 years old oak, good growth. Heavily thinned in 1894–95. Can be undersown in parts and underplanted in other places with beech. Brambles and fern on the surface. Will be included in new Blakeney Hill enclosure. |
| BRADLEY HILL Sandy loam over old red sandstone. Site of old quarries with stone on surface. | 60 | 25 years old oak and larch, planted in alternate rows of larch and larch and oak mixed, 4 feet apart. Larch has not done well. Most of it cut out. Those remaining not promising. Heavily thinned in 1895. Fern and brambles. Some beech, poplar, sycamore springing up. More beech will come up naturally. May be allowed to grow up. Very good growth, though few specimens of old oak miserable, showing that the treatment, and not the soil, makes the difference in vigour. Spruce along ride cut on one side. Should be kept wherever these protective belts are. Nothing to be done beyond removal of bad larch and pruning of old spreading beeches. |
| CHURCH HILL Loam, stiff and clayey in parts. Similar to Russell's. | 246 | 40 years old oak with larch and a few chestnuts. Larches numerous in south-west part where oaks failed. Deodars in rides and a few in crop. Good growth. Heavily thinned, with result that fern and brambles have got possession in parts, and there planting will have to be had recourse to. Elsewhere beech may be undersown. Many rides with lines of deodar and spruce, Scotch pine, lime and beech, forming good protective lines. Contains a number of fine old oaks, remnants of the crop removed in the fifties. |

**CHESTNUTS**      166
Sandy loam, but shallow.

Planted in 1812, therefore 85 years old. Very like Russell's Block, but overwood of oaks more open and less promising. Good in parts. Chestnuts show good growth, but many unsound have been cut out. Undergrowth consists mostly of hazel, with some chestnut and oak. Very little beech. Cut over partially 3 years ago.
Should have complete rest for 20 years, by which time leaf canopy will have become complete and condition of high forest be established.

**CINDERFORD**      6
Loam over rubble stone.

39 years old oak with a few larches and chestnuts. Fair growth except on west, where exposed. Little undergrowth of chestnuts. Undersow and plant with beech, then cut out bad oaks.

**CLEARWELL
MEEND**
(Three enclosures)
Easterly aspect. Sandy
soil over millstone grit.      36

53 years old oak in parts. Badly damaged by fires, and consequently there are large blanks. Some larch and chestnut.
Much of the area only fit for Scotch pines. Either clear and replant with Scotch pine and larch, or clear and replant bad parts in large patches and undersow best parts with beech.

**CLEMENTS-END-GREEN**      14
Partly on stiff loam and
partly on sandy soil.

53 years old oak and larch, incomplete. Burnt at different times and replanted 30 years ago. The younger wood is complete.
Undersow with beech and plant Scotch pine in blanks.

**CLEMENTS' TUMP**      16
Yellow loam somewhat
stiff.

38 years old oak and larch. Numerous larch allowed to remain over oaks till recently. Good growth. Undersow with beech.

**COVERHAM**      99
No. 1, 21 acres
No. 2, 78 acres
Flat. Good deep loam.

Oak and chestnut and some larch 51 years old. Excellent growth, chestnuts up to 3 feet and oaks 2 feet 4 inches in girth, with good clean stems. Complete underwood of chestnut and beech, cut over about 12 years ago. In No. 1 chestnut predominates, and in parts forms both the over- and underwood.
Capital example of a young wood in full production. Some 24 acres south and south-west of turnpike road are 17 years younger, and should be undersown with beech.
The old treatment of periodically thinning heavily the overwood and clear cutting the underwood should cease, and the whole be led on to high forest, being lightly thinned in about 10 years. The edges should be kept dense, especially on western boundaries, with walls of beech, which are appearing naturally, and should be encouraged and respected at the time of thinning.

**CRUMP MEADOW**
Flat. Yellow loam, with
shaly sandstone over clay
and bituminous shale.
Clay in parts near surface
Surface covered with
grass and brambles.

82

Oaks, with here and there a larch or spruce.
51 years old. Promising growth. Oaks with
30–35 feet of stem, 2 feet and even 3 feet in
girth. Very open. Has been thinned generally in
1867, 1884, and 1895, besides having undergone
some partial thinnings. The gross value of the
thinnings is kindly given by Mr. Johnston as
follows:-

|  | £ |
|---|---|
| 1867 | 448 |
| 1884 | 606 |
| 1895 | 392 |
| At different times | 175 |
|  | £1,621 |

This enormous return of nearly £20 an acre from
the thinnings of a wood 51 years old speaks for
itself, and explains the present state of
incompleteness of the woods.
Should be underplanted, and probably spruce or
hornbeam would succeed better than beech,
though beech may well be tried.

**DEAN'S MEEND**
Flat. Soil varying from the
sandy loam of the millstone
grit to stiff clay.

139

Oaks, and in places Scotch fir and larch
50 years old. Fair growth. Has been recently
thinned, and needs undersowing with beech.

**DELVES,**
Nos. 1, 2, 3 and 4
Loam, with clay near
surface.

158

Oak, with a few larch, and occasional spruce
50–53 years old. Oak short but of fair girth.
Heavily thinned. Suffers from frost in parts.
Wants underplanting badly. A few stray beech
indicate that that species will grow, though the
soil would seem to be better adapted to spruce
(which grows vigorously) or perhaps
hornbeam.

**DELVES,**
No. 5
As above.

33

Oak of 39 years with some larch and spruce. Fair
growth on west side. Poor growth on the east
where oak stunted. Underplant and gradually
remove bad oaks, letting beech or spruce take
their places. Convert worst 15 acres to pure
coniferous wood.

**EASTBACH MEEND**
Good sandy loam, partly
on millstone grit. Till
lately covered with leaf
mould, since last thinning
becoming covered with
grass and fern.

45

51 years old. Oak, and in places larch. Good
growth, but much thinned out in 1893–94.
Ought to have been underplanted or sown
before thinning. This operation should now be
done. Some little beech springing up naturally,
but nowhere sufficiently.

**GREAT KENSLEY**
Shallow loam over thick layer of clay, covered with luxuriant growth of coarse grass.

194

Oak, and in places larch. 53 years old. Open. Growth medium in places but generally poor. Unsuited for oak or beech. Spruce would probably grow better than anything else. Either clean and plant thickly with spruce or coppice, reserving such stores as have promise, and interplant with Scotch pine and larch. If to be coppiced, this should be done quickly, say in next 3 years, before trees get older.

**LITTLE KENSLEY**
Flat. Sandy loam with clay coming to surface in *b*, where it resembles part of Great Kensley.

138

28 years old.
*a.* 13 acres (south-west of spruce ride) oak, with here and there a spruce or larch. Complete, good growth, height 20 feet, girth 18 inches to 20 inches for dominant trees. The spruce might well be removed at any time as well as any larch not promising. Requires undersowing with beech within next 10 years. Contains an avenue of four rows of old oaks about 100 years old, known as 'Old Woman's Tump'.
*b.* 36 acres, burnt over recently, 4 years ago, and also prior to that. Oaks poor, some birch, and Scotch fir.
Clear of all burnt and defective trees and plant thickly with spruce or othere conifers.
*c.* 79 acres similar to *a* (north-east of spruce ride).
*d.* 10 acres burnt some 18 years ago, and replanted, therefore 10 years younger than *a* and *c*.
The undersowing, when carried out in *a*, should extend to *c* and *d*.

**HANGERBURY**
On slope with westerly aspect.

62

53 years old oaks and larch, with larch and Scotch pine on sandy part. Fair growth. Heavily thinned 1893–94, and so rendered open.
Some beech coming up naturally in the south, otherwise requires underplanting or sowing with beech. The planting of larch under such an overwood has been a mistake.
West side requires to be shut in with a dense growth of beech, as a protective windproof belt. The influence of the wind in the oaks is very marked, where the shelter of the adjacent private wood ceases.

**LEA BAILEY (OLD)**
Slope with northerly and westerly aspect. Deep sandy loam over red sandstone with corn-stones.

169

Said to date from 1815, but in reality the oaks of the overwood are older. They probably were then 40 or 50 years old, and short in stem, with branching crowns. 82 years ago the enclosure was formed, and open spaces planted up with larch and oak.
Good beech underwood, which it has been customary to cut over. Last cut and overwood thinned 16 years ago. The growing crop must be accepted and underwood allowed to grow up. Nothing required for 20 years.

| | | |
|---|---|---|
| **LEA BAILEY (NEW)** <br> On slope with south-west aspect. Deep sandy loam over red sandstone, with corn-stones. | 136 | Separated into two fairly equal parts, *a* and *b*, by the road to the lodge. 36–37 years old oak. Perfectly grown oaks with a complete underwood of self-sown beech. The oaks girth as much as 1 foot 9 inches to 1 foot 10 inches and 1 foot 11 inches, and have clean tall stems. A few old branching beeches scattered over the crop explain the presence of the underwood. In *b* the underwood of beech is not complete, a few larches remain, and the growth of the oaks is not so good. The underwood should be completed by planting in *b*. <br> The old beeches in *a* should have their side branches spreading 30 feet from the stem lopped, and be cut out entirely in the first thinning. May be ready for a thinning in 10 years. |
| **LIGHTMOOR** <br> Stiff loam, but clay appearing in parts. | 65 | 50 years old oak, with some larch spruce. Has been thinned, and requires undersowing or planting with beech. Growth poor, generally, particularly so on clay on south side. Might possibly be cleared and replanted with conifers. |
| **MILKWALL** <br> Loam of coal measures. | 14 | 56 years old oak, with some Scotch pine in places. Fair growth, and fairly complete. May be undersown with beech. |
| **MOSELEY GREEN** <br> Stiff loam, with clay near the surface in places. | 42 | 37 years old oak with some spruce and a few arch. Fair growth. Heavily thinned 6 or 7 years ago. Can still be undersown with beech. Good windproof belt of spruce and Scotch pine preserved on south-west. |
| **PARK HILL** <br> Loam over rubble sandstone. Stiff in parts. | 141 | 84 years old oak. Thinned in 1891. Open overwood of good growth with some underwood of young oaks, ash, sycamore and hazel. A little beech. Larches planted in groups after last thinning. <br> Beech might be planted under the oaks, where soil least encumbered with fern and brambles; then allowed to grow up, without further thinnings. |
| **PLUMP HILL** <br> Loam, stiff in parts to friable soft sandstone of millstone grit. | 18 | Planted in 1863, therefore 34 years old. Oaks and larch, in fact, few oaks, mostly larch. Good growth, oaks 2 feet in girth. Undersow with beech; possibly plant spruce instead in south corner. Part, an acre or two, on sand, poor growth, larches not succeeding. Burnt over. Partly repaired with Scotch pine. Sow Scotch pine in pits, removing bad larch to make room. |
| **RUARDEAN HILL** <br> Loam over rubble sandstone. | 50 | 35–37 years old oak and larch, larch numerous in parts and showing disease. Undersow with beech, and then cut out diseased larch and a few oaks. |

**RUSSELL'S**
Stiff loam and in places
clay, almost on surface.

990

*a.* 296 acres 87 years old oaks.
Open, with some chestnuts and larch over a thick
undergrowth of briars, blackthorn with some
oak, chestnut and beech; also birch, willow and
aspen. Oaks are not well shaped and do not show
good growth, being generally only 3 feet 6 inches
in girth. Thinned in 1891–92 but underwood
spared as not paying to cut.
Larch recently planted over several acres in south-
west corner, and in open places elsewhere.
*b.* 350 acres 87 years old oaks, thinned some
13 or 14 years ago. Part resembles coppice with
standards, but in greater part standards
predominate, and undergrowth is scanty or
incomplete.
*c.* 344 acres. South of the 'Three Brothers.' Much
of this is younger and denser than in *a* or *b*.
Apparently planted 40 years ago, when the last of
the old timber was removed. Some larch and
spruce in places. This is specially the case in the
south-east part.
The explanation of the underwood in Russell's,
which is absent in enclosures carrying woods of
the same age, e.g., Yew Tree Brake, is probably
that Russell's was enclosed from a more remote
date than 1810, when the majority of the trees
now standing were planted.
The wood on the whole is growing under
favourable conditions, and may be allowed to rest
for 20 years. It is true that the oaks are not all that
could be desired, but they must now be allowed
to grow to timber in order to get the best return
from them.

**YEW TREE BRAKE**
Good sandy loam over
rubble stone, but surface
covered with grass, fern
and brambles.

183

82 years old oak, regularly heavily thinned. Last
thinned in 1890–91. Thinning said to have been
heavy owing to number of broken and bad trees.
Crop reduced to about 70 trees per acre, with
average girth of 4 feet 3 inches about. Poor
height growth, and low branching crowns.
Openings after last thinning filled up with larch
and some patches of young oak. Underplant with
beech.

**BEECHENHURST (NEW)**
Made up of Kensley Ridge
Beechenhurst (part),
Serridge (part).
Slope, with north-west
aspect. Sandy loam on higher
part, gradually changing into
clay about the middle, and
stiff all over lower part.

667

81–87 years old oak, opened in 1855, and now
re-enclosed. It has been thinned, and openings
over half the area planted in 1896–97 with larch,
oak and sycamore. The area has to be generally
filled up with beech.
Other half remains to be planted. Very good
natural reproduction of oak showing, which
should be freed by cutting the fern.

## CROWN FREEHOLDS

| Name of Block; Situation and Soil | Area in Acres | Description of the Wood |
|---|---|---|
| **VALLETS GROUNDS** Goes with Perch, open wood to which it adjoins. | 78 | |
| **HERBERT'S LODGE** | 26 | Open grazing area. |
| **LATIMER LODGE** Stiff clay soil. | 17 | 57 years old oak and larch, most of the oak poor. Larch look fairly well, but they probably represent selection from a number. Scotch pine not doing well. Treat like Great Kensley. |
| **WORCESTER LODGE** | 6 | Open grazing area. |
| **DANBY LODGE** | 28 | Open grazing lands. |
| **OAKENHILL LODGE** | 5 | Open grazing lands. |
| **TERRINGHAM** Surface grazed over. Sandy loam. | 7 | 36 years old oak and larch. Good growth. Needs underplanting. |
| **WHITEMEAD** Stiff loam. | 240 | *a.* 67 acres of 88 years old oaks with some undergrowth of hazel, thorns, and a little beech. Good growth. At present let for grazing. Question whether it might not be treated for timber crop, and underplanted or sown with beech. *b.* 173 acres similar to *a* for the most part, but with more undergrowth. Hornbeam grows naturally in southern part. Introduce beech in groups, and encourage hornbeam in lower parts. |
| **ELLWOOD** Loam of coal measures. | 110 | 78 years old oak, open with some underwood. Let for grazing. |

## OPEN WOODS

| Name of Block; Situation and Soil | Area in Acres | Description of the Wood |
|---|---|---|
| **ASTONBRIDGE** Undulating main valley opening to south-west. Good loam over rubble and grey sandstone, but shallow in parts. Clay only in bottom of main valley where springs appear. | 474 | 85 years old oak, of good growth, having fairly tall stems and crowns still pyramidal, girth 3 feet 6 inches to 4 feet. Some beech in north-west part and scattered elsewhere. Thrown open at age of 49. If enclosed and simultaneously undersown with beech, would grow into a fine wood still. |

| | | |
|---|---|---|
| **BARNHILL**<br>A hill with gentle slopes to south and south-east. Loam over rubble stone and sandstone. Stiff soil near eastern boundary. | 354 | 88 years old oak of fair growth. Good growth of spruce in eastern part near railway.<br>Last thinned in 1891–92.<br>Thrown open at age of 46.<br>If enclosed and undersown with beech, except in openings caused by thinning, in which oaks and larch in patches should be planted a fair wood would result. |
| **BEECHENHURST**<br>Loam over rubble sandstone. | 309 | 87 years old oaks of fair growth, opened at age of 33. All but some 50 acres re-enclosed in 1896–97. (See Enclosures.) |
| **BIRCH WOOD**<br>Loam over rubble sandstone. Regular turf on surface. | 135 | 110 years old oak, poor growth of branching trees 4 feet 6 inches to 5 feet in girth. Very open. Hardly worth re-enclosing. |
| **BLAKENEY HILL**<br>Sandy loam over red sandstone. | 816 | 87 years old oak of fair growth, but very open. Few old larches in east ridge south of lodge.<br>A patch of old beech forest, fairly complete in south-east part west of Furnace Bottom, shows how much at home the beech is. The oaks intermixed with the beech do not show good growth, probably because they have been always dominated by the beech between which they have been planted. |
| **BROMLEY**<br>Good deep loam. | 259 | 82 years old oak of good growth for an open wood. Might be re-enclosed. |
| **BUCKHOLT**<br>Slope with easterly aspect. Deep sandy loam. | 368 | Said to be 100 years old, but does not appear more than 90. Somewhat irregular, having been many times filled up as old beeches, and perhaps oaks, removed. Good growth, and for open incomplete wood, long clean cylindrical stems. Old beech here and there, and few young beech in undergrowth.<br>About to be re-enclosed, when should be undersown generally with beech, patches of oak and larch being put out in open places. |
| **COCKSHOOT**<br>Soil varies from stiff loam on west to yellow loam of coal measures and fresh sandy loam on east. Surface hard and grazed over. | 628 | 82 years old oak. Incomplete. Fair growth. Fine beeches at Danby Lodge show how that tree thrives. |
| **CRABTREE HILL**<br>Slope with generally western aspect. Loam, stiff in parts. | 373 | 86 years old oaks. Very open. Poor growth. |

**EDGE HILLS**
Mostly easterly aspect.
Soil varies from sand of
millstone grit to clay over
limestone and sandy loam
of old red sandstone.

494

*a.* 40 acres of larch practically pure, planted after
a fire some 50 years ago. Good growth up to
3 feet 8 inches in girth and 40 feet in height.
In north-east corner some larch up to 60 feet
in height.
Remainder under oaks of 82–86 years,
incomplete, some poor hazel underwood in
places, and a few scattered beech. In two separate
old enclosures – Great and Little Edge Hills.
South-west corner much exposed, and oaks
stunted. Protective belt required, or Scotch pine
instead of oak should be planted in such a site.

**HAYWOOD**
Slope with westerly
aspect. Loam of coal
measures, except along
east where belt of
sandy loam.

407

87 years old oak of moderate growth in parts,
but generally poor.
A few Scotch pine and spruce growing well
along eastern boundary. If enclosed, the upper
eastern part might well be kept under conifers.

**HARRY HILL**
Loam, with caked
surface covered with turf.

91

53 years old oak of poor growth. Recently
thrown open. Might have been undersown
with beech. Fertility would then improve.

**HAZEL HILL**
Slope, with easterly
aspect. Deep fertile sandy
loam on red sandstone.

12

*a.* Part 34 years' old oak thinned in 1893.
Excellent growth 2 feet 4 inches girth, with
good clean stems.
*b.* Part 26 years old. Very good growth, 2 feet in
girth.
Recently thrown open. Should, I venture to
think, be re-enclosed owing to its exceptionally
good growth. If re-enclosed, a small patch on the
south planted at the same time should be
included.
Requires undersowing with beech.

**HOLLY HILL**
Stiff loam.

41

87 years old oak. Incomplete. Poor growth.

**KENSLEY RIDGE**
Loam.

356

Re-enclosed 1896–97 (*see* Beechenhurst).

**LEA BAILEY**
Slope, with north-
westerly aspect. Deep
fresh sandy loam on old
red sandstone near joint
with limestone.

178

82–84 years old oak, well grown in the north
part, 4 feet 6 inches to 5 feet in girth, with total
height of 60 feet. Much beech in the south in
both underwood and overwood; railway fence
protects on west side. Should be enclosed on first
opportunity.

**LEONARD'S HILL**
Stiff loam.

66

82 years old oak of poor growth.
Incomplete. Area reduced by pits and spoil banks.

**LINING WOOD**
Slope with easterly aspect;
same soil as Lea Bailey.

80

Said to have been planted in 1787, but it is really
much older. Mature open oak wood probably
160–200 years old. Trees with clean stems of

40 feet, and girth 7, 8, and 9 feet.
Could be reproduced naturally by establishing seed-felling and then hoeing up soil when crop of acorns appears.

| | | |
|---|---|---|
| LOQUIERS<br>Moist clay and sandy loam. | 43 | 50 years old oak with some larch. Wants underplanting. Site of fire might be repaired with Scotch pine. |
| NAG'S HEAD<br>Stiff loam. | 810 | 83 years old oak of fair growth, with some exceptionally fine larch. Might well be re-enclosed together with Barnhill. |
| OAKENHILL<br>Loam over rubble stone. | 478 | 84 years old oak. Incomplete to very open. Poor growth generally. Moderately good in parts. |
| OLDCROFTS<br>1, 2 and 3<br>Sandy loam. | 41 | 53 years old oak. Fair growth. Over-thinned 4 or 5 years ago. Thrown open in 1896. Good quick fences exist around greater part, and it seems a pity to have opened it before having established an underwood of beech, which could have assured its future development. |
| PERCH<br>Easterly aspect, with sandy loam. | 386 | 81 years old oak of good growth. Wood fairly complete with pure oak. Near the rifle range some beeches and a few chestnuts are found.<br>One of the best parts for re-enclosure. |
| RUARDEAN HILL<br>Loam over rubble stone and grey sandstone. | 314 | 85 years old oak. Poor for the most part. |
| STAPLE EDGE<br>Soil varies from loam on rubble sandstone to stiff clay on limestone and deep fresh sandy loam on red sandstone. | 1,127 | 83 years old oaks, mostly pure, now being thinned preparatory to enclosing. In north and east some old beeches and some young beeches planted 15 years ago. In these parts it will suffice to fill openings with oak and larch. Larch should be preferred in north-east opening where windfalls have left big open space.<br>On the eastern boundary is a patch of a few acres of complete beech wood, with a few good specimens of ash. Scotch pine grow well in the south, and that species should be sown in Tabber's Green, if included in enclosure. |
| SALLOW VALLETS<br>Loam over rubble stone. | 398 | 85 years old oak of fair growth, 3 feet 6 inches in girth, with straight clean stems. Open, park-like appearance. |
| SERRIDGE<br>Loam over rubble stone. | 388 | 87 years old oak, incomplete, open wood. Fair growth. Partly re-enclosed, some 300 acres remaining, of which Trafalgar Mine covers a part. |
| SHUTCASTLE<br>Deep loam. | 159 | 85 years old oak, open, incomplete. Good growth in parts. |

# APPENDIX VI

## COMMENTS ON AND CRITICISMS OF THE AFTER-MANAGEMENT OF THE 1808–18 PLANTATIONS

### BY H.C. HILL IN 1897[59]

The main crop of the Forest consists of oaks raised in plantations and the majority of these extending over 10,833 acres carry trees aged from 81–88 years [i.e. planted 1809–16]. They are for the most part pure, though some chestnut, ash and larch, and also a few scattered beeches, Scotch pine, and spruce are met with. The whole of the woods of this age are very open, and in only a few of the enclosures – viz. Russells, Chestnuts and Lea Bailey – is there any promising underwood [meaning under-storey] growing up to complete them. Such underwood consists of beech, chestnut, ash, and birch. Over 9,184 acres, now open, there is no underwood, and only the incomplete crop of isolated oaks.

There are 149 acres of older wood (110 years old) [planted *c.* 1787] in the same condition; and there are 80 acres still older (180–200 years) ['planted' *c.* 1697–1717] somewhat more complete, which is probably of natural origin. Aged from 50 to 56 years [planted *c.* 1841–47], there is an area of 2,082 acres, which has also been planted. These woods have all been gone over with more or less heavy thinnings, and with the one exception of Coverham, which is complete [i.e. fully stocked], they urgently require underplanting or undersowing. Where as in the Acorn Patch, rank grass and brambles have got possession of the soil, only a planting can succeed; elsewhere sowings promise to be successful.

There are 920 acres of woods aged from 25 to 40 years [planted *c.* 1857–72], and these are generally complete with oak and larch and a few spruce. In some instances a natural underwood of beech is springing up, and in the case of Lea Bailey the wood is complete with such growth.

*Past Management.* Going back to the last century [eighteenth], it is recorded that in 1787 the Forest carried a mixed crop of oak and beech in the proportion of two beeches to one oak, and this clearly indicates the conditions under which the fine oaks for which the Forest was renowned were produced. The small value of beech as compared with oak, and its tendency to outgrow the oak and suppress it, probably explain the attempts to substitute woods of fine oak for the original mixed woods. The crop of fine timber which grew up during the last century [eighteenth] was exploited early in the present century, and in 1849 no more than 500 acres of wood with old timber remained. It was believed to be 160 years old, and was valued at nearly £100 an acre. It stood mainly on Russells and Church Hill, and the felling of it in the years 1852 and 1853, as well as the fine quality of the timber yielded, are

[59] Hill, H.C., *Report on the Forest of Dean with Suggestions for its Management*, 19 July 1897, pp. ii–xvii. H.M.S.O. Relevant correspondence between Hill, Baylis and Schlich is in P.R.O., F3/327.

well described by the oldest woodmen as the great 'falls' of such timber as will hardly be seen again. There was a final felling a few years later in the Lea Bailey, and with that disappeared the last of the old crop, except some specially fine or quaint old specimens preserved in Church Hill and here and there elsewhere, which demonstrate unmistakeably the capabilities of the soil and climate.

The removal of the old mature crop was not affected without due consideration to its replacement, and plantations were undertaken as early as 1787. It was not, however, till 1809 that the work was begun on a large scale, and during that and the successive ten years the area of new plantations was brought up to 11,000 acres, all of which was enclosed.

That these plantations [made by Billington and Machen] were most excellently carried out there can be but one opinion. The sites were admirably chosen, the land was systematically drained, the choice of species and their arrangement in alternate lines, 8 feet apart, of oaks and conifers (larch, Scotch pine and spruce), the latter to serve as nurses to the oaks, were all that could be desired. The actual planting was so well done that, though certain failures and difficulties were at first met with, eventually the plants seem to have succeeded everywhere, and produced complete woods with not a blank or a necessity for repairs, except in cases where fires occurred on small areas. The Reports of 1849 and 1854 probably in no way exaggerated when they described the plantations as being 'in a good state and reflecting great credit on the parties concerned in their management', and when a Committee 'felt justified in representing that they were not surpassed by any forest property in the kingdom.'

At that period it was believed that the enclosures became fit for throwing open when the young trees [pole stage] 'had grown up sufficiently'. At the same time it was thought right to thin heavily. And the system of heavy thinnings, inaugurated in 1840 or 1850 was accepted as proper, became the custom, and was unfortunately pursued over a number of years till the plantations were reduced to the condition of open park-like woods, with isolated branching hide-bound oaks of little or no promise as regards the production of timber of fine size and quality. The plantations were not only heavily thinned, but everything in the shape of underwood [under-storey] was cut out, with the result that the trees stood far apart and the exposed soil became covered with a turf, fern, and brambles. The object in view was apparently to give to the oaks room to develop branches and produce crooked and curved timber for naval purposes. The fact that the fine timber which was then being felled had grown under quite different conditions, with 66 per cent of beeches to complete the leaf canopy and maintain the soil's fertility, was lost sight of. The law of nature under which pure woods of oak cease to thrive after the early stages of growth was disregarded, and finally any natural filling up of the woods and completion of the leaf canopy was prevented in the majority of the enclosures by their being thrown open. Had an underwood of beech been introduced, the thinnings would have been justifiable; and had the leaf canopy been allowed to become complete with oak *and* beech, the opening of the enclosures would not have resulted in such serious harm. It is an easy matter to point out, now that the results are apparent, the mistake that was made. Fifty years ago there was the laudable ambition to grow a maximum quantity of crooked oak rather than the less valuable beech, and though there may have been the recognition of the light-loving nature of the oak, there was also the erroneous idea of admitting sunlight on the boles. On the whole, and not without some reason at the time, conditions essential for the growth of fine oak timber came to be overlooked.

The process of throwing open the older plantations was continued till 1861, when 9,399 acres had been so dealt with, including the Lining Wood, which may or may not have been enclosed; and the only plantations remaining enclosed were 1,663 acres [named]. The temptation to throw open and so avoid the heavy cost of keeping up fences, as well as the payment of taxes, was unquestionably great, and doubtless the great loss in wood production was not appreciated. In all cases the thinnings were continued periodically, and the underwood was at the same time cut in the remaining enclosures. While the area of 9,399 acres was being thrown open the following new enclosures were formed and planted: 1841–47, 2,082 acres, 1657–63, 585 acres.[60]

## BY SIR WILLIAM SCHLICH IN 1904[61]

Any person with a pair of eyes, who visited the Dean eight or ten years ago, and made his way across the several woods, found on by far the greater part of the area a thin crop of oaks from 80 to 90 years old, of poor height growth, with rounded or flat tops, and the branches coming down low, so that only clear boles of small length were formed. Looking down on the ground, our observer would see the soil covered with a matting of grass and weeds, overrun with brambles, etc. Presently the wanderer would probably come across a solitary old oak or two of magnificent dimensions, towering high over the 80 to 90 years old crop; the idea would at once cross his mind that the flat-topped younger generation could never grow to the height of the few remaining old trees, and he would be sure to ask, 'What has brought about this change?' The answer is, 'The nineteenth-century foresters in charge of the Dean have ruined the former fertility of the soil by trying to grow oak pure beyond youth, by excessive thinning, and by unrestricted grazing.'

An enquiry into the past history of the Forest has revealed the fact that, up to the end of the eighteenth century, the Dean carried a mixed crop of oak and beech in the proportion of one oak to about two beeches; under these conditions the fine oaks of enormous size were produced which made the Forest renowned, and provided large quantities of first-class timber for the 'walls of oak' of Old England. This fine crop of timber was cut early in the nineteenth century, with the exception of about 500 acres, which were cut in 1852–53, yielding an average of 154 cubic feet of timber per tree, according to the quarter-girth measurement. The cleared areas were replanted [by Billington and Machen], so that most of these woods are now about 90 years old, and the rest 40 to 50 years. As far as is known, oak was planted with nurses, the latter having been cut out subsequently. And then the disastrous treatment commenced. When the woods had reached the age of 30 or 40 years, they were considered safe against cattle, and the greater part of the enclosures were thrown open, especially to extensive sheep grazing. About the same time it was considered the correct thing to thin heavily, and this was done during a number of years, until the trees were practically isolated. What the result of these operations is, has already been indicated. The soil, exposed to the unrestricted action of sun

---

[60] Hill may have been unaware that much of the 1808–18 planting was of almost pure oak without conifer nurses; also of the immense effort which had to be made after 1816 to fully stock many of the plantations. Some of the early throwing-open was probably due to pressure from the commoners, and the crown's desire to avoid the heavy cost of maintaining fences, gates, stiles, walls, mounds and hedges (Hart, *Royal Forest*, p. 228).

[61] Schlich, Sir William, *Forestry in the United Kingdom*, 1904, pp. 67–71.

and air currents, became in most parts practically unproductive, the result being a very inferior crop of unpromising oaks, short in height, and branched low down. How different might have been the results, if, instead of throwing open the enclosures and making senseless thinnings, the oak had been underplanted with beech at the age of 30 to 50 years, thus keeping the soil under constant protection, and causing a gradual accumulation of fertile leaf-mould on the soil.

It is due to Mr. Stafford Howard, Commissioner of Woods, and Mr. P. Baylis, Deputy Surveyor, Forest of Dean, to say that they recognised the unsatisfactory state of things, and set to work some ten years ago to mend matters. There were, however, great difficulties in the way. In the first place the areas, so ruthlessly thrown open, had to be re-enclosed, and this can only be done gradually; however, good progress has already been made, as several thousand acres have been fenced, and others will follow, until the whole area of 11,000 acres allowed by law has once more been brought under proper control. In the second place, the authorities had to consider what to do with the existing woods. In consultation with the late Mr. Hill, of the Indian Forest Department, they decided to underplant with beech the limited area of woods under fifty years old, where the mischief could still be remedied, as quickly as the occurrence of beechmast years permits. The older oak woods, about ninety years old, demand a somewhat different treatment, and this was commenced by Mr. Baylis about ten years ago. In these woods, only oaks of some promise are left, all others being cut out; then all blanks are filled up, chiefly with larch, oak, and other trees, such as sycamore and ash, and in suitable places spruce and Douglas fir. As soon as these young plantations have made a fair start, beech will be brought in over the whole area, so as to return to a state of affairs similar to that which existed a hundred years ago.

Some wiseacres have of late been writing about 'The New Forestry.' Alas! it seems to me what is really wanted is to return to 'The Old Forestry,' and to eliminate as quickly as possible the errors introduced into British forestry by the nineteenth century forest experts. These gentlemen were in too much of a hurry. 'Quick returns regardless of consequences' was their maxim, and now they have almost ruined national property of an enormous value, inasmuch as they have considerably reduced the fertility, or yield capacity, of the soil. It may indeed be said that the competency of a forester can be judged by examining the soil in his forests: if there is a good layer of leaf-mould on the ground, the management is sure to have been good; if not, undoubted mistakes have been made, which should be eliminated as quickly as possible.

No doubt, some readers will say, This is all very well, but what are we to do with so much beech, which fetches only a small price per cubic foot? The answer may be given by another questions: What is done with beech in Buckinghamshire and adjoining counties? Why, it is made into chairs and other articles of furniture, and it fetches at least a shilling a foot all round. In other words, provide the raw material, and industries to utilise it will soon spring up. They follow the raw material. Beechwood is coming into use more and more every year, for casks for dry goods, railway sleepers, pattens, heels for ladies' boots, and what not. Besides, the beech need not occupy more than half the crop, or it may be kept almost altogether below the oak.

Let us hope that the twentieth century foresters will profit by the lesson, and revert to methods of treatment which will secure the continued yield capacity of the soil, and thus lead to returns far higher than those which have been obtained of late from extensive woodlands in these islands.

Plate XX. 'The Verderers' Oak', west of the Speech House. 'A Monarch of the Forest',
approximately 320 years old, which has witnessed many of the events described in this book.
(Photograph by Chris Hughes, 1991)

## BY SIR WILLIAM SCHLICH IN 1910[62]

The Forest of Dean revisited. Having lately spent a couple of days in the Dean [June 1910], readers may care to hear what impressions I brought away. Since the year 1895 only 15 years have passed, and that is, in forestry, a short space of time, but I think substantial progress has been made. In the first place, 8,300 acres have been re-enclosed efficiently and are protected against sheep. It is hoped to bring the enclosed area up to 11,000 acres in the course of the next two years or so. The effect of this measure is very remarkable, there being already a decided difference in the vegetation and soil inside and outside the enclosures. . . . On the whole there can be no doubt that the management of the Dean is now being conducted on sound lines.

## BY C.O. HANSON IN 1911[63]

In the Forest of Dean . . . over large areas the present crop is poor, the trees are short in bole and much branched, and at first sight it might be assumed that the soil and climate are not suitable for oak. Nevertheless, this is not so; the previous crop consisted of fine tall oak, which produced much-prized timber. The poor condition of the present crop is due to different treatment, the woods having been thinned heavily in order to produce knees and crooks for the use of the Navy, in the days when the ships were built of oak. This sort of timber is now valueless.

---

[62] Schlich, Sir William, *Quarterly Journal of Forestry*, IV(3), July 1910, pp. 198–203. Schlich had accompanied his forestry students throughout a tour of Dean; the Report by one of them (E.A. Greswell, dated 6 July 1910) signed by Schlich is in the Forestry Library at Oxford University.

[63] Hanson, C.O., *Forestry for Woodmen*, 1911, p. 22.

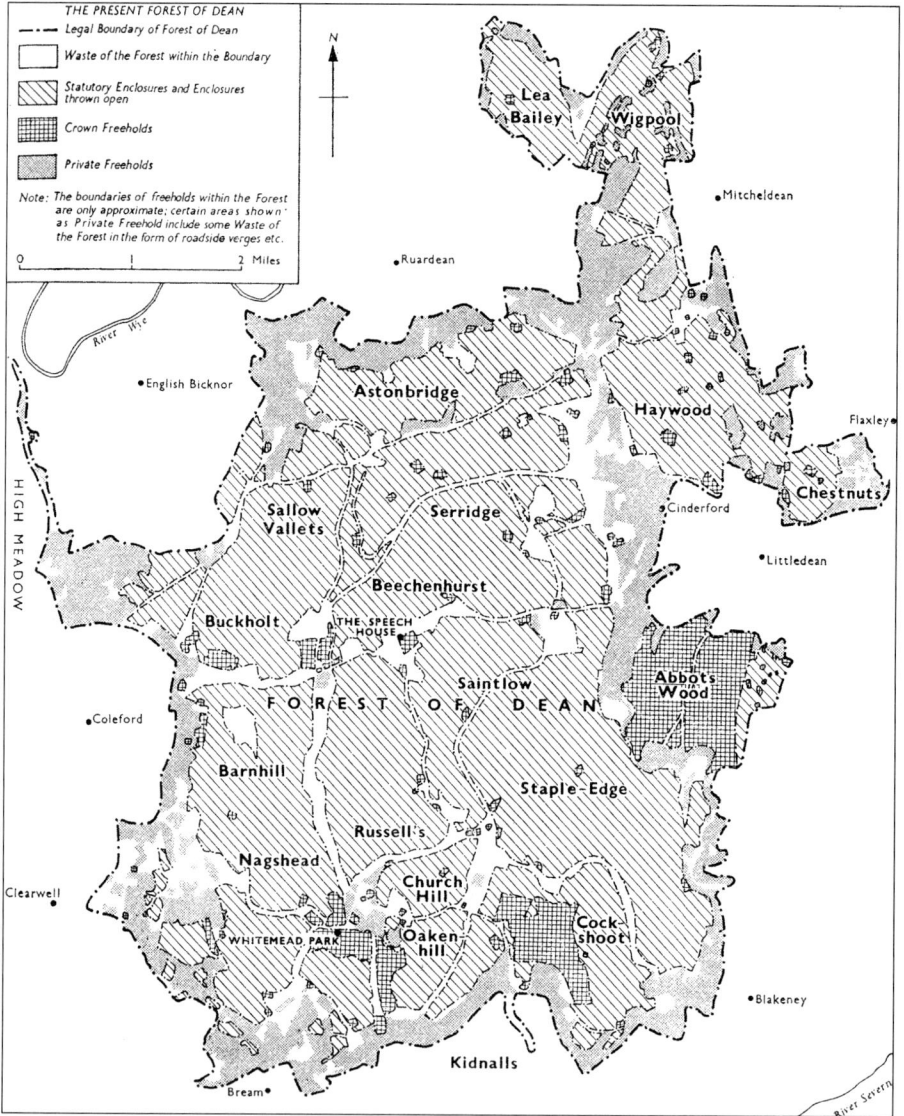

THE PRESENT FOREST OF DEAN
—·— Legal Boundary of Forest of Dean

Waste of the Forest within the Boundary

Statutory Enclosures and Enclosures thrown open

Crown Freeholds

Private Freeholds

Note: The boundaries of freeholds within the Forest are only approximate; certain areas shown as Private Freehold include some Waste of the Forest in the form of roadside verges etc.

0                    1                    2 Miles

N

River Wye

HIGH MEADOW

•English Bicknor

•Ruardean

Lea Bailey

Wigpool

•Mitcheldean

Astonbridge

Haywood

Flaxley•

Sallow Vallets

Serridge

Cinderford

Chestnuts

Beechenhurst

•Littledean

Buckholt

THE SPEECH HOUSE

Saintlow

Abbot's Wood

•Coleford

F O R E S T   O F   D E A N

Barnhill

Staple-Edge

Russell's

Nagshead

Church Hill

Clearwell•

WHITEMEAD PARK

Oaken hill

Cock-shoot

•Blakeney

Kidnalls

Bream•

River Severn

Map IX. The present Forest of Dean. This map will enable readers to note the location of some of the major woods.

# EPILOGUE

For countless years Dean provided for the hunter and the hunted. Later it yielded immense quantities of iron-ore, coal and stone, much at the expense of its abundance of trees. Its woods and beasts gave sport and food to kings and courtiers; people in the neighbourhood got necessary wood, pasture, pannage, and agricultural land. It furnished timber and iron to build and maintain upon the high seas a fleet that brought the nation through perils, that carried her trade and her colonists to the farthest corners of the earth, and that wrought the downfall of the Napoleonic empire. During two world wars it gave strength and sustenance to endure the strains of warfare on sea and land. Under modern conditions, some changes have been made in the uses to which parts of Dean is put, but through all these developments one can be sure it will continue a multi-purpose 'working Forest' of great national importance.

# GLOSSARY

## IN PARTICULAR

The forest
: The royal forest throughout the realm. Not necessarily woodland.

The Forest
: The Forest of Dean.

The Castle
: The Castle of St. Briavels, the administrative centre of the Forest of Dean from *c.* 1130 to *c.* 1800.

## IN GENERAL

Aeries, Eyries
: Nests of hawks, falcons and sparrow-hawks.

Afforest, Afforestation
: To apply forest law to a territory, thereby curtailing the freedom of the inhabitants. Not to be confused with its meaning from the eighteenth century – to establish a woodland on an area from which forest vegetation has always or long been absent.

Assart
: To uproot trees and other vegetation in forest and bring the land under agriculture.

Attachment Court
: The verderer's court. A court for preliminary hearing of forest offences. Sitting usually every sixth week, it was chiefly concerned in adjudicating cases of small trespasses to the vert. In the case of venison, the offences were recorded for presentation to the Justice in Eyre of the Forest. On some occasions the Attachment Court was called a Swanimote Court, or the two merged. In Dean, the Attachment Court became known as the Speech Court, where the local populace appeared to solicit wood and timber (estovers) for their needs.

Bailiwick
: A forest division to facilitate organization and management. The nine in Dean were in the charge of a forester-in-fee. The difference between bailiwicks and woodwardships is somewhat uncertain; they tended to merge. They are no longer extant.

'Battery'
: Iron sheets and plate, and goods made therefrom. Sometimes used also for the battering of copper or brass.

Beadle
: A minor official who *inter alia* acted as clerk to the Swanimote Court [Hart, *Royal Forest*, pp. 69, 78, 80, 147, 148]. The latest mention of a beadle in Dean is in 1713 [National Liby. of Wales, Dunraven MS 330].

| | |
|---|---|
| Botes | *See* Estovers. |
| Bowbearer | A forest official under the Chief Forester. |
| Cabbiners | (With their temporary cabins) often from afar, formed most of the labour force of the iron industry, especially in cutting, cording and charcoaling. Exceptions were the miners – they were local and more permanent. |
| Cattle | 'Commonable animals in forest', chiefly horses and cows. |
| Cinders (Slag) | Partly-smelted iron-ore, usually from the bloomery period, used for re-smelting in blast furnaces. They contained much iron, and acted as a flux in smelting. |
| Coal | Mineral coal; termed 'Seacole' in early times. |
| Cocket | A Custom House document relating to duty. |
| Cole | Charcoal. |
| Collet | An underwood or coppice cut on rotation, chiefly for charcoalburning. *See* Fellet. |
| Collier | Originally a charcoalburner; from the eighteenth century, a miner of mineral coal. *See* Free Miner. |
| Common, 'Rights' of | 'Rights' (or sometimes privileges only) of an individual or community to exercise 'Herbage' and 'Pannage'. |
| Commoners | Local populace claiming 'Rights' of common. |
| 'Commonable animals in forest' | Chiefly horses and cows (not sheep and goats). |
| Complement wood | Cordwood to complement leases/grants of the 'King's Ironworks'. *See* Delivery. |
| 'Concession', ('Concessionaire'; 'Patentee'; Farmer) | Refers in Dean to the 'King's Ironworks' and the cordwood necessary therefor. There was no reluctance to accept the 'concession'; for all the unpleasantness and rivalries generated, it remained a desirable and presumably profitable undertaking. It generated almost constant conflicts between conservative and positive administrators as well as between the local populace and the new industrial interests. The commoners, miners and other local populace maintained a stream of complaints, accusations, petitions and informations usually leading to litigation. From 1611 to 1642, at least twelve special Exchequer investigations were issued and returned to investigate the alleged misdemeanours of 'Concessionaires' and their employees, as well as of the forest officials engaged with them. The operation of each lease was investigated at least once – sometimes because the beneficiaries were Recusants or through the vigilance of the Throckmortons of Clearwell. |

| | |
|---|---|
| Constable-warden | The chief administrator in Dean, using St. Briavels Castle as headquarters. An office of some honour but little labour, with many perquisites. Sometimes the appointments did not included both offices. Most administration was by deputies, often two. |
| Coppice | An area of woodland managed as a coppice and cut on a rotation of about 15 to 30 years, largely dependent on growth. It needed to be enclosed, after cutting, against marauding cattle and deer, for about 9 to 12 years. In 1237 Henry III ordered the constable-warden of Dean 'to take care that in the season [presumably the growth "dormant" period October to March] when underwood should be cut, it should be so cut to grow again (*revenire*) and that no damage shall befall the coppice (*coepecia*)'. Underwood to sustain the king's eight movable furnaces/forges, was to be thorns, maple, hazel, and other species; no oak, chestnut, or ash was to be cut down, 'and the places so assigned shall be well and sufficiently enclosed so that no beasts shall enter to browse there'. [*Cal.* C54, 1234–7, p. 416; Hart, *Royal Forest*, pp. 29, 30.] See Section I footnote 74. |
| Cord (of wood) | A stack of sticks or billets of wood usually containing about 128 cubic feet and measuring about 8 feet 4 inches long × 4 feet 3 inches wide × 4 feet 3 inches high, sometimes referred to as a 'long' cord. The amount of wood was about 75 to 100 cubic feet according to quality. A 'short' cord was half a cord, usually of 2 feet 2 inches billets. A 'long' cord produced about 5cwt or 30 bushels of charcoal. |
| Cordwood | *See* Cord and Complement wood. Used for domestic fuel and (mainly) charcoal to smelt iron-ore. |
| Country, The | The local populace. |
| Cover, Covert | The woodland tree crop and other vegetation. |
| Defence Month | *See* Fence Month. |
| Deforest, Deforestation | Releasing all or part of a forest from forest law. Not to be confused with its meaning from the eighteenth century – to remove the tree crop from woodland without the intention of reforesting. |
| Delivery | Release, e.g. of estovers (botes) and pitwood, by the court of attachment; or of cordwood by forest officials to 'farmers' of the 'King's Ironworks'. |
| Demesne | Land held by the sovereign for his own use. |
| Dotard | A decayed tree unsuitable for construction work; no sound timber within it. |

| | |
|---|---|
| Encroachment | Encroachment on forest land; usually an illegal enclosure. *See* Assart and Purpresture. |
| Estovers (Botes) | An allowance of firewood, poles, timber and other necessaries released by the court of attachment as a privilege to the local populace. Included firebote, housebote, hedgebote and ploughbote. Not claimed in Dean since the Act of 1668. |
| Expeditation | The laming or lawing of dogs, usually mastiffs, whereby their legs or feet were mutilated so that they were unable to run fast enough to catch deer. |
| Eyre, Forest | (a) Judge's tour; (b) session of an Itinerant Judge's Court; (c) the principal forest court, due to be held every three years. *See* Justice Seat. Chiefly concerned with fines and amercements for breaches of forest law. Called into being by the sovereign's letters patent, appointing the justices to hear and determine pleas of the forest. The last held for Dean was in 1656. |
| Farm, Ferm | A right granted or leased in forest. |
| Farmer | A holder or patentee of a farm/ferm/'concession' significantly in the Dean iron industry. |
| Fee | A hereditary holding of land by feudal service. A fee farm rent was payment made for a fee. Holders were sometimes entitled to fee-deer and fee-trees along with other privileges. |
| Fellet (Vellet, Vallet) | A felling or felling area usually of all trees except timber-trees. Enclosed thereafter for regeneration by coppice shoots and natural seeding. |
| Fence Month | The closed or forbidden month because of the fawning of deer. Fifteen days before and fifteen days after the feast of St John the Baptist. The month contained thirty-one days, beginning fifteen days before Midsummer (24 June) and ending fifteen days after – i.e. from 9 June to 9 July (the fifteen days either side of Midsummer Day). |
| Forest | Territory designated by a perambulation and used by the sovereign for his, or his assigned, hunting, and subject to his will by forest law. The protection of deer and their habitat was paramount. |
| Forest law | Took precedence over common law and partly excluded it. It punished and restricted, but also maintained a system of husbandry well suited to the exploitation of woodland and waste. |
| Forester-of-fee, Forester-in-fee | A feudal holder of a forest bailiwick. There were usually nine. By 1637, 1676 and 1713 it is possible that not all the holders of the office were hereditary, in which case the |

method of appointment is not evident. Sometimes the office was purchased from the previous holder. The office was valued for its prestige and perquisites, and undertaken by a deputy. The difference between a forester-of-fee and a woodward is somewhat uncertain. The office, which had the entitlement of several perquisites, is now extinct.

'Four men' ('Fayre men')

Four men chosen from each forest township (vill) who, with the reeve, had to attend the Swanimote Court and the Justice Seat in Eyre. Significant mentions of them in Dean are in the Eyre of 1634 [see Section V], 1676 (sixteen townships) [Glos. R.O. D36 Colchester Papers Q2] and 1713 (nineteen townships) [see Section X]. See also list of townships in Hart, *Royal Forest*, p. 29 (C.54/38, m.10d, 1228, and E32/31, 1282) and, in 1221, Wright, E.C., *Common Law . . .*, 1928, pp 41–3.

Free Miner

A collier or miner with rights of mining coal, iron-ore and stone.

Great tree

Probably an ancient tree beyond its suitability for naval timber. More recently referred to as a 'Monarch of the Forest'.

Grove

A small wood, usually managed on a coppice rotation.

Herbage

(a) That which beasts feed on; (b) payment for putting beasts to graze in forest.

Ironmaking

(a) the 'direct process', a bloomery made decarbonized iron straight from the ore. (b) the 'indirect process' (from *c.* 1540) employed a blast furnace to smelt iron-ore, and a fining forge to decarbonize the iron.

Ironmaster

*See* 'Concessionaire' and Farmer. Sometimes they were 'financiers' and/or 'enterprising landowners' (with some financial backing) attempting to make profit from ironmaking, or at least to obtain an outlet for their woods and coppices which otherwise were virtually unsaleable.

Justice Seat

The location where the Chief Justice of the Forest or Justice-in-Eyre held his enquiries and administered forest law. The principal forest court. *See* Eyre.

Keeper (Under-Keeper)

A forester or woodman in charge of a walk.

Lawn

Open ground in forest, usually clear of trees, where horses and cows (not sheep and goats) were permitted to graze if the deer were not thereby disturbed. The prohibited periods were the Fence Month and the Winter Heyning. 'Forbidden lawns' are mentioned *c.* 1279–82 (P.R.O. E32/32). *See* Pasture Land.

Load

(a) Of shiptimber: 50 cubic feet – about 1 ton; (b) Of charcoal: twelve sacks, each of eight bushels.

| | |
|---|---|
| Lop and top | The branches and crown cut from a broadleaved tree felled or windthrown, more rarely, when standing (*see* Shredding). Usually used as cordwood, otherwise as firewood. |
| Logwood | The larger branches of a tree, yet unsuitable for construction. |
| Mast | Acorns and beech-mast, of value for (a) feeding swine (*see* Pannage); and (b) natural regeneration (*see* Spring). |
| Metes | The bounds or perambulation of a forest. |
| Mine, Myne | Iron-ore. |
| Miner, Myner | A digger of iron-ore. *See* Free Miner. |
| Natural Regeneration | Renewal of a woodland crop by self sown seed (*see* Mast and Spring), coppice shoots, or root suckers. |
| Offal wood | Lop, top and other branches unsuitable other than for cordwood or firewood. Also, the waste from axed (squared) or sawn timber. |
| Osmund iron | A special Swedish iron of high standard. |
| Pannage | Right or privilege of feeding swine in woods following fall of acorns and beech-mast. Money paid in acknowledgement was termed 'Swine Silver', usually one penny. The time of pannage was from 15 days before Michaelmas and 40 days after Michaelmas [Hart, *The Commoners* . . ., p. ix, n. 3 and p. 70, n.1; 1668 Act, S. 10; Turner (p. xxvi), 'about 14 September to 11 November']. In Dean the pannage season runs from 25 September to 22 November. |
| Pasture land (*landea*) | Open land, lawn, green or common in forest, where 'commonable animals' could graze on payment by their owners. |
| Perambulation | Delimitation of a forest by metes and bounds. Undertaken by walking/riding, but sometimes by consultation, enquiry and perusal of documents. Usually undertaken by a number of regarders, generally twelve. An example is Appendix I to Section IX. |
| 'Preservator' | Four officials appointed to supervise ironworks etc. in Dean 1650–3. |
| Purlieu | An area formerly forest but subsequently deforested, usually on the fringe of forest. |
| Purpresture | Illegal trespass or encroachment on forest by building or by otherwise disturbing land. |

| | |
|---|---|
| Ranger | An appointment by the king dealing with the beasts of the forest; sometimes a sinecure for courtiers. (Arthur Middleton appointed for Dean in 1581: D1677, GG1552) |
| Reeve | An official appointed by each forest township. |
| Regard, The | A periodical inspection of a forest made by regarders, usually knights. Once in every three years an inspection of the woods within the metes and bounds of the forest was or ought to have been made by twelve regarders chosen for the purpose. The inspection was known as The Regard. The duty of the twelve regarders was to find answers to a set of interrogatories entitled the Chapters of the Regard which included: herbage in the king's demesne, eyries of hawks and falcons, forges, mines, honey, assarts, purprestures, waste of woods, and other offences. Documents of 1637, 1676 and 1713 show that regarders were no longer knights but simply esquires or gentlemen of the Forest neighbourhood. They were not 'full-time'. |
| Regarder | *See* Regard. |
| Region, Dean | All or part of the land lying between the Severn and the Wye and bounded in the north by an approximate line Monmouth-Ross-Newent-Gloucester (outskirts). Not into Monmouthshire or Herefordshire. |
| Shredding | Debranching of a standing tree for firewood or cordwood. Much in evidence in the sixteenth and part of the seventeenth centuries. See Section I, footnote 74. |
| Spring | The young growth from germination of natural seedlings, and sometimes the shoots from broadleaved stools. |
| Standard | A tree reserved among coppice and underwood to reach full size and maturity as timber. Sometimes termed 'Standel', 'Store' or 'Teller'. The Statute of Woods, 1543, reserved 12 standards on each acre. *See* Great tree and Timber-tree. |
| Standel | *See* Standard. |
| Stogall | A tree 'cut short or broken down by the wind'. |
| Stool | A tree stump capable of putting forth shoots. |
| Store, Storer | *See* Standard. |
| Suit, Suitelands | Suit was owed for some lands to the Court of St. Briavels. |
| Swanimote Court | The forest court of presentment. In some documents spelled Swainmote. One of the two lesser courts of the forest (the other being the Attachment Court – in Dean the Speech Court). The Swanimote Court merged with the Attachment Court, significantly in Dean. Often the Swanimote was a vague word used both of the Attachment |

Court and forest inquisitions. The latest relevant references found for Dean are in 1713 [National Liby. of Wales, Dunraven MS 330] and 1739 [Gage MSS GG 1344].

Teller

A young Standard.

Timber-tree

A sound tree suitable for shipbuilding or other construction work, especially oaks and beeches. By ancient statute (Act of 35 Hen. VIII, C.17, c.V), at least 'one foot square at the stub'.

Township (Vill), Forest

*See* Four men, and Reeve.

Truck

A system of wage payment whereby workmen were paid in goods instead of money, or in money on the understanding that they would buy their provisions etc. off their employers.

'Uncommonable animals in forest'.

Chiefly sheep and goats.

Underwood

The lower storey of a woodland crop of trees; sometimes an alternative name for coppice.

Venison (*venatio*)

(a) Hunting; (b) the flesh of beasts hunted (chiefly deer and wild boar).

Verderer

A forest official with limited judicial power. Usually held the office for life. Four to each forest. Main duty to guard the venison and the vert. Elected under the sheriff by the freeholders of the county. *See* Attachment Court.

Vert (*viridis*)

Green vegetation and trees, growing in woodland and capable of serving as habitat or sustenance of beasts of the forest.

Walk

A forest division to facilitate organisation and management. Usually in the charge of a Keeper. There were six Walks in Dean.

Warden

*See* Constable-warden.

Wast, Waste

General term for unenclosed and uncultivated wooded forest.

Winter Heyning

The period when grazing was prohibited – to safeguard the sustenance of the deer. From 11 November to 23 April (i.e. from the feast of St Martin to that of St George). Since 1900, from 25 November to 7 May (Hart, *The Commoners* . . ., p. 70, n. 1); in the New Forest from 22 November to 4 May.

Wood

General term for produce of trees below timber quality. *See* Complement wood and Offal wood.

Woodward (and their deputy)  An hereditary forest official in charge of a woodwardship. There were usually 10. By 1637, 1676 and 1713 it appears that not all the holders of the office were hereditary. Sometimes the office was purchased from the previous holder. The office was valued for its prestige and perquisites, and undertaken by a deputy. The difference between a woodward and a forester-of-fee is somewhat uncertain. The office, which had the entitlement of several perquisites, is now extinct.

Woodwardship  A forest division to facilitate organisation and management. Usually in the charge of a Woodward. The difference between woodwardships and bailiwicks is somewhat uncertain; they tended to merge. They are no longer extant. An example is Appendix III to Section IX.

# BIBLIOGRAPHY

## (1) MAIN MANUSCRIPT SOURCES

### PUBLIC RECORD OFFICE

Chancery
|     |     |
| --- | --- |
| C54 | Close Rolls, Elizabeth I to Charles I |
| C66 | Patent Rolls, Elizabeth I to Charles II |
| C99 | Forest Proceedings, Modern |

Exchequer, King's Remembrancer
|     |     |
| --- | --- |
| E101 | Accounts various |
| E112 | Bills and Answers, Elizabeth I to Commonwealth and Protectorate |
| E124/125 | Decrees and Orders |
| E133 | Baron's Depositions |
| E134 | Depositions by Commission, Elizabeth I to Charles II |
| E137 | Estreats of Fines |
| E146 | Forest Proceedings |
| E159 | Memoranda Rolls, Elizabeth I to James I |
| E178 | Special Commissions and Returns, Elizabeth I to Charles II |

Exchequer of Receipt
|     |     |
| --- | --- |
| E401 | Pells of Receipt |

Land Revenues
|     |     |
| --- | --- |
| LR1 | Enrolment Books |
| LR12 | Receivers' Accounts, Series III |

State Paper Office
|     |     |
| --- | --- |
| SP12 | State Papers Domestic, Elizabeth I |
| SP14/15 | State Papers Domestic, James I |
| SP16 | State Papers Domestic, Charles I |
| SP18 | State Papers Domestic, Interregnum |
| SP25 | Council of State |
| SP29 | State Papers Addenda 1662 |
| SP39 | State Papers, Warrants |

Forestry Commission
|     |     |
| --- | --- |
| F16/17 | Dean Forest, Deputy Surveyor's Office |
| F20 | Dean Forest, Records |

Land Revenue Records
|     |     |
| --- | --- |
| LRR05 | Deeds and Evidences |

P.R.O. Maps    See end of this Bibliography

## BRITISH LIBRARY

Additional Manuscripts
            10038        Caesar Papers
            25302        Miscellaneous Papers
            36767        Caesar Papers
            69909        Coke Papers (Series II)

Harleian Manuscripts
            4850         Copy of Proceedings at the Forest of Dean Justice Seat, 1634

Lansdowne Manuscripts: various

## BODLEIAN LIBRARY MANUSCRIPTS

Bankes                          Papers of Sir John Bankes
Gough, Gloucestershire          'Customs etc. of the Forest of Dean . . .'
Rawlinson:    A21 & A24         Thurloe Papers
              A187              Pepys Papers
              D119              Forest of Dean Justice Seat, 1634

## GLOUCESTER LIBRARY MANUSCRIPTS

    L.F.1.1     Copies of records relating to the Forest of Dean
    L.F.6.2     Copy of Proceedings at the Forest of Dean Justice Seat, 1634
    L.F.6.3     Warrant, 29 March 1618, to the Farmers of the Dean ironworks
    LX.10.3     (1) Walmore Common. After 1668.
                (2) Proposals for a Supervisor of the Forest, 3 March 1674.
                (3) Proposals for an Overseer of the Forest to prevent abuses etc. After
                    1668.
                (4) Statement of forest officials regarding the Duke of Monmouth and
                    the Lea Bayly, 9 June 1676.

## GLOUCESTERSHIRE RECORD OFFICE

    D36         Colchester Papers
    D1557       Gage Manuscripts
    D421        Winter Papers
    D33         Wyrrall Papers
    D3921       Hart Forest of Dean Collection
    D2026       Bond Papers
    D23         Probyn Papers
    D4431       Phillipps Papers
    D1677       GG, various, Gage Manuscripts

## MARQUESS OF BATH AT LONGLEAT

        Devereux Papers:   1648 – Leases etc. relating to English Bicknor

## (2) MAIN PRINTED SOURCES

*Calendar of State Papers Domestic*, Edward VI – 1660

*Calendar of Treasury Papers*, I, 1557–1696

*Calendar of Treasury Books*, I–IV, 1660–1675

## HISTORICAL MANUSCRIPTS COMMISSION

Fourth Report, de la Warr MSS
Fifth Report, Cholmondeley MSS
Seventh Report, Sackville MSS, I, Cranfield Papers
Twelfth Report, Cowper MSS, Coke Papers
Salisbury Papers

## RECORDS

*The Third Report of the Commissioners appointed to enquire into the State and Condition of the Woods, Forests, and Land Revenues of the Crown* . . . (London) 3 June 1788 (cf. *Commons Journal*, 1787–8, XLIII, pp. 559–632)

I. Bromwich, *The Spoiles of the Forrest of Dean Asserted* . . . (London, 1650)

J. Manwood, *Treatise and Discourse of the Lawes of the Forest* (London, 1615)

## GENERAL

Sir John Winter     *Sir John Wintour's Vindication from the Aspersions of Destroying the Ship Timber of the Forrest of Deane* (London, 1660)

*A True Narrative concerning the Woods and Ironworks of the Forrest of Dean, and how they have been disposed since the year 1635* (London, c. 1667)

G. Hammersley     'The crown woods and their exploitation in the sixteenth and seventeenth centuries', *Bulletin of the Inst. of Historical Research*, XXX (1957), pp. 136–161

'The revival of the forest laws under Charles I,' *History*, XLV (1960)

'The charcoal iron industry and its fuel, 1540–1750', *The Economic History Review*, 2nd Series, XXVI (4), Nov. 1973, pp. 593–613

'Did it fall or was it pushed? The Foleys and the end of the charcoal iron industry in the eighteenth century', in *The Search for Wealth and Stability* (ed. T.C. Smout, 1979)

Rhys Jenkins     'Ironmaking in the Forest of Dean', *Trans. Newcomen Soc.*, VI (1925–6), pp. 42–65

H.G. Nicholls     *The Forest of Dean*, 1858

*The Personalities of the Forest of Dean*, 1863

*Iron Making in the Olden Times*, 1866

H.R. Schubert     'The king's ironworks in the Forest of Dean', *Journ. of Iron and Steel Inst.*, CLXXIII (1953)

*History of the British Iron and Steel Industry from c.450 B.C. to A.D. 1775* (London, 1957)

W.B. Wilcox          *Gloucestershire: A Study in Local Government 1590–1640*, (Yale
                     University Press, 1940), Section VII, The Forest of Dean,
                     pp. 179–203.

Edward Machen        The *Machen Notes, 1818*, written in two 'exercise books', were studied
(deputy              by the present author, who took copies of many of the pages. The
surveyor)            two books were then returned to H.A. Machen of English Bicknor.
                     He was assumed to have deposited them in the Gloucestershire
                     Record Office; this was not done, and their present location is
                     unknown.

## MAPS

1608: P.R.O. F17/1, MR 879, Glos.
1608: P.R.O., MPC 108, Mon.
*c.* 1710: P.R.O. F17/7.
1782: T. Pinnell: P.R.O. F17/14.
1787: Drivers': P.R.O. F16/47 MR 415; F16/59; F17/5 and 6 (copy in Glos. R.O., Hart
Collection D3921).
1842: J. Atkinson (copy in Glos. R.O., Hart Collection D3921).
1847: J. Atkinson (copy held by the present author).
1848: In *Report of the Select Committee on the Woods, Forests, and Land Revenues of the Crown*
– relating to the 'Duncan Committee' of 1848/9. (Incidentally, the copy map held by the
present author was produced for the debates in the House of Lords relevant to 'the saving
of the Forest from sale' resulting by the Forestry Act 1981.)
1897: H.C. Hill: *Report on the Forest of Dean, and Suggestions for its Management*, Appendix B.
H.M.S.O. 1897.

# INDEX OF SUBJECTS

The main group-headings include: Acts, Administration, Animals, Bailiwicks, Birds, 'Forest', Forest Officials, Forges, Furnaces, Houses, Industries, Iron, Lodges, Manors, Pools/Ponds, Timber, Trades, Trees, Walks, Woods (Crown), Woods (Private), and Woodwardships.

* The present deputy surveyor is J.E. Everard; and the four verderers are Dr C.E. Hart, Messrs. Melville Watts, Robert Jenkins, and Ray Wright.

# INDEX OF PLACE-NAMES

1. Woods and Enclosures are named under Woods (Crown) and Woods (Private). Other main group-headings include: Streams/Brooks, Lanes/Paths/Ways, Wells, Lawns, and Groves (some of the latter being included under other place-names).

2. The place-names sometimes refer to the township or village, and sometimes to the bailiwick, woodwardship, manor or parish.

3. The following main group-headings in the Index of Subjects should also be noted: Bailiwicks, Castles, Houses, Pasture Lands, Pools, Walks, and Woodwardships.

4. Not all the variants in spellings of place-names are given. The spellings in relevant documents and maps vary throughout the centuries. Cartographers, surveyors and lawyers often used for such spellings their own interpretation of the pronounciations of the local populace at any point in time.

# INDEX OF PERSONAL NAMES